The Lawyer's Guide to the INTERNET

by G. Burgess Allison

with a Foreword by ROBERTA COOPER RAMO,
President-Elect of the American Bar Association

Section of Law Practice Management
American Bar Association

Book design by Catherine Zaccarine.

The Section of Law Practice Management, American Bar Association, offers an educational program for lawyers in practice. Books and other materials are published in furtherance of that program. Authors and editors of publications may express their own legal interpretations and opinions, which are not necessarily those of either the American Bar Association or the Section of Law Practice Management unless adopted pursuant to the bylaws of the Association. The opinions expressed do not reflect in any way a position of the Section or the American Bar Association, or of The MITRE Corporation.

Library of Congress Catalog Card Number 95-75479
ISBN 1-57073-149-7

00 99 98 97 96   5 4 3

A Vanguard of Technology Production. No lawyers were harmed during the testing of this product.

Dedication

To my Mother and Father, who still know everything.

About the Author

G. Burgess Allison is the Technical Editor of *Law Practice Management*—the magazine of the American Bar Association's Law Practice Management Section (LPMS). He is also the author of "Technology Update," the magazine's featured column on technology-related issues. The column focuses on the latest popular hardware and software products; it also covers broader-ranging industry developments that affect the strategic use of technology in law offices— including the Internet. Mr. Allison has been writing "Technology Update" since 1983 and received the LPMS Distinguished Writing Award in 1992.

Mr. Allison is employed as a systems engineer at The MITRE Corporation, a not-for-profit corporation that operates Federally Funded Research and Development Centers for the Air Force and the Federal Aviation Administration and provides systems engineering services to many other government sponsors.

He earned his J.D. from the University of Michigan in 1976 and is a member of the Delaware bar.

Much more importantly, he is the assistant basketball coach of his daughter's basketball team, his son's biggest fan, his wife's best friend, and nothing but trouble for his two beagles. His wife still thinks that he's trainable, but his mother knows better. And he is a proud co-founder of the Law Practice Management Section's Team Attitude.

He can be reached at allison@mitre.org.

Acknowledgments

I am indebted to *many* people who made this book possible:

To Jane Johnston, Paula Tsurutani, and Beverly Loder—who did much more than just shepherd this project (and me) from start to finish. The production was an enormous team effort; these three recruited and led an *outstanding* team of talented individuals to make it all work (including Tim Johnson, Catherine Zaccarine, and Sara Drummond). I couldn't have asked for anything better.

To the Law Practice Management Section Publishing Board and Gary Munneke, its indefatigable chair who simply wouldn't leave me alone until I agreed to this project. To Ernie Schaal, my Publishing Board Project Manager, and the many reviewers and editors who contributed substantive corrections and suggestions for improving early manuscripts. And to Roberta Cooper Ramo, who to this day both inspires and surprises, and who did *much* more for this book than write its Foreword.

To Erik Heels, Lyonette Louis-Jacques, Terese Austin, and Kim Bayer, whose contribution of resource listings to *The Lawyer's Guide* barely scratches the surface of what they've really done. To develop and compile those listings has required a level of dedication, and innovation, that marks them as true net.pioneers on the e-frontier of law-related Internet resources. Their efforts have contributed substantially to the community of net.connected lawyers.

Special thanks to Al Moses and John DeCarlo, who never realize how much they contribute to my writing. And to the denizens of aba-unix-list and network2d-l who refuse to give me an inch (knowing full well that I will take the proverbial mile).

And especially to the many readers of *Technology Update* who send me comments and stories, relating their own firsthand experiences with the successes and failures of technology. These are the people I must listen closest to; ultimately, these are the people who shaped the specifics and direction of this book.

Finally—and foremost—to my wife, Dawn, and my children, Tracy and Jack. They contributed to this book *every single day*. They *are* the best.

Contents

Internet Specifics: PALEOTECHNOLOGIES

Choosing a Role: E-FLATLAND SETTLERS

Executive Foreword to
The Lawyer's Guide to the Internet

"Mingle some small folly with your wisdom."
—Horace (I think)

The mistake that may be made about this book (depending upon the person making the mistake) is to think that it focuses on a transitory technology or that it is too basic for someone currently fluent in the popular technogibberish, or that it is not important to the person who can hire someone else to "do technology."[1] The fact is that *The Lawyer's Guide to the Internet* is a combination Baedekers, scout manual, book of lists, glossary, and slightly crazed Emily Post introduction to the newest American Frontier.[2]

The use of technology is as fundamental to a rapid change in the modern law as the combination of the first written legal codes and the printing press. The Internet is perhaps the most potentially pervasive and influential form that technological change has taken to date.

What is remarkable about the Internet is that it creates a real-time, worldwide community. Like the first communities of all cultures, but particularly those of America's Old West, it is a community without laws, judges, or even sheriffs. It is a global village where the citizens are made up of good Samaritans, holy monks, and evil Rasputins, where they devise self-help solutions to problems, and use capital punishment with no due process. An entire world exists on your home or office computer screen. In the electronic window you can see American ingenuity, public-spirited volunteers that rival the Red Cross, and a can-do attitude along with the rough-and-ready behavior of the OK Corral. It is place without race, gender, or age. The global economy was made possible by modern transportation. The global society exists in its earliest primitive stage on the Internet.

If, in addition to integrity, wit, and compassion, there is a single quality that lawyers need to succeed, it is a hunger for knowledge of the world around them. It is impossible to be a first-rate advocate or scrivener or interpreter of the law if one does not understand the society in which the lawyer lives.

Today's lawyer requires an understanding of the fact that space on earth has been reduced to the distance between the computer on your desk or lap to the phone jack. To understand the world in which our laws are being made,

---

1. If G. Burgess Allison can have footnotes that do whatever in the world he wants, R. Cooper Ramo can have sentences of many clauses!

2. Which really isn't American, but more about that later.

tested, and negotiated, lawyers must inhabit this cyberspace with their intellect, even if they are not the least bit interested in applying it to their practice. If you are computer-illiterate, you risk being unable to comprehend the world of your clients, many of whom are already sophisticated in the ways of the interactive world. Often it is not possible to understand key front-page articles in today's *New York Times* without a basic understanding of the communications made possible through the Internet.[3]

This book is a map showing the entrance to the global village, so you can see the Internet frontier for yourself. Lawyer/anthropologists can observe what happens in a world where there are no laws and no lawyers acting in their normal roles. However, the importance of this guide is the explanation that technology is no longer focused on hardware. That very fact may be the most important lesson parsed in this guide. It is an explanation that lawyers must heed, or cease to survive. The Internet offers us the lesson that buggy-whip manufacturers failed to learn. They were in the transportation business and we are in the knowledge and communication business. When lawyers become masters of the arcane rather than effective communicators, they fail to serve society. The Internet is a vehicle of communication that lawyers must use in order to serve their clients and society well.

Technology in current life offers lawyers an opportunity to improve their skills because of greater research capabilities and communication with others solving similar problems. It offers a chance to interact closely with clients and the courts and to be economically efficient. It makes the boundaries of states seem ephemeral and the barriers of distance across the oceans nonexistent.

But those serious thoughts miss a whole nother[4] attraction of this book: the fun factor. What lawyer could resist getting into the libraries of those law schools that may have foolishly rejected her, or spending time seeing what the American Bankers Association or American Birding Association have in common with the American Bar Association.[5] If you never want to touch a com-

---

3. For example, the second lead article in a recent edition of the *Times* was about the capture of a criminal computer hacker (burglar/thief/artful dodger/felon, in this case) who (just to get your interest up) through the telephone wires stole thousands of credit card numbers, reprogrammed telephones to masquerade as pay phones, and put the nation's defense and some scientific capability at grave risk, among other things.

4. "Nother" and "Bejeebers" (see text) deserve one another. :-) as they say.

5. Internet names that start with ABA. Just to give you an idea of how fast this is all moving, the author notes that "ABA" is the "domain" name of the American Bankers Association, but didn't pick up the new domain name of the American Bar Association "abanet" so I had to write this foreword to bring the reader up to date. Such are the burdens of foreword writers. Forward we must. [*OK, OK. Having the last shot at this book, I stuck in the correct address for the American Bar Association—abanet.org. The birders, by the way, are aba.org; the bankers are aba.com. I am in.debted.—GBA*]

puter, but might masquerade as an Internet sophisticate, this book tells you how to explain the difference between gopher and Mosaic. If you have an entomologist's interest, it explains flaming and spamming, FAQ files and cancelbots. It is a good Rorschach test for telling who will enjoy trying to get on the Internet now and who might be more comfortable later. Inside are the secrets of that remarkable expert (Burgess Allison) who understands the difference between people who repair their own cars or homes and those with a very important phone list of mechanics and plumbers. You should read this book whether you plan to be an armchair traveler or to hit the highway yourself.

If you are a lawyer who is embarrassed to admit to technological illiteracy, you can read this guide in the privacy of your home and stand proudly when you have finished its brief but clear explanations. If the Internet has frustrated you or you have questioned what application it might have in your real practicing life, you have the analysis and help of an expert who speaks plain English. If you have pondered exactly what is meant by the "information superhighway," you can join in on the discussion after reading Burgess's cogent explanation. If you wondered why this isn't as easy as picking up a telephone, this book explains why, and predicts that soon it will be as easy. As it used to say in *The Saturday Evening Post,* "The other lawyers laughed when I sat down to enter the World Wide Web, but after reading *The Lawyer's Guide to the Internet . . .*"

Roberta Cooper Ramo
President-Elect
American Bar Association
March 1995

Foreword

For regular readers of Law Practice Management magazine, Burgess Allison is the popular author of the long-running "Technology Update" column. Month after month, Allison tracks the breaking trends in legal technology, or more precisely the application of technology to the practice of law. His witty and incisive observations offer readers a novel perspective on everything from the latest release of a popular software package to the latest computer industry gossip about why IBM is really (this time) at the end of its ropes. Allison gives all of his readers a feeling of joining the techno-cognoscenti, even those who don't know RAM from ROM.

Now Burgess Allison takes on the biggest trend to come down the pike since the PC—the Internet. Or so it would seem from media accounts. Newspaper, magazine, television, and radio stories regale the joys of surfing the net. From on-line sex to perusal of obscure tomes in distant libraries to watching frog dissections for med school students, the Internet is touted as the great meeting house for McLuhan's global village. Internet aficionados seem to claim that if you know where to look on the net, you can find a cure for the common cold. In the midst of this cyber-hype, Allison provides down-to-earth explanations and sound analysis. He debunks the myths, reins in the hyperbole, and cuts through the techno-jargon.

Instead of pie-in-the-sky, Burgess Allison gives the reader meat and potatoes—down-to-earth practical answers to the questions all of us ask. As a practicing lawyer, can the Internet help me? Is this serious stuff or just fun and games? Is Internet access feasible today or will it be in the near future? Is it for tekkies only or can anyone use it? Will I need to understand the Internet in order to practice effectively? Will my clients expect me to do so? Are there any shortcuts, or is the learning curve interminable? What will it cost?

The Lawyer's Guide to the Internet is written for legal practitioners who want to know the answers to their questions, who want to separate the wheat from the chaff, who want straightforward answers they can understand. For years Burgess Allison has demonstrated a unique ability to communicate with practicing lawyers and legal professionals in terms that are both comprehensible and relevant on a variety of topics involving technology. This book is no exception; while he addresses many of the questions that lawyers are asking about the Internet, he does not try to sugarcoat the "not-ready-for-prime-time" nature of the medium. While he clarifies many of the basic concepts needed to go on line, he quickly admits that the technology is evolving rapidly, making definitive statements all but impossible to make.

This book is organized into several sections: an introduction that explores why the reader might be interested in the Internet, an overview of the Internet environment explaining what the Internet is (and isn't), a discussion of Internet services and capabilities geared to a legal audience, a description of how to get connected and use the Internet, and a reference section that describes a variety of Internet service providers. If *The Lawyer's Guide to the Internet* is not the final word on how to use the Internet, it is certainly a good start—and it is a good read, too, unlike many of the guidebooks and manuals on the market.

Professor Gary A. Munneke
Chair, LPM Publishing

Introduction

"No matter where you go,
there you are."

—Buckaroo Bonzai

Chapter 1

Why This Might Be Interesting

This joint is *jumpin'*.

Entertainment, education, information—the content is there and growing. The hype machines are going *crazy*. And the users are just plain *swarming* to the net: 1994 saw more than 2.6 *million* new host computers connected to the Internet. That's more than 7,000 new connections *every single day*. And those numbers don't count the millions of users on the major online services like Compuserve and America Online, because each one of those services is counted as just *one* host computer.

Email is bordering on ubiquitous, online discussion groups seem to be exploding on the net—many covering substantive, useful topics—and frankly, the stuff that's showing up on World Wide Web servers around the world is simply phenomenal: exhibits at the Louvre with full-color point-and-click graphics, a tour of the White House with graphics *and* sound, stock-market graphs with detailed historical stock-price charts, the full text of bills introduced in Congress, the *U.S. Code*, the *Federal Register*, and searchable text of just-published Supreme Court decisions. Government agencies and other sources of original data are coming to the net just as fast as they can.

The ease of setting up graphics-and-hypertext web servers on the net seems to have inspired a whole generation of researchers, e-publishers—and just plain *strange people with too much time on their hands*—to establish a network of web sites that staggers the imagination. The growth of the web is almost as pervasive as the newfound connectivity that binds the net together. They can't even *total* the number of web sites any more (although one service at Stanford University has references to more than 25,000 sites).

Amid the din, the popular press and the hype machines are simply *beside themselves*. There's so much going on, they *just can't sit still*—I'm afraid they're risking some kind of internal injury.

(It's *really* jumpin'.)

But with this much hype and this much activity, it's a real challenge to figure out what's really going on. How much is hype, and how much of the attention is coming from the usual hype-inflation in which attention generates more attention? What's the point, and dare I say it out loud, what's in it for the would-be net.connected lawyer?

Sure, you've seen it in *Doonesbury* and read about it in *Time*, and you may have concluded that there's *not* much in it that's important to what you do as a lawyer. And of course you're right.

Partially.

Many think the Internet still isn't ready for prime time: It's certainly not well organized, it's difficult to find your way around, and it's a challenge just to get connected. And the Internet isn't *even in the same quadrant of deep space* with user-friendly. If you think programming your VCR is hard, the Internet will be a *real* shock. The Internet is *not* a consumer product—there's no one to take you by the hand and bring you in. This is not your teenager's Compuserve.

On the other hand, the Internet is already delivering key information from original government sources to thousands of lawyers around the country, and virtually every state court system in the country is actively considering a project or experiment to put some portion of court records online.

In fact, most of the significant information suppliers already on the Internet are government agencies, or someone posting results of government action. When one goes back to the fundamental role of the lawyer—helping individuals and corporations deal with the rules and actions of the several branches of government—then the swarm of government agencies moving to the Internet provides a very real and powerful incentive for the legal professional to be aware of what's available, and what this technology is all about.

Indeed, if there is any profession that can make immediate use of the Internet, it is the legal profession.

If your geek glass is half-empty, this could be trouble

Not to put too fine a point on it, but when the courts or agencies you deal with announce that certain information will be available through the Internet, your clients will be looking *to you* for answers. They'll want to know what's being made available, what impact it's going to have, and what *you* plan to do about it.

They'll also want to know that you're *already* connected, of course. (Better get your excuses ready now. Because if your local courthouse gets to the Internet before you do, your clients will want to know *why*. And be prepared for that insufferable geekier-than-thou question, "You mean you don't have a *modem?*") (Like, you probably don't even have a *fax machine*.)

Hey! Gimme a day or two, all right?

As unusual as it sounds, there is a very real possibility that the legal profession is going to be dragged into the 21st century—kicking and screaming if necessary—*by the government*.

(I know, I know. I can hardly stand it myself.)

The purpose of this book is to help the legal professional understand enough about Internet technology—and its high-politics vaporware cousin, the information superhighway—to be able to recognize what's coming, and to be able to develop a plan for working with it when it comes knocking at the door. The intent is to help with the *strategic decision* of whether the Internet is something you should try to deal with right now. And if so—how?

If your geek glass is half-full, this is a golden opportunity

Many courts and agencies are already connected—as are many clients. The Internet represents a real opportunity to gain and keep a competitive advantage within the profession. It can give you access to better and more timely information—direct from original sources. It can improve your ability to communicate with clients (and others) without getting lost in the tangle of endless telephone tag. It can help you exchange data files with your colleagues and with your clients. And many offices are finding that the technologies (and public-domain software) made popular on the Internet can be implemented *within the law office* to make immediate improvements in the office's automation environment. Ultimately, it gives you an opportunity to provide more effective service to your clients—possibly at a lower cost.

Make no mistake—the Internet is no panacea, and it isn't easy. It takes a lot of time: a lot of time to learn it, a lot of time to set it up, and a lot of time to become effective. And once you're up and running, you might find that in *your* particular situation, the storied advantages just aren't there.

But by going through the process, you will have learned quite a bit about the technology and its features. You'll make mistakes, and you'll learn to avoid them in the future. But perhaps most importantly, you'll learn to tell what's a real opportunity and what's a waste of time.

(Now wait a minute, isn't that what *this book* is supposed to do?)
Nope.

There are just too many different lawyers and law offices—each with its own unique interests, specialties, and clients. There are too many different features and services on the Internet. Trying to tell you what's important *for you* would be presumptuous and misleading at best. (It would also be out-of-date almost instantly.)

What this book *does* set out to do is to show you enough about the Internet—within the context of the legal profession—to help *you* decide what's a real opportunity (for you) and what's a waste of time. The detail focuses on the Internet itself: the services; the law-related starting points; and the community in which the net.connected lawyer has an opportunity to participate (these are fundamental characteristics that are likely to remain *somewhat* stable over the next few years). *The Lawyer's Guide to the Internet* is intended to help you find new features *as* they're being introduced, and to help you *evaluate* those features for yourself.[1] The intent is to help with the *strategic decision* of whether the Internet is something you should try to deal with right now. And if so—how?

Being an Early Adopter

Is there an advantage to learning this stuff early—before things are completely settled and everything is ready to go? Of course

---

❶ ...not to mention, to help *me* try to set new single-sentence records for the use of italics, hyphenated-phrases-pretending-to-be-words, split infinitives, run-on sentences, and metaphors mixed to within an inch of their collective lives. Hi! Welcome to the footnotes section of the book. Ordinarily a book's footnotes simply supply reference or contextual detail to illuminate the point or points being discussed in the main body of the text. In *this* book, I will thoroughly abuse the footnote paradigm—using it to branch off into completely different topics from time to time, and occasionally adding a point or two—or a counterpoint to completely discredit the assertions being made in the body of the text. Consider this departure from standard footnote practices and norms as an introduction to the Internet's blatant disregard for normal paradigms that have been established in traditional printed constructs. One of the Internet's most annoying and yet occasionally endearing qualities is its willingness to commandeer a technology or medium and redirect it to a completely different—often unintended—purpose. A related quality is that the Internet almost always offers multiple paths or threads to a single topic. (What a perfect technology for lawyers. The answer to *every* question is, "Well, there are many different ways you can do that.") Sometimes the alternatives are simply mechanical—several different ways to get the exact same file. But at other times, the differences are substantive—offering similar-but-not-identical information, with overlapping coverage. Discussion groups, for example, frequently spring up in a variety of different Internet services. The different groups cover many of the same topics, and you might find some *participants* are in several related groups. But each group has its own perspectives, and its own dynamic. And each gives you a slightly different take on the subject. As a library science, this is *not* a model of efficiency—but new technologies rarely are. The footnotes in this book are modeled after this brave-new-technology paradigm: off-point, almost-but-not-quite duplicative, and inefficient (footnotes with at least a trace of attitude). Come down here if you're interested, but don't feel that you *need* to. After all, it's just a book.

there is. But there are disadvantages as well: There's a considerable learning curve associated with these technologies, and a lot of what you learn can become quickly obsolete. As the technologies continue to change—and as the Internet matures—the skills you need to be effective on the net today might be Old News in just a few years, or in just a few months.

The question is whether you can establish an advantage that will *survive* your temporary mastery of specific skills.

The situation is *entirely* analogous to the PC industry in the early 1980s: maybe not completely ready for prime time, sometimes difficult to use, but showing lots of potential and some pretty astonishing capabilities. The early-PC-adopters accomplished quite a bit with fairly rudimentary tools. Some used the tools to carve out an advantage over their competitors—an advantage that they were able to exploit during the course of the decade. Others found themselves wasting time, spinning their wheels, investing the money and effort but never quite getting the payoffs.

The Internet represents an *identical* opportunity: maybe not completely ready for prime time, sometimes difficult to use, but showing lots of potential and some pretty astonishing capabilities. Some have already used it to establish an advantage that should hold up for quite some time; others, inevitably, will waste time and resources, and come up empty.

What will be the difference? Good question.

Think about what made the difference when we started to implement PCs in the 1980s? How did *your* office react? Was it worth it to struggle through the early-adopter learning curve for PCs—perhaps just to be a part of the revolution— or was it smarter to sit on the sidelines (with your mag-card typewriters and dedicated word processors) and watch while other people worked out the bugs?

If you had it to do over again, which would you do?[2]

The early-adopter costs—both for PCs and the Internet—are nontrivial. In the 1980s, many offices were fortunate enough to find a PC champion—someone who had the energy to spend

2 I hate to say it, but this is a terrific first question to ask yourself if you're now facing the strategic question of what to do about the Internet. On the other hand, if you never went through that process with PCs (and there are, of course, quite a few who didn't), then the question isn't—shall we say—quite as helpful. If, for whatever reason, you weren't part of those decision processes back then, and didn't have to live through the painful lessons of guessing wrong and guessing right, then you're in the traditional quandary of guessing what to do when analogous first-hand experience isn't right at hand. Certainly, you would do well to talk to friends and colleagues whose opinions you respect, and who may have been through that process in the 1980s. But do make sure that your would-be technology-mentors are people with whom you share philosophies about technology and automation investments. If you respect some-one's legal skills, for example, but you *just can't believe* that person is still using a creaky old 386, then you're looking at a difference that's significant. Listen to the experience about PCs, but make sure you tailor it to what level of early-adopter effort *you're* willing to do.

thankless hours in research and debugging, and then in trial and error. The results may have come up empty as often as not, but eventually the successes started to come in. Certainly many lawyers who labored in the role of PC champion found themselves on the receiving end of snide comments about "wasting time" as a PC technician, and about being the world's most expensive PC repairpersons. Clients wanted to be assured that they weren't being billed for the time *you* spent learning office technologies. And senior partners seemed to relish asking when you were going to get back to your *real* job. Some offices tried to avoid the lawyer-as-champion syndrome by assigning the "champion" task to a nonlawyer microcomputer specialist. And sometimes that worked. But that type of end-around process avoids the critical issue: The learning curve isn't about learning the specific details for *operating* the early-adopter technologies—no one cares whether you knew the difference between DMA channels and interrupts.[3]

The critical issue is that you become familiar with what the technology offers —and figure out what the *strategic* benefit might be to you and your practice.

There might be cost savings, it might offer operational efficiencies, or you might find new opportunities for working with certain clients. But more likely, the strategic benefit won't be something that jumps out at you the first time you see it. Instead, like so many other opportunities that a lawyer must take advantage of, it'll be one of a hundred apparently unimportant things that you notice, learn about, and almost forget to use in your day-to-day business. But at some point an opportunity will come along where a particular tidbit of technical understanding will pay its dividends—an opportunity where the difference between guessing that someone probably knows the answer and knowing the answer yourself (and being able to actually *do* what needs to be done) might prove to be the difference between winning and losing (regardless of whether it's a case, a client, or just an internal operating efficiency that you're trying to win).

Those are the advantages that survive the temporary mastery of early-adopter skills. Unfortunately, those are the advantages that it often takes a lawyer—or a nonlawyer with an exceptional understanding of the law office's strategic needs and opportunities—to understand.

What was it that made the difference in taking advantage during the PC revolution? Usually, what made the difference was understanding *both* the technologies and the strategic objectives of the law office. And figuring out where the two could be matched up effectively. What will make the difference in taking advantage during the Internet revolution? Exactly the same thing.

Let's try a quick example. The hypothetical law firm of

3 OK, I care, and your mother cares. We're both very proud of you. But that's still not the point.

John's Toe and Stepson in Washington, D.C., has assigned a partner to look into the costs of getting access to the Securities and Exchange Commission's electronic database of public filings, called EDGAR. The partner has learned that the cost of access is about $40,000 a year—pretty steep for what they need it for, but they really do need it, and they can't charge it back to some client. During a staff meeting, the issue is discussed at length—weighing the out-of-pocket costs versus the costs of doing without. Finally, that scraggly looking new-hire associate who hasn't said a word since he[4] started six months ago, almost sheepishly raises his hand and asks, "Is there something wrong with getting it off the Internet?" All heads turn, a suitable grilling is performed, and sure enough the firm learns that the SEC's EDGAR database is republished on the Internet, nightly, at no cost to users. (Except of course, that they have to be connected to the Internet.) Sure the data is "a day late." But a day late versus $40,000 a year might be an easy choice to make.

Let's try one more example. Hypothetical Mark has been talking recently with a prospective-and-equally-hypothetical multinational client—let's call 'em Deep & Pockets, Ltd. They do a lot of work in Mark's field, and we think they're opening a major facility in Mark's town as well. Normally, they stick with the Big Name Firms in the same city where their corporate headquarters are. Mark has had a chance to talk with them a few times—they know him and they like his work, but it's pretty clear that they're uncomfortable working with a lawyer so far from headquarters. At one of the meetings they happen to mention something about email—they're *uuencoding* files to exchange word-processing documents among branch offices, and using *PGP* to maintain security. Mark's eyes glaze over and he writes himself a note to figure out *what the heck* that was all about. A few days later, Mark learns that Susan— just down the street from Mark—has just landed the D&PL account for the upcoming transaction. And that they're thinking of using her as a specialist in *Mark's* area of expertise! The next time Mark sees her, he congratulates her (naturally) on landing the account. "Oh, that DP&L thing?" she explains, "It turns out they've been using uuencoded email over the Internet—with PGP for security—to keep in touch with all their branches around the world. I turned around a couple of document reviews for 'em pretty quickly and now they're saying I'm just as convenient as their in-town counsel—but at a fraction of the cost." As Mark sits there trying to figure out how to even *pronounce* uuencode, she adds, "I think they're really comfortable working with me, even though I'm pretty far from their headquarters."

This isn't about being reactive. It's about being proactive.

Some institutional clients are now *requiring* counsel to use email. But of course, that's the easy part—you can react

4 Or "she," if you prefer. *Trust me,* it could be either one.

to that. What you *can't* react to are the clients that don't consciously use that as criteria—the clients that think of email as just part of their day-to-day business routine.

The Internet represents no less a revolution than did the emergence of PCs in the 1980s. The task is to become familiar with what the technology offers—and figure out what the *strategic* benefits might be to you and your practice. The intent of this book is to assist you in that process.

One Special Early-Adopter Advantage—Domain Names

One special word of advice to people who may be unsure about whether to start early: There is one special advantage that early adopters *will* have over latecomers. The "domain names" that make up an Internet address are assigned on a first-come first-served basis.[5] If you think your office will want its own name on the Internet—so that your Internet address can include the name of your firm or office (such as johns-toe.com or whitehouse.gov)—then you'd better get started now. Early adopters will be more likely than latecomers to get the domain name they want.

5 An Internet address is usually made up of several components, including the domain names. The names are separated by periods. For example, the address "www.abanet.org" can be interpreted by looking at the last part of the address first—".org". That's the top-level domain and it indicates that the owner of the address is a not-for-profit institution. (Other top-level domains include .edu for schools and universities, .com for commercial entities, .gov for government, and .net for network operators. There's also an entire hierarchy of top-level domains determined by what country the host is located in.) The second part of the address—again, counting from the end of the address—is ".abanet". That's the domain name selected by the organization that has registered the name—in this case, the American Bar Association. That's also the key when it comes to selecting your own domain name. That's what you get to choose if you register your choice before anyone else does.

Chapter 2

About This Book

This book has two main parts. The first part is the guide itself—materials intended to introduce lawyers to the strategic issues of how and whether to participate on the Internet. The second part includes three reference listings that contain descriptions and specific pointers to law-related online resources (including specific addresses and instructions for reaching the listed items) that have been compiled by some of the leading pioneers in this industry. These listings are normally accessible online—the authors have graciously given us permission to include them in *The Lawyer's Guide to the Internet*. These represent some of the best and most important listings of law-related resources on the Internet.

What's in Here—The Guide

The "guide" portion of the book is divided into five parts:

Introduction. This section discusses why the Internet might be interesting or useful, and gives a few perspectives on how the Internet might be best approached.

The E-Frontier. The second section of the book describes the basic operating paradigms of the Internet—what the Internet is and isn't, how it functions without a central authority, and the basic Internet ethics that pervade day-to-day participation. Some might think the philosophy and "netiquette" of this environment is a secondary topic, but it's more fundamental than that. To answer the strategic question—what's in it for me?—you need to understand the rules of the game—before you start fiddling with the nuts and bolts.

Paleotechnologies. The third section of the book gets into the details—describing what those nuts and bolts really are. It introduces the specific Internet services that make up the suite of available tools, and then presents my own compilation of Internet starting points—not the exhaustive listings of law-related resources that you'll find in the reference lists, but my own "short list" of places to go and things to get when you first get connected. From these starting points, you should be able to find most of the resources described in the exhaustive listings, and you should be able to find the latest versions of the listings themselves. These starting points are called "Burge's Bookmarks."

E-Flatland Settlers. This section of the book gets to the heart of the strategic decision—the different ways in which one might participate or use Internet technologies. The three primary roles include:

- Internet user—This includes accessing the many materials, data, and other resources that others have published or made available, as well as participating in numerous discussion groups (a different kind of *networking*).
- Information provider—This includes supplying information to others on the net—as part of marketing, advertising, or simply to provide a service. Being an e-publisher on the net has some very distinct advantages, and disadvantages.
- User of Internet technologies in-house—These technologies represent a real breakthrough in standards-based, ubiquitously available, platform-independent information distribution capabilities. Under certain circumstances, these can offer some real advantages (and save a lot of money in the process).

"The User's Internet" describes the details of how to get connected, find your way around, and find an Internet service provider. It also introduces some of the security concerns that any net.connected lawyer should be aware of.

"The Provider's Internet" presents practical considerations regarding advertising on the net, and detailed netiquette-driven constraints that apply to *any* information provider that participates in the several different Internet services. It also includes tips on how best to start and position an e-publishing effort.

"The Internal Internet" describes how Internet-based software can be used as a Keep It Simple solution to some of the thorniest problems with today's client/server technologies. This includes the problem of how to disseminate information to lots of people who might be using different types of computers—without forcing everyone to conform to a single type of "client," and without committing the office to expensive proprietary solutions.

Learning More. The last section of the guide contains appendices and reference materials that can help the net.connected lawyer learn more about specific Internet-related topics. "Book Reviews," in particular, should be a good source of pointers if you decide to go further with these technologies.

What's in Here—The Listings

The second part of the book presents three resource listings. I consider each of these to be a must-have resource for the net.connected lawyer.

Legallist. This includes excerpts from Erik Heels's comprehensive online listing of law-related resources. (The full *Legal List* is an enormous list of specific law-related resources—both on the Internet and off.)

Lawlists. This is the full text of Lyonette Louis-Jacques's online listing of law-related discussion groups.

Govdocs. This is the full text of Austin & Tsang's online listing and bibliography of government-related Internet resources.

I've included these lists because I know readers want to *see* what we're talking about—and not just come away from this book with a homework assignment to go look them up. However, it's important to remember that these lists, as printed, are dated. (And Heels's *Legal List* is only excerpted.) Once you get ready to use these lists for real, you should get the latest up-to-date versions—online.

What's Not in Here

You'll notice that I didn't mention a single word about setting up your computer and telling you what buttons to push.

OK, in "The User's Internet," I succumb to the temptation and do a little bit of how-to button pushing. But frankly, there are many different ways to reach the net, many different things to do, and many different ways to get things done. And each involves different ways of setting up your computer and different sets of instructions. And of course, none of those instructions are unique to how a *lawyer* would use the Internet.

Getting connected is a key issue and this book has a section on it (see "The User's Internet"). But to cover all the how-to-connect topics thoroughly would have expanded the book significantly (duplicating many excellent books that are already on the bookstore shelves) and wouldn't have been lawyer-specific. I point you to what I believe are the industry's best and most comprehensive how-to-connect titles, but I don't try to duplicate their exhaustive coverage.

A second area that I've touched on only briefly is the ever-fluctuating marketplace of Internet service providers. There are hundreds of providers in the market; they are coming and going faster (and changing their products faster) than most *magazines* can keep up with; and the most cost-effective services are usually regional providers that serve fairly local geographic areas. I supply a brief listing of some of the major Internet service providers, but the most important references I give on this topic are the pointers to other listings and sources where you might find current information about providers that you can choose from—especially in your local area.

Finally, I want to emphasize that this book can't be everything for everyone. The subject of "the Internet" is so broad and far-reaching that no single book is going to cover it all. As you end up participating on the net in one way or another, you'll undoubtedly need to go to other sources for specific instructions and guidance. (Indeed, I included the "Book Reviews" chapter specifically to point you toward the best sources for that kind of additional information.) If you end up working on the net extensively, you'll no doubt end up with a bookshelf *full* of specific how-to guides—each describing a different aspect of the net.

Frequently Asked Questions for the Pragmatist

Q. So how come you're making such a big deal about what this book isn't?

A. Partly because the popular hype surrounding the net is so pervasive (and there are so many people looking for quick-and-easy answers) that it's tempting to position a book or an article as "Everything You Ever Wanted To Know." But that's misleading at best—and dangerous at worst.[1] On the other hand, when there's this much hype on a subject, there's a natural tendency to try to find out what the fuss is all about. I'm trying to answer that question, and to focus on the obvious followup—the strategic aspects of participating on the net. But you need to realize that we're just scratching the surface. The Internet is *huge*—thousands of networks, hundreds of thousands of information providers, and probably billions of accessible computer files. And there are millions of users trying to reach those services—trying to sort through them and find their way around, and trying to interact with one another in a way that's useful (or at least entertaining).

I envision the Internet first-timer with a shovel in his hand, making that first tentative push into the ground—trying to dig up something useful, and at the same time trying to figure out how hard

[1] The problem of describing the "Internet" is completely analogous to the various how-to legal books that ostensibly teach people how to write their own wills or start their own corporations. The most responsible books in that genre make a special point of telling the reader when the subject is getting too complex to be handled by the book, and that you should see a lawyer. The most dangerous books in that genre try to pretend that lawyers don't exist—and when the reader starts to do something that the book can't handle, the author *keeps it a secret!* To avoid a similar misimpression, I'm trying to make sure you're aware of *this* book's limits and scope.

this stuff is. Maybe he hits a rock, or maybe he hits gold on the very first try! But then the mind's camera pulls back to reveal the scale of this little mining expedition. As the view expands—further and further—and as the user and the little shovel become a tiny speck in a vast panorama, it becomes clear that the would-be Internaut is trying to dig up *an entire mountain*. From that perspective, it's easy to see that the first couple of shovelfuls won't mean a thing.

Q. How is this different from other law-related Internet guides?

A. This book is about strategies: Are you going to play in this game—at all— and if so, what role do you want to take? And once you decide, what's the next step?

Are you going to focus on legal research? Email? Grabbing free software? Are you looking for technical support, or to join a discussion group? Quite a few guides will give you the detailed how-tos, and the bibliographies will give you extensive descriptions of Internet resources—much more detailed than you'll find in this book. But I believe that few other books cover the pros and cons of participating as an information provider. Few deal with the special issues that *lawyers* face in this environment. And *very* few seem to acknowledge even the possibility—and significance—of using Internet service software for internal systems.

Q. If I'm new to this technology, should I skip around to different parts of the book?

A. Hey—it's your book. Read it however you like. And tell me what worked best for you so I can tailor the next edition to match your preferences. Because that's how this book was written—specifically for the net.newcomer. OK, you might be anxious to get past the introductory stuff, but if you're going to focus on the strategic questions, that introductory "stuff" is significant.

Q. If I'm a net.denizen and I already know my Internet specifics, should I skip around to different parts of the book?

A. Well, it's your book, too. But my advice is to go straight to the sections on netiquette and Internet ethics. And before you stick your advertising toe in the Internet waters, *please* read the section "The Special Case of Lawyers on the Internet" (in "The Provider's Internet" chapter).

Q. If I'm a consultant and I know this stuff backward and forward, should I skip around to different parts of the book?

A. Do not pass Go. Do not collect $200. Go directly to "The Internal Internet." For years, I was astonished that computer consultants were studiously avoiding the Internet—pointing out to me that there wasn't anything useful on the Internet for themselves, meanwhile ignoring the fact that their *clients* were clamoring for Internet technology capabilities. Now, I fear that these same consultants are studiously avoiding Internet service technologies and their applicability to solving heterogeneous client/server problems—at a comparatively low cost. It's not a panacea, but in certain situations it's a very real alternative and can offer *dramatic* cost savings.

Q. C'mon, level with me. Why don't you have just a one-page summary that tells me how to find stuff on the net? How hard can it be?

A. "Burge's Bookmarks" gives pointers to key *starting points*. But the problem is a real one: The Internet represents a *huge* virtual library with no centralized card catalog. It *can* be hard to find something, and once you do find it, it can be very difficult to find *again*. So some of the virtual library's virtual patrons (especially those who are very real professional librarians) have taken on the task of cataloging the uncatalogable. Unfortunately, even with boundless energy and limitless resources, the constantly changing and fundamentally anarchic Internet would represent an enormous challenge to track. With limited resources, it really is quite difficult.

Frankly, this is an immature marketplace. No one has stepped in with a single definitive guide or guides. Instead, we have twenty-five million would-be librarians on the job. Dare I demean my own effort . . .

Q. Dare you demean your own effort?

A. Why, yes I do. (And, uh, thanks for asking.) But this book is just one of many efforts to answer these where-do-I-go-and-how-do-I-find-it questions. In *The Lawyer's Guide to the Internet*, obviously, I'm trying to answer those questions for lawyers in particular.

I'm interested in whether you think I've helped or hindered—and whether I've given you what you were looking for. Please feel free to write to me in care of the American Bar Association, ABA Publications Planning, and Marketing, 750 N. Lake Shore Drive, Chicago, IL 60611. Or use the Reader Comments form in the back of this book. Or send comments directly to me via email, at either allisongb@attmail.com or allison@mitre.org.[2]

2 I guess if I get a lot of comments delivered by the U.S. Postal Service, that'll tell me something, eh?

Q. Any last words of advice before I start out on this journey?

A. Buckle up. You're in for a wild ride.

The Internet Environment

The E-Frontier

Chapter 3

The Basic
Internet Intro

The Internet is the largest network of computer systems on the planet.

Technically, it's the global network that connects huge numbers of networks to one another. It links together the massive online service bureaus, such as Compuserve, Prodigy, and America Online. It links together hundreds of thousands of universities, government agencies, and corporations located in almost a hundred countries around the world. It reaches out to small offices, school rooms—even individual homes. According to the Internet Society (ISOC), the net reached nearly five million host computers and twenty-five million users in 1994. Those numbers have seen a steady doubling *every year since 1983*.

From the user's perspective, the Internet is a truly massive resource of services. This network gives you access to the world's largest online source of reference information, publicly distributed software, and discussion groups—covering virtually every topic one could reasonably imagine (and an embarrassingly high number of topics that one could *not*, or at least *should* not, reasonably imagine).[1] The net.connected lawyer can find a wealth of information—including Supreme Court decisions, government agency filings, and discussion groups on specific fields of law. On both legal and nonlegal topics, the Internet is a significant reference library. In some areas of the country, even local court dockets are accessible on the Internet.

What makes the Internet difficult is that no one is in charge. It's not a single service that you sign up for—there's no vendor or government agency that's responsible for making sure there's useful information on the net, or deciding

[1] If you even come close, you should do some thinking about whether you've got too much time on your hands. *Way* too much time on your hands.

what information goes where. And there's no one whose job it is to make sure you can find what you need. The Internet is inherently disorganized—made so by its fundamental lack of structure. Organizationally, it is anarchy—plain and simple. In a group where everyone is a user, nothing happens unless individuals from that group step forward and help.

And what a group. Twenty-five million users—with varying ranges of technical and professional expertise (and some with rather remarkable skills)— give the Internet a powerful potential. Of course, to realize that potential, there has to be something more than just the numbers.

What seems to make the Internet work is a singularly strong sense of community. In the absence of authority, the anarchy *must* develop a group-wide ethic—of sharing and cooperation. Without this cooperation, without a strong community sense of what represents the "public" good, and without the volunteers who put in time and effort to serve that perceived public good, nothing would happen, and the net would turn into just another common carrier—a telephone system for interconnected networks.

Of course, the Internet is much more than that.

Chapter 4

A Tour of the E-Frontier

Let's go for a little ride.

Let's see what's happening just a *little bit* out on the edge. No multimedia or groupware—I promise—and no 32-bit vaporware, wireless pen computing, or virtual-reality Power Gloves (give me a *break*).

Just a little tour of the electronic outback—a no-wimps Frontier where reluctant pioneers are inventing new ways of doing things because they can't afford to do 'em the old way any more. A place where necessity is still the mother of invention. (A place where innovations are put on the fast track so they'll be up and running before management finds out!)

Keep your hands and feet inside the car at all times, remain seated, and don't raise the bar while the car is moving. Hang on folks, and welcome to the first part of the tour. Internet is the name, and *Too Much Information* is the game.

InternetLand

Meet Julia. She'll be your tour guide. Just out of high school, she's a freshman now—at Enormous State University (ESU). Bright kid. Wants to be a lawyer—or maybe a politician. (No accounting for tastes, eh?) No money, of course, and she doesn't own her own computer, but she's in computer class right now and she's logged onto the university computer. She's going to take you out for a little net-surfing ride.

She types in the word *gopher*. A menu of information sources appears on the screen. There's also a notice that shows we're connected to the gopher server at the University of Minnesota.[1]

Let's see if she can at least get your attention.

Here's an interesting item: "U.S. Supreme Court."

She selects it and we're in.[2] (Actually, we're connected to Case Western Reserve University—one of the distribution points in the Supreme Court's Project Hermes.) Lessee, now, what'll we look at? Here's one. Just a few minutes ago,[3] the Supreme Court announced the decision in No. 91-8199, *Thomas Lee Deal v. United States. It's already available.* Full text. ASCII format, WordPerfect format, or the Supreme Court's own Atex format if we want it that way.

What'll we look for next?

Browsing with an Attitude

How about looking for all the recent decisions on abortion? OK—let's get out of gopher and try a little "WAISsearch" for the word *abortion.*

1 **Why the University of Minnesota? Because** that's where this Internet service was developed, and when the programmers made copies of the software available (to *everyone on the net*), they specified the U. of M. gopher server as the default starting point. Most gopher software programs that run on PCs or Macs or Unix host computers (the gopher "clients") start by connecting to the server at Minnesota unless you specify something different. Why is it called gopher? Oh, a hundred different reasons that represent what passes for folklore on the net. But it's no coincidence at all that the University of Minnesota mascot is the Golden Gopher. (And no, gopher is not the same as that Personal Information Manager software called Gofer.)

2 That was quick. One of the basic concepts implemented in gopher is that picking a menu choice—depending on the menu choice—can take you to another computer on the net. (Other menu choices may take you to documents, or to text search programs.) The gopher "servers" on the two host computers automatically handle the logins required—all in the background. The user doesn't have to type in a user ID or a password—the connection process works like any other menu choice.

3 Oh, give me a break. *Of course* it wasn't just a few minutes ago. This is an *example.* You gotta work with me here. In real life™, many decisions are posted within minutes or hours of being released by the Court.

Yow! We got back about a *zillion* cases that contain the word *abortion.* They're sorted, so that the cases with the most occurrences of the word are at the top of the list, but that doesn't really help a lot. Let's try something else. How about *confrontation clause* AND *child witness* AND *adversariness? That's* a lot more obscure. Sure enough— only three cases this time, and again they're sorted by what WAIS (Wide Area Information Servers) refers to as "relevance."

WAIS isn't in the same league with most of the commercial text-search databases. LEXIS, WEST-LAW, and ZyIndex (just to name a few) all have more sophisticated searching capabilities. Also, the Internet's legal research databases are rather limited: Supreme Court cases only go back to 1990, lower court and state court decisions are just starting to come online, and for the most part, decisions are being published on a go-forward-from-this-date basis. This *isn't* a LEXIS clone. (Just a little tiny *part* of one.)

Anything else? How about the daily list of Supreme Court orders? OK. (That was quick.) This thing is mostly one-line orders. Certs granted and denied, habeas corpus, mandamus, admissions to the Supreme Court bar, and Way Too Many Disbarments. And the Court will recess 'til next Monday.

Let's go somewhere else. University of Virginia's law library? Temple's? There's one in Australia. "How about Cornell?" Julia suggests, "They've got a pretty good gopher server there." Cornell gives us these menu choices:

```
   1. Directory of Legal Academia
   2. U.S. Law: Primary Documents and Commentary
   3. Foreign and International Law: Primary Documents and Commentary
   4. Other References Useful in Legal Education and Research
-->5. Other Internet Law Sites
   6. Government Agencies: Information and Reports
   7. Library Resources (online catalogs)
   8. Periodicals, News, and Journals
```

Paleotechnologies

What you're watching is a demonstration of just two of the more *elementary* services available on the Internet—gopher and WAIS. There are more than 3,000 publicly accessible gopher servers in about seventy countries around the world.[4] There are also more than 500 WAIS-searchable databases. And the really fancy stuff—such as World Wide Web (WWW), with its hypertext links, graphics, and an attractive little point-and-click user interface—is outpacing them all, with a meaningless-because-it's-so-new doubling-every-two-months growth rate and the usual it's-out-of-date-already count of 25,000 WWW servers.[5]

One of the pioneers of these "resource discovery" technologies, Paul

4 By the time you read this, these numbers are out-of-date. Most of the more popular services on the net are just now being invented. They grow at spectacular rates—usually expressed as "doubling every *n* months." Of course, the "forever-doubling" measure is unrealistic. In some cases, since the services are so new, the very high growth rates merely reflect the usual Internet start-ups (A typical popular service grows from zero to a significant number, for example, in just one year. That infinity-percent growth rate, however, is a *bit* hard to sustain.) On the other hand, some of these "forever-doubling" growth rates are *very* real—maybe not as predictors but at least to reflect historical growth. As I've mentioned already (and will again several more times until this horse is *completely* dead), the number of host computers connected to the net, has roughly doubled each year since 1983—the annual rate of growth is running between 80 and 90 percent.

5 It really *is* difficult to try to express the growth of these services. Part of the reason is that the numbers are hard to get on anything other than an anecdotal basis. Here's an
continued next page ➤

Evan Peters,[6] refers to the burgeoning tools of the Internet as "paleotechnologies"—crude tools that appeal to the hunters, gatherers, and storytellers of this developing e-civilization. He describes the emerging Internet services as settlements on the e-frontier—intended to attract those *flatland settlers* who might be more interested in husbanding the natural resources of the net, than in the simple pleasures of exploring it.[7]

Two significant advances are represented by the Internet service technologies. One is the Internet itself—the network of databases, servers, and discussion groups that people are building and discovering. The other is the use of resource access software *within* an organization—converting the Internet's technologies to your *own* use.

Let's take a quick look at both.

E-Library to the World

Three thousand gopher servers? What could they *possibly* have to tell us?

In a matter of seconds, Julia takes us on a tour of the world.

Instantly, we're connected to TECHNET in Singapore. Now, to the Bioinformatics database at the Australian National University—and to the Japan Cancer Research Resources Bank. Here in the United States, we reach out to the National Institutes of Health and a host of medical, educational, and scientific databases.

And for those who want to travel *in flagrante*, rather than electronically, let's take a look at the *CIA World Factbook* or the State Department's travel advisories for foreign locations. And here are weather reports and forecasts from every weather station in the country.

➤ example: In December 1994, the National Center for Supercomputing Applications (NCSA)—which maintains a popular *What's New* list of World Wide Web sites—noted that it was receiving submissions for more than 400 new web sites each week. That semi-statistic was no doubt true, but it was just one number. It may have been a peak that NCSA ran into for just one or two weeks, or it may have been a "snapshot" of a dramatic trend. And since the number was submitted as just one data point—and not as part of a real growth analysis—we have no way of putting it in context. The other reason it's difficult to express growth rates is that we *do* know that the rates—at least for the newer services—change quickly and dramatically. After just a few months, the rate will be different. Maybe higher, maybe lower. Maybe by a little, maybe by a lot. At this point in the history of the net, we really don't have much of an historical basis for predicting even rough *patterns* of growth. But I think I can predict with a fair amount of certainty that by the time you read the words on these pages, the number of web servers will be something other than 25,000, and that the growth rate will not be 400 new sites per week.

6 Peters is the founder and executive director of the Coalition for Networked Information. CNI was established to promote the creation and use of networked information resources and services that advance scholarship and intellectual productivity. CNI is sponsored by three associations: the Association of Research Libraries (ARL), CAUSE, and EDUCOM.

7 Just in case you had any doubts at all, the phrase "flatland settlers" in this sentence is said in the most patronizing tone available. Obviously, Mr. Peters does not think of himself as a flatlander, but he clearly acknowledges that *those people* do have a place (albeit a boring place) in the grand scheme of things. Personally, I like to think of *myself* as just such a flatlander. Boring? *You bet.* In the Peters paleotechnology context, I'm an e-flatland settler *and proud of it!*

More than fifty law schools operate gopher and web servers. They offer full-text downloading and searching of statutes (copyright, patent, trademark, the UCC), as well as discussion groups and materials for specific subject areas (disability law, environmental law, privacy).

The White House is online. Here's the full text of speeches, press releases, budgets, and proposals. You'll even find the president's daily schedule! (Email to the White House? Oh come on, that's *old news*—send it to president@ whitehouse.gov.)

Indeed, the government is on the net *en masse*. While we're just "wandering around," let's go to the Government Printing Office's ACCESS system, the Securities and Exchange Commission's EDGAR system, or the House and Senate gophers. There are 325 state and federal agencies that supply data and resources to the net.[8] Even the Library of Congress has opened up its massive card catalogs, and photographs of new exhibits, to the Internet. Clearly, the intent is to turn the Internet into an electronic library of enormous proportions.

Then that brat Julia reminds us, "And the number of databases is *doubling* every six months. . . ."

What about the *Intranet?*

The prospect of a publicly accessible worldwide e-library is getting a lot of attention. But the more telling impact may come when the Internet service technologies—or their successors and derivatives—are used for *internal* information systems.

Julia says that she'd *like* to show you the internal services that she's helped one local law firm implement; but since it's an internal system only and really quite secure—the standard Internet tools *can't get into it*.[9] Building an internal system doesn't mean that you're publishing your client list for the world to see. In fact, you don't need to be connected to the Internet *at all* to utilize the Internet's resource-access technologies.

OK, OK, let's not go to *that* law firm, but there are many firms—even large corporations—that use these technologies for simple point-and-click access to basic firm resources: a client phone book, a list of file numbers, conflicts-of-interest checking. They start out

8 *Of course* that number is out-of-date. I keep telling you—this stuff is growing faster than printed write-ups can keep up with (except maybe in a daily newspaper). To help me out, and to keep me from qualifying every number I put in this book, I'd appreciate it if you would just translate any numbers you see (throughout the rest of this book) into a suitable descriptive phrase. Something like "quite a few." Or "Wow, more than <whatever the number was>?!" If the actual number is interesting to you, you can check the online resource guides or the sources listed in the chapter "Fun with Statistics" in "References."

9 Actually, the last time she gave this tour, someone really pressed her on the point. She stopped, turned to the guy, and said in a sort of conspiratorial half-whisper, "Well, I *could* show it to you. But then I'd have to kill you." Julia scares me some times.

with something small and obvious—like that phone book—but once they figure out the power of these ubiquitous little information-browsing tools, they find themselves asking how hard it would be to add in something with a little more meat on it: each client's billing and receivables status, full text of the most recent bill, key names and addresses, or upcoming milestones in related case-tickler files. The hypertext-based WWW servers are *especially* well suited to this sort of start-at-one-point-then-depending-on-what-you're-looking-for-drill-down-to-something-else functionality. Each time you want to add something new, you just add a link to another set of menus or files. With a little imagination, the hypertext services can realize a lot of potential—including (dare I suggest it?) search and retrieval of internal work product. Almost any reference material is a legitimate candidate for these technologies. Of course, to get *access* to the data, someone has to be in charge of *entering* the data and keeping it up-to-date. If you have to build the information from scratch, that can be a real chore (and it's what dooms most of these fancy pie-in-the-sky all-you-gotta-do-is systems). In that case, you get to the heart of the question right away: How badly do you want that information—just how important is it? On the other hand, if the data is already in a database somewhere—billing, conflicts, whatever—then making it available through the browsers shouldn't be that difficult.

So why would you use these unassuming little half-baked utilities when the Microsofts and Lotuses of the world can sell you something *really* sexy that knocks your *socks* off?[10] One reason is that the Really Sexy Stuff usually requires a lot of effort just to set it up. You waste a ton of time building the technology, then you barely have enough time to focus on collecting, entering, and maintaining *the data*. Of course the data is what's useful, so every minute spent on building menus, queries, and forms is taken away from building the content. Also, when you go for the sexy stuff, you eventually figure out that you have to switch *everyone* over to Enormous Software Company's *proprietary* database and forms environment. Which is expensive. And which invariably causes a conflict with Some Other Plan.

The reason so many firms are moving to Internet-based services for these ubiquitous query tools is that they're simple (albeit simplistic), they're inexpensive (freeware or shareware), and they're standardized (*nonproprietary*, and usually available for every major operating system).

[10] Somehow, I always seem to be able to keep my socks on during demos. It's not until the stuff goes out to real live users and they either decide to actually do something with it or relegate it to the back of the software shelf that I'm convinced. And it's not until some users come back to show *me* what they're doing with it and how they can't live without it that I find myself suddenly wandering around barefoot (or at least sockless). If I'm going to avoid the so-called productivity paradox, I want to see time saved, questions answered, or better results. Exploring is fun, but it's results that count. Yes, I'm an e-flat-land settler and I'm *still* proud of it.

Oh? Did I mention that they're nonproprietary? That means that if you get *just fed up* with That Stupid Gopher Software from Some Dumb University, you can dump it and get someone else's version of the software that promises to do something a little nicer or a little faster. Or if *you* like one, but Jane Down-the-Hall likes another, that's fine. You can use the one, and she can use the other. They work together because they're following standards that have been developed for supporting *twenty-five million Internet users*.

Typically, to set up internal Internet services, you *do* have to set your machines up to be running TCP/IP—usually on Ethernet. Ethernet is fairly commonplace—especially if your office uses Novell Netware for its local area network—but TCP/IP is something that many Novell-only offices will have to add. TCP/IP is a network protocol that's different from the one used in Netware, but you can set it up to run simultaneously with Netware (and yes, over the same wires).

Once the network is set up, the Internet services are extremely efficient.

"Did I mention that the gopher server we went through," Julia points out, "You remember—the one at the University of Minnesota? It handles 50,000 transactions a day on a Macintosh IIci."[11]

Thanks, Julia—that was fun, but we've got to be going now.

"But you haven't seen *the web yet!*" she protests. "You haven't seen Mosaic,[12] or the terrific web server that the Legal Information Institute put up at Cornell, or the list of legal resources at Indiana's law school![13] You haven't seen the newsgroups, or the listserv digests, or the sites full of shareware."

(Pretty pushy for some youngster fresh out of high school, eh?) Sorry. We've got to get going.

11 Actually, that was a long time ago—back when the gopher traffic could be counted in merely tens-of-thousands of transactions per day. At the 50,000-a-day mark, it was being run on a Mac IIci. Now that the transactions have skyrocketed, it runs on much more powerful workstations. Even so, 50,000 per day on a Mac IIci is pretty efficient.

12 She actually means, "you haven't seen the World Wide Web Internet service through NCSA's Mosaic WWW browser software." Mosaic is just one of several WWW browsers—or "web" browsers. But it's the most popular, so you'll often hear people refer to the WWW Internet service as simply Mosaic. As others—such as Netscape—catch up in popularity, you may hear the references to Mosaic drop. But they are likely to be replaced by more references to the individual browsers—like Netscape—instead of to the service itself.

13 You also haven't seen the interactive frog dissection she was planning to show you at http://curry.edschool.virginia.edu/~insttech/frog (complete with full-color photographs and gratuitously gross and disgusting movies), or the Russian Archives exhibit put up by the Library of Congress, or a hundred other astonishing and scary net sites—but I guess she figured you'd find the legal resources potentially more enticing. What she *wasn't* going to show you, but what might have been *painfully* enticing, were the net sites being put up on the net by your colleagues and competitors. Venable, Baetjer, Howard & Civiletti, for example, has set up a WWW server. In fact, O'Reilly & Associates' Global Network Navigator (GNN) lists several law firms in the GNN marketplace. It's like watching another law firm marketing to *your* prospective clients, and it's more than just a little disquieting. Maybe we shouldn't mention this to Julia.

Chapter 5

How Does the Internet Work?

Like I said, the Internet is the largest network of computer systems on the planet.

But what makes it work are the people—the users and the developers that seem to be energized with a sort of guerrilla can-do attitude that seems to insist that it *will* work. This is what seems to make the Internet more than just another group of wires—more than just a large network of computer systems.

You'll find good Samaritans on the net who will go out of their way to help a newcomer. You'll find people helping to organize and map out the net for us e-flatland settlers. (As a public service, thank-you-very-much.) You'll find universities and government agencies—even for-profit corporations—that are publishing information on the net simply because they think that providing information is good and useful—part of their charter, if you will.

OK, you'll also find people who *don't* share the community spirit, *and* you'll find an interesting interplay between those who do and those who don't. Indeed, in the absence of an externally established authority, the anarchy must turn to its own users to resolve these problems.

Instead of threatening the viability of the net, this anarchic lack of structure seems to give its users an extra incentive to make it work. They not only seem to *like* this anti-authoritarian model, but they embrace it—by developing and encouraging the necessary community ethic (frequently referred to as "netiquette") to establish the standards and practices for working on the net. And they protect it—with a fierce devotion that ranges from zealous peer pressure (usually in the form of vitriolic email messages, or "flames"), to targeted destructive hacking.

It's an interesting contradiction: The pervasiveness of the Internet ethic and the vehemence with which it is "encouraged" seem diametrically opposed to its anti-authoritarian ideals. The contradiction not only stands as a key part of the Internet environment, but it seems to flourish. And it's not the last contradiction we'll run across while checking out this e-frontier.

Who Owns the Internet?

No one.

No one owns the Internet, and no one runs it. No single vendor sells it; the government doesn't run it; it's not a government-regulated monopoly. There's no central authority that enforces proper behavior, censors transgressors, or imposes sanctions on net.miscreants.

This is something that a lot of people can't accept. How can something this big run without someone *in charge?* How can it operate? How can it function? *Where's the Internet's Al Haig?* Some people just don't believe it. And in a sense, I can understand the resistance—most services are offered to customers as a product. Or at least as a government service.

One way to reconcile this dilemma is to consider the Internet's similarity—at least in terms of "ownership"—to faxing. No one is "in charge" of faxing. No one "owns" it. And yet people the world over use it effectively. You need to own your own equipment, and you pay for whatever telephone bills you run up. You rely on suppliers of basic services to make it work (*especially* the telephone companies). And there are semi-official international organizations that set the "voluntary" technical standards to make sure that all the fax machines in the world will talk to each other—standards that the manufacturers are supposed to adhere to carefully.

The Internet follows a *roughly* similar model. As long as you've got the equipment that's technically capable of connecting, all you really need is the communications link and you're in. The vendor who sells you the connection is simply selling connectivity—not unlike the phone company in the faxing example.[1]

1 As with faxing, the Internet is more of a logical network—rather than a physical set of wires that you can point to. Most of the net is implemented through standard connectivity services offered by the telephone companies and other standard carriers.

The Internet also has its own international organization—the Internet Society (abbreviated, curiously, as "ISOC")—that's responsible for setting "voluntary" technical standards. The one substantive difference is that ISOC not only recommends the standards, it also manages the Internet addresses—the domain names—that are used to identify a particular host or computer network. Presumably, since ISOC controls the addresses, it could withhold or revoke an address from a net.miscreant, but it has fiercely avoided any such enforcement role (so far, at least).[2]

Who Pays for the Internet?

Some people, still uncomfortable with the no-one-in-charge model, try to "follow the money"—confident that the trail of money will *reveal* the "true Internet." As it turns out, this investigative path *does* reveal quite a bit about the Internet, but not in the ways that our follow-the-money cynics would expect.

First and foremost, there is no single entity that collects money for using the Internet. Just as with faxing, there are costs associated with using the net, but what you're paying for are all of the bits and pieces.

Part of the reason the Internet model works is that the underlying network technologies were specifically designed to operate in the *absence* of centralized control. The forerunner of today's Internet[3] was a U.S. Defense Department network called the ARPAnet, developed in 1969 as an experiment (in part at least) to test network technologies that could withstand partial outages—such as you might get with, oh, *global thermonuclear war.*[4] The TCP/IP network protocol was designed with the assumption that the network is unreliable, that any portion of the network could disappear at any moment, and that any individual computer or group of computers might be unavailable for lengthy periods of time. The resulting technology is a network protocol that constantly tries to deliver packets of information from the source computer to the destination computer—automatically bouncing from node to node to node, looking for whatever route might reach the destination. Certainly, there is no central hub that could be knocked out and bring down the entire net. Instead, the connectivity model is for each node on the network to run its wire to the next closest node (sometimes to the next two or three closest nodes, to ensure that the network isn't vulnerable to a simple break in the chain). A high-speed network backbone helps with overall network performance

2 ISOC does officially encourage adherence to standards and practices that constitute "electronically correct" behavior on the net—netiquette. Recently, ISOC has started an initiative to codify those standards. This is an ongoing evolutionary process—as is much of the Internet—and the actual progress of this initiative could be very interesting to watch.

3 Time out. You're kidding! We're gonna get a *boring history lesson?* Hey! Does a kid looking for Sega Genesis care even *one whit* about Atari's first game of Pong? Of course not. Is it even of any *use?* Like, I don't think so. Like, not any more than hearing about *Grandad* who had to walk *fifty-three miles* back and forth to school every day through snow drifts that were at least a *couple of hundred feet deep.* (And he *liked* it.) OK, OK, I'll try to mention the history only when it's relevant, and I'll try to throw in some cool stuff—like maybe blowing things up? How about if I try to mention global thermonuclear war? Very *War Games*-ish, eh? OK, time back in.

4 Wait a minute. That wasn't *War Games*-ish. That's what they were really testing for, wasn't it? Yow.

—connecting together different regions of the country. The backbone is operated and funded by the National Science Foundation (NSF), an agency of the U.S. government. The National Science Foundation Network (NSFNET) is an important part of the Internet in the United States—but the network could operate without it. Thus, no giant mainframe runs this thing, no network manager ties it all together, and no single entity cashes checks written to "the Internet."

Who pays for the network? Every organization that participates in the Internet with a full-time connection (rather than a simple dial-in capability) establishes a dedicated line between it and its nearest neighbor (or neighbors)—usually through the local telephone carrier. This implements the basic network links, and it has the side benefit of minimizing participants' costs. The cost of connecting to a neighbor is almost always less than running those expensive dedicated lines all the way to a central hub. (Phone companies charge for those dedicated lines by the mile.) Also, with dedicated lines, there are no usage fees. Whether you're online for just a few minutes a day or whether the Internet is filling your local link with the entire traffic of the Eastern seaboard, your local link costs the same.

Who pays for the network? Each organization pays for its own equipment, and for a short link in the net. (NSFNET, supported by government funds, represents a tiny fraction of the total networking costs.) It's not very much, individually, and it tends to go to the phone companies who—until recently—didn't seem to recognize the magnitude of what was being carried over this innocuous group of otherwise unrelated leased lines. Now that they *do* know what's going on—now that they realize they're providing the last-mile infrastructure for a global network of extraordinary capacity—they're pretty sure they're being underpaid. Follow the money? As the politics of the so-called information superhighway are discussed and lobbied, there are a lot of commercial carriers that want the trail of money to be a *bigger* trail, thank-you-very-much, pointing directly at them.

What about the data? What about the software? What about the services? Who pays for those?

These questions can be hard to explain—at least to people who insist on keeping their follow-the-money bias. That's because virtually all of the resources on the net are free. Once you've got your connection, you can reach out to literally thousands of sources—to get data, software, and services—at no additional cost. No LEXIS- or WESTLAW-like usage fees.[5] No Prodigy-like omnipresent advertising. No visible means of support of any kind.

5 Actually *some* services *do* require LEXIS- or WESTLAW-like usage fees: LEXIS and WESTLAW, just to name two. But the norm on the net is to avoid those charges. At least for now.

How can this be? What's in it for the information providers? What kind of quality can I expect if I'm not paying the information provider?[6] Those are difficult questions. For a clue, let's look at the PC user groups that started up during the 1980s. Certainly, there wasn't much money-to-be-followed in those groups. Should we look at what was in it for *those* volunteers? Indeed, why would anyone spend time and effort simply sharing information with others? Maybe they all hoped to start lucrative PC consulting careers!

Geesh! Just give it a rest!

Some people share information simply because they think there's a net gain for everyone involved. Maybe some will gain more than others, but as long as there's a critical mass of people willing to try, the group as a whole comes out ahead. This fundamental principal of cooperation is a cornerstone of the Internet ethic. If you think you'll trick the system and just grab what you can get (this is referred to as "lurking"), *that's fine*. No one will care, no one will notice, and it won't cost anybody anything.[7]

Some organizations share information as part of academic research: More than a quarter of the host computers attached to the Internet are located at universities, and a substantial number of the services available—and the supporting software they use—were originally developed as part of academic projects. In some cases, this can be a little disconcerting—I'd hate to find out that I'm *relying* on a software product that some graduate student wrote as an extra-credit homework assignment. (Worse yet, I'd hate to find out that the student only got a C on the project.) But in many cases, the consortia among academia and government are the ones that produce the most powerful results—such as the Supreme Court decisions that are reposted by Case Western Reserve University and the extensive resources organized at Cornell's School of Law. True, these efforts may lack the breadth and polish of full-fledged commercial databases (such as LEXIS and Dialog), but they can provide real value—at dramatically reasonable costs.

Of course, some of the more visible participants on the net are government agencies—at both the state and federal level. In most cases, the agencies have a charter that requires them to disseminate information to

6 Have you noticed the cognitive disconnect between capitalism and the Internet ethic? Frankly, most traditional economic theories have a difficult time with the Internet. Of course, getting things done without a profit-based motive flies in the face of good capitalist doctrine. But cooperating without government direction wasn't exactly what Karl Marx had in mind. Discussions on the net often find the Libertarians taking credit for having the Internet Idea all along, but as soon as you get sucked into that trap you're talking politics—not economics. Suffice it to say that the would-be vendor community is having an especially hard time understanding what's going on and why. It should come as No Surprise At All that Bill Gates—ironically, one of the first to tout the information super*hype*way—admits that he misjudged the Internet completely.

7 Who knows—if you lurk long enough, maybe you'll actually help someone someday. Accidentally, of course.

the public, and an Internet site can help them meet that charter with an automated tool that's relatively inexpensive, requires little of their ever-dwindling labor resources, and carefully tracks inquiries and accesses so the sponsoring agency can actually measure and track the service's performance. Other government agencies have migrated to the Internet for wholly selfish and straightforward reasons—they can work more efficiently (both with other agencies and with the public) if they have an Internet capability. The network in Kansas, for example, was driven in large part by the state courts' belief that they could work better with local attorneys if those attorneys had electronic access to court dockets—rather than requiring taxpayer-paid staff to field a constant flow of docket-related questions.[8]

To be fair, some organizations share because there *is* something in it for them. Quite a few companies have established Internet-based services (technical support, basic questions and answers, some reference materials) to encourage use of their products. Some software companies distribute free demonstration copies of their commercial products in hopes that it will encourage sales. Some vendors even set up online catalogs for would-be customers to browse and order from. Indeed, some law firms have set up Internet-based sites that allow people to check out what services the firm may offer. Most of these commercial sites have a fairly low-key tone to them, because the Internet community seems to respond best to vendors who present information about their offerings as a service to would-be customers. The infamous "Green Card Incident"—in which an Arizona law firm advertised their immigration-law legal services by posting an unsolicited advertisement in thousands of discussion groups (a process that's referred to as "spamming")—invoked the collective wrath of the Internet community, and served notice that intrusive commercial advertising violates the cooperative spirit of the community and is pointedly unwelcome.

Some visionaries predict a time when commercial advantage on the Internet will be gained not by direct sales and client contact, but rather by sponsoring popular services and getting the advertiser's name in front of users in a positive

[8] See "INK: The Information Network of Kansas—A Model for Public Access Through Public-Private Partnerships that Really Work," William F. Bradley, Jr., *Law Practice Management,* March 1995.

[9] Prodigy—the online service and joint venture between IBM and Sears—attempted to implement this television model of advertiser support. Unfortunately, Prodigy suffers from a severe case of not-invented-here syndrome: It seems to have assumed that it should and can provide everything the users might want (in terms of electronic content). It also seems to assume that the primary role of its service is to deliver users to advertisers, rather than providing services—and content—to users. But whether you like Prodigy or not (it certainly has its strengths and advantages), I don't believe that its relative success or failure should be used as an indicator of the viability of the advertiser-supported model. Prodigy's strengths and weaknesses are focused more on its content and features—taken as a whole—than on its use of an advertiser-supported revenue model.

light. In the early days of television, half-hour advertisements just didn't draw viewers. But Milton Berle did. And the advertisers paid handsomely to have their name and products prominently displayed on shows that people wanted to watch. Some suggest that the Internet may move towards a similar model—in which would-be advertisers pay to support popular services.[9]

Aren't There *Any* Rules?

OK, so no one is in charge, no one runs it, and no one pays for it. So, how can it possibly work?

It works because of the enormous sense of community and cooperation that characterizes the net. It rides on the backs of volunteers who make things happen—even when there's "nothing in it for them." It flies in the face of conventional me-first selfishness of the advertising stereotype. And it stands as something of an example—held in high esteem by the net.connected would-be technocrats—that a society based on nothing more than ethics, fair play, and cooperation can exist and work effectively without the intervention (the more vocal participants would say interference) of government, laws, or enforcement agencies.

It works—at least for the moment. But most recognize that the foundation is more than just a bit fragile. Hoping that twenty-five million people[10] will unilaterally follow an unwritten code of ethics—without any threat of censure or enforcement whatsoever—is entirely naive. And frankly, the ethic carries within it several internal inconsistencies.

Netiquette

Typically, discussions of electronically correct behavior—or "netiquette" in the lexicon of today's media hype—focus on the day-to-day rules for playing well with others.[11] Most articles

10 "People." That would be distinguished from—at least in the minds of many net.denizens—lawyers. Regrettably, the Green Card Incident represented a breach of Internet ethics that fits all too well into the popular-culture negative stereotype that the legal profession suffers from these days. The Green Card lawyers weren't the first to break these unwritten rules (others have run chain letters and various get-rich-quick scams). But they were one of the first to show no remorse. (The others at least had the common decency to *pretend* that it was an accident, or that they didn't understand the standards and practices.) Instead of showing contrition and understanding, the Green Card lawyers argued that they weren't breaking any laws, that they planned to do it again, and that they were planning to show others how to do it, as well. There were reports that the law firm had threatened to sue those that might interfere. Unfortunately, this response reinforced *exactly* the stereotyped negative images that the legal profession strives to overcome. Following the Green Card Incident, expectations in the Internet community are fallen to the point where lawyers fall *beneath* the level of chain letters and Skinny Dip Thigh Cream. Obviously, it will take some time and effort to rebuild our reputation.

11 Everything I ever needed to know, I learned in my netiquette FAQ file. A FAQ file is an online resource—usually a text file—that contains the answers to Frequently Asked Questions (FAQs). You can always find a good group of netiquette-related guides and FAQ files at the Electronic Frontier Foundation: ftp://ftp.eff.org/pub/Net_info/Net_ culture or http://www.eff.org/pub/Net_info/ Net_culture.

or write-ups that try to cover the rules of netiquette (and there seem to be hundreds of them) are very detailed, very how-to, and very Miss Manners-esque[12]—telling you how to put smiley faces[13] in your email :-), why you should always read the FAQ file (Frequently Asked Questions), and that you should NEVER TYPE IN ALL CAPS BECAUSE IT LOOKS LIKE YOU'RE SHOUTING! They're easy enough to follow and almost entertaining.

But this type of day-to-day focus tends to miss the more substantive principles of the Internet ethic—i.e., the fundamental standards and practices of the community that are likely to have a strategic effect on what the Internet might offer to you or your office. Or *vice versa*.

Most popular-press pieces tend to shy away from this occasionally darker side of netiquette.[14] Write-ups on the underlying Internet ethic are few and far between—in part because it's more entertaining to turn your head sideways and look at a hundred different smiley faces and try to figure out who has the time—or the twisted imagination—to think up these things. But there are other more substantive reasons as well: There are some internal inconsistencies in the generally accepted netiquette, there are some things in it that don't exactly adhere to international copyright laws, and frankly, there are some noticeable disagreements over how the rules of netiquette should be applied—fundamental differences over what's perceived as right and wrong.

What follows then, is my

12 By contrast, the Emily.Post Rules of Netiquette teach by sarcastic anti-examples. Strangely enough, the Emily.Post entirely-rude-and-sarcastic approach is not out of line with the limits of netiquette—illustrating by its very approach that netiquette has much more to do with what you should and shouldn't do when using Internet services, than with having good manners and being polite.

13 You'll frequently hear about the use of "emoticons"—smiley faces and other graphical icons created using punctuation marks and letters. These *emotion constructs*—from which we get the term, *emoticon*—are inserted into the text of email messages and other net postings to convey sarcasm or humorous intent—especially when the author isn't sure that the text alone has conveyed the intended emotion (or when the author wants to laugh at his or her own humor). Typically, emoticons are either a variation on the basic :-) smiley face (which, at its best, can look like a smiley face fallen over on its side), or is represented by an expression written within angle brackets, such as <grin>. Because the smiley face emoticons work best in the fixed-width fonts that are generally used for email and related applications, and because they work poorly in the proportional and stylized fonts that most magazine and book publishers use, the utility and value of the device is rarely communicated well in published materials. This book will fail as well. :-)

14 This division of netiquette into two distinct parts (day-to-day versus standards and practices) is a source of considerable discussion and controversy. Since the vernacular seems to be stuck with just one word to describe the entire range of acceptable and unacceptable behavior, the participants don't really have a lexicon for distinguishing between the Green Card Incident and TYPING IN ALL CAPS. Both are violations of netiquette. But by lumping the Incident into a category that sounds like it was written by Miss Manners, you're equating it (or one might *argue* that you're equating it) with chewing with your mouth open. It's of use to note that some have made exactly that assessment; while many others feel the Incident, and the attitude behind it, represent a threat to the viability of the net.

own subjective assessment of the two guiding principles of the Internet ethic: freedom of speech and self-determination. I'll try to point out places where I'm making things up, and places where the "rules" conflict with one another.

Most of the Internet ethic, in my opinion, can be attributed to one of two basic principles:

- Freedom of speech is absolute.
- Self-determination is absolute.

As you might imagine, those pesky "absolutes" tacked on to the end of each ideal can set up some pretty dramatic confrontations. And those of you who specialize in consitutional law will notice the nontrivial absence of key qualifying phrases, such as "the government shall make no law. . . ." On the net, there is no government, there is no law. Oxymoron or not, "anarchy rules."

Freedom of Speech

To a limited extent, this basic principle is just what you would expect—it represents the "right" of participants on the net to discuss and yell and scream and express their opinions with as much zeal as you'd find at any idealized political soap box. But there are a number of corollaries to this basic principle that you might not expect.

- If you put something out on the net, it's generally treated as though you've turned it over to the public domain. The Internet community has an expansive and what I'm sure some would call a "novel" perspective on the fair-use exception to copyright law. Not to put too fine a point on it, but if a net.user can somehow grab an electronic copy of something—by scanning it, running it through OCR, or grabbing a copy off a newspaper wire service—then that text or picture is likely to be spread around the net without regard to copyright protections or intellectual property rights. The ability to send anything captured electronically is perceived as fair game and—through the community's special brand of logic—anything that one can "use" must therefore be "fair-use."[15] The practice is

15 Oh, don't even try to follow it. Knowledgeable professionals recognize that copyright extends to electronic copies, and most companies establish policies against violating copyright laws on the net. Indeed, you'll occasionally find a few would-be scholars ranting about the potential copyright violations contained in the common email option of including a copy of an original email message with the reply—even though you probably didn't get permission to electronically forward or "republish" the original note. Admittedly, a number of common Internet practices raise some interesting and complex copyright issues, but there is nothing complex about the rampant, unapologetic, and deliberate copyright violations that are pervasive on the net. They are a part of the culture. Indeed, a few Internet "newsgroups" openly describe their contents as "thousands of copyright violations." You'll also find lengthy verbatim copies of newspaper and magazine articles—and they're specifically tagged, "reprinted without permission." Fair-use goes a long, long way on the Internet.

frequently likened to sharing a newspaper with a friend—with the only difference being, from the users' perspective, that they're using a bit of technology to do the sharing. Of course, when you share your newspaper with *twenty-five million* friends, the concept of fair-use suffers a bit.

- The limits of copyright abuse seem to stop at the edges of the net. Users won't think twice about sending copies of entire books out to everyone on the net. But if you take something *off* the net and print it as part of a commercial endeavor, you'd better get permission from every attributable author you can find. In fact, most electronic products and publications specify this particular implementation of the Internet ethic in their all-rights-reserved copyright paragraphs. Most Internet products give blanket permissions to copy and distribute the product electronically, but require express written consent if the product is going to be used in any publication that involves paper and ink, or in any enterprise that has a profit-making objective.

- Users are encouraged to express their opinions—without qualification and without fear of reprisal. This, of course, generates lively discussions and impassioned rebuttals, but the minute that any participant is attacked for expressing an opinion—rather than for the *content* of that opinion—you'll find legions of otherwise silent defenders rushing to the rescue with countless variations on "I disagree with what you say, but I'll defend to the death your right to say it." Attacking *what* someone says is always fair game. But don't attack someone's right to participate.

- The "without fear of reprisal" has an interesting variation. Many net.denizens are on the net through the good graces (not to mention dedicated high-speed Internet connection) of their employers. A person's signature block often identifies the employer—in some cases, the person's email address is enough to identify the corporate source. But the presence of an identifier is not the same as "speaking on behalf of." In fact, the generally accepted rule—within the Internet community at least—is that an individual doesn't speak for the employer unless that's expressly pointed out.[16] Many signature blocks include an express (and occasionally colorful) disclaimer, but even

16 Participants need to understand—would-be Internet ethics notwithstanding—that if someone is expressing an opinion that even arguably falls within the scope of the employer's domain, others might reasonably perceive the expression of opinion as that of the employer. If an employee of General Motors expresses an opinion on pending handgun legislation, for example, it's reasonable to expect that the opinion is the individual's own. But if an employee of the National Rifle Association expresses the exact same opinion (even if the person works in the MIS department or some other non-policy-making capacity) the individual would do well to make it completely clear—in the text of the message, not just the boilerplate disclaimer—whether the opinion belongs to the employee or the employer.

without the disclaimer, it's considered an especially egregious breach of ethics to bring a person's employer into a discussion—even if you think you've been grievously wounded in e-battle. As you might guess, most employers show a decided lack of understanding when confronted with an angry net.correspondent. Attacking a person's employer is at least as bad as attacking someone's right to participate—made worse by the threat of interference from *outside*. It also represents an attack on the second key principle of Internet ethics.

Self-Determination

Think of the Internet as a great big TV set. If you're watching a channel you don't like, *then change the channel.*

In a nutshell, that sums up the prevailing attitude of net.participants who struggle with the fact that absolute freedom of speech inevitably generates what some will consider "inappropriate" content. The assumption is that every participant on the net should have absolute control over what comes in from the Internet.

- Discussion groups have a very clear grasp of this concept. If you don't like the content of a particular group, you should be able to determine that *very* quickly, and you're expected to keep your disapprovals to yourself. Expect to get lambasted if you disparage a group for its subject matter. It is generally perceived that "we're all adults on the net" (even though "we're" not[17]), with a right to discuss and say anything at all—as long as it's kept within the group. If you don't like the content or the group, then change the channel.
- The obverse of this principle is also true: If you join a discussion group, keep your contributions within the limits *of* that group. This is the basic premise of playing well with others. *You* get to choose what you want to see on *your* TV. But you have to respect the rights of others to have the same control over *their* TVs. If you burst into a group with a completely off-topic rant, you're violating the

[17] Yes, kids are on the net. But the ethic is very clear about this: If you are a parent concerned about what your child might find on the net, then it's your responsibility to monitor what your child is doing. The net has no mechanism for "carding" participants, and no patience for parents who want someone else to take responsibility for their children. The emphasis and clarity of this position is probably related to the fact that many participants are college students—away from home for the first time ever—with memories of parental censorship (or the lack thereof) still fresh in their collective minds. And you have to believe that the vision of some youngster with enough intellectual curiosity and technical ability to browse the net for contraband—all the while keeping parental units In The Dark—has a certain counterculture appeal to it. Self-determination, in this context, is a right conferred by access, not by age.

others' right of self-determination.[18]

- Of course, the most notorious confrontation over netiquette—with special applicability to the legal profession—was the Green Card Incident. In that case, two Arizona lawyers—a small husband-and-wife law firm— "spammed" the Internet by posting an advertisement for their immigration-related legal services (i.e., help with getting green cards) into every one of several thousand newsgroups on the net. In so doing, the Green Card lawyers violated the Internet's leave-me-alone ethic in several different ways and on several different levels:

1. They interrupted each discussion group with an off-topic posting that, alone, would have earned them a public censure or two from the various self-appointed *topic police* that seem to inhabit the groups.

2. Worse, the interruption was a commercial advertisement. An interruption for "good cause"[19] would have been objectionable, but an interruption for an ad is considered worse. A purely political posting, for example, would be reviled as off-topic, but would likely draw less ire because the posting would be perceived as closer to the traditional ideals of free speech. Also, of course, a purely political posting would be censured by its own bad publicity—the posting would certainly generate far more negative publicity than positive. In a political context, negative publicity counts for something. But with a purely commercial posting, the negative publicity might not really count—as long as the ad generates a significant amount of business. In a political contest, if you generate a 99-to-1 disapproval rating, it's a disaster. But

[18] One of the more infamous such events was when the members of a discussion group called alt.tasteless organized an attack on another group called rec.pets.cats. They did it just for fun. They had run out of people on alt.tasteless who would be grossed out by their particular brand of fun, so they decided to go on a "net.panty.raid" and look for someone who would react with the appropriate level of shock and horror. They arranged for one person to post a fictitious story about two pets that were difficult to "housebreak" (not their words), then the rest of the net.bullies chimed in with gross and disparaging "suggestions" about what could be done to "fix" the problem. Well, the folks at alt.tasteless got what they were after: The members of rec.pets.cats were *shocked*. It was a childish stunt—petty, unattractive, and almost by definition, sophomoric. Of course, as soon as rec.pets.cats figured out what had happened, they were outraged—and the rest of the net backed them up. Although the alt.tasteless denizens argued and whined that they had done no real damage, they eventually went away—if not actually repentant— never to return. Because what was done to rec.pets.cats wasn't just perceived as a harmless prank. It wasn't just bad manners. It was an attack on a basic ethic of the system. And if it were repeated on a regular basis, it would "ruin things for everyone." In a community that relies on cooperation to get things done, "ruining things for everyone" is not taken lightly.

[19] Whatever that means. Each group has its own separate charter—including groups whose topics include dismantling the Internet and destroying the earth. (*Not* necessarily in that order.) There is probably no single issue that can safely be considered on-topic for every group on the net.

if you're selling a product, a 99-to-1 disapproval rating can still be a success if any of the 1 percent who are interested bring money to the bottom line—and if the disapproval of the other 99 percent doesn't cost you anything.[20] The economics of this analysis would seem to *encourage* this type of abuse by advertisers. Therefore, if "spam" advertising is successful, the threat of "ruining it for everyone" is once again very real.

3. Worse still, the posting went to *every single newsgroup on the net*. An off-topic posting to five or ten groups is one thing, but an off-topic posting to everything represents an attack on the system—not just on one or two groups. (It also indicates just how dedicated the attack is. A higher level of effort indicates that the attack is deliberate, with malice aforethought, and likely to be repeated.)

4. *Worse even more still*, the lawyers who set off the Green Card Incident were completely unrepentant. Confronted with the arguments that they're breaching the standards and practices of the Internet, the lawyers have argued that they've done no wrong and committed no crime. They've repeated the spamming—time after time. They've *moved* from location to location to avoid reprisals. They are pursuing an effort to "teach" others how to do what they have done. This is not an attack by a prankster with too much time on his hands, this is perceived as a systemwide attack that's targeted at cutting out at least one piece of the Internet ethic foundation.

In theory, the Incident highlights an internal contradiction of the Internet ethic. Freedom of speech—if it really was absolute—would accommodate commercial speech as readily as any other. But that principle runs smack up against the principle of absolute self-determination. You can't have both. Either you let people say what they want—to whomever, and whenever they want, *including spam advertising*—or you let the participants exercise some control over what they will or won't have to listen to. In theory, it's an inherent conflict between the freedom of speech and the freedom not to listen.

In practice, though, there is no conflict—the Internet ethic clearly falls on the side of freedom not to listen. On this otherwise *laissez-faire* frontier, the Green Card Incident was universally derided as an abuse of the common standards and practices.

Of course, what the Incident *did* reveal is that without a *technical* ability to enforce these ethics, and faced with participants that refused to cooperate,

[20] As you might imagine, this analysis tends to appeal more to fly-by-night one-time advertisers who are more interested in sales than in a good "public image." Most of corporate America, where Good Will is often carried on a company's balance sheet, couldn't afford this type of disapproval rating. Don't expect Nike or Coca-Cola, for example, to start a "spam" advertising campaign anytime soon.

the only remaining enforcement mechanisms are—themselves—violations of the Internet ethic.

Vigilante Justice on the E-Frontier

The Green Card Incident challenged the community to its core. The lawyers violated the rules of a society that has no means of enforcement. In an electronic frontier that doesn't have any sheriffs, guns, or jails, the cavalry can't come in and save the day—there's simply no mechanism for shutting people off.

Justice Brandeis once wrote that the answer to "evil speech" is "more speech." And that's exactly what the Green Card lawyers got. Thousands of angry email responses were directed at the lawyers; the responses flooded the network and the volume of email shut down the system the lawyers were using. Not surprisingly, the lawyers' Internet service provider promptly kicked them off the system.[21] In the vernacular, this is referred to as the net.death.penalty.

Some net.denizens constructed electronic spring guns that would automatically send out thousands of email replies if another note came out from the Green Card lawyers. In this context, free speech became a weapon: If you carpet-bomb the net with your free-speech posting, we'll target your site with a cruise missile of free-speech email. The intent was to shut down the lawyers' host computer in retaliation for perceived and anticipated net transgressions. In an interesting twist of logic, fighting free speech with free speech seemed to have a certain poetic-justice appeal—irrespective of the fact that the net.death.penalty is entirely destructive and, itself, violates the Internet ethic.

Eventually, a hacker in Norway developed a "cancelbot" program that looks for messages from the Green Card lawyers and automatically deletes them from any network discussion groups they might show up in.

Under different circumstances, the mere existence of such a program would be treated as a threat, and the author of the program would be treated as a net.vandal. But since it was developed in response to a perceived attack—since it was employed in an approximation of "self-defense"—the cancelbot was generally well accepted.

But who gets to say when the cancelbots will be used? There's no Committee on Un-Internet Activities. There's no Internet Tribunal. There's no Court of Appeals. Right now, the person who decides whether to use it is the author of the program. How will he use it?

21 As it turns out, the lawyers moved from provider to provider to spam the network repeatedly. Each time, they generated a firestorm of protest, and each time they got kicked off by their Internet service provider. The story continues, and at this writing has not yet been resolved.

What if he uses it in ways the "public" doesn't like? What if he uses the weapon for personal gain or benefit? Who shall guard the guardians themselves?[22]

Of course, the fundamental problems with the cancelbot are that it's basically antiethical, and there's no authority for using it. The only thing that supports it is popular opinion—the vocal and surging outrage of a lynch mob. Sensing the mood of the mob, self-appointed vigilantes step in to dispense what passes for justice on the electronic frontier. Deputized by nothing more than the perception of public opinion, outlaws are brought in to fight outlaws. You ask for a cooperative solution in a society that doesn't have the technology for enforcing cooperation, and I give you Wyatt Earp.

Frankly, this is a society that has not yet formed the very basics of self-rule. It's still a seething, disorganized mob. It is struggling, even now, to establish a foundation upon which the structure of self-government can be built: to find some way to discern the will of the group—as a whole—and then find some way to enforce that will. These are the basics that will define the net as it grows. These are the basics that will lead the net past its anarchy (eventually). And these are the basics that are being *invented*—as we sit here and watch.

This is a fascinating time. (Of course, for the e-flatland settler, "fascinating" doesn't exactly translate into "stable.")

The curse of living in interesting times doesn't mean that the Internet isn't *usable* by for-profit enterprises. It just means that you need to be aware of what's going on, and where the potential conflicts are. Despite the unsettled nature of issues facing commercial use on the net, most commercial users are welcomed. (Albeit cautiously.) But that welcome is *definitely* limited to activity that fits within the Internet standards and practices.

Since the rules aren't written down, businesses need to understand the *nature* of the different types of Internet services, and then apply the Internet ethic *principles* to the particular service or role that the business is considering.

[22] Why doesn't the government step in to fill this enforcement role? One reason, of course, is that the Internet is a global network—one country's government simply doesn't have jurisdiction over the entire net. But the more compelling reason is that government intervention would represent a complete failure of the Internet's operational model. Self-determination is *defined* by the absence of government control. Two basic fears seem to be built into the foundation of the Internet as it exists today: One is that someone will eventually figure out an effective way to put meters on the net and start charging for Internet services on some sort of Internet-wide usage basis—which, the argument goes, would have the effect of turning the Internet over to commercial participants only, since only they could afford to participate. The second is that the government (e.g., the U.S. government) will take over the net, prompted by some hype-driven event that stirs up outrage from the disconnected public—sex, or drugs, or protecting our children from themselves, no doubt. With the popularity of "war on crime" rhetoric, the government is not perceived as a zealous guardian of free speech. The fear is that the government would turn the Internet into a watered-down Prodigy—suitable for children of all ages—in which government-sponsored *thought police* would monitor the net for abuses and keep the net "safe" for everyone.

Chapter 6

What the Internet Is and Isn't—The Players

Over the last few years, the Internet has changed—from a valuable-but-difficult-to-use technology with significant promise and potential—into a meaningless techno-geek buzzword burdened by the usual hyperbole and shallow reporting that comes with being a media "discovery."

Unfortunately, the publicity and hype have reached way beyond ridiculous, into the land of embarrassing. Showing up in everything from comic strips and soap operas to advertisements for toaster ovens, the net and its all-buzzword cousins, "cyberspace" and "the information superhighway," are the current darlings of the popular press. I guess it's a sign of success that the press is full of articles by reporters who just discovered the net—touting "innovations" that were old hat a zillion years ago, and yet somehow failing to report what really *is* new and astonishing.[1]

With everyone from telephone companies to toothbrush manufacturers selling the information super*hype*way, it's even more difficult to figure out just who is selling what and where the offered services fit within the marketplace. We'll cover the specific services in another chapter, but right now, let's look at who the online service providers are.

Time out. Wow. How can we talk about Internet service providers without having

1 Coming back to the Internet-as-another-PC-revolution analogy, this pattern of look-what-I-discovered news coverage—written by reporters who are apparently selected because they don't know what they're talking about—is distressingly reminiscent of the early 1980s coverage of microcomputer topics. In those days, typewriter-bound curmudgeons discovered the marvels of word processing ("Look Fred! I just change one or two words and I don't have to type everything over again!") and felt somehow compelled to share with us the fact that they *hadn't been paying attention for the past ten years*. OK, so maybe some of those here's-how-I-got-dragged-into-the-twentieth-century articles had a place in the overall coverage of technology developments, but the number of slap-on-the-forehead Gee Whiz articles always seemed to outnumber the Real News articles in disappointing proportions.

talked about the various Internet services? OK, here's a quick Internet Services Refresher: "Full Internet access" usually includes five key features—electronic mail (*email*), logging onto Internet-connected computers (*telnet*), transferring files from Internet-connected computers (*ftp*), getting access to discussion groups (*usenet* or *newsgroups*), and a host of information-research tools (e.g., *gopher*, *WAIS*, and *World Wide Web*—especially the web). Sometimes a commercial online service offers "partial Internet access" by establishing a "gateway" between their own email system and Internet email. But it's not the same: It ain't Internet 'til it's telnet. I want my ftp. A day without newsgroups is a day without... You get the point. OK, *time back in.*

Commercial Online Service Vendors

These providers include some well-known names—such as Compuserve, Prodigy, and America Online (AOL). But they are *not* the Internet.[2] They are proprietary online services in which all of the software, services, and content are either supplied by the vendor or through arrangements with the vendor.

Each has at least an email gateway to the Internet—supporting the exchange of email to and from Internet addresses[3]—but each is a primarily captive universe (albeit a very large one)[4] in which the expectation is that users will play within the confines of the local schoolyard. Typically, these vendors offer a carefully structured, user-tailored online environment. They have lots of software that make things easy to use (or at least "easier" to use),[5] they have carefully moderated discussion areas—sometimes sponsored by major vendors—and they often have links to well-known information research services (e.g., Dialog

[2] At least not yet. Faced with increasingly strident customer demands—not to mention users leaving to sign up with true Internet service providers—some of the big online services are starting to offer bits and pieces of the Internet.

[3] Some users of online services—especially those who may be limited to using a particular service (because, oh just as an example, that's the only service *that the employer is paying for*)—have found that many Internet-based resources can be obtained through email gateways. (For details, see the sidebar "Using Email to Get ftp and www Files" in the "Internet Specifics" section of this book.) Of course, using the gateways this way can be especially expensive—depending on the vendor's pricing scheme—but it's a useful thing to look for if you're trying to be resourceful.

[4] Reportedly, both Compuserve and AOL have more than a million-and-a-half subscribers each.

[5] In most calling areas, online vendors set up a local phone number to connect your computer through—using a modem and a local phone call. In cases where you're out of the local-access areas, some of these vendors can give you an 800 number to connect through. Not to be *too cynical* about it, but by offering local phone numbers in most calling areas and by setting up 800-number long distance access, the online service vendor is simply transferring your long distance payments from your phone bill to your online services bill. We *hope* that the vendor is reselling the long distance services to us at a reasonable price so that we can fool ourselves into thinking that we're not being gouged for this undoubtedly convenient service. (Cynical? *Me?*)

and LEXIS). But they also have two big limitations: One, they typically *don't* give you full access to the Internet. And two, they don't *want* to give you full access to the Internet (or at least, they don't seem to).[6] The no-fee-for-information-services Internet scares the living bejeebers[7] out of them because it contains more information than any vendor can ever hope to provide (by several orders of magnitude), and there's usually no surcharge for access to that information. The commercial online vendors charge a premium for access to their services—over and above the basic costs of just connecting—because the vendor has had to make considerable investments in writing the software, arranging for and organizing the content, and providing technical support to users.

On the commercial online services, there *is* someone in charge, there *is* someone to yell at when things go wrong, and there's a convenient benevolent dictatorship that can and does enforce rules of behavior. The Internet paradigm challenges every revenue-generating construct of a commercial service, and in the process, threatens the very survival of those services—in their current form at least.

Frankly, the online commercial services have the name recognition clout, the economies of scale, and the technical capacity to step in and virtually dominate the Internet service provider marketplace—if they chose to do so. But in so doing, they would have to underprice their own bread-and-butter product, and they would undercut their own captive user base. For the online service vendors, the Internet is either competition or opportunity—it's up to each vendor to decide which it will be.

Bulletin Board Systems

Bulletin board systems (BBSs) have a basic concept of *operation* that is roughly similar to the commercial online services: A user dials in, uses software running on the BBS host computer, then contributes to the discussions and file exchanges that are available within the BBS-provided

[6] Many of the online service vendors are finally offering partial Internet services. (I like to think of this as setting up diplomatic relations with the Internet.) They haven't exactly bestowed Most Favored Nation Status on the net, but they *have* realized that the largest operating network on the planet needs to be formally recognized. Compuserve and Prodigy, for example, offer limited-service gateways to the Internet (i.e., more than just email), including access to the popular usenet newsgroups and just a few of the other basics. Others, such as AOL and Delphi, seem to be flirting with true Internet access. Of course, the punishing anti-Internet pricing is frequently still there. Perhaps they're hoping that newbie Internet surfers will go out in the rough waters, fall off their boards a few times, and decide it's too dangerous (or too expensive)—presumably without noticing the hundreds of alternative services that can supply access to the Internet for a lot less money. Go ahead and splurge—blow your entire Internet-email budget in one fell swoop and send a message containing the words "Send PDIAL" to info-deli-server@netcom.com. You'll receive a Very Lengthy List of Internet service providers. Of course, the true highway warrior wannabe uses the first couple hours of free connect time on a commercial online service to snag a copy of *PDIAL*.

[7] Bejeebers—that's a technical term. Oh, just grab the jargon file from http://www.ccil.org/jargon/jarginfo.html.

services. However, the similarity between the BBS and the online giants ends pretty abruptly.

Most BBSs are run by volunteers, hobbyists, user groups, or corporations and government agencies that want to be available to any computer user with a modem. Typically, there are no fees for accessing a BBS,[8] prearranged user accounts are unnecessary, and they tend to be run very nicely on business-sized PCs.

BBSs are *not* the Internet—and for the most part, they're not *on* the Internet.[9] Interestingly, many BBSs have established usenet-like networks to exchange discussions and email among the individual systems.[10] Many BBS networks also support gateways to the Internet—again, allowing email to and from Internet addresses, and in some cases mirroring discussions in selected Internet newsgroups. Although the BBS technology no longer represents the leading edge of online connectivity that it once did, it still supports an active community of participants, sysops (BBS system operators), and information providers.[11]

For would-be information providers, a BBS can still play an important role—because virtually any PC user in the country, equipped with little more than a modem and a phone line, can dial

[8] Or very modest fees—maybe $10, $20, or $30 per year. The fees are almost always structured as a membership or subscription—once you pay your fee, you're allowed on as often as you'd like (rarely will you find usage fees on a BBS). And with a BBS, you'll almost always have to foot the bill for any long-distance phone calls to reach the system—no local-calling-area access and no 800 numbers. Inevitably, that means that most BBSs tend to attract users within a single calling area.

[9] Actually, a few of the early "Freenet" Internet access providers were originally set up as BBSs—torturing the usual BBS software into allowing pass-through access to some selected Internet services. To this day, many of these hybrids still retain their local BBS character (i.e., fee structure and local phone numbers) and user interface. Also, many BBSs are providing this hybrid technology to allow BBS users to access the suddenly popular web sites on the Internet. In this context, though, these hybrids represent another type of Internet service provider—with a special set of capabilities and limitations.

[10] In the late evening hours, affiliated BBSs automatically call one another, using redistribution points and daisy chains of short-hop phone calls to exchange messages and contributions to discussions. Functionally, the BBS networks work in a manner similar to the Internet's usenet newsgroups, but it usually takes longer for a BBS network to distribute its messages out to the farthest reaches of its network—as long as several days.

[11] Some have said that BBS technology is "the CP/M" of online services—referring to the CP/M operating system that once dominated the microcomputer industry before the IBM PC and MS-DOS took over. (Yes, that's before time began.) To be fair, one reason why the analogy might be apt is that the CP/M user community was active and effective for many years after the IBM PC showed up (indeed, the financial systems of many businesses—and many law firms—were operated on CP/M-based machines for quite some time). Ultimately, of course, CP/M gave way to DOS and its successors, but I guess I don't believe that BBSs will suffer the same fate. That's because the basic BBS paradigm—local dial-in, no-fee, ad hoc access—meets the requirements profile of a very large community of users. If the only problem is building an effective bridge to the Internet (or whatever form the information superhypeway eventually takes), then I sure wouldn't count this community out.

into a BBS. It can be a bit clunky—but no other service in the online community can provide that same level of universal accessibility.

Internet Service Providers

This *is* the Internet. There are literally hundreds of Internet service providers (ISPs)—sometimes referred to as Internet access providers—and the field is growing so fast that it's a real challenge to keep up with who's playing, who isn't, and who is offering what for how much. The offerings vary considerably, ranging from the freenets with local dial-in, no-fee, and ad hoc access, to the big providers with custom software, 800 numbers,[12] technical support for users, and service-by-service usage charges. Whether you're an individual or small business dialing in to the service using a PC and a modem, or a large multinational corporation with wide area networks spanning the globe, connecting to the net using dedicated hosts and routers, the ISP is the vendor that supplies the needed connection point.[13] You might get some software for your PC that lets you run Internet software directly through the connection, or maybe the ISP will have you connect to its own host computer, then let you access the Internet services from there. Some providers make you use just the software they have; others support only selected services.

Certainly, none of the ISPs can impose a structure on the ruthlessly decentralized Internet, or present it to you in a way that suddenly "makes sense." And they usually *don't* have the same type of hand-holding software or user-support services that the big commercial vendors use to make "dialing in" a consumer-market product.

But the biggest problem the ISPs face is that they're still comparatively small and dispersed. They're like PC clone makers in a market that's still dominated by a few namebrands. There's no One Big Name that has imprinted itself on the computer-geek consciousness—the way Compuserve *et al* have done in the commercial online field. And the Internet service industry, as a whole, still hasn't been able to establish itself as a significant market presence. Frankly, without that kind of high-visibility provider (say, for example, *Microsoft* or *MCI*, or one of the commercial-vendors-turned-ISP), the Internet will likely continue to elude the consumer marketplace.

The Information Superhypeway

Probably the most abused buzzword in this industry is *the information superhighway*. The term is used promiscuously—to mean just about anything and everything—and it's becoming more and more difficult

[12] By the way, I'm just as cynical about the ISPs gouging us when they resell long distance services as I am about the online service vendors. I just don't have any *facts* to back up either suspicion.

[13] For dial-in users, the ISP mostly gives you a local-access phone number to connect to.

to use it to actually express a particular thought or concept.

By most definitions, the Internet would be considered a *part* of today's information superhighway. (Many would say it's the only *working* part.) By some definitions, the highway is a concept for things that haven't been invented yet, and the Internet—at best—is just part of the early prototype. Indeed, because the term is used to describe so many different visions, it would never be correct to say that the Internet *is* the information superhighway. So let's take a look at some of those visions, and see where the Internet fits in (and where it doesn't).

- If your vision of the hypeway is high-definition TV and 500 channels of digital video on demand, then your vision is something different from the Internet.[14] That's not to say your vision is wrong, or that you shouldn't use the term *information superhighway* to describe it, or even that the Internet will never be part of such a vision. But a brave new world of TV *isn't* the Internet.

- If your idea of the hypeway is "all that multimedia and CD-ROM stuff," that's something different from the Internet, too.[15]

- If your hypeway is Phone Phreaks and Clipper Chips, you've got the right attitude, but the wrong technologies.

- Virtual reality power-gloves? Super-Duper Nintendo? Fancy new telephone services? Nope, more nope, and you-need-to-start-looking-for-a-life.

- If your hypeway is "*anything at all with a computer in it*," then you've been dragged into the marketing hype completely. The same is true if your hypeway is "anything that has a digital readout" or "anything that uses electricity."

- What about the U.S. government's National Information Infrastructure (NII) proposal? Well, that's actually getting quite close. The NII's definition of the *infobahn* certainly contains all the right words: "A seamless web of communications networks, computers, databases, and consumer electronics that will put vast amounts of information at users' fingertips." Well, the Internet isn't exactly "seamless." And there's that tricky

[14] By the way, this *is*—by most accounts—Bill Gates's vision of the hypeway. His vision also includes a device that sits on the top of your TV (running Microsoft software, *naturally*) to handle the interface with whatever service supplies the video signals. Reportedly, Microsoft's prototype for this "set-top" device is code-named Penguin—taken from a Monty Python sketch in which the answer to the question "Wot's on the telly?" describes what's on *top* of the television set, not what program happens to be playing at the moment. Of course, wot is on the telly is a penguin (*naturally*). Wot isn't *quite* so natural, and what gives me the chilly willys when I extend the Monty Python sketch to the Microsoft Über Alles example, is that the penguin eventually *explodes*.

[15] Yes, you might find multimedia *on* the Internet. And you might find the Internet accessed through some sort of multimedia device or presentation. But the Internet and multimedia are two different things. They're not necessarily linked—and not mutually exclusive. Ditto the hardware technology of CD-ROM.

phrase in there about "consumer electronics." If the Internet isn't the NII, then it's a pretty good first start.[16] What's discouraging about the NII is that it's being proposed as something *completely new* by people who know the Internet quite well. And then there's that worrisome part about the NII being implemented in true politically correct fashion—by promoting private-sector involvement and investment.

Private sector is the key phrase here. Within minutes after NII was announced, the telephone and cable giants started positioning themselves to stake out territorial claims to the NII highways' on-ramps.[17] They keep offering to "help" the government "build" the highway (an easy offer—since the highway seems to be already built). The newly formed Information Technology Association warned that the NII should be operated in the *exclusive*

domain of the private sector, and that the government's role should be limited to that of "paying customer." Bill Gates *admonishes us* that the government "shouldn't spend another red cent" on the information highway.

I hate to see the NII (in whatever form it eventually takes) postured as a public-dole albatross that needs to be privatized to be effective.[18] The current Internet is built on a system of privately owned and maintained networks in which only a small percentage of the total net is funded by the government.[19]

And personally, hearing Bill Gates tell the government *not* to spend money in an industry where he plans to have a significant role instinctively makes me grab for my wallet. It makes me think he has a grander plan, that the price tag for that plan is higher than the government can afford (yow!), and that the

16 Consider the Internet to be the beta version of NII.

17 I really do hate the highway metaphor, but this is one case where it's too apt to avoid. And make no mistake, there's no fight over who will run the gas stations and service areas on the *infobahn*—the fight is over who will run the toll booths.

18 The politics of this situation wouldn't have any relevance in this book—except that the financial and operational structure of the net will have a direct impact on the availability of government-originated data and on the nature of the Internet-access marketplace. Depending on what changes do or don't get made, those factors would dramatically affect both the size and the demographics of the user population, and thereby, virtually every aspect of what makes the Internet valuable at this time.

19 I *have* seen arguments asserting that a much larger percentage of the net is funded using what are referred to as "taxpayer dollars." But the arguments carry follow-the-money tunnel vision to specious ends: The extensive networks operated by universities are attributed to taxpayer dollars because most universities receive federal grant money of some kind; and networks operated by corporations that do business with the federal government are attributed to taxpayer dollars because that's where the corporations get their revenues from. Both arguments miss the fact that all of these organizations—and the user-agencies in government, as well—would still have to pay *someone* for those networking services if they didn't get them through the Internet. Unless of course the private sector is proposing to give all those services to the agencies and universities and government contractors for free :-) (See, now *there's* a good use of a smiley face.)

money for that plan is supposed to come from my own pockets (double-yow!).

Howard Rheingold posits exactly that concern in his timely perspective on the information highway—*The Virtual Community: Homesteading on the Electronic Frontier* (Addison Wesley). For the highway to be effective, Rheingold suggests, we need to establish a basic set of connectivity goals and ground rules quickly—"before the political and economic big boys seize it, censor it, meter it, and sell it back to us."

What-the-market-will-bear pricing works for manufactured consumer goods. But does it work for fundamental components of the national infrastructure—roads, telephones, data?

I'll admit that I'm encouraged by Al Gore's attempt to establish at least a vision for an information infrastructure. But the details of "privatization" will be crucial: Does privatize mean that the government hires private industry to build and maintain the government-designed interstate highway system? Or does it mean that the government abdicates control over the system, letting private-industry providers build their own competing sets of roads?[20] The highway metaphor breaks down pretty quickly, but the underlying principles remain: Is there a commitment to system-wide connectivity? Or not.

Unfortunately, there's a pretty glaring difference between the interests of the providers and the customers. The government (and we assume at least some of the customers) has expressed the need for an infrastructure that serves as a foundation to give U.S. interests a significant advantage in the ever-more-competitive global village. But the providers can't shake the image of *millions of paying customers*—each coughing up the kind of money that turned the cable TV and cellular telephone industries into metaphorical gold mines. (The phone companies, for example, are *apoplectic* over the fact that simple telephone lines are being used to support all this digital traffic. And the specter of the government simply picking up the tab for a nationwide public-access network absolutely *terrifies* them.) The two models for implementation are diametrically opposed: interstate highway system, or yet another cable TV industry.

One more Tidbit From The E-Frontier can help to put an entirely unnecessary edge on the point.[21] The ABA's own ABA/net—operated as a part of AT&T's online commercial service—has separate pricing rules for email coming in from the Internet. Unlike email *within* ABA/net, which is charged for on a straightforward the-more-you-send-the-more-you-pay basis, there is a sepa-

[20] Or at least set up a competing set of toll booths.

[21] It also helps show how all of this buzzword-speak posturing translates into money-coming-out-of-the-checkbook.

rate surcharge on Internet email that gets charged to the person who *receives* the mail.[22] "Conveniently," ABA/net offers a feature for *blocking* all messages that come in from the Internet.

This would be like AT&T charging you for a collect phone call anytime a call comes in from MCI—and offering to block out MCI-originated phone calls as a money-saving convenience! Hmmm, *I'm just guessing now*, but somehow I don't think that approach would survive judicial review in today's long distance phone service market. Maybe that approach can help a vendor build its customer base. (Maybe not.) But as public policy, it sure flies in the face of system-wide connectivity.

I hope that Bill Gates's not-another-red-cent approach builds a better infrastructure than this.

State and Local Information Highways

Despite the high-concept *infobahn* rhetoric that seems to come in at the federal government level, there are some especially *tangible* programs that are being developed—and *delivered*—at the state level (albeit with much less press coverage.) Iowa, Kansas, and Texas, just to name a few, are setting up fully operational and effective public-service networks.

The Iowa Communications Network (ICN) received *Network World's* 1994 User Excellence Award for the public sector, among 600 entries in that category. Kansas's network was started up, in part at least, for the express purpose of helping the courts and lawyers work together more effectively. And when TexasOne was announced, more than 2,800 applications flooded in—from companies, schools, and other state governments—all wanting to join in.

One more example seems to set the tone for many aspects that surround state and local information highway networks: At last report, the Enoch Pratt Free Library in Baltimore was preparing to offer an Internet access service to Maryland's five million residents. (It was part of a program to make the library's databases accessible to anyone who is already on the Internet.) Obviously, this was good news for Marylanders (since the fees Enoch Pratt plans to charge seem to be decidedly consumer-oriented), and it

22 Email to and from the Internet goes through AT&T's Internet gateway. Ostensibly, the additional charges for Internet email are used to defray the costs of buying, maintaining, and operating that gateway. To be almost fair, given the amount of email that can be generated from the Internet—automatically and in very large quantities—tracking the inbound Internet email might be (arguably) a rough gauge for Internet usage. On the other hand, if you're running the gateway—and we assume that AT&T is—then you could certainly determine actual usage instead of rough gauges. And of course, the discussion about *how* one determines Internet usage certainly diverts attention away from questioning *how much* is being charged. By the way, I'm not trying to pick on ABA/net or AT&T in this example—many other commercial online services also charge for inbound email from the Internet.

established yet another model for how public institutions might participate in making the information highway a reality. Unfortunately, it also gave the snake-oil side of the hypeway an opportunity to raise its slimy little head.

The proposal generated a firestorm of complaints—primarily from commercial providers who wanted a piece of the franchise for Maryland's *infobahn*. Amazingly, the complaints were completely transparent: "I'm concerned," said one, "that public institutions are being given a license to undercut the rates from private providers."

I guess it depends on whether you think the government should help provide low-cost services to citizens in a fiscally responsible cost-effective manner, or whether its role is to *ensure that net.carpetbaggers will be able to gouge the public for whatever exorbitant prices the free market will bear.*

Geesh.

The library is planning to offer basic email access for $35 per year (compared to the $35 *per month* that some access providers charge), as well as expanded Internet services for a completely reasonable $100 per year. The state's Department of Education explains that it's an offshoot of the networking facilities the library system was installing anyway, and that the services are being priced on a full cost-recovery basis.

To me, that's *entirely* persuasive. If the commercial vendors want to keep something out of government hands, then they'd better be offering the same service for *less*—not more. (Certainly not *twelve times more!*) Or they should demonstrate why their service is worth the extra money, rather than lobbying to cut the government out of the game.[23] This is why I get so worked up about the talk of turning over the *infobahn* franchise exclusively to the private sector. In case after case—especially at the state and local level—the public sector is proving an effective channel for connectivity. And occasionally we get a little glimpse of just how greedy the infohypeway-wannabes really wanna be.

[23] If Federal Express, for example, can't offer something better than the U.S. Postal Service offers, then Federal Express is dead-ola. Toast. This is life in the bigs—we're building a highway here and you're either part of the steamroller or part of the pavement. If your Imus-quotient is "can't-suck-enough," then you're pavement. (And you kids out there—don't mix these metaphors at home. Something might catch fire.)

Internet Specifics
Paleotechnologies

Chapter 7

What Is the Internet?

Let's try this again.[1] What *is* the Internet? What's really out there? What can we actually *do* on it?

As we noted earlier, the touts and information highway hype make it difficult to figure out just who is selling what and how the offered services fit within the Internet marketplace.

Specific what-to-do and what-to-buy answers, of course, change daily with the winds of market maturity (or, in this case, the overwhelming lack thereof). But *strategic* decisions about the Internet require a good understanding of the basic *services* that make it up—because the Internet, for all of its user IDs and modems and fancy information-surfing robots, is still defined by its services, i.e., what can it do and how does it do it?

You need to understand the different services to decide what type of participation you want your office to consider. You also need to know the services if you want to compare offerings from different service vendors. And if you *do* get caught up in day-to-day activities on the net, you need to know how the services fit together—because any time you ask the question, "How can I get *that?*" the very *first* part of the answer is the name of the service that's used to reach it.

❶ Enough with this philosophical meandering!

Chapter 8

Internet Services as Public Utilities

"What *is* the Internet?" The reason this question is hard to answer is that there's such a broad range of services that make it up. It would be like someone looking at all the wires and pipes leading into your home, and asking "What are those?" Yow. Where to start? Water, sewer, telephone, electricity, cable TV—it's a whole host of services, with various purposes, delivered in a variety of ways. The Internet services are analogous.

Open up the manhole cover on your information superhypeway metaphor and you'll find an infrastructure made up of *various* services—file transfer, electronic mail, remote logon, information "browsing"—each having a different purpose, each delivered in many different ways. Depending on what your service provider offers, you may have access to all, some, or just a few of the basic services. You may be connected to the net with just one wire, but what makes a difference is what part of that network infrastructure you can tap into.

In the following description of services—and how they fit together—it's useful to look at certain characteristics of each service:

- What is the service typically used for (discussion groups, file exchange, "browsers," or resource discovery)?
- Does it require special software?
- Is the user interface graphical point-and-click or plain old text?
- What is the URL (uniform resource locator) identifier?

Categorizing a service by what it's used for is cheating a little bit—because almost *any* service can be tortured into fitting a particular use (*cf.*, "To a man with a hammer, everything is a nail"). Also, many services are hybrids that provide multiple uses. For example, the browsers—which are used to look for and browse through sources of information on the network—are usually tied in with an ability to retrieve the information (i.e., a file exchange capability).

The URL System for Locating Internet Resources

The URL (uniform resource locator) is the Internet's basic citation system. Almost every file, every database, and every resource on the net can be identified by a URL address.

The format for a URL is service:username:password@hostname/directory path/filename. The first part of the URL is the name of the Internet service. The second—optional—part is the username and password, if the service needs one (in most URLs, usernames and passwords aren't required, so this part is just skipped). The third part is the Internet address of the host computer. Everything after that is the path to the specific item.

For example, the URL for documentation describing the URL system itself is ftp://cnri.reston.va.us/internet-drafts/draft-ietf-uri-url-08.txt.[1]

That address tells you to use the "ftp" file transfer *service* to reach the *host computer* named "cnri.reston.va.us". And on that computer, you would look in the "/internet-drafts" *subdirectory* for a *file* named "draft-ietf-uri-url-08.txt".[2]

Each Internet service is identified by a shorthand notation, and each of the following descriptions of Internet services begins with the URL preface that identifies the particular service. For example, the URL preface for using email is shown in the title as "mailto:"—accordingly, the URL for an email address begins with "mailto:", e.g., mailto:allison@mitre.org.

The Basics

At the very bottom of the network services food chain[3] are the fundamental services that tend to show the worst of their Unix

[1] Actually, that's the URL for an early *draft* of the documentation that has since been released as a technical standard. (The drafts, of course, are located in the *internet-drafts* subdirectory.) The no-longer-a-draft form of the document is available at ftp://ftp.ds.internic.net/rfc/rfc1738.txt. "RFC," by the way, stands for Request For Comments. The people who are responsible for coordinating these standards—the Internet Architecture Board's Internet Engineering Task Force (IETF)—are wary of labeling any standards as "final" since the standards must be updated from time to time as need arises. In fact, the name itself—Request For Comments—reflects the obligation to update the standards, rather than let them stagnate.

[2] If the long file and directory names seem a bit unusual for your favorite DOS and Windows operating system, that's because *we're not in DOS anymore, Toto.* Most of the net has roots in the Unix operating system—where long file names are fine, where all-lowercase names are the norm, and where meaningless-bizarre-cryptic-shorthand-acronyms take the place of almost-understandable-by-human-being commands, turning what should be simple operations into macho ritualistic rites of passage shrouded in mystery and revered by geek wannabes. But I digress.

[3] Oh, you didn't think we'd start with the fun stuff right away, did you? Of course we can't, because most of the fun things are the hybrids—built up from the basics. Don't worry, this won't take too long.

origins. These include a simple mail transfer protocol, a file transfer protocol (ftp), and a protocol for logging onto to other computers (telnet).

Electronic Mail—mailto:

Email is the foundation for most services associated with discussions and discussion groups (e.g., listserv lists and newsgroups). Internet email doesn't require that you use a particular email system (you can use your own local email), but it *does* require that your email be connected to the net—usually through a gateway. Most online services, such as Compuserve and Prodigy, give you access to Internet email through a gateway—even if you can't get access to all the other Internet services.

Email is a primary mechanism for participating in discussion groups, but it's also used as an alternate delivery mechanism for many other services (primarily because email is more widely available than any other type of service).

It's also of special note that email represents one of the most powerful features of the net, in that it represents a key mechanism for communicating with clients, colleagues, researchers, and other people you may need to work with. You need to be careful not to exchange confidential or secret information with clients using unencrypted Internet email (see "Security as an Oxymoron" in "The User's Internet" chapter of this book). You also need to be careful about the potential for intended-jokes-and-humor coming across as unthinking or mean-spirited criticism—the text-only format of email frequently hides the good-natured intent of a friendly comment,[4] and your well-thought-out sarcasm can be taken at face value, twisting your meaning completely. (You also need to watch your temper—the anonymity of the faceless email screen sometimes dehumanizes the people who are the other end of your email link.[5]) Even with these caveats, though, the power of email is considerable. Not only

4 So there you are, minding your own email business, when you start to notice certain acronyms creeping into the language of your correspondents. The correspondent obviously thinks you're familiar with them, but they seem to have no etymological basis whatsoever and they contain precious few contextual clues as to their meaning. As it turns out, there's a fairly common set of acronyms that punctuate email traffic (much in the way smiley faces and other emoticons have been added to the email lexicon). Here are some of the more common net.connected acronyms: BTW (by the way), IMHO (in my humble opinion)—which rarely means humble, RSN (real soon now)—which rarely means soon, TIA (thanks in advance), NRN (no response necessary), ROTFL (rolling on the floor laughing), TANSTAAFL (there ain't no such thing as a free lunch), and one that you might have some trouble using, IANAL (I am not a lawyer)—which usually precedes a statement that looks for all the world like an assertion of legal opinion. BTW, if you are engaged in face-to-face conversation with an especially geek-possessed net.denizen, you might find some of these terms slipping into the conversation. Bizarrely, a few of these are pronounced as *words*—especially Imhoe, Rotfull, and Tans-Taafull.

5 OK, my very favorite Internet cartoon shows two dogs, furiously typing away at a computer keyboard. One of them says to the other, "On the Internet, nobody knows we're dogs."

Using Email to Get ftp and WWW Files

If all you've got access to is an email account, you shouldn't feel completely isolated—there are other ways to access other Internet services.

Specifically, there are a number of different gateway services that let you get files (even binary files) that are normally accessible only through ftp or World Wide Web—via email. The two most popular email gateway services are the ftpmail servers and the wwwmail servers.

- You can reach ftpmail gateways at mail-server@rtfm.mit.edu, ftpmail@sunsite.unc.edu, and bitftp@pucc.princeton.edu. When you create your email message, put nothing in the subject line, but put commands in the text of the message, such as "send pub/usenet/news.answers/internet-services/access-via-email". If you want to get fancy with ftpmail, you can put other ftp commands in the message as well—such as "open ftp.eff.org", "cd pub", "dir", and "quit"—all on separate lines. It's like running an ftp session via email.
- The two wwwmail gateways are both at CERN in Switzerland: listserv@www0.cern.ch and listproc@www0.cern.ch. Again, put nothing in the subject, but the command in the text of the message should be in the form "send http://www.law.cornell.edu".

To use the email gateways, you'll need to know the file's specific URL. If you're having trouble, maybe the site has changed. Even if a URL changes by just one letter in the name, most email gateways will produce error messages instead of files. Also, remember that capitalization counts ("govdocs" is different from "Govdocs"). If you're using an ftpmail gateway, try running a directory command (DIR) to look for nearby files. If you're using a wwwmail gateway, look for an index.html file that might have the latest URL for a particular file.

For more details about using the various email gateways, get a copy of Bob Rankin's excellent "access-via-email" guide (via email, of course!):

- mailto:mail-server@rtfm.mit.edu, put nothing in the subject, but enter the following line of text—as the only text—in the body of the note: send usenet/news.answers/internet-services/access-via-email
- mailto:listserv@ubvm.cc.buffalo.edu, put nothing in the subject, but enter the following line of text—as the only text—in the body of the note: GET INTERNET BY-EMAIL NETTRAIN F=MAIL

is it one more weapon in the battle against telephone tag, but it also represents a key capability in making yourself available to your clients. Some institutional clients are actually requiring email access to their counsel; others, of course, don't need it and wouldn't use it if they had it. But making yourself accessible through this medium at least communicates to your clientele that you're committed to making yourself available.

File Transfer—ftp://

Ftp—pronounced by saying the letters individually, rather than "pfftphph"— is a software utility that's part of most Unix operating systems, and it's included with most full-featured Internet access services. It provides a very basic interface for logging onto a remote host computer, moving among directories (similar to the CD and DIR commands in DOS) and copying files to and from the host computer. Ftp can be used to transfer software and other binary files (such as word-processing files), as well as text files.

Note, though, that there are some very large files available on the net. If you're dialing in from home using a 1,200 bits per second modem, that "neat little software utility" might take you *several hours* to download. A lot of Internet users are connected through leased lines at universities and large corporations, so the information providers will often put up files or services that are quite large. If your link is limited, you need to be careful about those.

Some of the most useful collections of files and information on the net are maintained on so-called anonymous ftp servers. These allow anyone on the net to log onto the server, using "anonymous" as the user ID.

```
======================== anonymous ftp ========================
Unix prompt > ftp ftp.cwru.edu
Connected to po.CWRU.Edu.
220 po FTP server (Version 5.53 Mon Jul 19 09:37:14 EDT 1993) ready.
Name: anonymous
331 Guest login ok, send ident as password.
Password:
230 Guest login ok, access restrictions apply.
ftp> dir hermes
200 PORT command successful.
150 Opening ASCII mode data connection for /bin/ls.
total 197
-rw-r--r--   1 uucp     daemon      77936 Nov 14 14:23 Index
-r--r--r--   1 root     wheel         878 Feb  8  1993 README.FIRST
-r--r--r--   1 root     wheel        2255 Sep  8 15:19 README.SECOND
-r--r--r--   1 root     daemon        998 Feb  8  1993 README.UPDATE
drwxrwxr-x   2 uucp     daemon      45568 Nov 14 14:23 ascii
drwxrwxr-x   2 uucp     daemon      15360 Nov 14 14:18 ascii-orig
drwxrwxr-x   2 uucp     daemon      10752 Jan 25  1994 atex
drwxrwxr-x   5 uucp     daemon        512 Aug  5  1993 briefs
drwxrwxr-x   2 uucp     daemon      32768 Nov 14 14:23 word-perfect
drwxrwxr-x   2 uucp     daemon      11264 Jan 25  1994 xywrite
226 Transfer complete.
658 bytes received in 0.36 seconds (1.8 Kbytes/s)
ftp> get hermes/Index
```

If you're looking for a particular file, there is a "resource discovery" service—called archie—which serves as a fairly-good-but-not-*complete*-complete directory of anonymous ftp sites. To use archie, you have to have a version of the archie software and its database, or you need to log onto one of the several publicly accessible archie servers (such as telnet://archie@archie.mcgill.ca).

Remote Logon—telnet://

Telnet is another basic utility; its purpose is to let you log onto a remote host computer. As a service, it doesn't really provide very much—just a simple text interface—and once you get to the other computer, there's not much to do unless someone is offering a program there for you to use.

Telnet applications almost always run on the remote host computer, so they're not very sensitive to how fast your Internet connection is.

A few of the newer information sources, or services that require extensive dedicated databases (such as resource discovery services), are best accessed by logging onto a computer that someone has made available for public access. Typically, the instructions for reaching public-access telnet sites will include instructions for logging on (e.g., log on as "archie" or "guest").

There is a directory of telnet-accessible resources, called hytelnet (telnet://hytelnet@access.usask.ca).

Discussion Groups

For many solos and small-firm practitioners, in particular, the art of networking (that would be the personal-not-electronic form of networking thank-you-very-much) is an important part of practicing in a specific field or area. Meeting people and making the right connections—it's all part of learning who to know and knowing who to ask. As it turns out, one of the key *strengths* of the net is exactly this type of networking—using net-based discussion groups that cover a broad range of legal specialties and interest groups.

Of course, the most elementary discussion is an exchange between just two people. Obviously, email is the service of choice for one-on-one discussions—you just need to know your correspondent's email address (or at least how to push the "reply" button). Indeed, by sending email to a number of people on a related subject, you have built a rudimentary distribution list—which, with careful use of the "reply all" button, becomes an almost-organized mailing list. Most email systems support user-defined distribution lists that can also be used to support discussions. But maintaining distribution lists is a time-consuming chore—something that computers can handle quite well. Two Internet services address this role directly: listserv lists and newsgroups.

Note that discussion groups are not seriously affected by the speed of a user's Internet link. Both of these two discussion group technologies follow a limited email-like mostly-text paradigm, so the speed of accessing individual items in a discussion is about as fast as using standard email. The only thing to be careful of is that the discussion groups can generate a *lot* of discussion.[6]

Listserv Lists

Listserv lists are the product of automated distribution list handlers. Typically, these are referred to by the name of the handler—such as LISTPROC, MAJORDOMO, or the original LISTSERV. (There is no URL identifier for listserv mailing lists—yet.) To join a discussion group, you send an email message to the list handler at a sponsoring host computer,[7] and the listserver automatically puts you on the distribution list. All email sent to that list's address gets automatically sent to you, as well as to everyone else on the list, of course.

This makes for discussions that tend to be immediate and fairly personal—since the entire discussion shows up in your own email inbox. Listserv lists can be tailored somewhat—by putting someone in charge of what goes out to the list (this would be a "moderated" list), and by letting people request that individual notes be combined into a single "digest" before sending. Most listservs can be joined by anyone who has an Internet-accessible email address (although membership *can* be controlled by whoever runs the list).

There are listserv lists on literally thousands of topics, and since they're so easy to set up, they can come and go fairly quickly. They are not centrally registered and can be very difficult to keep track of. Lyonette Louis-Jacques at the University of Chicago maintains a noteworthy list of listserv lists that are related to legal topics (gopher://lawnext.uchicago.edu or mailto:llou@midway. uchicago.edu)—although there are other sources of law-related lists as well.

Technically, the biggest problem with listserv lists is that they generate a huge amount of email traffic on the network. If a thousand users are subscribed to a list, the listserv generates a thousand individual copies of every email message that gets contributed to the discussion. Even if all the subscribers are on a single host computer, the listserv generates separate email messages for each individual subscriber. This generates lots of traffic, and fills your inbox. In response to this troublesome inefficiency, the early developers of Internet services (usenet) developed an alternative service.

6 Subscribing to a discussion group through your email account may be fast and easy to use, but depending on your service provider's chargeback mechanisms for Internet email, it can also be expensive.

7 Typically, you would send an email message to an address like listproc@bitnic.educom.edu. You wouldn't put anything in the subject line of the message, but the first line of text in the body of the message would say: SUB EDUPAGE firstname lastname. (Do I have to say this? Don't send the words "firstname" or "lastname." Send your real first name and your real last name.) (Or at least your *favorite* first name and last name.)

```
┌─────────────────────── email to listserv ───────────────────────┐
│ Command: create                                                 ↑│
│                                                                  │
│ To: listserv@fatty.law.cornell.edu                              │
│ Cc:                                                              │
│ Subject:                                                         │
│ Text:                                                            │
│ subscribe liibulletin Burgess Allison                           │
│                                                                  │
│ Command: send                                                   │
│                                                                  │
│                                                                  │
│                                                                  │
│                                                                  │
│                                                                 ↓│
└──────────────────────────────────────────────────────────────────┘
```

Newsgroups—news:

Rather than flooding host computers with multiple copies of the exact same message (repeated for every list subscriber), newsgroups let each host keep just a single copy of each discussion, and let the participants browse through the stored messages. Individual participants use special "newsreader" software to read through messages and to post replies; meanwhile, in the background, the host computers that support newsgroups handle the task of distributing individual postings to other host computers. (This collective process of exchanging newsgroup postings is often referred to as the "usenet.")

For the user, this means that the newsgroup is analogous to a community bulletin board—you log onto it, browse, and post replies that everyone who reads the newsgroup will see. These discussions are a bit more removed than listserv lists, but the newsgroups don't fill up your email inbox, and you can browse the discussions at your convenience.

There are newsgroups on thousands of topics (9,500 by a recent count), and they contain some of the more infamous discussion groups on the net (particularly within the free-for-all "alt" topic categories). Some newsgroups (such as newsfeeds from major wire services) are provided on a for-fee basis; i.e., the people who run your host computers must pay a fee for receiving those newsgroups. As you would guess, not every host computer is subscribed to all newsgroups.

Most listservs and newsgroups ask newcomers to review the group's FAQ file before filling the discussion traffic with, well, frequently asked questions. In most cases, you will need ftp or some other file exchange capability to get the FAQ.

```
┌─────────────────────────────────────────────┐
│            Newsreader                        │
├─────────────────────────────────────────────┤
│ 3 groups                                     │
├─────────────────────────────────────────────┤
│ 15  news.announce.newusers                   │
│ 16┌──────────────────────────────────────────────────────────┐
   │            news.announce.newusers                        │
   ├──────────────────────────────────────────────────────────┤
   │ 18 articles, 15 unread                                   │
   ├──────────────────────────────────────────────────────────┤
 - │  ✓ David C Lawrence   How to Create a New Usenet Newsgroup│
 - │    Ron Dippold        Usenet Newsgroup Creation Companion │
 - │  ✓ Perry Rovers       Anonymous FTP: Frequently Asked Questions (FAQ) List
 - │    Chris Lewis        How to become a Usenet site         │
 - │    the *.answers m…   Introduction to the *.answers newsgroups
 - │  ✓ Russ Hersch        FAQs about FAQs                     │
 - │    Aliza R. Panitz    How to find the right place to post (FAQ)
 - │    Mark Moraes        Emily Postnews Answers Your Questions on Netiquette
 - │    Mark Moraes        A Primer on How to Work With the Usenet Community
 - ┌──────────────────────────────────────────────────────────┐
 - │              ✓FAQs about FAQs                             │
 - ├──────────────────────────────────────────────────────────┤
 - │  From: sibit@datasrv.co.il (Russ Hersch)                 │
 - │  Organization: none                                      │
 - │  Date: 10 Nov 1994 01:38:09 GMT                          │
 - │  Newsgroups: news.announce.newusers,news.questions.newusers,news.answers
 - ├──────────────────────────────────────────────────────────┤
 - │      1.1)  What does FAQ stand for?                       │
 - │      1.2)  How is FAQ pronounced?                         │
   │      1.3)  What do FAQs contain?                          │
   │      1.4)  What are FAQs used for?                        │
   │      1.5)  Where are FAQs found/kept/hidden?              │
   │                                                          │
   └──────────────────────────────────────────────────────────┘
```

Browsers

Ftp, of course, is the original browser. But ftp is entirely clunky (yes, that's a technical term)—you have to download each file to read it, and your only browsable-hint as to the content of each file comes from the long-but-still-terse file name.

Some of the most exciting *new* developments in Internet services are the browsers—World Wide Web, gopher, and WAIS—sometimes described as network information retrieval (NIR) tools.

Full-Text Searching—wais://

It's a little unfair to call WAIS (Wide Area Information Servers) a "browser," but it *is* part of the suite of services that helps you look for and locate information. It should be noted, though, that the standard WAIS interface tends to more closely follow the Unix model for user-hostility than that any of other Internet service. As an Internet service, WAIS provides full-text searching of WAIS databases across the Internet.[8] A WAIS provider will establish a database, and any user on the net can send queries to that database.

Most WAIS databases support only rudimentary search algorithms—exact match, wildcard

8 WAIS is also used to support other Internet services, rather than as an Internet service itself. In fact, WAIS is probably most frequently used not as an Internet service, but as the search engine used by gopher and WWW when those services need to do full-text searching. In that way, the user is protected from the less-than-friendly WAIS user interface, but the search capability is delivered.

characters, case-sensitive or not. Some WAIS databases (not all) also provide a *very limited* boolean search capability—simple ANDs, ORs and NOTs.[9] The more sophisticated boolean algebra and proximity searching that you get with most commercial full-text searching tools—such as LEXIS, WESTLAW and ZyIndex—are simply not part of WAIS. The one place where WAIS does get sophisticated is in the determination of a "relevancy" score for each qualifying document. The relevancy score is used to rank-order the retrieved documents based on the number of "hits" or qualifying matches found within each document. In a one-word search, relevancy is determined by the number of hits, but in a multi-word search, relevancy also considers how *many* of the requested terms are found. WAIS *will* retrieve documents that only have some (or just one) of the requested terms, but those will get assigned lower relevancy scores.

When you're running a WAIS search, most of the retrieval time (and it can be a long time) is spent waiting for the server to come back with an answer. That isn't affected by the speed of your Internet connection. But if you ask WAIS to send you a file that it found, then you're in a mode similar to ftp file transfers: Obviously, if you happen to choose a very large file, the speed of your Internet connection comes into play.

Dedicated WAIS databases *do* tend to be registered with a number of different *directory-of-servers* around the net (which are, themselves, WAIS databases).

Menu-Based Browsing—gopher://

Gopher was the first browser on the net to use in-the-background anonymous logons as part of a basic menu interface.

Here's how that works: gopher presents to you a very simple text menu. Some of the menu options may take you to a document stored on the host computer, or to local searching programs (such as WAIS). But many of the menu options take you to other gopher sites on other host computers. If you select an option that takes you to another host computer, then all of the connections are handled in the background by the separate gopher servers; no passwords or user IDs are required, and the user doesn't have to do anything else to get connected. In fact, the process is *usually* quick enough that—from the user's perspective—connecting to the other machine is no different from simply bringing up another

[9] "Boolean" search capabilities are one of the key features that distinguish different full-text searching systems. Simple systems may support only some fundamental boolean operators (such as AND, OR, and NOT) that let you combine search terms (e.g., search for documents that contain the words *Internet* AND *lawyer*). More sophisticated boolean algebra gives you additional operators and "wildcard" characters, and lets you control the precedence of operators with parenthetical expressions.

```
┌─────────────────────────────────────────────────────────────────────┐
│ ▤□▤            ▤▤▤▤▤▤ gopher ▤▤▤▤▤▤            ▯▤│
├─────────────────────────────────────────────────────────────────────┤
│            Internet Gopher Information Client v1.12S              ⬆ │
│                                                                      │
│            Root gopher server: gopher.law.cornell.edu                │
│                                                                      │
│   -->█ 1.  Cornell Law School Information/                           │
│        2.  Directory of Legal Academia/                              │
│        3.  Discusions and Listserv Archives/                         │
│        4.  U.S. Law: Primary Documents and Commentary/               │
│        5.  Foreign and International Law: Primary Documents and Commentary/ │
│        6.  Government (US) and Agency Information/                    │
│        7.  Information Services: Academic Institutions/              │
│        8.  Library Resources (online catalogs)/                      │
│        9.  Periodicals, News, and Journals/                          │
│       10.  Other Gophers and Information Services/                   │
│       11.  Internet (FTP sources, Archie, etc)/                      │
│       12.  Locators (where to find people and things)/              │
│       13.  Miscellaneous/                                            │
│       14.  Other Internet Law Sites/                                 │
│       15.  +---+ Please give us feedback! +---+.                    │
│                                                                      │
├─────────────────────────────────────────────────────────────────────┤
│ Press ? for Help, q to Quit, u to go up a menu      Page: 1/1    ⬇ │
├─────────────────────────────────────────────────────────────────────┤
│ ⬅ │                                                           ➡ ▯ │
└─────────────────────────────────────────────────────────────────────┘
```

menu. (Dare we say it?—the connection process is "transparent to the user." Usually, anyway.) With a few quick menu choices, you may find yourself jumping to different host computers around the world: Minnesota, Japan, Singapore, Australia, and back to the United States again.

The operation of gopher menus is quick, and the background linking is handled without much traffic to the user's host computer, so most of gopher is not affected by the speed of your Internet link. But again, like WAIS, if you happen to choose a very large file to be retrieved, the speed of your link becomes very important.

Gopher does require special software,[10] but once you're in "gopher-space," all of the gopher sites on the planet are available to you. In fact, it's very easy, using gopher, to "wander around" from site to site to site. It's easier still to lose track of where you are and forget the path you used to get there. (As one might imagine, wandering around is not an especially *precise* library science. The phrase, "surfing for information," is sometimes *painfully* accurate.)

If you're looking for a particular file, or if you remember the name of a gopher menu option, there are two gopher-specific resource discovery services—"veronica" and "jughead"—which serve as limited

[10] There are a number of different gopher software packages—at least one for almost every platform on the market. But just to clarify one potential misunderstanding: gopher and the various Internet gopher software packages are *completely different* from the commercial software product—Gofer—that has enjoyed some popularity in the Personal Information Manager (PIM) marketplace. The products and services are fundamentally different. If you really pushed it, you might be able to torture the gopher Internet service into acting like a PIM. But no amount of pain or suffering could turn the Gopher PIM into the Internet service.

searchable directories of gopher listings. Most of the veronica or jughead servers are accessible using either telnet or gopher.[11]

Full-Graphics Browsing—http://

World Wide Web (also known as "WWW," "W3," or simply "the web") is a logical extension of gopher. The web adds two significant features to the world of browsing: embedded "hypertext" links that replace fixed-format menus, and a fairly sophisticated use of graphics, sound, movies, and other multimedia—all tied together with a point-and-click graphical user interface.

The web is flashy, but it consumes bandwidth voraciously. To be fair, there is an all-text mode that is boring-but-still-useful. Even in graphics mode, the graphical point-and-click interface is remarkably efficient—because it's implemented primarily on *your* computer, rather than sending all the fonts and look-and-feel interface back and forth across your Internet link.[12] But the opportunity to send glorious and colorful bitmapped graphics—as part of the web page decorations and as the buttons to be pushed—is apparently irresistible. Not only will web servers send you giant files at the drop of a bit bucket, but they also seem inclined to send you huge graphics files just to make the interface look pretty.[13] If you use the web in all its resplendent glory, it will make even the latest 28.8 Kbps (thousands of bits per second) modem seem slow.

The hypertext linking in the web is a well-established technology (see for example, "Building and Using Hypertext Systems," David R. Johnson, *Law Practice Management*, May/June 1991). It allows the author of a document (or annotator) to set up certain words, phrases, or graphics in a document as push-button links to another document, a definition, or even another host computer. Thus, the concepts of cross-referencing and drill-down to specific detail are inherent in a hypertext-based system. As you might imagine, several academic initiatives have already been sponsored to cross-reference selected legal materials. (It's a rare perfect fit for technology.)

Like gopher, WWW requires special software. (NCSA's Mosaic is the most popular web browser—so much so that it's often mistaken as a synonym for World Wide Web.) Also like

[11] Archie? Veronica? *Jughead?* It helps if you try *not* to visualize.

[12] That's why each different web browser has its own different look and feel. The specific fonts, buttons, and other graphical pieces that make up the web browser interface are programmed into the browser *client*. The web *server* sends the same text and formatting tags to every web browser client—then the browser interprets those tags and displays the text, buttons, and links in whatever way the browser's programmer thought "best." If the programmer's idea of best matches yours, then you'll probably be pleased with that browser. If not, then you can look for a browser that's more to your liking. Or you can look for a browser that's been programmed to let the user control some parts of the user interface—such as typeface and font size.

[13] Yes, most browsers will let you turn off the automatic downloading of images—but if you want to get a particular image, you can ask for it.

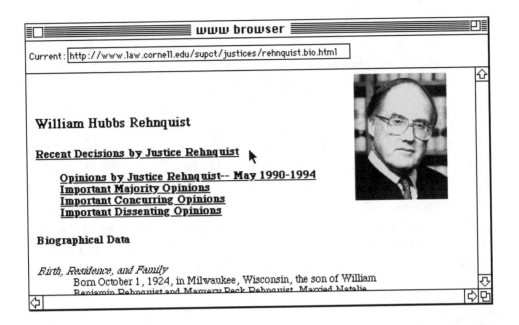

gopher, once you're in the web, all of the Internet's web sites ("home pages") are accessible. It's easy enough to wander around aimlessly, but at least the web browsers do a little better job of helping you keep track of where you are.

The web is the latest new service to take the Internet by storm. (Invented in 1992, usage of the web is now responsible for 16 percent of *all traffic on the net*—that's the second largest among all Internet services.) The features it offers are fairly mature: searchable indices, links to documents and files, links to other servers—even a "forms" capability that lets the user enter comments (by filing out a form) during a web session. Web browsers can also link particular documents to applications software on your desktop computer—so when a sound file is downloaded, for example, your sound-playing software can be automatically started. Other software—such as spreadsheets, word-processing programs, and graphics software—can also be linked to specific file types.

How the Services Fit Together

Frequently, several Internet services are linked together. For example, gopher browsers usually give you access to WAIS, ftp, and telnet (but not webs), as well as to other gopher sites. Web browsers let you access both web and gopher sites, as well as the basic WAIS, ftp, and telnet. Web browsers also let you access newsgroups, assuming that you've got access to a local host that subscribes to newsgroups.

Most content providers on the net offer several alternative services that allow you to reach the same information in different ways. Typically, the information provider is trying to strike a balance between making the service as powerful as possible and making it accessible to as many people as possible. Either way, it's a compromise: The latest, most powerful software (WWW, recently) isn't available to everyone; but the lowest common denominator (email) doesn't really offer the functionality of even a rudimentary browser. The solution for some providers, therefore, is to offer multiple services.

For example, two of the biggest software exchange sites on the Internet (ftp://oak.oakland.edu for PC software and ftp://sumex-aim.stanford.edu for Macintosh software) use *listserv digests* (INFO-IBMPC and INFO-MAC) to collect and distribute information about what is being posted on the site. Then the software files themselves are typically accessed through a huge *anonymous ftp* site—one that doubles as a *gopher* site. Those two listserv digests also happen to include some of the most prolific and extensive discussions related to software and developments for their respective platforms.

Accessing Supreme Court Information through Cornell Law School's Several Internet Services

The Legal Information Institute at Cornell Law School provides access to recent Supreme Court decisions that have been supplied electronically through the Supreme Court's own Project Hermes. Internet users can access archived decisions through four search methods: 1) the standard citation, 2) a topic index, 3) party-name indices by year (including both first-party and second-party names), and 4) key-word search. The decisions of the most recent term are listed by date of decision as well. The LII also presents a feature called Gallery of the Justices that offers biographic material and photographs of all current members of the Court, together with hypertext links to their decisions (including separate concurring opinions and dissents).

These materials (or subsets of the materials—depending on the service) can be accessed through:

- Web server, at http://www.law.cornell.edu/supct/supct.table.html
- Gopher server, at gopher://gopher.law.cornell.edu
- Telnet, at telnet://www@www.law.cornell.edu or telnet://gopher@gopher.law.cornell.edu
- File transfer, through an exchange program with Case Western Reserve University and the Supreme Court's Project Hermes, using either ftp://ftp.cwru.edu/hermes or email by sending requests to mailto:liideliver@fatty.law.cornell.edu
- Recent developments in the LII are discussed through the LIIBulletin listserv, subscribing through mailto:listserv@fatty.law.cornell.edu

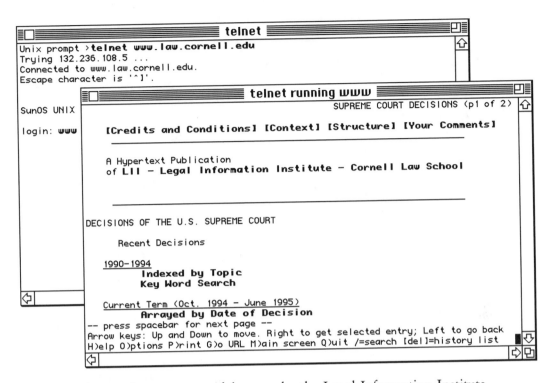

In another, perhaps more useful example, the Legal Information Institute (LII) at Cornell Law School maintains one of the most advanced suites of law-related services accessible on the Internet. LII's hypertext-based search engines for finding recent Supreme Court decisions present a perfect example of just how easy—and powerful—these tools can be. But LII knows that there are a lot of people who just don't have all the Internet services. Therefore, while LII's Supreme Court *web server* is at http://www.law.cornell.edu/supct/supct .table.html, you can also reach most of the same information through *telnet, gopher, ftp,* and *email* (though not as easily searchable, nor as effectively cross-referenced). You can also subscribe to the LII's electronic newsletter by joining the liibulletin *listserv*.

This high-level overview has covered the major Internet services. Once you start using the net on a day-to-day basis, however, you might want to look for some of the basic navigation aid services (such as whois and finger). Also, as the net continues to evolve (in its own sudden nanotrends way), look for still more new and interesting services.**14** But some of the more intriguing new services seem especially focused on resource discovery technologies—finding out what's-hiding-where. The painful absence of a definitive Index to the Internet has encouraged hundreds of initiatives to survey and map out this electronic frontier.

14 New-and-emerging services include email-to-fax servers, Internet "radio" shows, and other sound-and-graphics experiments that seem intent on using up all the bandwidth on the planet—thereby verifying the net.corollary to Parkinson's Law: Data expands to fill available bandwidth.

Chapter 9

Library Science on the E-Frontier

The instant you try to use the Internet as a reference tool, you'll run smack up against the fact that it's a very poor library. There's no Dewey Decimal system and no card catalog. Simply wandering through the stacks would be inefficient enough—but in this case you'll be lucky if you can even *find* all the stacks. The Internet presents a terrible challenge to professional librarians—there's an *enormous* wealth of riches, but those resources are basically uncataloged.

The bibliographic scientists are further challenged by the fact that the *content* from the different sources varies dramatically. Many gopher sites and web pages contain raw data, full text of reports, and other valuable original-resource materials. Other sites are only "under construction"—and contain little more than an announcement that the provider has discovered the Internet and plans to participate. Not only is it difficult to assess the comparative content of the different resource providers unless you actually try to use each one, but the content can change substantially, rapidly, without notice, and sometimes without any visible signs of change. With traditional printed publications, it's comparatively easy to notice whether the publication has been changed—usually, new and updated editions tend to show up as *new books*. (Or at least pocket parts.) But there's no similar construct or tangible evidence that lets the Internet librarian know, for example, whether the Federal Communications Commission Online Archive finally delivered on its plans to provide access to the *FCC Daily Digest* and related public notices.

How can you find out which sites have content and which have fluff? How can you find what sites might even be *candidates* for valuable content? And how can you keep current on all the latest changes?

Welcome to the world of trying to be your own librarian. These are exactly the questions that define the role of library science—and exactly the questions that virtually every Internet newcomer[1] seems destined to ask.[2] This is what librarians *do for a living*—people devote entire careers to it. Yes, the questions are frequently asked, but the answers will be essay answers—not multiple choice.

Resource Discovery Utilities

Sometimes, all you're looking for is a good index. The net is full of electronic indices, but the question is whether they're good or not. Most are simple lists of resources—usually specifying a file name or Internet address—and most require that you know the exact URL (sometimes the exact spelling *and capitalization*) that you're looking for. That can be useful when you *know* exactly what you're looking for, but it's usually pretty lousy for general subject-matter research. Most in the archie-veronica-jughead series work that way, so do the finger, whois, nslookup, netfind, and hytelnet utilities for email and telnet.

Online Guides and Bibliographies

To find substantive subject-matter collections and evaluations of individual resources, you'll usually need to track down the appropriate online guides and bibliographies. These are where library science meets the user. Some are easier to use than others, some are just lists of names, some are descriptive, and some contain subjective assessments. In each case, the guides and bibliographies reflect

[1] In the vernacular, a new Internet user who reveals his lack of knowledge or experience is deemed a "newbie." (No, there is no corresponding label for "oldbie.") It's not necessarily bad to get the newbie label—we're all new to different things at different times. Sometimes, you'll even see experienced Internet users refer to themselves as newbies as a way of explaining that they're new to a group, or new to a technology. Still, the newbie label does get used in disparaging tones—especially at newbies who haven't yet figured out the customs and practices of the group. One time-honored way to avoid making a newbie gaffe is to "lurk"—watch and listen long enough to figure things out. Just remember newbie is as newbie does.

[2] "How can I find what I need on the net?" is a TANSTAAFL question—There Ain't No Such Thing As A Free Lunch. It's a simple question, and it's completely understandable that a new user would ask it. But the answer is more than what the questioner wants to hear. It would be like someone coming up to a lawyer at a cocktail party and asking "How do you find out whether something is legal or not?" Wow. The questioner would love to hear that there's some little *secret book somewhere* with all of the answers in it, and if the questioner could just *find that book* then life would be easy. Sometimes, the group will patiently explain the situation, many times the question will just be ignored, and once in a while, someone in the group will accidentally start to supply the two-thousand-page answer. "How can I find what I need on the net?" is a TANSTAAFL classic: The task of finding what you're looking for is exactly what makes the Internet hard to use.

the labors of individual researchers, and in every case you'll find trade-offs driven by how much time it takes to do the necessary research.

Obviously, a list of URLs is the easiest to compile,[3] so in most cases, those are more extensive and more frequently updated than other resource guides. On the other end of the bibliographic spectrum you'll find thoroughly researched reviews containing descriptions of the various sites' contents, with subjective assessments of each. As you would expect, the more lengthy subjective assessments tend to be updated less frequently, and they're also more susceptible to being out-of-date: A simple listing merely lists the site's URL (or just the URL itself)—which is less likely to change than its contents. An assessment of a site's contents is instantly out-of-date as soon as those contents have changed. (And the contents change all the time.)

One of the most important characteristics of a guide or bibliography is how current it is. Not surprisingly, printed materials (such as this book) usually represent the least up-to-date resource guides. The most up-to-date listings are those that are updated and accessible through the net.

In "Burge's Bookmarks," I've included references to all of the leading online guides and bibliographies for law-related Internet resources.

Also, in "References," I've included the full text (or excerpts) of what I believe are the *key* online guides and bibliographies for law-related Internet resources. It's important to note that the listings are *not* included for the purpose of pointing you to specific resources on the net. As I said, that information will be at least partially out-of-date before the book is printed.[4] (And it will degrade over the years.) Instead, I've included them for two reasons: 1) to show you the breadth of coverage, and the type of information you can find in these guides, and 2) to *highlight* a few of the listings that I believe are must-have resources for the Internet-connected lawyer. Here's what's included:

- *Legallist*—excerpt. Erik Heels' *legallist* is one of the most extensive listings available, with an enormous breadth of coverage. (*The Legal List, Law-Related Resources on the Internet and Elsewhere.*)
- *Lawlists*—full text. Lyonette Louis-Jacques' *lawlists* covers only discussion groups (law-related), but within that scope it delivers the most complete listings. (*Law Lists.*)
- *Govdocs*—full text. Austin and Tsang's *govdocs* lists government sites, with excellent breadth of

[3] *Easiest*: That's a comparative adjective not to be confused with *easy*. The number of sites on the net is growing at a tremendous rate. (Remember that December 1994 statistic: More than 400 new web sites were being submitted to NCSA—*each week*—for inclusion in NCSA's *What's New* web page.) Trying to maintain even a simple listing of *unevaluated* locations is a difficult task.

[4] It's important to remember that when you want to actually work with these sources, you should get the latest copy of the lists from the net. They are freely available—without copyright restriction for making electronic copies—and they are *always* more likely to be up-to-date.

coverage and substantive evaluations. (*Government Sources of Business and Economic Information on the Internet.*)

Of course, these are just a few of the relevant guides and bibliographies, and what's useful and valuable for some might not meet the preferences of another. Which brings us to the third category of resource discovery technologies.

Meta-Sources

Several research initiatives have taken on the task of cataloging the guides and bibliographies themselves. Unfortunately, right now at least, most of the meta-guides are simple listings of guides and bibliographies—rather than subjective evaluations.

Most meta-guides are accessible through gopher or web services—which are ideal for presenting lists of choices, then allowing the user to browse. Being able to browse through the different guides and bibliographies doesn't replace a good evaluation, but it at least gives you a chance to check out the basic format and form of presentation.

The best-known meta-guide on the net is on the WWW server where WWW was developed—at CERN, the European Laboratory for Particle Physics in Switzerland (telnet or http://info.cern.ch). CERN's meta-guide is one of the most exhaustive and comprehensive subject-matter indices for information on the net. For law-related references, CERN's index points to the comprehensive web-based meta-guide that was set up at the Indiana University School of Law by Will Sadler (http://www.law.indiana.edu). These two meta-guide sites aren't the most visually stimulating web pages you'll ever run across (OK, I'll say it, their looks are almost *entirely* boring)—but that's not their purpose. Instead, they're all business (or, more accurately, all research)—immersed in the task of trying to be card catalogs to the world.

Books

Printed books tend to make poor "card catalogs."

Still, you'll find the bookstores chock full of titles that would lead you to believe (in 72-point headlines) that they'll be your surrogate librarian for the Internet. These seem clearly targeted at promising what everyone would like to hear—that this business of finding resources on the net is easy. Unfortunately, the promise is little more than hype—the library science of tracking what's on the net is hardly trivial, the basic resources are growing wildly and they're fundamentally disorganized, and your best shot at finding a specific piece of legal research is just what it has almost always been—finding a good law librarian who knows the subject matter thoroughly. Failing that, the online resources (everything from meta-guides to discussion groups) have the usual advantages of frequent updating and immediacy.

The book format is certainly better suited toward presenting "guides" than card catalogs.

That said, there are a few printed bibliographies that have a special value —either because of the special quality of the evaluations or because the authors aggressively try to match the scope of content with the frequency of new editions. (Erik Heels's *The Legal List* and Josh Blackman's *The Legal Researcher's Internet Directory* sort of come leaping to mind.) And indeed, some guides include reference listings—as does *this* book—because it's helpful to the readers to have the information at hand rather than be told to simply *imagine* the nature and content of online bibliographic resources.

With respect to book-format guides, I've included a set of reviews (see "Book Reviews") of what I consider to be some of the industry's better guides and tutorials.

There are also many general-purpose guides to the Internet that are available online—complete with detailed how-to information and explanations of bizarre Unix-oid rituals that *your* Internet service provider may expect you to master. *The Big Dummy's Guide to the Internet* is one of the better-known online guides.[5] It's now called the *EFF's Guide to the Internet* and it's available online at ftp://ftp.eff.org/pub/Net_info/EFF_Net_Guide or http://www.eff.org/pub/Net_info/00-links.html.

Some popular guides are available in both online and printed form. In most such cases, the online version is either an early draft or a subset of the printed work. For example, the original working draft of Brendan Kehoe's excellent overview of the net—*Zen and the Art of the Internet*—is available online at ftp://ftp.eff.org/pub/Net_info/Guidebooks/Zen_and_Internet. Tracy LaQuey and Jeanne Ryer have made *part* of their highly regarded beginners' guide for the net—*The Internet Companion*—available online at ftp://ftp.eff.org/pub/Net_info/Guidebooks/Internet_Companion.[6]

Finding online materials

5 After some initial popularity with the *Big Dummy* title, Adam Gaffin's guide has subsequently been retitled to avoid confusion with the popular series of software guides, *<Your Software Named Here> for Dummies*.

6 So have you noticed that ftp://ftp.eff.org and http://www.eff.org are getting mentioned a lot? The Electronic Frontier Foundation has some of the most extensive, easy-to-reach publications about how to use the Internet. Their *resource listings* are sometimes a little bit out-of-date, but their *guides* are usually quite current. The site is generally well organized, thorough, and easy to navigate. Some other Internet-reference-material sites have more materials and more up-to-the-minute updates (such as ftp://rtfm.mit.edu), but they tend to be much more voluminous and can be intimidating for the first-time Internaut. EFF is a great place for beginners to start.

published as printed books can be disconcerting.[7] Sometimes, as with *Zen* and *Companion*, it's obviously the same author and there's a clear if incomplete connection between the printed and online versions. Some authors, though, have simply grabbed public-domain material off the net and republished it.[8] I guess it wouldn't be so bad if those books were clearly labeled—maybe with the unavoidable 72-point headlines, "Reprint of the usenet newsgroups file! Available online at thousands of sites around the world!"

[7] Some of the reprint-from-online books are just-for-fun little snippets. The ubiquitous smiley directories, for example—showing a thousand different variations on the basic colon-hyphen-parentheses smiley ":-)" with humorous comments and flights of imaginative interpretation—are readily available at thousands of sites on the Internet (for example, look in ftp://ftp.eff.org/pub/Net_info/Net_culture/Humor). Others, such as Eric Raymond's well-distributed jargon file, are reprinted by the source's author as a way to defray expenses (in hard copy form, the jargon file is *The New Hacker's Dictionary*—online, you can get it at ftp://prep.ai.mit.edu/pub/gnu or at http://www.ccil.org/jargon/jarginfo.html).

[8] If you're interested in what's original and what's grabbed, read through Kevin Savetz's online book reviews—he covers that particular phenomenon with a certain flair. See *book-list*, #21 in "Burge's Bookmarks."

Chapter 10

Burge's Bookmarks

"Where should I look—to start?"

The question comes from so many places—from the recently net.connected lawyer, the net.denizen trying to solve a specific problem, or someone who just wants to do a little law-related browsing. And frankly, the answers are a lot more straightforward than one would expect.

Yes, I know that the net is changing minute by minute. New sites are being installed, new services are coming online, and new applications are being invented.[1]

But a few major law-related sites have proven to be quite stable. They don't move around, they keep up with the latest technologies, and they're maintained by dedicated individuals and institutions[2] who are committed to making Internet technologies and online law-related

1 Now here's a use for the Internet that you *might* not have thought about. Researchers at England's Cambridge University wanted to keep an eye on their coffee pot (gotta top it off every now and then). So, *naturally*, they set up a video camera, connected the camera to a web site, and now they can *watch the coffee pot using their Internet connection.* (The picture is updated every second.) *You* can watch their coffee pot, too. It's at http://www.cf.cam.ac.uk/coffee/coffee/html. Or if you'd rather check something else, you can check the supply of Jolt cola at the Rochester Institute of Technology, or the M&M's in a vending machine at Carnegie Mellon. (*Don't even ask.*) (At least those are text, not video.) Maybe watching coffee pots and aquariums and throwing virtual snowballs won't have an effect on your day-to-day life, but when someone decides to train a bunch of cameras on the freeways during rush hour (San Diego is already working on this)—and you can get a firsthand view of what the traffic is actually like before you venture forth into the Rush Hour Inferno—maybe this capability will take on a new-found relevance.

2 In the pre-history of the Internet (you know—two or three years ago), many institutions and universities had *no idea at all* that one of their students or professors or employees was establishing that institution as a leader in the field of Internet research. In some cases, upper management didn't know the institution even *had* an Internet connection—much less that some worker-bee night-shift system operator had started to use the neglected connection to provide valuable services to the community at large. Sometimes, when management finally figured out what was going on, the operator was summarily dismissed—for "misappropriating" computer resources—and the net would suddenly lose an important site. These days—with the profession of "Internaut" now becoming almost *respectable*—most institutions are well aware of their Internet involvement, so it's much less likely that a site will be suddenly yanked off the air.

resources an essential part of the legal profession.[3] In addition to the law-related sites, there are some others that are good starting points for general-purpose research.

Here, then, is my own list of Internet starting points for the net.connected lawyer.[4] These—in my own thoroughly subjective opinion, of course—are the starting points I've found to be the most useful or the most frequently referred to. In *my* bookmark file at least, these are all must-haves. (At the end of this section is a short summary list with site names and basic URLs—the detailed list has descriptions and more extensive URL alternatives.)

Criteria for inclusion in Burge's Bookmarks?

- First and foremost, it *has* to be stable. If I can't rely on a site to be there month after month—even year after year—then I'll have to keep checking and updating the list. I just don't have the time.[5] And when I give this list out to others, I don't want to stick *them* with the problem of having to figure out what happened to one site or another. Since many people save this list for Way Too Long, the list has to be survivable.

- Second and just as foremost, it has to be *short*. A thorough list of a hundred URLs defeats the purpose of a starting point. A very long list would just give people another chore—wading through the list to find what's interesting.[6]

- I try to include the best of the meta-guides. Since I don't have the time to keep up with the latest and the mostest, the pointer should point to someone who *is* keeping up with the latest and the mostest. To me, that's the *measure* of a good starting point.

- It includes the more noteworthy law-related bibliographies and listings. Yes, you can find them at the meta-guide sites, but they're sufficiently unique within the community that they warrant inclusion.

- It includes a few discussion groups and ftp sites. If a service is significant, but might take Way Too Long to find it in a meta-guide, I'll go ahead and just name it out loud.

- OK, so I've also caved in to the peer pressure and included a few "popular" sites.

[3] It is, of course, no coincidence at all that the more stable, valuable sites are maintained by people who have been doing this for a very long time.

[4] Personally, I maintain this list of URLs within my own web browser. Both gopher and WWW offer a feature that lets you mark a location when you have logged onto it. Given how easy it is to jump from site to site to site, it's really important to use this feature—early and often—as you go past things that look interesting. Later—once you've finished the task at hand—you can go back to the saved locations and review then at length. Unfortunately, as you save more and more locations, the list becomes longer and longer. (It's important to keep your day-to-day working list fairly short.) In both gopher and WWW, the feature for saving locations is called a bookmark. That's why this list is called "Burge's Bookmarks"—because that's just what they are.

[5] Remember—I'm an e-flatland settler. Not an explorer.

[6] Of course, a long list also happens to be harder to keep up-to-date. But since I have boundless energy, that has nothing to do with why I keep my list *as short as humanly possible.*

Some places are so frequently mentioned that people invariably ask about them. And others are there for no good reason whatsoever—other than to scare you. (Well, they frighten the bejeebers out of *me*.)

How to Get What's on the List

Each listing in "Bookmarks" includes one or more URLs for finding the items on the list.

These are the URLs for the *original* site or primary distribution point for the item. But you should be aware that some of the items are available in a lot of other places as well—not just the original site. A little looking with archie or veronica—or searching through the meta-guides—might show you some alternate locations if the originals are unaccessible.[7]

Remember that even at the primary distribution point, many different techniques can be used to reach a particular item. Indeed, many sites are actively working to set up additional Internet services for reaching their materials, so if you don't have access to a particular network service, you may have success experimenting with any services that you *do* have access to—even if the additional service is not listed here. For example, if an item is shown at http://www.esu.edu and all you have access to is ftp, you might try to connect to ftp://ftp.esu.edu, or ftp://esu.edu, or even ftp://www.esu.edu. It never hurts to try.

Of course, people who only have access to email accounts can use the ftpmail and wwwmail gateways, as described in the chapter "Internet Services as Public Utilities" in the "Internet Specifics" section:[8]

- You can reach ftpmail gateways at mail-server@rtfm.mit.edu, ftpmail@sunsite.unc.edu, and bitftp@pucc.princeton.edu. When you create your email message, put nothing in the subject line, but put commands in the text of the message, such as "send pub/usenet/news.answers/internet-services/access-via-email". If you want to get fancy with ftpmail, you can put other ftp commands in the message as well—such as "open ftp.eff.org", "cd pub", "dir", and "quit"—all on separate lines. It's like running an ftp session via email.
- The two wwwmail gateways are both at CERN in Switzerland: listserv@www0.cern.ch and listproc@www0.cern.ch. Again, put nothing in the subject, but the command in the text of the message should be in the form "send http://www.law.cornell.edu".

7 The alternate locations *occasionally* have the most up-to-date versions of the item—but sometimes not. The original sites have the latest.

8 Yes, I know this is a repeat of what was in the Internet Services chapter—almost word for word. I do this because I think it's useful for people who may be skipping around the book. The astute reader will also notice when I start repeating my reviews of related books and places to learn additional information.

Remember, to use the email gateways, you'll need to know the file's specific URL. Also remember that capitalization counts—"govdocs" is different from "Govdocs".[9]

Well, here they are—the best of the best—in my I-wish-I-could-pretend-it-was-humble opinion.

Law-Related Starting Points

1. The Legal Information Institute at Cornell Law School. LII is one
of the most comprehensive starting points for law-related services on the net. It's home to the best search engines for finding recent Supreme Court decisions,[10] and it includes pointers to virtually every other law-related service you're likely to be looking for.[11] It includes access points for most of the other Bookmarks, as well.

- http://www.law.cornell.edu
- gopher://gopher.law.cornell.edu
- telnet://www@www.law.cornell.edu
- telnet://gopher@gopher.law.cornell.edu
- see also listserv mailto:listserv@fatty.law.cornell.edu, body of note: subscribe LIIBULLETIN <name>

2. The House of Representatives Law Library. The House gopher and
web servers maintained by Elliot Chabot are best known for making the full text of pending legislation and congressional testimony available online. For me, though, the real gem of the site is the Law Library section. As you might guess, it's especially strong for federal legal resources, but the coverage of the Law Library extends well beyond the federal sector—the site is comprehensive and well laid out. By the way, don't confuse this with http://thomas.loc.gov, the Library of Congress's separate House server that duplicates some of the services but doesn't have the Law Library.

- http://www.house.gov
- gopher://gopher.house.gov

[9] Also, when you're trying to use the list, be sure to use the specific URLs rather than the textual descriptions. For example, *govdocs* gets capitalized in the textual description of Bookmark #10—as *Govdocs*—only to match the style constraints of traditional printed-material publishing. In the URL, though, the reference instructs you to use "govdocs"—all in lowercase. That's the one to use—all in lowercase.

[10] Supreme Court decisions show up first at Case Western Reserve University, ftp://ftp.c wru.edu/hermes. It sometimes takes a while—a few hours or days—before they're moved over to LII.

[11] Notably, LII includes links to several government-service locators, such as the ones at the University of California Irvine (gopher://peg.cwis.uci.edu) and at the Villanova Center for Information Law and Policy (http://www.law.vill.edu/Fed-Agency/fedwebloc.html).

Law-Related Meta-Guides

3. *The Indiana University School of Law.* This is the extensive subject matter–based index of law-related topics that is referenced, in turn, by the top-level subject matter–based index for WWW maintained at CERN, in Switzerland. The references that Will Sadler set up at this site are up-to-date and positively enormous.

- http://www.law.indiana.edu
- telnet://www@www.law.indiana.edu

Law-Related Listings

4. *Legallist.* Maintained and updated by Erik Heels, this listing has extraordinary breadth of coverage. The full title of the listing is *The Legal List, Law-Related Resources on the Internet and Elsewhere* (and it is excerpted in the Reference section of this book). He's quite serious about the "and Elsewhere" part of the title—it covers everything from the Internet to bulletin boards, online services, and printed journals. The latest edition even includes listings of law firms that are on the net.

- gopher://gopher.usmacs.maine.edu/11e%3a/usm/law
- ftp://ftp.midnight.com/pub/Legallist
- listserv mailto:listserv@justice.eliot.me.us, body of note: subscribe LEGAL-LIST <name>
- printed version directly from Erik J. Heels, 39 Main Street, Eliot, ME, 03903-2234

5. *Lawlists.* Maintained and updated by Lyonette Louis-Jacques at the University of Chicago, *Law Lists* is the most comprehensive listing of law-related discussion groups that I'm aware of—more extensive than *The Legal List*. (*Law Lists* is included in the Reference section of this book.) The latest compilation includes 406 separate Internet mailing lists and 82 Internet newsgroups. The newsgroups are simply listed, but the mailing lists are described in some detail.

- http://www.kentlaw.edu/lawlinks/listservs.html
- gopher://lawnext.uchicago.edu:70/00/.internetfiles/lawlists

6. *Interlaw.* Maintained and updated by James Milles at the Saint Louis University School of Law, this is ostensibly an introduction to using the Internet on the VAX machines at his particular school, but it is much more than that. Milles does an excellent job of assessing and highlighting a very broad range of law-related and Internet-related resources. The full title is *An Introduction to Using the Internet at Saint Louis University School of Law*. Milles is prolific, and you can usually find several other useful guides and listings at his ftp site.

- ftp://sluaxa.slu.edu/pub/millesjg/interlaw.txt

Law-Related Discussion Groups

7. LAWSRC-L. This is the Internet Law Sources list, intended for exchange of information about law-related Internet resources. By subscribing to this list, you'll receive virtually every announcement of new or updated law-related resources, as it happens. The list also has discussions about the relative merits of specific sites, and occasionally fields questions about where to find a particular item. As you might guess, the list is heavily populated with law librarians who really know their stuff. (It's their job.) Another list, TEKNOIDS (also at listserv.law.cornell.edu) covers new Internet resources as well, but it also covers other law library technology issues and it generates a lot more traffic. TEKNOIDS is more of a user group; LAWSRC-L carries the announcements. If you're just interested in the new sources, stick with LAWSRC-L.

- listserv mailto:listserv@listserv.law.cornell.edu, body of note: subscribe LAWSRC-L <name>

8. ABA-UNIX-LIST and NETWORK2D-L. These groups concentrate on the use of the Internet, and technologies generally by practicing lawyers. (The focus is usually more along strategic lines rather than nuts-and-bolts "how-to.") Nominally, each was set up as a discussion list for a special-interest group in the American Bar Association's Law Practice Management Section. They aren't huge lists, but membership is open to all. The discussion usually stays on topic—applicability of technology and strategic alternatives in a legal setting, with a very strong practicing-attorney bias. There are other law-related discussion groups that have a lot more members and a lot more traffic (such as the newsgroup at news:misc.legal) but they often stray from the topic, and they sometimes seem dominated by nonlawyers who are looking for free legal advice, wanting to complain about "the system," or hoping that some recently received slight is grounds for a million-dollar lawsuit against some deep-pockets defendant (frequently the university that they are attending). Personally, I can't stand the noise, and rarely do you find a gem on a general-purpose newsgroup that isn't also referenced on source-focused lists, like LAWSRC-L.

- listserv mailto:listserv@austin.onu.edu, body of note: subscribe ABA-UNIX-LIST <name>
- listserv mailto:listserv@austin.onu.edu, body of note: subscribe NETWORK2D-L <name>

9. NET-LAWYERS. This is a relatively new list that's already many times larger than N2D or ABA-UNIX. The focus is how-to Internet details for the practicing attorney, and it seems to have quickly turned into a gathering spot for attorneys who are new to the Internet and want to put it to good use. Sure, there's a fair amount of repetition as newcomers frequently ask the same questions, and as other newcomers share their discoveries of well-known sites. But the enthusiasm is just plain infectious and you won't find another group anywhere that's more inclined to help newcomers find their way around. Frankly, everyone seems to be at least lurking here and this is where the action is—with all the attendant advantages and disadvantages that entails.

- listserv mailto:net-lawyers-request@webcom.com, body of note: subscribe

Government-Related Listings

10. Govdocs. Developed by Terese Austin and Kim Tsang at the University of Michigan, this is not only one of the most comprehensive listings of government resources on the net, but it also contains some of the most extensive subjective assessments about the value and utility of the content at each site. You may not agree with all of the assessments, but with so many government agencies putting "under construction" sites on the net, it's important to know which ones really have something of value. Unfortunately, with this much subjective evaluation, it will be difficult to keep this list up-to-date. The full title is *Government Sources of Business and Economic Information on the Internet* (and it is included in the Reference section of this book).

- ftp://una.hh.lib.umich.edu/inetdirsstacks/govdocs:tsangaustin
- gopher://una.hh.lib.umich.edu/00/inetdirsstacks/govdocs:tsangaustin
- http://www.lib.umich.edu/chhome.html

11. Government. Maintained and updated by Blake Gumprecht at Temple University, this also boasts a comprehensive listing with substantive assessments about the content. The full title is *Internet Sources of Government Information.* The coverage and style differ only slightly from *govdocs*—probably in ways obvious to a librarian but not so much to me. Personally, I prefer to use *govdocs* because the citations in the reference are usable as URLs—in *government*, the citations include extra blank characters in between each of the path elements in the URL, so you have to fix each citation before using it. *Government*'s bibliographic style is a little less subjective than *govdocs*, so it probably has a better chance of being updated frequently. (Be sure to also check the gopher- and web-based government-service locators referenced at Cornell's LII. See Bookmark #1.)

- ftp://una.hh.lib.umich.edu/inetdirsstacks/government:gumprecht

- gopher://una.hh.lib.umich.edu/00/inetdirsstacks/government:gumprecht
- http://www.lib.umich.edu/chhome.html

Government-Related Discussion Groups

12. GOVDOC-L. This is the Government Documents list, intended for ex-change of information related to the administration of government-document and related resource collections. There's a fairly high volume of traffic on this list—targeted primarily at government document librarians—but when there's a new government source on the net, this is where you'll hear about it first.

- listserv mailto:listserv@psuvm.psu.edu, body of note: subscribe GOVDOC-L <name>
- listserv mailto:listserv@psuvm.bitnet, body of note: subscribe GOVDOC-L <name>

General-Purpose Starting Points

13. NCSA's Starting Points. This is the very best starting point I know of—bar none. It's for World Wide Web users only, but I've found nothing else that comes close to presenting high-quality starting points in a way that's as easy to understand and work with as NCSA's Starting Points. You'll find every major meta-guide, all the massive search engines, resource discovery tools – everything. CERN's top-level page attempts to deliver the same breadth of coverage, but it sometimes comes across as a huge card catalog. NCSA's Start-ing Points seems to take better advantage of the web technology to deliver something different.

- http://www.ncsa.uiuc.edu/SDG/Software/Mosaic/StartingPoints/ NetworkStartingPoints.html

14. Yahoo at Stanford University. David Filo and Jerry Yang's Yahoo web server at Stanford University has what is probably the most extensive col-lection of URLs on the planet. The Yahoo site is frequently named as a place to find funny stuff, or things that are more than just a little off the wall, but that reputation belies the enormous wealth of resources that are collected here, including one of the larger lists of net.connected law firms. At the begin-ning of 1995, Yahoo listed more than *25,000* web locations around the globe. New locations were being added at a rate of 100 to 200 *per day*.

- http://akebono.stanford.edu/yahoo

15. Internet-tools and internet-cmc. John December's seminal works list virtually every network information service available on the Internet (some of which are quite obscure) and every major service provider (i.e., resource discovery databases). There is a web version, but when I use these documents, I find it best to simply open them in a word processor and search them to find what I'm looking for—together with all of the relevant URLs. The documents don't have much in the way of tutorial explanations, but the URL listings are the meat. December distinguishes between Network Information Retrieval (NIR) *Tools* (internet-tools) and Computer-Mediated Communication (CMC) *Forums* (internet-cmc). His work always seems to be scrupulously updated.

- ftp://ftp.rpi.edu/pub/communications/internet-tools
- ftp://ftp.rpi.edu/pub/communications/internet-cmc
- http://www.rpi.edu/Internet/Guides/decemj/text.html

General-Purpose Meta-Guides

16. CERN's Overview. This is the most extensive effort on the net to deliver a complete card catalog—for everything. Although it sometimes seems stuck in traditional library paradigms, it seems to attract the very best of that breed. This is the top-level subject-matter index for most sources on the net. In most cases, it simply routes the user to a subject-matter index maintained somewhere else on a particular subcategory.[12] For many research projects, this is the *best* starting point available.[13]

- http://info.cern.ch/hypertext/DataSources/bySubject/Overview.html
- telnet://www@info.cern.ch

17. Clearinghouse for Subject-Oriented Internet Resource Guides. This is also a subject-matter index, but it focuses on Internet guides and bibliographies. Sometimes, the Clearinghouse is a little late in getting things, but probably no other collection has as many different guides onsite. Lots of other meta-guides just point you to some other place—the Clearinghouse actually has them. (In fact, a lot of other meta-guides actually point to the Clearinghouse.)

- ftp://una.hh.lib.umich.edu
- http://www.lib.umich.edu/chhome.html
- http://http2.sils.umich.edu/~lou/chhome.html
- gopher://una.hh.lib.umich.edu

General-Purpose Collections

18. MIT. The ftp site at rtfm.mit.edu is home to what is certainly the most extensive collection of instructional materials and FAQ files about the Internet and usenet newsgroups. If someone tells you to "read the FAQ," you'll usually find it here. The

[12] For the subcategory of law, CERN's subject-matter meta-guide links you directly to the subject-matter index at the Indiana University School of Law. See Bookmark #3.

[13] OK, so the link to CERN—in Switzerland—takes you halfway around the world and squeezes you through sometimes-slow international network links. If you can start at the NCSA Starting Points, you might be able to find useful alternatives without the trans-oceanic link. If you need to use telnet, try Cornell (also a little closer to home) at telnet://www@fatty.law.cornell.edu.

organization of the collection attempts to mirror the structure of the usenet,[14] which is helpful if you already know that structure. But if you're new to the net and looking for FAQs—which is a likely situation for people who have been pointed at rtfm—then the structure is positively baffling.[15] This is another place that many meta-guides point to.

- ftp://rtfm.mit.edu

19. EFF. The collection of Internet instructional materials at the Electronic Frontier Foundation has the same basic purpose as rtfm.mit.edu, but it's not as extensive (or as up-to-date). On the other hand, it's about a thousand times easier to use. The resulting misconception—and it's a common one—is that EFF is where the net.saints live, while rtfm is stomping grounds for the dreaded newsgroup.flamers. That's not true—both of these sites are run by dedicated people who put in enormous time and energy to make things work better. (But EFF is *still* easier to use.)

- ftp://ftp.eff.org
- http://www.eff.org

20. Software ftp sites. Anonymous ftp sites are all over the net for finding shareware and freeware software, and they cover virtually every type of computer on the planet. (The archie servers can help you find ftp sites for the various computer platforms. The meta-guides will also point you to lists of anonymous ftp sites.) But the Big Two are the ftp sites for DOS-compatible and Macintosh-compatible software—related to the listserv digests INFO-IBMPC and INFO-MAC, respectively. Both sites have enormous resources—but they also have an enormous number of people trying to reach them. Use archie to find other copies of the primary sites, called *mirrors*. (The mirrors can be easier to get into, and may run faster because there are fewer people on them.) In fact, the IBMPC site at SIMTEL is on a military branch of the Internet and almost never acces-

---

14 *Structure.* Once again, that term of art shouldn't be confused with any implication that usenet is *actually* structured. Or even in the same quadrant of deep space with structured.

15 This fits the net.wizard and net.geek paradigms just *perfectly*: The default is that you *hide* all information about how to use a system unless the user knows how to use it already. (This is like putting word processor installation instructions in a file you can't read until you've installed the word processor.) But if someone actually goes to the trouble of writing something down, you can't really just throw it away—someone will notice and someone else might actually make it available to the *users.* The best you can do is hide it someplace where the users can't find it—unless they already know how to find it. The logic is both simple and elegant. The extra bonus is that when someone asks a question, you can act horrified and be indignant that they "didn't even bother to read the manual." Stupid users. The name of MIT's ftp site says it all. The "rtm" part stands for "Read The Manual." The rest is just attitude. By the way, you *can* find net.saints who will step in and help—but you have to ask. And if you're going to play in the newsgroups, you'd better keep rtfm's URL handy.

sible—the listed site at oak.oakland.edu is a SIMTEL mirror—one that seems to be the most commonly referenced.

- ftp://oak.oakland.edu (INFO-IBMPC)
- ftp://sumex-aim.stanford.edu (INFO-MAC)

General-Purpose Listings

21. Book-list and internet-press. Maintained and updated by the prolific Kevin Savetz (and sponsored by the Computer Literacy Bookshops and The Electric Bookstore), *book-list* tries to cover and review every book in print that covers the Internet (over 200 in the latest count). *Internet-press*, co-authored with John Higgins, tries to list every online "magazine" on the net. Both of these are huge tasks, but he takes them on with gusto and the updates come out pretty regularly. But the most important part of these lists is their candor. If a "magazine" is nothing more than an electrified press release, he'll say so. And he's quick to point out which books are fluff, outdated, or lean too heavily on reprints of online materials. If you're interested in reading more about the net, these lists are mandatory.

- ftp://rtfm.mit.edu:/pub/usenet/news.answers/internet-services/book-list
- ftp://rtfm.mit.edu:/pub/usenet/news.answers/internet-services/
  internet-press
- http://www.northcoast.com/savetz/savetz.html

22. PDIAL. Maintained and updated by Peter Kaminski, the *Public Dialup Internet Access List (PDIAL)* is the most comprehensive list of Internet service providers available.[16] Unfortunately, updating a list of access providers is very difficult, so if *PDIAL* is out-of-date, you might want to look at several other similar listings that may be in the /providers directory at NIC.MERIT.EDU. Phil Eschallier's *nixpub* list, in particular, is one of those and it's a very good list—but it includes quite a few sites that don't offer full Internet access (some are limited to just email).

- mailserver mailto:info-deli-server@netcom.com,
  body of note: Send PDIAL
- ftp://NIC.MERIT.EDU/internet/providers/pdial
- mailserver mailto:mail-server@bts.com, body of
  note: get PUB nixpub
- ftp://rtfm.mit.edu/pub/usenet/alt.bbs/Nixpub_
  Posting_(Long)

[16] Of course, you have to be connected before you can get this list for getting connected. The irony of this smug circular reference—in fact, *any* online guide for getting connected—is entirely entertaining. But hey—if you're connected, you're connected. OK, to be fair, *PDIAL* is useful when you're trying to find alternative providers that you might want to *switch to.* Especially if you're using your free-trial "introductory" time on one service to grab *PDIAL*—looking for other Internet service providers.

General-Purpose Electronic Magazines

23. EDUPAGE. This is a twice-a-week news-clipping summary that focuses on stories and new products related to the Internet. It chronicles who's doing what to help people reach the net, and it announces new and interesting net resources. It covers what the outside world is trying to do to the net, and what the net is trying to do to the outside. Twice a week is actually a lot if you really read it. But it's the best on the net. Before subscribing to any other online "magazine," sign up for EDUPAGE.

- listproc mailto:listproc@ bitnic.educom.edu, body of note: subscribe EDUPAGE <name>
- ftp://educom.edu/pub/ edupage.new
- http://www.educom.edu

Other Popular Sites

24. The Supreme Court at Case Western Reserve University (CWRU). Published decisions come to the net as part of the Court's Project Hermes. Often within a day, the decisions are available at CWRU—one of the project's partners.[17] CWRU has the decisions themselves, but if you want any searching or browsing capability, you should connect to The Legal Information Institute at Cornell Law School (see Bookmark #1). If you still want to try to get the decision from CWRU, or if you need to grab it just as soon as it's available, you can get it from CWRU—but you'll need to know the specific case number.

- ftp://ftp.cwru.edu/hermes

17 Project Hermes was originally sponsored with twelve participants, one of which was a noncommercial, nonprofit consortium composed of CWRU, EDUCOM, and the National Public Telecomputing Network (NPTN).

18 The data in the archive consists of electronic filings by corporations to the SEC, since the beginning of 1994. Not all corporations currently file electronically, but those that do participate in the SEC's EDGAR filing system. The project to make EDGAR data available is called The Internet EDGAR Dissemination project.

19 *Federal Computer Week* reports that the decision to make EDGAR Internet-accessible and free of charge was a surprise to the SEC! Which explains the apparent disconnect when the SEC and Mead Data went on record dismissing the Internet as "too expensive" just a short time before EDGAR showed up on the net. Reportedly, the National Science Foundation received an unsolicited proposal suggesting a way to disseminate EDGAR for a fraction of the costs that the SEC and Mead were estimating for an Internet service. The NSF *foolishly* assumed that saving money and providing a public service was "good," then went ahead and awarded the grant to try it as an experiment—*without bothering to mention it to the SEC.* FCW called it "Gearheads Meet Policy Wonks" and speculated that NSF was operating with the mindset of engineers—guilelessly supplying a how-to solution without considering the politics or policies. Well, the gearheads got their hands slapped (just to show who's really in charge), but the wonks may have lost the war: It'll take some real fancy wonkwork to explain why the NSF "experiment" shouldn't be allowed to continue. On the other side of this *infobahn* paradox, the arrangement between the SEC and Mead is being put under considerable strain. Mead's deal with the SEC, of course, was based on an assumption that Mead would get a slice of those access fees. But if the Internet project cuts substantially into Mead's projected revenues, then the next time this EDGAR contract comes around, the SEC won't get the same "discount" for letting Mead charge user-access fees. Ironically, if Mead can't hit up the big users of the EDGAR database for user fees, then the cost of running EDGAR—to the SEC and to us taxpayers—will go up.

25. The Securities and Exchange Commission's (SEC) EDGAR database. New York University and the Internet Multicasting Service operate an Internet-accessible data archive containing electronic filings from the SEC's EDGAR database.[18] The interest and publicity surrounding this project are driven more by what it represents to the user community (frequently, EDGAR's users are lawyers)—as a new paradigm for access to government-collected data—rather than by the contents of the archive itself. Under prior arrangements, EDGAR filings are (or were) made available through Mead Data (now LEXIS-Nexis). The price for getting this data through Mead was in excess of $40,000 per year. But the Internet project makes this data directly available on the Internet—the next day—for no additional fees. The services are quite different—Mead adds a lot of value for that $40 grand. But the opening of EDGAR databases to the Internet raised quite a stink,[19] and the questions surrounding this experiment have not been resolved. If you want to see the object of all this fuss:

- http://www.town.hall.org/ edgar/edgar.html
- ftp://ftp.town.hall.org
- gopher://gopher.town.hall.org

26. GPO Access. This is another database more famous for the fight surrounding Internet access than for what's in the database itself. But what's in it is pretty noticeable—the Government Printing Office's GPO Access database includes the full text of the *Congressional Record*, the *Federal Register* (with graphics), all versions of all bills introduced in Congress, a locator service, and more than 6,000 files from twenty-five federal agencies. Initially, GPO Access was going to be available only on a subscription fee basis, but after much arm-twisting,[20] GPO announced a process for obtaining Internet access to the GPO titles free of charge—through sharing

[20] GPO Access is still a subscription service with per-user, per-database pricing that starts at $60 per year per person for the bills database—up to $375 for the *Congressional Record* (for more information, log onto telnet://newuser@wais.access.gpo.gov or mail-to:help@eids05.eids.gpo.gov). Partly because this was a completely new service—rather than one that has been running as an online service already—the subscription announcement set GPO Access into lightning rod mode. Ralph Nader's Taxpayer Assets Project, of course, said the subscriptions "create an unsurmountable barrier for episodic users of the databases" and fail to fulfill the mandate of providing access to citizens. GPO responded that a subscription to GPO Access is less than the cost of a subscription to the printed materials. Certainly, GPO Access compares *unfavorably* to the approach used by the Supreme Court. But it sure got to the heart of the matter in a hurry: Is the government going to charge for access to government data and prevent others from republishing that data? Of course, it's not just dollars and cents—one government agency's cost-recovery plan may be another office's public-service charter. Almost immediately after the subscription announcement—which included the database of pending legislation—the House of Representatives decided to e-publish the House's *own* database of pending legislation. Free of charge, of course. The House sites (see Bookmark #2) are at http://www.house.gov and http://thomas.loc.gov. The WAIS full-text database is at WAIS://diamond.house.gov. (And GPO is stuck at cross.purposes.)

arrangements with selected freenet-based libraries. Missouri and Seattle are two of the sites—they are telnet only, and the interface is a tad on the user-hostile side.

- telnet://guest@bigcat.missouri.edu
- telnet://library@spl.lib.wa.us

27. NCSA's *What's New*. Frankly, if you've got a web browser with a high-speed link—fast enough to support the huge images that web pages often use—the new pages listed on NCSA's What's New page can be absolutely fascinating. It really takes the Internet to an new level of creativity and publishing. It's not overly well organized (remember, this is the place that's getting 400 new submissions each week), but it's always amazing. NCSA[21] and GNN[22] are cooperatively publishing this page. So look in either of these two places:

- http://www.ncsa.uiuc.edu/SDG/Software/Mosaic/Docs/whats-new.html
- http://nearnet.gnn.com/gnn/wn/whats-new.html

28. MCOM's *What's Cool*. This isn't amazing—it's just plain frightening. This is the place where net.explorers come to see if they can scare the e-flatland settlers. Any time you think you've got a handle on what the Internet is and can be, come to this page. It'll show you that all of your preconceptions about life in general (well, some of them at least) are wrong. And be careful not to waste too much time in here—depending on your sense of humor and your taste for the extreme, this can use up all your time without even trying hard.

- http://home.mcom.com/home/whats-cool.html
- see also http://home.mcom.com/home/whats-new.html

[21] The National Center for Supercomputing Applications in Illinois is where Mosaic—currently the most popular web browser—was developed.

[22] O'Reilly and Associates' Global Network Navigator is one of the leading sites for businesses to establish a commercial presence on the net.

The Quick List

Law-Related Starting Points

1. The Legal Information Institute at Cornell Law School
   http://www.law.cornell.edu
2. The House of Representatives Law Library
   http://www.house.gov

Law-Related Meta-Guides

3. The Indiana University School of Law
   http://www.law.indiana.edu

Law-Related Listings

4. *Legallist*
   ftp://ftp.midnight.com/pub/Legallist
5. *Lawlists*
   http://www.kentlaw.edu/lawlinks/listservs.html
6. *Interlaw*
   ftp://sluaxa.slu.edu/pub/millesjg/interlaw.txt

Law-Related Discussion Groups

7. LAWSRC-L
   mailto:listserv@listserv.law.cornell.edu/subscribe LAWSRC-L <name>
8. ABA-UNIX-LIST and NETWORK2D-L
   mailto:listserv@austin.onu.edu/subscribe ABA-UNIX-LIST <name>
   mailto:listserv@austin.onu.edu/subscribe NETWORK2D-L <name>
9. NET-LAWYERS
   mailto:net-lawyers-request@webcom.com/subscribe

Government-Related Listings

10. *Govdocs*
    ftp://una.hh.lib.umich.edu/inetdirsstacks/govdocs:tsangaustin
11. *Government*
    ftp://una.hh.lib.umich.edu/inetdirsstacks/government:gumprecht

Government-Related Discussion Groups

12. GOVDOC-L
    mailto:listserv@psuvm.psu.edu/subscribe GOVDOC-L <name>

General-Purpose Starting Points

13. NCSA's Starting Points
    http://www.ncsa.uiuc.edu/SDG/Software/Mosaic/StartingPoints/
    NetworkStartingPoints.html

14. Yahoo at Stanford University
    http://akebono.stanford.edu/yahoo
15. *Internet-tools* and *internet-cmc*
    http://www.rpi.edu/Internet/Guides/decemj/text.html

General-Purpose Meta-Guides

16. CERN's Overview
    http://info.cern.ch/hypertext/DataSources/bySubject/Overview.html
17. Clearinghouse for Subject-Oriented Internet Resource Guides
    http://www.lib.umich.edu/chhome.html

General-Purpose Collections

18. MIT
    ftp://rtfm.mit.edu
19. EFF
    http://www.eff.org
20. Software ftp sites
    ftp://oak.oakland.edu (INFO-IBMPC)
    ftp://sumex-aim.stanford.edu (INFO-MAC)

General-Purpose Listings

21. *Book-list* and *internet-press*
    ftp://rtfm.mit.edu:/pub/usenet/news.answers/internet-services
22. *PDIAL*
    mailto:info-deli-server@netcom.com/Send PDIAL
    mailto:mail-server@bts.com/get PUB nixpub
    ftp://NIC.MERIT.EDU/internet/providers

General-Purpose Electronic Magazines

23. EDUPAGE
    mailto:listproc@bitnic.educom.edu/subscribe EDUPAGE <name>

Other Popular Sites

24. The Supreme Court at CWRU
    ftp://ftp.cwru.edu/hermes
25. SEC's EDGAR
    http://www.town.hall.org/edgar/edgar.html
26. GPO Access
    telnet://guest@bigcat.missouri.edu
    telnet://library@spl.lib.wa.us

27. NCSA's What's New
    http://www.ncsa.uiuc.edu/SDG/Software/Mosaic/Docs/whats-new.html
    http://nearnet.gnn.com/gnn/wn/whats-new.html
28. MCOM's What's Cool
    http://home.mcom.com/home/whats-cool.html
    http://home.mcom.com/home/whats-new.html

If you use this list and find that it sends you off on an Internet wild goose chase, please let me know (mailto:allison@mitre.org). Or if you find some new or overlooked site that you think is just a drop dead *lock* for this list, please let me know about that as well. Like I said, I try to keep the list fairly stable, but I'm always on the lookout for something better.

Hope it helps.

Choosing a Role

E-Flatland Settlers

Chapter 11

The User's Internet

OK, so you're anxious to get started, you've got your credit card in one hand and your modem in the other. What can you do to get started *right away?*

Well, for starters, put the modem down[1]—you can keep the credit card out, though. Maybe you can pick up the telephone if you really want to.

Getting Connected

There are four basic options for *how* to get connected:

- Connect through a commercial online service, such as Compuserve or America Online, which can give you a limited-service gateway to the Internet.
- Connect to a "shell" account—provided on a host computer operated by one of the many Internet service providers.
- Use a "SLIP" account—or better yet, a "PPP" account—to connect your home or office computer directly to the Internet networks through one of several Internet service providers.
- Establish a network connection, usually through a high-speed ISDN or leased telephone line, to connect your entire local area network with one of several Internet service providers.

Your choice of these options affects what level of Internet service you'll get. Also, each can differ substantially in terms of price, speed, hardware requirements, software set-up, and how much help you can expect from your vendor. And of course, the biggest difference comes when we answer the question, "How easy is it?"

Frankly, there are a lot of choices, and the choices are changing fast. In any market that seems over-endowed with choices, consumers tend to lean toward vendors who wave

1 You shouldn't be waving that thing around in the air anyway. Just leave it on the desk, or for heaven's sake, if you took it out of the computer just to participate in the opening paragraph, *put it back!*

their hands with the authority of superior-technology-magic and pretend to supply the "one easy answer." The fact is that there *are* some easy answers, and if what the easy-answer-vendor offers is what you want, then by all means, use it. The trick, of course, is knowing enough about the technology to understand what's being offered, to know what you want, and to find the vendor or vendors who can do the best job of giving you what you want.[2]

Online Service Gateways

Technically, connecting to a commercial online service is not the same as connecting to the Internet. What you're connecting to is the service's own host computers where they've established a proprietary, self-contained electronic environment for you to wander around in. Any links to the Internet are controlled through specially constructed gateways.[3]

With online services, you get an account on their computer, the software you use is either your own telecommunications package or the vendor's proprietary software, and you dial in using a modem and a standard telephone line. The speed of your connection depends entirely on what speed the vendor's modems are set up to handle—usually somewhere between 2,400 and 14,400 bits per second (bps).[4] The costs for using online services are usually calculated as a fixed monthly fee plus connect-time charges. The hourly fees frequently vary by time of day[5] or by the speed of the line that you're connecting through. Also, once you start using the Internet gateways, you may find special Internet-related surcharges (especially for email).

The strength of the online services is that the vendors have been in the business of supplying connec-

[2] That might be easy to say, but it can be hard to do. Sort of like "Buy low, sell high."

[3] Most online service vendors are aggressively boasting about their plans to offer full Internet access—rather than just Internet gateways. Some are forging new alliances with key Internet participants, some are building on their own established infrastructures, others are just making noise. Technically, there's nothing to prevent an online services vendor from offering Internet shell accounts, SLIP or PPP accounts, or direct Internet connections. But at this writing, the talk has been mostly that—just talk. As the industry matures further, one should expect at least some online service vendors to make the jump successfully. (Of course when the dedicated word processing market was forced to shift to PCs in the early 1980s, not a single dedicated-WP vendor successfully made the jump. I hope the online service vendors are a little more agile.) In the context of this discussion, therefore, it's important to distinguish between the vendor and the type of service. It's entirely likely, for example, that America Online will offer both an online service and a shell account service. That won't change the nature of "commercial online services"—which in the Internet context are *defined* by the use of gateways. In that example, it will mean that the vendor is offering *both* an Internet service provider capability and an online services gateway.

[4] A *few* online services are starting to experiment with 28.8 Kbps dial-in modems, and with ISDN telephone lines that offer speeds that *start* at 64 Kbps.

[5] Thereby encouraging an entire generation of sleep-deprived online junkies recognizable by daytime lethargy, a killer caffeine habit, and an unnatural familiarity with late late late night talk shows.

tivity to large numbers of consumers for quite some time. Their software tends to be targeted at the computer neophyte—easy to use, easy to install, and with plenty of help just a phone call (or email message) away. Discussion groups within the confines of the service tend to be ruly and generally better behaved than the free-wheeling affairs out on the net. The features, resources, and discussion groups—again, *within* the service—tend to be better organized than those you'll find on the net.

The weakness of the online services is that Internet access is provided exclusively through gateways. Internet email should be fairly easy to use,[6] but the other Internet services can be either limited or completely missing. Most online services provide some sort of selectively republished newsgroup discussions, but the software tends to be the vendor's own, the list of newsgroups is frequently limited, and participating in a newsgroup (by posting new messages) may be only partially supported. Other services, such as telnet, ftp, gopher and WWW, are only rarely included. When the services *are* included, you'll often find that the vendor has put its own proprietary software between you and the service. If you don't know anything about the Internet, this custom front-end might actually help;[7] but for someone who is already familiar with parts of the Internet, the custom front-ends can be confusing and disruptive.

An easy answer? If all you really need is email, or if you'd prefer to get comfortable with email before tackling some of the more powerful Internet services, the commercial online services do an excellent job of getting you started and making things easy. And if we believe the recent promises that the online service vendors are moving towards improved access to the Internet, then you might find that the vendor is delivering that capability just about the time that you're ready for it.

Shell Accounts

To use an Internet access shell account, you dial in and connect your computer to the vendor's own Internet-connected host computers. The user interface software that's running on the vendor's computer is the "shell"—and it can vary dramatically from vendor to vendor. Some shell accounts use text-and-command-line Unix as the shell—which gives you a fair amount of power, but requires familiarity with Unix's notoriously user-hostile command set. At the other end of the ease-of-use spectrum, some shells are proprietary point-and-click graphical interfaces that blur the line between online service and Internet service provider. With all shell accounts, though, you're getting a true

[6] Remember to pay attention to any surcharges that are imposed on Internet email. The surcharges are frequently applied to *incoming* email.

[7] Certainly, it helps the vendor lock you into the vendor's own service, by ensuring that your familiarity with Internet services is filtered through the vendor's proprietary process and terminology.

Internet connection, complete with the ability to log onto other Internet hosts and services.

With shell accounts, you get an account on the Internet service provider's computer, the software might be either your own telecommunications package or the vendor's proprietary software, and you dial in using a modem and a standard telephone line. The speed of your connection depends on what speed the vendor's modems are set up to handle—usually somewhere between 2,400 bps and 28.8 Kbps. Some Internet service providers also support ISDN or leased telephone lines, although those high-speed links are usually used with SLIP/PPP accounts or full-time LAN connections. The costs for shell account Internet access are among the lowest in the industry. In most cases where the shell is command-line Unix, charges are set as a fixed monthly fee—with variations based on the speed on the dial-in line connection (sometimes, pricing varies with the range of Internet services supported). Some shell accounts, especially those with more sophisticated graphical shells, charge both a fixed fee and an hourly fee for connect time.

The strength of a shell account is that you're getting true Internet access at some of the best rates in the business. If you're willing to live with the Unix command line interface, you might be able to find some local providers who will give you access for a *very* nominal flat-rate monthly charge. If you're interested in more sophisticated user interfaces,[8] some of the shell providers—notably Pipeline and Netcom—do a good job of providing an easy-to-use interface, as well as a decent level of user support during installation and day-to-day operations.

The weaknesses of a shell account are usually found in the trade-offs you make to get the low prices. Unix can be both difficult and intimidating (although it doesn't have to be). Also, some of the more basic command-line shells can't support the full-graphic capability of services like World Wide Web—or if they are supported, slow dial-in speeds can make the graphics operations so *painfully* slow as to be irrelevant.[9] And the lack of graphics can be significant. With the astonishing growth of the web, some are now suggesting that if you're missing the web, you're missing everything—and graphics are a key part of the web.[10] Final-

8 Read: "less user-hostile."

9 Some web pages are absolutely *filled* with graphics—as much as several M-bytes (megabytes, or millions of characters) on a single page—put there by people who obviously have a corporate or university connection that's using a "T1" link or better. Using a T1 link, at 1.544 Mbps (millions of bits per second), a 2 M-byte image can be downloaded in just fifteen or twenty seconds. Try that at home with your trusty 2,400 bps modem and you'll sit there for about *two hours* waiting for what turns out to be nothing more than a decorative border. It gets old, fast.

10 Of course the web supports a text-only interface that works with most web servers (not all). If you're in this for the research only, text should be enough. In my opinion, the impact of the graphical images can tell a compelling the-medium-is-the-message story. But to be fair, hearing the story and doing research are two very different tasks. It's up to you. But it's an unattractive choice.

ly, the Internet service providers are not as well organized or as well established as the online service vendors. It's generally harder to find the Internet service providers, harder to evaluate their longevity or reputation, and harder still to find published comparisons.

An easy answer? This is the entry level for true Internet access: basic, inexpensive, fairly easy to install—but it can be difficult to use. If you're trying to keep costs down to a minimum (which can be difficult if you're using it a lot and your service provider charges by the hour), this is the service of choice—for both newcomers and experts alike. On the other hand, if you're looking for easy all-in-one-place answers, you won't find many in this group. Probably the two most likely chances for that type of answer could come from either Netcom or Pipeline—two of the better-known shell account providers that offer nationwide access. Both have fairly sophisticated graphical interfaces, and a better-than-average reputation for technical support.

SLIP/PPP Accounts

To use a "SLIP" or "PPP" account, you install one of two types of networking software on your computer—either SLIP (Serial Line Internet Protocol) or PPP (Point to Point Protocol)—to make your computer compatible with the TCP/IP networking software that's used on the Internet. Once you're set up, you use the software to dial in and connect your computer to the vendor's own Internet-connected routers. The routers connect you directly to the Internet, through the providers' own link to the Internet networks. At this point, your computer is now a fully connected Internet host computer—complete with the ability to log onto all other Internet hosts and services using telnet, ftp, gopher, full-graphics web—whatever. To use the Internet services, you use your own software—frequently supplied as part of the SLIP or PPP bundle, or whatever other variations on TCP/IP supported software that you decide to use. Like the different user interfaces in the shell accounts, there's a fairly wide difference among the TCP/IP tools for use with SLIP and PPP accounts. Some are downright painful, while others are the best in the market. In this case, though, it's up to you to find and choose what you think is best. If you have a choice between SLIP and PPP, go with PPP—it's a more reliable technology.[11]

With SLIP/PPP accounts, you get an account on the Internet service provider's gateway (which lets you connect to the router), the software might be yours or theirs (but the key is the SLIP or PPP networking software), and you dial in using a modem

11 PPP constantly monitors the network connection and retransmits any packets that get garbled in transmission—which can happen quite frequently on a "noisy" telephone line. The older SLIP technology doesn't do retransmissions. This can make it a little bit faster in some situations, but the loss in reliability (especially if you're using graphics-intensive point-and-click operations) just isn't worth it.

and a standard telephone line. The speed of your connection depends on what speed the vendor's modems are set up to handle—usually somewhere between 14.4 Kbps and 28.8 Kbps—in some cases you can also get ISDN or leased telephone lines. The costs for SLIP/PPP accounts tend to be a bit higher than that for shell accounts. You'll find a mix of flat-rate monthly fees and flat-fee plus hourly connections.

The strength of SLIP/PPP is that this is a true Internet connection. It means you get to use native Internet software directly on the Internet, and you're not constrained by the limited services developed by some vendor who thinks they know better than you what you really want. When some new service comes out, you don't have to wait for your vendor to come up to speed and figure out how to make it acceptable to the masses—you can download it immediately and try whatever is there for the trying. If you don't like the software that came with your TCP/IP package, you can probably download and try out several different alternatives—mostly as freeware or shareware. Obviously, you can mix and match different utilities until you've got exactly what you like best (assuming that you want to take the time). Another significant advantage of the SLIP/PPP account is that you almost always get set up with your own domain name. If you want your Internet address to be your-name-goes-here.com, this is way to play.

The weaknesses of SLIP/PPP are found in the trade-offs you make to get the true Internet connection—mostly during installation and set-up. Installing SLIP/PPP can be fairly challenging, unless your SLIP/PPP vendor happens to have guessed most of the details about your particular configuration and your particular access provider ahead of time. (With some of the packages at the far end of the user-friendly scale, installation is unconscionably difficult.) The second part of the process—choosing your own software—is great if you're an expert in the field. But if you don't know your *awk* from your *grep*, the terrible price of freedom is freedom. Even knowing *what* you're supposed to collect can be a chore; trying to choose the best among seemingly unconstrained choices can make the job impossible. To make matters even more—uh—challenging, most of the vendors who write this type of software assume that you're already a TCP/IP expert. So they're less likely to make the interfaces user-friendly, they're more likely to bury key configuration options in hidden nooks and crannies and leave "technical support" to the never-especially-talkative readme files. The Internet service providers for SLIP/PPP accounts, as for shell accounts, are not as well organized or as well established as the online service vendors. It's generally harder to find the Internet service providers, harder to evaluate their longevity or reputation, and harder still to find published comparisons.

An easy answer? This is the real thing—extensive and extensible, not necessarily easy to install and not necessarily easy to use. But it gives you full connectivity to the Internet—web pages, downloadable movies, sound bites, all of the standard Internet services plus the hundreds of obscure services and in-the-process-of-being-developed services that make this environment so dynamic. If you're connecting computers one at a time, *this is* where the action is. Interestingly, if you're looking for easy all-in-one answers, the SLIP/PPP option actually seems to have more choices than the shell account option. Spry's *Internet in a Box*[12] and NetManage's *Internet Chameleon*[13] try to take on the task of making SLIP and PPP connections positively easy. Also a number of books (most notably, the *Starter Kit* series—for both Windows and Macintosh[14]—by Adam Engst) contain most of the software you'll need to set up a full SLIP/PPP connection. In most cases, the kits come with well-written books or guides that describe the software and installation process in detail. In a few cases, the packages come with decent technical support (from a variety of vendors) as well. Engst's Starter Kits are very competitively priced, but aren't as preconfigured as the in-a-box offerings. On the other hand, the in-a-boxes tend to be a little more expensive and they don't come with the extensive guides.

LAN Connections

To connect your entire local area network (LAN) to the Internet, the process involves establishing a LAN connection with one of the several Internet service providers. In most cases, this involves setting up a router of some kind on your own LAN (sometimes combined with a PC or other computer running Unix),[15] then making sure that all the computers on your LAN (well, all the ones that will be connecting to the net at least) are running TCP/IP. The router can either be set up to maintain a full-time connection over an ISDN or leased telephone line, or to automatically dial out to the Internet service provider whenever a user tries to start an Internet service. Once the connection is established (either full-time or as a dial-out session) all of the users on your network can use that one connection to request and operate Internet services. There is no separate logon

[12] Oh, by the time you read this, it'll be out-of-date. But just in case, Spry is at 800-557-9614. *Internet in a Box* lists for $149.

[13] NetManage is at 408-973-7171. *Internet Chameleon* lists for $199.

[14] *Internet Starter Kit for Windows* and *Internet Starter Kit for Macintosh*, both by Adam Engst and others, Hayden Books, ISBN 1-56830-094-8 and ISBN 1-56830-064-6, respectively.

[15] Yet another option when trying to connect all the computers on a LAN is to set up your own internal shell-account server. In this scenario, you would configure a Unix host on your network, connect the Unix server as a single node attached to an Internet service provider, then set up all of your LAN-connected computers to be able to log onto the Unix host. Instead of having users log onto your provider's host, they would log onto your internal host. The shell they would be able to use would be the shell you provide.

process for your individual users (unless you set one up internally). At this point, the computers on your LAN are all fully connected nodes on the Internet—complete with the ability to log onto all other Internet hosts and services using telnet, ftp, gopher, full-graphics web—whatever. As with SLIP/PPP accounts (actually, more so), you'll be on your own for selecting and installing the Internet software packages on your LAN-connected machines.

With a LAN connection, you establish a relationship with an Internet service provider to be able to connect your router to the provider's gateway, the software is almost always yours,[16] and the process of dialing in is carefully negotiated between you and your provider. Some providers offer dial-in modem service that starts at 14.4 Kbps, but trying to pump several simultaneous Internet sessions—supporting however many people you might have on your LAN—through a 14.4 Kbps pipe will be a noticeable constraint. Some providers support 28.8 Kbps over standard telephone lines, but most LAN connections should be set up with ISDN or leased telephone lines. ISDN starts at 64 Kbps, and both technologies readily support connections of up to 1.544 Mbps (a T1 link). Higher-speed links are also available. The costs for LAN connections tend to be flat rates—but comparatively *high* flat rates.[17] But the real cost of the LAN connection can be the telephone line. A leased line can cost several thousand dollars a year. By *comparison*, ISDN is becoming almost reasonable.

The strength of the LAN connection is that you've enabled your entire office with true Internet connectivity. You get to use native Internet software directly on the Internet, and you're not constrained—either by some Internet service provider or by what Fred-down-the-hall is using. Your users can use different software products to reach the different Internet services—if that makes sense in your environment. This approach also opens up the entire breadth and richness of the network. With the higher speed links, you don't have to worry about point-and-click graphics slowing your connection to a crawl. Also, with the full-time connection (or with on-demand dial-out service), you can leave your email accounts open for new mail constantly. No longer do you have to dial out to an outside service to get external email; it shows up in your inbasket the same way your internal email shows up—as soon as the Internet delivers it. As with SLIP/PPP accounts, a LAN connection will get you your own domain name.

The weaknesses of the LAN connection are nontrivial. You need to know what you're doing and you need to give

[16] Note that NetManage's *Internet Chameleon* can be configured to support this type of LAN connection.

[17] The rates are high only when you compare them to single-user rates for things like shell accounts and SLIP/PPP services. If you consider the cost of buying a shell account or SLIP/PPP service for every computer on your LAN, then the bulk-rate fees for a LAN connection are bargains.

some serious attention to the security concerns raised by having a full-time Internet connection attached to your LAN. In fact—given those security considerations—the simple model of connecting a LAN to a router, then the router to the Internet, is probably irresponsible. Especially in a law office. Installing a LAN connection, choosing the software, administering the service, and answering questions from your users are all noticeable undertakings. Most offices assign these types of activities to a LAN administrator or other technical specialist(s). That's not to say they can't be understood or handled by a smart user who's willing to spend the time and energy to make it happen, but don't be tricked into thinking this is just Internet-in-a-Box: The Sequel. Don't expect much help from the access providers or other software vendors—they'll all assume that you're already a TCP/IP expert. As before, the Internet service providers for LAN connections are not especially well known outside the basic circle of administrators (although UUnet and PSINet may be the market leaders). It'll generally be harder to find Internet service providers that provide this service, and harder still to find published comparisons.

An easy answer? Not really. But if you're in a position to build this type of infrastructure, this is the Real Deal. LAN connection gives you top-of-the-line, no-excuses no-compromises access. Of course, if all you want to do is try this Internet *thing* out and take it for a spin, a LAN connection isn't the way to do it. But if you've tried it out, if you're serious about playing in this field full time, then this is what it takes to do it right. It'll cost you several thousand dollars. Perhaps several thousand a year. Oddly enough, if you're looking for easy all-in-one answers, there *are* some easy answers here—not always reliable, but sure-enough *easy*: the new horde of Internet consultants. With as many organizations as there are now desperately racing to move to the Internet full time, a *huge* cottage industry has built up—a group of consultants who hold themselves out as capable and experienced in setting up these types of full-time LAN-based Internet connections. There are many excellent Internet consultancies—some even specialize in doing this work with law offices. They can take you from start to finish and get you up and running in a re-

sponsible, well-thought-out manner (using your money of course, and charging you a fee on top of that). As with any suddenly popular, demand-driven cottage industry, however, the quality of these consultants can vary—rather spectacularly. Until the industry matures a bit, you would do well to rely on personal references, or references from your Internet service provider.[18]

18 *Whatever* you do, make sure that you ask the consultant for references, and more importantly—actually *call the references!* An Internet access consultant can spend an awful lot of your time, effort, and money; and with just a little bit of effort, can actually hurt *your reputation* on the net before you've gotten a chance to go out there yourself. Check those references, and check *all* of them—even the fly-by-nighters will have one or two happy customers.

Making Your Choice—Easiest, Fastest, Cheapest?

It's not an easy decision, and there *are* way too many choices. I know you want to pick up that modem again, but if you really want to do this right— and not be disappointed because of a mismatch between what you want to do and what the service offers—it's important to understand the different characteristics of the different options (described above), and apply them to your own situation and preferences.

If you need more detailed information, look through the "Book Reviews" section of this book, or get a copy of Savetz's Internet *book-list* (see #21 in the "Burge's Bookmarks") for an update on the latest available guides.

The following books are especially helpful in the process of getting connected:

- Susan Estrada's definitive work on the topic, *Connecting to the Internet— An O'Reilly Buyer's Guide* (O'Reilly and Associates, ISBN 1-56592-061-9), is detailed, hands-on, how-to, specific and directly on point. This guide covers just one thing—getting connected—and it does that one thing very well. It does assume that you're already familiar with the Internet basics and that you know exactly what you're going to do once you get connected. But if what you're trying to do is get into the details of the different connectivity alternatives, this is the book that lays it all out.
- If you *don't* have all the bits and pieces ready to go (maybe you're not even sure what all the bits and pieces *are*), then a better bet would probably be one of the two Engst starter-kit books—*Internet Starter Kit for Windows* or *Internet Starter Kit for Macintosh* (both Hayden Books, ISBN 1-56830-094-8 and ISBN 1-56830-064-6, respectively). Both starter kits come with instructions, lists of providers, and all the software you'll need to get started. These books are really what they say they are: complete starter kits— designed to get you from holding the modem in the air to surfing the Internet curl.

Choosing a Service Provider

Before you *choose* an Internet service provider, you've got to *find* one. (OK, that makes sense.)

Unfortunately, in an emerging industry like this, there are precious few directories or listings of industry participants (and most of *those* are online). Most don't even make an effort to supply substantive or comparative information *about* the offered services, and frankly, the services are changing so fast that any such effort would likely be futile.

Also unfortunately, most of the ubiquitous computer magazines and trade journals—where you would normally expect to find massive comparative lists of rapidly changing, probably-out-of-date-by-now-but-something-is-better-than-nothing technology-related products and services—have been painfully silent on this topic (at least to date). Perhaps the problem is that so many of the vendors in this market are regional vendors—offering services only within a few states, a few area codes, or even just a single area code. Or perhaps the magazines feel daunted by the number and different types of products (although that doesn't seem to daunt *PC Magazine*'s blockbuster printer issue every year). Or perhaps the magazines are already gearing up for this dauntful task, and next year's hotbed of testbeds will be chock-full of Internet service providers. Maybe *in the very next issue.* (Maybe.)

The best place to look for a *comprehensive* list of Internet service providers is, at least for now, online. The lists are *occasionally* updated, though not with the type of frequency that one would prefer. When you look for them (if you look for them), you might find that some of the lists haven't been updated in a very long time—so much so that the list may have lapsed from out-of-date into unreliable (except perhaps to give you the *names* of at least some of the vendors and their disconnected telephone numbers). The best thing to do is to check the more popular *locations* where provider lists are collected. If a once-well-known list is missing, it was probably pulled because it was getting too old. If you find some new list—especially one with a fairly recent last-updated-date—maybe someone has published a completely new compilation. Most of the key Internet sites will try to get the latest lists of Internet service providers.

Here are some of the better lists, and places to look for Internet service provider listings:

- The MERIT.EDU provider lists. Look in the entire directory at ftp://NIC.MERIT.EDU/internet/providers.
- The internic.net provider lists. Look in the appropriate country subdirectories at ftp://is.internic.net/infoguide/getting-connected.
- *PDIAL (Public Dialup Internet Access List)*. This is (or was, depending on how recently it's been updated) one of the most comprehensive listings of Internet service providers available. Try ftp://NIC.MERIT.EDU/internet/providers/pdial, or mailto:info-deli-server@netcom.com with the message "Send PDIAL".
- *Nixpub*. This list concentrates on public access providers, including Bulletin Board Systems (BBSs) and sites that don't offer full Internet access (some are limited to just email). Try ftp://rtfm.mit.edu/pub/usenet/alt.bbs/Nixpub_Posting_(Long), or mailto:mail-server@bts.com with the message "get PUB nixpub".

The two best places to look for current information about local and national Internet service providers—which may be more meaningful than a more comprehensive listing that's maybe-almost-up-to-date and online—are two decidedly *offline* sources of information:

- Magazines tend to attract advertising by both the established and wannabe Internet service providers.[19] My favorite magazine for this purpose is *Wired*, but many of the other Internet or online-service-oriented titles carry a fair amount of advertising as well.

- Local sources. Be *sure* to check the ads in the business section of your local newspaper. Look for local computer magazines or newsletters. Talk to staff at local computer stores. Check with local computer user groups. In fact, some user groups operate their own shell account or SLIP/PPP Internet access services.

Pick the vendors that seem to offer what you're looking for, and call 'em up to get more details. And be aware that some vendors—even if they advertise nationally—may only offer their services in certain parts of the country.

What to Ask About

Ask about the type of service offered—shell account, SLIP, PPP—since the provider might offer several different options. Ask about prices for each different level of service: one-time setup charges, monthly flat-rates, hourly charges, surcharges for high-speed links, storage, separate Internet services (including either outbound or *incoming* email), or "toll-free" long distance access.[20] Check for discounts if you dial in "after hours," or for flat-rate unlimited-usage plans if you agree to a certain minimum. Find out if there's a charge for software you have to buy. Ask about the Internet services you'll get access to, and what sort of limitations there might be. Make sure you find out if you need to supply any of your own software. Also ask about documentation and technical support for users—both online and "offline."[21] Do you have to have a specific modem? How fast can you connect in? (14.4 Kbps? 28.8 Kbps? Can you get ISDN? Is ISDN planned?) And go ahead, dare to ask it: How fast is the Internet service provider's own connection? If the provider doesn't have a T1 or T3 leased-line link—if they're trying to get by with a modem-based link themselves—then you're likely to run into serious performance problems.

[19] As testimony to the efficiency of capitalist incentives, advertising has the highest likelihood of providing *current* information through traditional print media mechanisms. Both the vendors and the publishers have an incentive to get the most up-to-date information distributed to the would-be buying public. Accordingly, advertising tends to have shortest lead time of almost any content in a print media product. On the other hand, accuracy and comparability to competitor products aren't exactly hallmark features of quick-to-press advertising.

[20] OK, I *love* it when they charge you a fee for "toll-free" access.

[21] If the only way to reach your technical support Help Line is through email, it won't do you a lick of good until you've got your email up and running.

Getting Started Now—Let's Get Ready to Rum-mble!

Still got that modem in your hand? Got an itchy Internet finger?

OK, if you really want to get started now, let's go ahead and take a look at that list of "Internet Service Providers" in the Reference section of this book. You'll notice very quickly that the list is neither comprehensive nor especially detailed. (That's the job of other people and other lists.) The providers in that listing are just a few of the ones that—in *my* opinion—appear to have developed some level of reputation and stability over the years.

My list of providers is organized just a little bit differently than by the type of Internet access service—I tried to use this list to highlight a few of the special purpose services available. Here's how the reference list of providers is organized:

- Full-Service Providers. These providers not only offer all Internet services—usually including shell account, SLIP/PPP account, and LAN connectivity—but they also offer the important service of being able to register a domain name for you. Almost all can give you an 800 number for using the service. Prices vary, of course. UUnet[22] and PSINet may be the market leaders in this class, but they're also some of the more expensive.

- No-Fee Access Providers. You've got to pay for the long distance phone call if one of these is not in your area, and the type of service can be fairly limited, but these can be just about the quickest way to get started.

- Other Internet Service Providers. These are some of the most prolific of advertisers, and they seem to be among the most interested in making this process easy for you. They are usually shell account and SLIP/PPP providers. Pipeline and Netcom are fairly common choices, and probably a good easy choice if you're starting out completely from scratch (i.e., no Internet-in-a-Box or Starter Kit) and really want the Internet instead of an online service.

- Special Law-Related Networks. Some of these aren't really Internet service providers, but they have special applicability to the legal community and are included. Each is very different from its neighbors.

- Commercial Online Service Vendors. Most of these give you gateways rather than the Internet itself, but they're promising great things. If you're looking for true Internet access, you might consider what these vendors are offering—but be very careful to find out the details behind advertised "features." Many gateways are advertised as the features themselves. To be fair, these folks are the most likely to get you up and running the fastest. They have the biggest budgets, the biggest computers, and the biggest technical support staffs. Some novices start with these, get familiar with the

[22] Microsoft recently purchased an equity interest in UUnet. Industry analysts speculate whether or not this will cause a fundamental change in the services UUnet offers, but nothing is really settled yet.

technologies, and then move up to full Internet access after they've gotten comfortable with the basics. Compuserve is certainly the biggest, America Online is probably the best all-around service, and Delphi tries to deliver the most extensive list of Internet services (albeit with a more cumbersome user interface than most of its competitors).

Obviously, the best approach is to go back now and try to get a better list of service providers. Call 'em. And ask the whole range of gimme-the-details questions. Heck, at least pick up a copy of *Wired* and check for the latest advertisers and special deals.

Well, that was your last chance. If you really have to jump in right now, here goes.

Setting up the Account

By whatever means, choose one of the providers from the whatever list you're using.

If you're using the list from the Reference section of this book, you'll notice that some of the listings only show a voice telephone number, while others show a number for "dialup:".[23] The availability of a dialup number means that you can dial in and try the system out. If there's no dialup number, you'll need to use that credit card you've still got waving in the air. Put it down long enough to dial the voice number, then find out from the vendor exactly what they'll need from you to get an account set up.[24]

Typically, you need to know eight things:

1. What's the dialup phone number? Can they give you one that's local to your calling area, or are you going to have to pay for the long distance call yourself? Are there different charges for different phone numbers?[25]

2. Are there any special modem settings you'll need to use? The default that almost everyone uses is 8-N-1 (8-bits, no parity, one stop bit).[26]

[23] Although I've presented the dialup information in a format that follows the model for URL, there is no true URL preface for dialup services. Consistency being the hobgoblin of *this* little mind, I've made this format up completely—to try to *build* on the basic URL form and format, rather than introducing a completely different mechanism for describing how to reach a target service.

[24] In turn, they'll probably ask *you* to pick up that piece of plastic that you so carelessly left on the table beside the phone.

[25] Lots of services charge more for higher-speed links, and the different speed links are usually reached by dialing into different telephone numbers.

[26] Do you need to know what this means? *Of course not!* But that's the language that's used to set the modem and communications software correctly. If you don't know how to check or change the communications settings, then you might be in trouble. (Well, maybe not *real* trouble. I mean, there aren't any *modem police* that'll come knock-knock-knocking on your back door.) But you're going to be stuck for a while until you can figure it out. Unless of course you just go ahead and try it. As I said, 8-N-1 is a fairly common default.

3. How fast will this link be? Again, this is used in setting up your modem and communications software. But also again, your computer is probably already set up for the fastest possible speed, and if the link is slower, most systems will adjust automatically. When they give you the answer to this question, they'll say something like 2,400 or 9.6 or 14.4. *Sometimes*, they'll include a unit-of-measure as well. Usually the unit of measure is bits per second—expressed as either bits per second (bps) or baud.[27] Indeed, if the number is expressed in hundreds (like 2,400), that'll be bits per second. But if the number is expressed in single digits, or with decimals (such as nine-dot-six)—or in *K*—then they're telling you thousands of bits per second.

4. Do I need SLIP or PPP? If you do, then you're hosed (for now, at least). You'll need additional software to make this thing work. Of course, SLIP and PPP are *good* signs, not *bad*. Even though it's extra software, it's the *exact* software you need to get the most full-service operation of Internet features (even though it's going to take you a little longer to get started).

5. What's the user ID for your account? When you log on, you'll need to have a user ID and a password. The user ID identifies who you are, and the password says that it's really you.

6. What's the password you'll need to use? Will you have to change it the very first time you log on, or will you have a few grace logons? If you have to change it, what are the rules for making up passwords?[28]

7. When will the account be ready? Immediately? Or do you have to wait a couple of hours (or a couple of days) before you can use it?

8. Here comes the Ugly Question: What can I do once I log on? Here, the options literally explode before your very eyes. If this is a Unix-based shell account, you're going to log on and get nothing more than a heartless command line prompt that'll make you yearn for the friendliness of DOS. If they tell you

27 Technically, baud is different from bits per second, but at the comparatively slow speeds that modems *used to* run at (you know, back in the *old days* before 1990), the two terms were effectively identical and everyone got used to using the terms interchangeably, albeit inaccurately. Now, unless we want to send those modem police out again, we just have to live with the fact that people will say "baud" when they mean "bps." Bps is the correct term in this context. Aren't you glad you asked?

28 It always amazes me when I run across a new Internet service provider that's trying to win my business, but then the first thing they make me do is make up a new password according to some completely mandatory rules that they decline or neglect to tell me about. That makes them *secret* rules. Later (sometimes *much* later, thanks), I learn that the password had to contain a minimum number of characters, or at least one "special" character from an unpublished list of special characters. Rather than get stymied at the logon prompt, ask about the password rules (if there are any) ahead of time.

it's Unix or a shell, be sure to ask them for *help*, and ask what commands are available for accessing Internet services. (And resolve to buy a copy of Ed Krol's *Whole Internet*.) Actually, in one sense, the Unix prompt is good (in a way). It means that you're at least working in a nonproprietary environment that millions of *other* people are familiar with. If you are directed towards a custom user interface, it probably means that you've got to get the software before you can get started, and it means that you *still* need instructions on what to do and how to do it. If the software is proprietary, only they will be able to help you out. Each system is different; your mileage may vary.

9.[29]Now comes the *Really Ugly Question*: Did any of my instructions and explanations make sense to you? Maybe I assumed that you already have a computer and a modem (you know—the one you were waving in the air) that's already set up and ready to use. If those are bad assumptions, or if you've never actually *used* any of those features, then you're going to have to figure out those basics. If they didn't make sense because they're options and configurations that you don't normally change or even deal with—then that's not such a problem. Like I said, a lot of those will be handled by the system defaults.[30]

OK, now that you've gotten the information from the vendor (and presumably, now that they've gotten your plastic) and you've waited for however long they told you to wait, you're ready to go.

Start your computer, fire up the communications software, make sure the modem set-up is correct (speed and line protocol settings) and do whatever your software requires to dial the phone number they gave you. The vendor's system will ask you for your user ID and then for your password.

If you're following some of the dialup instructions that are listed with each provider in the Reference section (rather than having talked to the vendor personally) assume that your modem setup settings are all the defaults and that the vendor's system will tell you what you need to know to log on as a new user. If my dialup instructions show something like this

dialup://visitor@217-255-9000

that means that the *phone number* is "217-255-9000," and that you should use "visitor" as your *user ID* when the system asks for one. If this is the logon instruction, then the system isn't supposed to ask you for a *password*. (If it does, it should give you specific instructions on what to do. If it asks for a password but doesn't give you instructions, then just make one up—or use the user

29 Yes, I know I said eight questions. But this one doesn't count :-)

30 If they didn't make sense because I'm just not clear when I write about this geekazoid stuff, then that's my responsibility. Which isn't a lot of help. But I'm willing to take the blame.

ID again—but remember what you used. You'll probably need it the next time you dial in.) If the logon instructions show something more detailed, like this

dialup://JOINDELPHI:WRD949@800-365-4636

the first half of the logon information is the user ID, the second half (after the colon) is the password they want you to use. In this example, the *phone number* would be 800-365-4636, the *user ID* would be JOINDELPHI, and the *password* would be WRD949.[31]

OK! Let's assume that you made it past the password prompt, and you're in! Terrific.

Welcome to Unix.Hell

Of course, if you've connected to some user-friendly place where your every need is anticipated and met,[32] then you're up and running now with no more need to follow any more of the instructions in this chapter. You should tear these pages out of the book, recycle them, and get on with using your new-found tools. Congratulations!

On the other hand, if you're now staring at the unblinking eye of a single-character prompt (like % or $), then you've probably entered the command-line world of a Unix shell. This isn't going to be impossible (easy for me to say), but it really isn't going to be intuitive, either.

Unix was written for programmers[33]—programmers who were expected to already know what they needed to know, so the only issue was how fast the programmer could enter the commands and get their work done. First and foremost, therefore, Unix commands are terse. (Brutally terse.) The COPY function is written as cp, MOVE is written as mv, and DELETE is rm. Many commands have switches that let you specify options for how the command should operate. For example, the command to list all the files in a directory (similar to the DOS command, DIR) is "ls". But if you want to see a nondefault view of the files, one where all the information about a file is listed instead of just the filenames, you would use the "l" switch, like this: "ls -l". And if you wanted to see all files, including hidden files, you would add the "a" switch, like this: "ls -al". Also, be aware that Unix treats upper- and lowercase characters differently from one another. For example, the

31 The passwords are usually designed to supply marketing information. The listed password, for example—WRD949—came out of an advertisement in the September 1994 issue of *Wired* magazine. Wired, '94, month 9 gets translated to "WRD" + "94" + "9". With that information, they can track which of their ads are producing the best response. Of course if everyone reading this book uses WRD949, the folks at Delphi will wonder why that particular issue of *Wired* seems to have enjoyed a sudden resurgence.

32 Please let me know if this happens to you. Ever. In your entire life.

33 Or operators. Or system administrators. But not for users. At least not for *untrained* users. And certainly not for lawyers.

filename "readme" is completely different from the filename "README"—and both are different from the filename "Readme". Also, the switch -r is different from the switch -R. Finally, be *very* careful about using wildcards and switches. Unix is *not* going to ask you whether you're sure you want to erase all the files on your hard disk. If you tell it to do it, it does it. If you tell it "rm -R *", those files are gone.[34]

This is a world where *it's hard to learn something unless you already know it*. That's just the way it works. One sometimes useful hint is that the HELP command is called man (it comes from the word *manual*, as in "get me the manual pages for such and such"). So if you're trying to figure out how to use the ftp command, you could enter: man ftp. If you want to figure out how man works, enter: man man.

But that hint is only sometimes useful, because there's *no* command for "please give me a list of all the commands." (That would be *too* helpful.) And of course, if you don't already know the name of the command, then you can't run man against it. Like I said—unless you already know about a command, there's no way to find out about it.[35]

Here's a short cheat sheet on the evils of Unix. If you have questions on how to actually use any of these commands, use man to find out (e.g., to find out how to use grep, enter: man grep). In many cases, though, if you just type the command with nothing else on the line, the system will tell you the basic usage options.

[34] By the way, there is no "undelete" feature in Unix. DOS and Macintosh users may have been spoiled by this capability that made the Norton utilities famous, but in the Unix world, Homey don't play that game. The only good news is that most Unix machines are backed up every night—unlike their less disciplined "personal computer" brethren.

[35] Unless of course, you just happen to guess what it might be. Which *can* actually work sometimes. If you're a DOS user, for example—familiar with the CD command for changing directories—try man cd. By coincidence, it's there. Also, if you're really stuck, run man against the commands that you *do* know—especially any that are similar or related to what you want to do. At the very end of each man listing is a reference to related commands. By running man against those related commands (and looking at the bottom of *those* listings for *more* related commands), you just might find something useful.

cp	Copy a file.
rm	Delete a file.
mv	Move a file (i.e., copy, then delete original), or Rename a file (mv is used for both move and rename).
cat	Display a file on the screen.
more	Display a file, one page at a time.
grep	Search for text in a file.
man	Display instructions on a supported command or program.
pwd	Show your current directory (i.e., the path).
cd	Change to a different directory.
ls	Display the contents of the directory (short form).
ls -al	Display all files in the directory (long form).

passwd	Change your password.
exit	Quit your Unix session.
ftp	Start an ftp session.
telnet	Start a telnet session.
gopher	Start a gopher session.
[backspace]	A common problem is that the [backspace] key generates ^H characters on the screen. Try pressing the [delete] key instead. Or start going through your communications software to change the emulation.
Ctrl-C	This key combination stops a process (such as an ls or ftp).
Ctrl-Y	This key combination also stops a process, and can sometimes work if Ctrl-C doesn't.
Ctrl-Z	This key combination interrupts a process and switches you back to the Unix command prompt. This is useful in emergencies, but don't just walk away from a Ctrl-Z. It means you've left some process (or "job") running on the system—usually one that's in trouble since you bailed out that way. Talk to an administrator to figure out how to kill the job.
Ctrl-D	This key combination is sometimes required as an "I'm done typing text in my email message" indicator. Your email system may vary.

At this point, if your Internet connection is really set up, all you need to do is start up one of the Internet services. For email, newsreaders, and web browsers, you'll need to talk to your system administrator. What you use and how you use it depends entirely on what software has been set up. But for the other basic services—telnet, ftp and gopher—simply type the command and specify the applicable part of the URL.

Using Internet Services

Just as a reminder, the format for the URLs used in this book (as described earlier) is: service:username:password@hostname/directorypath/filename. The first part of the URL is the name of the Internet service. The second part is the username and password—if the service needs one (in most URLs, usernames and passwords aren't required, so this part is just skipped). The third part is the Internet address of the host computer. Everything after that is the path to the specific item.

Telnet. So in the case of telnet, if the URL was telnet://www@www.law .cornell.edu, then "telnet" is the *Internet service*, "www" is the *username*, and "www.law.cornell.edu" is the Internet address of the *host computer* you're trying to connect to. You would issue the following commands to start a telnet session:

telnet www.law.cornell.edu	Connects you to the host computer
www	This is the user ID

That's it! You've connected to Cornell and you're logged in. As it happens, this particular telnet session takes you automatically to Cornell's *telnet* version of their World Wide Web server. So you're logged in to Cornell, using telnet. And on *that machine*, they've set things up so that when you log on, you're immediately running a copy of World Wide Web.[36]

There's not much more to using telnet. When you finish with the session, the system will usually stop telnet automatically. If you need to force your way out of a telnet session, press the key combination Ctrl-[. That'll give you a telnet prompt ("telnet>"), then you can enter "close" or "quit" to quit.

Gopher. For gopher, the URL translation is similar to telnet, but there's no user ID. If the URL is gopher://gopher.law.cornell.edu, then you would issue the following command from your[37] Unix prompt:

gopher gopher.law.cornell.edu	Connects you to the gopher server

Again, that's it. You're now connected to Cornell's gopher server, using the basic gopher menus to pick and choose and connect to other gopher servers. Up and down arrow keys move you from choice to choice (or type a number if that's more convenient). Press the [return] key to select a choice. Press "?" to get help on specific options. The most useful option is to use the "a" command to set bookmarks as you travel around from place to place. The most difficult thing in gopherspace is trying to figure out where you are (and how you got there). The bookmark operation will save that location in your bookmarks file.[38]

Ftp. For ftp, the basic URL is translated as before, but in this case the added wrinkle is that it assumes you are using anonymous

36 The copy of WWW you're running in that scenario is running locally on the *Cornell* machine. The machine that *you* originally logged onto is still running telnet. If you happen to choose a particular type of menu option, you might find that the Cornell server will start up its own session of telnet to connect to yet another Internet service—to connect to GPO Access at a freenet library site, for example—and the freenet library will need to run its own session of telnet to get to the main GPO site. With only a little bit of effort, therefore, from your computer at home (connected to your Internet service provider) you've started off a chain of events in which the provider is running telnet, Cornell is running www *and* telnet, Seattle is running telnet, and GPO is running its own custom software. And *you're* running it all. Ain't life grand? (It ain't simple. But it's grand.)

37 See how quickly this bastion of user hostility is suddenly becoming *yours*? It'll *grow* on you. (Or *onto* you, if you're not careful.)

38 Press "a" to mark a menu item, press "A" to mark the menu itself. When you want to go back later, use the "v" command. (I *told* you these folks were terse.)

ftp. That means your user ID will be "anonymous"—even though "anonymous" is not written out in the URL. Anonymous ftp does require a password (which, again, isn't mentioned in the URL, but the ftp site will give you instructions during the logon process)—the password you use is usually your *own* Internet address. If the URL is ftp://NIC.MERIT.EDU/internet/providers/pdial (and if your own Internet address was allison@mitre.org) then you would issue the following commands to run your ftp session:

unix>	ftp NIC.MERIT.EDU	Connects you to the ftp server
Name:	anonymous	This is the user ID
Password:	allison@mitre.org	This is the password
ftp>	cd /internet/providers	Change directory to the URL path
ftp>	dir	Check to make sure the file is there
ftp>	get pdial	Download the URL-specified file name
ftp>	close	Finish up
ftp>	quit	

As you can see, this can be a bit tedious. Many ftp servers also support a gopher server so that users can log on and download files by choosing the files from menus. Also, there's quite a lot to watch out for when you're using ftp. If you're downloading certain kinds of files (software, images, compressed files), you'll need to use the binary command, so ftp will copy the file correctly. Also, if you download a compressed file, or a uuencoded file, you will have to uncompress it or uudecode it.[39] And of course, once you've downloaded the files, all you've really done is copy them from the ftp server to your Internet access server. They're not on your desktop computer—not yet at least. That'll be yet another process, and it'll depend entirely on your software link to the access provider (who you should talk to about this). Of course, if you're running one of those SLIP or PPP accounts, or if you've got a direct LAN connection, then the download *did* go directly to your desktop machine.[40]

39 No, there is no quick-and-dirty explanation that will cover the subject of compression completely. There are a *lot* of different compression schemes and there are even *more* different uncompression techniques—some of which are described in the next section "Working with Compressed Files". Also, look in ftp://ftp.cso.uiuc.edu/doc/pcnet/compression for David Lemson's FAQ describing detailed compression and encoding techniques. It should be fairly up-to-date and comprehensive, but this technology changes so fast that it's hard to handle everything an ingenious file-compressor might throw at you.

40 The difference in these accounts becomes most apparent when you try to get big files down to your desktop. Until you get a high-speed link, at least *one* of the hops in this file transfer process will be slow. If you're in a shell account, a file transfer from the Internet service to your shell account provider was probably very fast—most access providers have *very* high-speed links to the net. But copying to your local machine will have to squeeze through whatever modem you've got on your desk. If you're connected through SLIP or PPP—using a modem—you'll find that the process is

continued next page ➤

There are some shortcuts available in ftp. If you use the mget command instead of get, you can download a whole *group* of files—by specifying a wildcard character.**41** Mget (actually, mget) can also help when you're trying to get a file—even just one file—with a very long name. For example, if I'm trying to download a copy of draft-ietf-uri-url-08.txt, but my fumble fingers can't seem to type that many letters in a row correctly, I can use this instead: "mget draft-ietf*". That command will grab all of the files that begin with "draft-ietf"**42**—including the one I'm trying to get.

Other commands that you can issue from the Unix prompt may include the many resource discovery commands: archie, finger, nslookup, netfind, fred, whois, and WAIS (or WAISsearch). Try the man approach for each (e.g., man finger) to find out how it works. Get Ed Krol's *Whole Internet* or the Engst *Starter Kits* if you want a reference manual for using them.

Working with Compressed Files

To reduce the amount of storage space that large file archives take up, to reduce the amount of time and bandwidth it takes to transfer certain types of files, and to handle some of the peculiarities of Internet file transfers, there are a number of different compression utilities that reduce the size of a file or that format a file for file transfer.

The first time you run into this, you'll probably find a file with a filename that ends, curiously, with a ".Z" file extension. Or you'll open up an email message, only to discover that it's just a bunch of garbage—apparently random letters and special characters. Unfortunately, figuring out what's going on, and learning how to deal with it, can be a real challenge.

The first clue in deciphering a compression technique is to look at the filename it-

➤ slow *right away*. This sounds like a great argument for shell accounts, and it is if what you're doing mostly is ftp. But if you're headed for the mountains of web, all those graphics have to squeeze through your modem regardless, and the shell account will make it a two-hop process. That high-speed LAN connection becomes more and more attractive as you use the Internet more and more.

41 For example, if a directory has 100 files in it, and the ten you want all start with the letter *r* (not the uppercase *R*—remember they're different) then you could issue the command "mget r*" and ftp would get them all. Unfortunately, if you didn't specify the -i option when you started ftp(!), the software will prompt you as it goes through the list of files in the specified group—one by one: Do you want to copy *that* file, yes or no? If you *do* specify the -i option (e.g., ftp -i NIC.MERIT.EDU), then it will assume the answer is yes to all of your mget questions.

42 Actually, in this particular example, issuing the command "mget draft-ietf*" at ftp://cnri.reston.va.us/internet-drafts would select a lot more files than just the one I want (there are a lot of files that begin with "draft-ietf". That's why I sometimes *don't* use the -i option. If I omit the -i option, mget will go through the entire list of files, prompting me for which ones I want copied and which ones I don't. I wait for the one I want to come around, tell it Yes, and I'm done! By the way, gratuitous exclamation points notwithstanding, you should never take pride in being able to torture this horrible interface into doing what you want it to do. It would be a false geek pride, and a hollow one indeed.

self. Most compression utilities append an identifying extension on the end of the filename. (For example, if you compressed a file named README using ZIP, the new file would be called README.ZIP.) In cases where multiple utilities have been used, file extensions will be cascaded—making a longer and longer file name. (Frequently, for example, BINHEX is used to convert a compressed file so it can be sent through limited Internet gateways. It's common, therefore to see a file that has been compressed, and then BINHEXed—which appends a file extension of .hqx. The resulting filename would be README .ZIP.hqx.)

Once you know the compression technique, then you need to find the compression utility that will let you uncompress the type of file you've got. There are many utilities that try to uncompress a lot of different formats, but if the utilities you have don't handle a particular format, use the resource discovery program archie to try to find the software you need. Use archie to search for something with the compression name in it, or look in David Lemson's latest "compression" guide for pointers to specific tools and utilities (ftp://ftp.cso.uiuc.edu/doc/pcnet/compression). For most compression techniques, there is a freeware version of the software for uncompressing files.

Here are some of the more common file extensions associated with different compression utilities:

Original Files (uncompressed):

.txt or .TXT   This usually indicates that the file is stored in "straight ASCII" file format—i.e., no special word-processing control characters or anything beyond the basic ASCII character set. This apparent *lingua franca* of the computer industry is generally considered the lowest common denominator that everything can read, but even with "ASCII" documents, different platforms handle line-endings differently. Some require an ASCII line feed code, some require a carriage return code, and some require both. Good word processors should be able to handle all the different line feed combinations, but if yours can't, look for one of the many "strip" programs that convert line-ending codes.

.doc or .DOC   This usually indicates that the file is stored in "straight ASCII" file format—although the .DOC file extension is also used by Microsoft Word.

Special-Format Files (uncompressed):

.ps or .PS | This is a PostScript document—prepared using Adobe's page description language and ready to be sent to a Post-Script-compatible printer. It's usually stored in a straight ASCII format, but it's usually *difficult* to convert these back to editable word-processing documents. You can print .ps files, or you can find PostScript viewer utilities (like GNU project's GhostScript) to view them onscreen.

.hqx or .Hqx | This is a BINHEX file. The purpose of a BINHEX file is to deal with the fact that many Internet links (especially email) cannot send so-called 8-bit files. (8-bit files, sometimes called binary files, are files that contain characters that use all 8 bits of a byte that represent the character.) Some links support only 7-bit transfer, or strip off the 8th bit—thereby changing the meaning of an 8-bit character. BINHEX converts a file so that it is all in 7-bit characters—immune to the effects of stripping the 8th bit. It has to be converted back, to use it, but the resulting file will make it through the transmission correctly. You can recognize a BINHEX file, regardless of whether it's got the .hqx file extension, because it begins with a line like this, "(This file must be converted with BinHex 4.0)", and all subsequent lines in the file are exactly 64 characters long. Almost every compression utility includes a BINHEX converter. Unix users should look for a program called mcvert.

[uuencoded] | This is a file that has been converted for 7-bit transfer, identical in function to BINHEX, but different in format. There really is no set standard file extension for uuencoded files. They are usually found embedded in email messages or newsgroup postings, so it's somewhat rare to find a file specifically saved in uuencoded format. You can recognize a uuencoded file because it begins with a line like this, "begin 0700 README.TXT", and all subsequent lines in the file are exactly 61 characters long, beginning with the letter "M". If you're on a Unix system, uncompress uuencoded files by using the uudecode command. (Enter man uuencode or man uudecode to get instructions.)

Compressed Files:

.ARC
: This has been compressed in a common (but old) MS-DOS compression format. Quite a few programs for PCs will uncompress .ARC files, but the original program is called ARC. There are Unix and Macintosh utilities that will uncompress ARC files as well, but they're not very common.

.cpt
: This has been compressed in a common Macintosh compression format. Quite a few programs for Macintoshes will uncompress .cpt files, but the original program is called Compact Pro.

.dd
: This has been compressed in a Macintosh compression format using a commercial product called DiskDoubler. DiskDoubler files are frequently stored as self-extracting archives (see .sea).

.exe or .EXE
: Most MS-DOS software programs have this common file extension, but if you find a self-extracting archive (see also .sea) for use with MS-DOS, it will also have this extension. Very few programs will uncompress self-extracting files stored as .EXE files, but the primary mechanism for extracting such an archive is to execute it—then it will uncompress itself. (Since they are software programs, self-extracting archives represent a special risk with respect to viruses—make sure you have checked *any* executable file before letting it run on your system.)

.gz
: This has been compressed using the ZIP compression format—commonly found on MS-DOS platforms, but it has been compressed on a Unix system using gzip. If you're on a Unix system, uncompress .gz files using the gunzip command. (Enter man gzip or man gunzip to get instructions.)

.LHZ
: This has been compressed in a common MS-DOS compression format. Quite a few programs for PCs will uncompress .LHZ files, but the original program is called LHARC. Other uncompression utilities (such as lharc for Unix and MacLHarc for Macintoshes) can uncompress LHZ files as well.

.pit
: This has been compressed in a common (but old) compression format. Some programs will uncompress .pit

files, but the original programs are called PackIt (and its companion, UnPackIt). On Unix systems, there is an un-pit utility that can uncompress pit files as well.

.sea	This is a self-extracting archive that has been compressed in one of many different Macintosh compression formats. Quite a few programs for Macintoshes will uncompress .sea files, but the primary mechanism for extracting the contents of an sea file is to execute it (by double-clicking)—then it will uncompress itself. (Since they are software programs, self-extracting archives represent a special risk with respect to viruses—make sure you have checked *any* executable file before letting it run on your system.)
.shar or .Shar	This has been compressed in a common Unix compression format. If you're on a Unix system, uncompress .shar files using the unshar command. (Enter man shar or man unshar to get instructions.)
.sit	This has been compressed in a common Macintosh compression format. Quite a few programs for Macintoshes will uncompress .sit files, but the original program is called StuffIt (and its companion, UnStuffIt).
.tar	This has been compressed in a common Unix compression format. If you're on a Unix system, uncompress .tar files using the tar command. This is a standard Unix utility—intended originally for moving files to tape for backups and archives. Accordingly, it's a little more hostile than most other uncompression utilities—be careful. (Enter man tar to get instructions.)
.TAZ	This is an MS-DOS version of a file that has been compressed using a combination of .tar and .Z compression formats. On a Unix system, this will be shown as .tar.Z, but since DOS doesn't support cascaded extensions, .TAZ is used to show this common combination.
.Z	This has been compressed in a common Unix compression format. If you're on a Unix system, uncompress .Z files by using the "uncompress" command. (Enter man compress or man uncompress to get instructions.) Other uncompression utilities (such as MacCompress for Macintoshes) can uncompress .Z files as well.

.zip or .ZIP   This has been compressed in a common MS-DOS compression format. Quite a few programs for PCs will uncompress .ZIP files, but the original program is called PKZIP (and its companion, PKUNZIP). There are Unix and Macintosh utilities that will unzip ZIP files as well.

But enough with the bits and pieces. Let's see if we can struggle back to something resembling a strategic perspective.

You Can Never Have Too Much Bandwidth

Unfortunately, one of the hard lessons in connecting to the net comes once we start trying to work with large files and images. Dialing in, even with a fastest-on-the-market V.34 modem (V.Fast), still sticks you with a pokey little 28.8 Kbps speed limit. That works great for text, email and a little file transfer. But graphics, movies, and a full-featured point-and-click interface eat bandwidth for lunch. (Bandwidth—it's not just for breakfast any more.)

Some offices feel that the connectivity is important enough to justify that dedicated line for a LAN connection, running from your office to the next link in the Internet daisychain. But that can cost you several thousand dollars a year.

A fairly attractive alternative is ISDN. Prices for an ISDN line from your local phone company tend to be almost reasonable (as low as $23/month[43]), but the important features that ISDN delivers are bandwidth, bandwidth, and more bandwidth. It supports at least 64 Kbps, and can go as fast as 1.544 Mbps (giving you access to a full T1 link). You'll need a special ISDN adapter to move up—even to the entry-level 64 and 128 Kbps speeds—but that bandwidth should be enough to handle a lot of what the Internet dishes out.[44] Unfortunately, like caller ID and various other telephone services, ISDN is being implemented sporadically around the country. So check with your local phone company for availability and prices.[45]

Getting Your Own Domain Name

Probably the most overlooked trap on the Internet playing field is neglecting to pay attention to the *name* of your Internet address. Internet address names—particularly the last part of the name, the

[43] Watch out for additional per-minute charges that can move ISDN up into the leased-line price ranges.

[44] How much attention is the issue of bandwidth getting? Here's a hint: The vice president of the United States actually uttered the phrase "two-way broadband access" in a speech. Yow.

[45] At long last, ISDN may finally have a reason for living. Derisively referred to as I Still Don't kNow, this long-touted but poorly understood service is finally emerging from the obscuring shrouds of telephone company marketing (although not without a fight). So don't be discouraged when the first person who answers the phone has never heard of ISDN. That's still pretty common.

"domain"—are something you get to choose for yourself *if* you're connecting through a full-service Internet service provider.[46] But when it comes to registering a domain name, it's first come first served.

So for example, IBM was able to choose "ibm.com" and the University of Michigan was able to choose "umich.edu". But with just a little oblivious neglect, someone else could snap up mcdonalds.com or coke.com. As it turns out, until just recently, more than *half* of the Fortune 500 had *not* registered their most obvious domain names. So mcdonalds.com went to a reporter who was writing an exposé on companies who weren't registering their domain names, coke.com didn't go to Coca-Cola, and aba.com now belongs to the American *Bankers* Association. (The American Bar Association *has* registered abanet.org as its domain name.)

If you decide that you want a specific domain name for your firm or office—or just for yourself—*now* is the time to act.[47]

No it's *not* free. Registration is free, but you actually have to have a computer that you can connect to the net, and of course you need the connection itself—which may cost you a monthly fee. But the *process* for grabbing a domain name is trivially easy. Simply call one of the full-service Internet service providers—one that includes domain-name registration with their service (that's the key)—and just set up an account. Try UUnet or PSINet (see the list of Internet service providers for phone numbers). Or check with one of the many other providers that provide domain registration services. If you're feeling especially geek-enabled, you can register directly with the InterNIC Registration Services, managed by Network Solutions Inc. (703-742-4777, or email to hostmaster@rs.internic.net).

Security as an Oxymoron

A lawyer or law office planning to use the net needs to be *completely* aware that the Internet is not a secure environment. Your email can be read by others, files you might store on some Internet service provider's machine can be hacked into, and if you establish a full-time connection to the net, your connected host computer can be the target of a concerted break-in.

That's not to say that the net is substantially worse than other means of communication. You

[46] If you connect through something other than a full-service provider, your Internet address will include the provider's domain. For example, the address for a Compuserve user uses a domain of "compuserve.com", users of Pipeline get an address that ends with pipeline.com.

[47] Assuming that it's not already too late. Just as little Internet side trip, you might want to take this same lesson to your institutional clients—making sure that they consider registering appropriate domain names. (Registering now can save a lot of headaches later.) And be proactive. Spin-offs, subsidiaries, or major customer service initiatives might all represent special opportunities. You might advise clients to consider a domain-name check as part of naming a new business.

already know that your phone can be tapped, your mail can be read, your faxes can be intercepted, and your conversations can be recorded.

Still, we don't let those realities of life in an unsecure world paralyze us into inactivity.[48] We figure out where the risks are and we take precautions. We lock the doors when we go home at night, we challenge strangers walking through the office, and we don't discuss secrets over cellular telephones.

Working on the net is similar. We need to understand the specifics of the risks, so we can take appropriate measures to protect against them.

Here are some of the specifics:

Email

Your email is readily available to the information service providers and other system administrators that help make the network work. Indeed, with almost no effort at all, the system administrator for your host email system, or any reasonably adept snoop can snag and browse through your email as it goes around the net. However, the situation is not too dissimilar from cellular phones: Casual eavesdroppers are out there, but the sheer volume of traffic lessens the likelihood of a serious breach.

Unless someone has a reason for thinking that they might find something useful or valuable (or unless someone is pursuing a grudge), it's unlikely that *your* email will be specifically sought out.

If you really want to use email as a secure channel, you can—but you'd better know exactly what you're doing. Some people are using fairly sophisticated public-key cryptography, such as Paul Zimmerman's PGP encryption software (Pretty Good Privacy). And some email services offer either encryption (either PGP or RSA) as part of the service.

If you do it right, you should be able to achieve a fairly high level of security (barring the possibilities of stolen passwords or someone

[48] Indeed, it's easy to get carried away with finding potential security problems. One consultant for example recently ranted, "Never put data on the Internet that you wouldn't want your worst enemy to know. The only 100 percent secure systems are unplugged, encased in concrete, at the bottom of the ocean." Actually, as it turns out, if the hard disk in that submerged lump of high-tech-trade-secrets-concrete hasn't been completely erased and over-written, a little salvage operation could pull it up, crack it open and reveal all. Military organizations reportedly erase-and-overwrite hard disks, and then run the hard disk platters through a military-grade shredder and then *burn the pieces*. I *love* the imagery of some spy—who has cleverly grabbed the hard disk pieces after they've been shredded but *before* they got burned—gluing the pieces together, miraculously turning it into something that is machine readable, then somehow evaluating the *residual electromagnetic shadows* beneath the overwritten text (especially since the overwriting process requires that the disk be overwritten three times) to successfully reveal the original text. If that spy then says to his comrade-at-arms, "Boy, I'm glad I got those pieces when I did—if the pieces had been burned, *this would have been impossible!*" then the imagery will be complete. Now that the Cold War is over, maybe this spy should go into the hard disk repair business.

going after your message with a Cray supercomputer). But doing it right can be a nontrivial process. Certainly inconvenient.

Here's an example: If you tried to use PGP to send me an encrypted email message, you and I would both have to have "public keys" assigned and registered. As it turns out, I already have one. (You'll need a "private key," too—I've already got one.) Assuming that you get one too, you can send me an encrypted message by using both *your* private key and *my* public key. That way, only you and I can read it. To read it, all I have to do is supply *my* private key and *your* public key. In principle, it's an easy process. In practice, it's—shall we say—encumbered a bit by the length of these keys. Here's *my* public key: mQCPAy8cChYAAAEEAN8MnVwpWHEz7NoYN0I9qC/sgItp+5dD cxtyd6rOi3cQRjnYRDy2023WKFxESVINrnl8XhCaSGeJcNntZHtcP6wW7 sxJIxvvwGDKUeBtaMC5i85rp8qgAD9LrCAcvxtzB0mt4fGgU9EQEy POAkPYBYT+tpNgIpheEKc941ukjEs1ABEBAAG0JkcuIEJ1cmdlc3MgQWx saXNvbiA8YWxsaXNvbkBtaXRyZS5vcmc+=or9g. (Whatever you do, don't make a mistake in typing that in. The whole system fails if you miss even one letter.) It's secure, but it's not especially easy.

For the legal community in particular, the issue of email security is turning into a special problem. Since unencrypted email is *completely* readable by your host computer system administrators—in the normal course of day-to-day operations and without any special effort to "break into" your email account, some people are asking whether email-based communications with your client might *not* be protected under the attorney-client privilege. There is no precedent on point (yet), but the principles that protect (and don't-protect) client communications using other never-completely-secure technologies would seem applicable.

Accidental Email

In most email systems, once you push the send button your email is gone. Like toothpaste out of the tube, there's no way to get it back again.

Ordinarily, this wouldn't really be a security concern, but I'm reminded of the Wall Street mergers and acquisitions law firm that was trying to fax the details of a proposed takeover to its client. The fax machine was set up with those speed-dial buttons that let you program in the fax numbers of several common fax destinations. As it turned out, the speed dial number of the client was right next to the speed dial number of *The Wall Street Journal*, the fax operator pushed the wrong button, thereby sending the takeover details straight to the press, and the takeover (reportedly) had to be abandoned. Another misaddressing adventure sparked a lawsuit when a damaging communique was sent via messenger to a corporate officer staying at a particular hotel. The messenger had the recipient paged and it just so happened that there was an employee of the company's arch-rival in the lobby—an employee with the exact same name as the corporate officer. The memo was misdelivered, it happened to contain evidence of actionable malfeasance, and the lawsuits were on. I tell these stories to say this: Accidental email isn't really a security issue, but obviously, a misaddressed email message would be just as devastating as a misdelivered fax or note. Consider email as yet another opportunity to make a mistake.

A second aspect of accidental email happens when email "cascades." A common feature of most email systems is the ability to attach a copy of the email message being replied to, so the recipients have an opportunity to see the entire thread of discussion without having to repeat or summarize everything that went before. Of course, as an email conversation goes on and on, the attached email messages that represent the history of the conversation can get quite lengthy. Indeed, as the conversation develops and more and more people get involved, the topic can wander significantly—to the point where the original email message bears little resemblance to the "active" topic of conversation. Be careful of this, because the original message (or some of the intervening replies) may contain information or characterizations that are inappropriate for the current discussion. If you wanted to gently remind someone of his or her responsibilities, for example, it might turn into a real problem if you accidentally attached the email notes that originally brought the matter to your attention.

Be careful of what you send, and to whom you send it.

Remote File Storage

If you get your Internet access through a third-party Internet service provider that gives you an account on their machine, don't think for even an instant that your files, on that machine, are secure.

Many Internet host computers use some variation of Unix as the operating system, and Unix is specifically designed to *facilitate* sharing of information among users, rather than keeping it secure. While some providers implement privileges and procedures to help keep your information protected from other users, the success of that process will vary. Some providers try harder than others, and some are more likely than others to be attacked by curious hackers, interesting in finding what they can. In no case will your files be protected from either the system administrator or from any hacker who's able to get system administrator privileges.

Your only real hope of security in that type of environment is to encrypt your files. As you can see, though, while that's doable it's not always convenient.

Passwords

This is my very favorite security subject. Most computer break-ins are achieved by finding or guessing a user's password. I can usually find passwords just by walking through an office, looking for post-it notes next to computers. The best notes are the ones that have just one word on them,[49] usually in all caps—words like GREEN4, JULIA, or my personal favorite, SYSTEM. Or better yet, something so convoluted it just *has* to be a password, like ZY25JQX.

Studies indicate that the most common password selected by users is no password at all. Other very common passwords include their own name, their user ID, the name of the system being logged onto, a single letter (e.g., "A" or "B"), or (if people are feeling *really* tricky) a family member's name instead of their own. Also, many systems come with preconfigured default accounts and passwords (for system administration or maintenance), and many of those defaults are never changed or disabled.

Unfortunately, there are WarGames-esque programs[50] that repeatedly try different passwords, using huge dictionaries of common passwords, known defaults, and algorithms to build possible passwords through common tricks (such as adding a single digit to the end of a common word).

Another trick—one that's very hard to detect, and one that takes advantage of Internet architectures that involve people logging onto remote computers—is to build a password "sniffer" that either listens for passwords being transmitted over the net (as part of a logon process) or a "spoofer" that surreptitiously intercepts a user who is trying to log on, mimics the logon process, grabs the password when the user supplies it, then (sometimes) passes control back to the targeted system. Fortunately, these technologies aren't commonplace, so you're not likely to get attacked with one of these unless you've been specifically targeted.

One of the most insidious tricks for getting passwords is to get them from *another* system that the user may have logged onto. This works because many users define the same password for every different system they use. If you're the system administrator for System *A,* for example (or if you've broken into the system and given yourself enough privileges), then you can set things up so you can read your users' passwords. When

---

[49] Sometimes, people are especially helpful—they'll even write down their user ID next to the password.

[50] Interestingly, some of the best versions of these programs are written for use by system administrators. The administrators use these programs to check the passwords that have been set by their own users. Obviously, the integrity of a system is compromised by the weakest link in the fence—so the administrators use these programs to look for easy-to-guess passwords. Of course, the *exact same* password-guessing programs are available to both the hackers and the system administrators—so the better and better the system administrator programs get (for *checking system security*), the better and better the hacker programs get (thereby *reducing system security*).

someone logs onto your system and uses the same password that they use on System *B*, then you may have exactly what you need. Even if the person doesn't use *exactly* the same password, you may have the core of what you need to figure it out. Ordinarily, we don't expect system administrators of well-run systems to commit this type of security breach. And in most well-run systems, user passwords are stored in a form that even the system administrator can't read. But there are many systems that you might log onto, on an occasional or one-time basis, where the administrator might not be so scrupulous (or careful). Maybe you're trying out some local BBS—just to see what they've got. Maybe it's a vendor's BBS that requires you to set up a password the first time you log on. One of the most famous password-grabbing incidents on the Internet happened when the system administrator of a popular game site— one that required you to log on (via telnet) to use it—started collecting and using passwords of the people who logged on to play. Obviously, the best approach is to use a different password for each different system.

My favorite rule for passwords is to treat them like toothbrushes: Don't share them with others and get a new one regularly.

Your Internet Servers

If you want to set up a server on the Internet—for you to connect to, for others to connect to, or even if you're setting up a full-time bridge that lets *you* connect to the Internet—that server represents a *potential* target for a security breach.

Frankly, there are a lot of *myths* about the risks associated with putting a bridge or a server on the Internet—and there are plenty of anecdotes and horror stories that got those myths started. But putting up a link to the net does *not* open up your office's files to random browsing by every hacker who turns the doorknob.

You *do* need to make sure that you deal with the standard "firewall" security concerns[51] when you connect to the net, but the basics are fairly straightforward.[52] You'll never achieve "perfect computer security,"[53] but you can achieve a very good level of protection against external non-password-assisted attack.

51 An Internet firewall is a method of configuring a server or bridge, so that there is only one machine—a gateway—connected to the net. If someone breaks into the gateway, that's as far as they can get. If you try to send something to the Internet, your internal network automatically routes that message to the gateway, and the gateway passes it on. If something from the Internet comes in for you, it goes to the gateway, then the gateway routes it to you on the internal network. The gateway is connected to the internal network through a very controlled environment—the only thing it can do is send and forward specific types of messages. It does not pass through services that would be used in an ordinary security attack.

52 For details about setting up a firewall, see Cheswick-Bellovin's *Firewalls and Internet Security*, Addison-Wesley, ISBN 0-201-63357-4.

53 There's that oxymoron again. Consider it more of a goal or objective, rather than an achievable endstate.

Mything Viruses

Another type of "security" concern about the net that falls into the "popular fable" category is the touted risk of getting viruses from the Internet.[54]

The fact is that the Internet represents one way of receiving new software, and so if you download a piece of software that has a virus—using the Internet—you will get that virus. But it's really incorrect to classify that situation as "getting a virus *from* the Internet." Clearly, the virus came from the software, not the Internet. If you got that same software on a diskette, you would get the exact same virus. It would be like saying that you got a virus from the U.S. Postal Service if the disk was delivered through the mail.

There are a few electronic anomalies that, indeed, live only on the Internet. The famous Internet Worm Incident, in which a Cornell computer science student accidentally flooded the net with a program that generated email[55] was one such anomaly. When the Worm hit, the flood of email traffic was so great that the Internet itself was unable to operate for quite some time.

Although the effect of this incident was disastrous for the Internet itself, the infection did not destroy data files or corrupt applications software. The Internet Worm did not infect normal PCs and Macintoshes being used for everyday work—mostly, it shut down the Internet host communications.

You *should be* concerned about protecting your computing environment against the introduction of viruses, but the Internet should fall

[54] *Virus* is the term generally misused in the popular press to describe *any* type of computer-to-computer operation that automatically affects the target computer in some negative way. This would include viruses that copy themselves into a key part of your operating system or applications, then replicate to "infect" other operating systems and applications. These types of viruses can be expected to do something—like pop up a little message or try to erase your hard disk—at specific intervals or when the user performs a certain action. Things that have this type of negative effect on your computers or networks are often defined by example, rather than by general principle, because there are many different things that can cause harm to your computer, not just viruses. A software package with a bug in it, for example, might do the exact same damage that a virus is intended to do, but because the developer didn't *intend* for the problem to happen (or just didn't care), we try to give the developer the benefit of the doubt and declare the defect a bug instead of a virus. (More than one industry wag has cracked that some very prominent software packages are taking up so much hard disk space, and slowing things down so much, that they should be labeled "viruses.") Some vendors have actually installed "time bomb" viruses in their software, to disable it after a certain period of time if the user doesn't keep making timely software license payments. The line between copy protection and virus can be quite fuzzy.

[55] Actually, the Worm not only generated large volumes of email, but it also replicated itself on many other machines. The replicants started generating large volumes of email as well, and replicating further. Growing exponentially, the total volume of traffic on the net became impossibly large, and all infected Internet hosts had to be disconnected and reconfigured (to eliminate the replicated software). Ironically, the college student who built this didn't intend this effect. He was, admittedly, try to build an email-generating virus, but he made a mistake in his programming and the bug-in-the-virus-under-development caused the runaway condition that proved so harmful.

into that concern primarily as a yet-another distribution method, rather than a new and foreboding risk.

General Guidelines

Clearly, you shouldn't use the Internet for truly confidential communications unless you take special precautions, you shouldn't put sensitive materials in places where others can reach them, and if you're going to open up a full-time Internet connection, you need to take appropriate security measures.

However, for the day-to-day logistics and discussions that frequently make up communications with clients and colleagues, even an unsecure email link represents a strong client-service opportunity.

Be careful, but don't feel paralyzed by the risks.

Chapter 12

The Provider's Internet

One of the most intriguing opportunities on the net, right now, is that of becoming an information provider. The global e-library is an exciting place to browse, but as an e-publisher, you have an opportunity to reach out to an enormous Internet audience.

If any of your plans include marketing, publicity, or providing the public with either information or services, then you should consider the possibility—the opportunity—for reaching a certain segment of the public through this medium. It doesn't matter whether your aims are altruistic or profit-inspired—public service or bottom line—the e-publisher's Internet is just another medium for reaching people. Of course, to be effective as an e-publisher, you need to be aware of the environment within which you're playing and to learn from the mistakes of others.

Because this medium is so new, unfortunately, there's much more that we *don't* know about these opportunities than what we *do*. Clearly, with twenty-five million potential readers, there's a very strong feeling of "untapped potential." But the challenge is to figure out how to reach those people, and how to do it in a way that doesn't violate the standards and practices of the group. *This is* the oft-touted "ground floor"—the place where e-publishing is being invented.

What It Takes to Set Up a Full-Time Server

It's not too difficult to set up your own Internet server. For example, if you wanted to set up your own web server that would let people log on and read your materials at any time of day or night, here's what you'd need—the four Cs:

- Computer: In this scenario, you'll need to assign a computer that won't be used for something else. A 486 PC, a Macintosh, a Unix machine (like a Sun)—any should work just fine for an initial effort. (Obviously, if you're planning on several million simultaneous users, you'll need just a *little* more horsepower.)

- Connection: You'll need a full-time connection to the net, usually by getting a leased line from your local telephone company. These start at speeds of 56 Kbps (thousands of bits per second); ISDN can offer higher speeds, sometimes for less money; a full-scale T1 link runs at 1.544 Mbps (millions of bits per second), but is significantly more expensive. You'll also need to make arrangements with a local Internet service provider who will set up the other end of the link. Depending on your provider and how much line speed you buy, you can expect this connection to cost more than the computer itself. (Don't be surprised. Also, don't be disillusioned, if you want to go with something less quick, or with less than 24-hour-per-day connectivity, there are many less expensive options.)

- Communications software: Your computer will need to be running TCP/IP—in some form that's compatible with the type of connection you've purchased, and compatible with the Internet service provider you've signed up with. If it's a web server you want to set up, you'll also need some form of World Wide Web server software (http) for your particular platform. In most cases, the server software is inexpensive, readily available, and easy to use: Install it, start it, and you're up and running with a real-live web server.

- Content: And more content. You'll change the default html document to point to other documents. You'll learn the simple basics of preparing documents with html formats. And you'll learn the method for defining a word or a phrase in one document to take the user to another document. The technology is easy. What's hard is figuring out what you have that others want to see. (And keeping it up-to-date.)

Certainly, another option is to pay a consultant to set one of these things up for you. With the startling popularity of the net these days (and with setting up a server being as easy as it is—once you know what you're doing) Internet server consultants are becoming quite popular. (Be sure to double-check my litany of caveats about using Internet consultants, in "LAN Connections" in "The User's Internet" chapter.)

Also, if you'd like to avoid even these setup steps, there are a number of businesses that already have servers on the net, and they'll let you set up your home page on one of their servers. It might not have *your* domain name, but it will let you get a start in the process of building and maintaining content, and it will give users a way to reach you.

Entrepreneurial Spirit

If your entrepreneurial[1] glass is half-full, this is a startling opportunity: All those people, not too many competitors—this is a market just *waiting* for new ideas.

Don't confuse this with a *user base* that's waiting for more *advertising*. The users are already getting a level of service at what they perceive as a justifiable cost—without the intrusion of obvious advertising. If you have an advertising objective, you'd better figure out how to raise the level of a service, add value to that service, or lower the costs to the user before your presence will be accepted.[2]

Gopher sites? Web sites? Listserv lists? There are a handful of e-publishing constructs that are being used right now, but certainly more are coming (including many that haven't been invented yet, no doubt).

If your entrepreneurial glass is half-empty, this is still a pretty good opportunity. It doesn't cost too much to at least stake out a presence on the net—in a way that will meet the standards and practices of the community. If it succeeds, then you're ahead; if it fails, you haven't lost too much.

E-publishing is not about inventing new tools—it's about *using* the tools that are already available, in a way that effectively communicates to the target audience you're trying to reach. That requires an understanding of the tools themselves, how they relate to the standards and practices of the community, and any lessons learned from prior efforts—both good and bad.

Whether you want to explore brave new worlds, or just set up shop in this e-flatland settlement, you should know the basics and how they relate to participating as a provider on the net.

The Special Case of Lawyers on the Internet

The Bad News for any law firm or office that wants to establish a presence on the Internet is that the trail has already been blazed during the Green Card Incident.[3]

The Internet community's overwhelming

1 Don't confuse "entrepreneurial" with "for-profit." Many not-for-profits and public service organizations are trying to apply this same entrepreneurial spirit to invent positive new ways of reaching out to the public.

2 Advertising might very well not be your objective. Consider the public service aspects for your local bar association. Consider the public relations objectives of your corporate sponsors or clients. Consider the possibility of tapping into Internet discussion groups to find worthwhile *pro bono* activities. The possibilities are intriguing—but they don't all have to be profit-motivated.

3 If you've been skipping ahead, go back and read "Aren't There *Any* Rules?" in "The Internet Environment" section of this book.

negative reaction to the Green Card Incident has been so pervasive that there is a presumption of sleaze—among many in the Internet community—that attaches itself to *any* lawyers on the net (and especially to lawyers involved in immigration law).

The Green Card lawyers were not the *first* Internet abusers to spam the network with junk email. But they were the first to defend their abuse as a "right," the first to do it repeatedly, and the first to raise the abuse to the attention of the popular press. Then they followed it up with a book professing to teach others how to do the same thing. This was certainly not the *only* spamming incident, nor the first, but it was one of the most notorious. Unfortunately, this is the only contact that many on the net have had with lawyers—which has generated some very disappointing misconceptions: that this is how all lawyers act, that lawyers never found the net until this one law firm told us all about it, and that everything that we lawyers know about working on the net we learned from this firm. Not surprisingly, within this community, expectations about lawyers are particularly low. To overcome this Ugly American-esque perception, you may actually find that the first part of an Internet-related introduction will have to include, "No, I'm not affiliated with the Green Card lawyers."

If you would like to participate as an Internet provider, you need to deal with the effects of the Green Card Incident carefully:

- Be especially sensitive to the standards and the practices of the net—focus on being a responsible net.citizen. This is one reason why I went into so much detail, in the early chapters of the book, describing the foundations and underlying principles upon which the Internet ethic is built.

- To participate as an e-publisher, you need to understand the *principles* well enough to apply them in the individual cases and opportunities that you will be presented with as the Internet services mature.

- If you are going to try to invent something new, you need to know these ethics thoroughly—they will determine how well your e-publications will be received, and therefore how effective your message can be. Be fully aware, though, that if you try something completely new, you will have to overcome an initial level of distrust that other professions would not have to deal with. Also be aware that your actions can affect millions of people who are paying—by the minute or by the character—to download things that reach them. A failure in the new-invention category can cost everyone money, will undoubtedly hurt your own effort and reputation, and—depending on the scale of the effort—could further tarnish the reputation of lawyers on the net.

The Internet is a powerful, empowering tool. The Green Card Incident shows that individuals—armed with standard Internet tools—can singlehandedly produce a fairly wide-ranging effect (both positive and negative). I encourage you to be careful in how you use these tools.

The Internet succeeds, or fails, on the ability of the users to cooperate in the day-to-day application of the Internet ethic.

A Services-Based Guide to Commercial Netiquette

Let's go through each of the basic Internet services from the perspective of using the net as an e-publisher. We'll cover the basics of applying netiquette[4] in the particular service, and try to highlight any special lessons learned.

Electronic Mail

Email is one of the most powerful services on the net—not because it does so many things, but because it's so ubiquitous. If you've got net.connected clients who are comfortable using email, having that link can make all the difference.[5] Also, email is the foundation for so many other services, and an alternative for many others (through the ftpmail and wwwmail gateways).

If all you're going to do is participate as an Internet user, having an Internet email address is the important first step (even if it's through an online services Internet gateway). But if you're planning to set up something more than just an experimental Internet server, it's especially helpful to have your own domain name that identifies you specifically (e.g., ibm.com)—it indicates that you're serious about the net and have gone to the trouble of establishing a permanent address.

Finding the Internet addresses of people that you're looking to reach is sometimes possible—using the utilities finger, whois or netfind—but more often than not, you're simply out of luck unless your correspondent tells you the address.[6]

It's important not to use people's individual email addresses for unsolicited advertisements, solicitations, or notifications. This goes to the very heart of the self-determination principle. Violations of this ethic are treated as uninvited junk email, and your communications will suffer precipitously. Vendors who have

4 As mentioned earlier, our focus on "netiquette" applies to the broad application of fundamental Internet ethics, rather than the incidental how-to examples of email manners and when-to-use-smiley-faces.

5 Internet folklore already includes the apocryphal stories about lawyers who landed clients because the lawyers had Internet addresses. Although I happen to know some of these stories are true, it's important to remember that you don't land a client *just* because you've got an Internet address—obviously—the issue of connectivity is one of many factors that the client might care about. But it *is* fair to conclude that there are at least some lawyers who have *lost* a client just because the lawyer isn't accessible via email.

6 For simple person-to-person communications, an easy approach is to tell your correspondent what *your* Internet address is, then have them send you an email message. Usually (not always), the email message will include the person's reply-to Internet address.

collected lists of email addresses as part of product registrations can be expected to use those lists to send out mailings. Organizations that solicit email addresses at a conference or presentation might be expected to send out related announcements. But in every case, the sender should give the recipients a way to "opt out" of future mailings, and they should make sure the mailings are related to the purpose of the original list.[7] Specifically, if you give people an opportunity to give you their email address or not, you are giving them the opportunity to choose whether they will or won't get unsolicited email from you. You shouldn't later violate that self-selection process. And you should never sell that list to someone else who will violate that process.

There is no white pages directory of email addresses. If you are going to use email addresses as part of an information-provider role, then you should treat your recipients' email addresses the same way you would treat their unlisted telephone numbers.[8]

File Transfer

Running an anonymous ftp service is one of several ways to let people reach you or your organization. As an information-distribution construct, ftp is fairly crude. (All it does is let the user log on—anonymously—then browse through available files and download those that appear applicable.) Usually, an anonymous ftp server is considered part of a full-scale Internet e-publishing operation—since it enables people who don't have access to the more elegant browsers to still get access to the information.

If you set up an anonymous ftp server, you can set your own limitations on the number of users and what files those users can see. You can also request that users avoid using the service during certain times of the day. Assume, however, that users will download anything they have access to, and that they will *not* follow the time-of-day constraints voluntarily. Be sure to include README and INDEX files that tell the users what they can find on the server and where to find it, as well as the name, email address, and, possibly, a phone number for people to call if they are having problems (or if they notice that something isn't working properly).

7 For more on this subject, see the discussion of Listserv lists that follows.

8 The unlisted phone number analogy falls apart pretty quickly. Many people publicly advertise their email address, so it doesn't always need to be treated as "confidential." But in your role as an information provider—rather than as just another member of the Internet community—you need to take special precautions.

Remote Logon

This is another lowest-common denominator service. In this case, you are letting people log onto your own machine, usually to let them run a special software program that you've set up on that machine. The advantage, of course, is that the software is accessible to every telnet user—not just the users who have access to some special Internet service software package.

Operationally, this may be the most complex approach—since you're inviting other people to run your computer.[9] And functionally, a telnet service may deliver the very least of all the Internet services—most telnet-based services work with very rudimentary user interfaces. But if your objective is reach a very broad user population, telnet can be an important part of an e-publishing venture.

Listserv Lists

This is one of the Big Two Internet services for the would-be e-publisher.

A listserv, of course, is simply a fancy email distribution list, managed by an automated list handler. It fits the self-determination ethic perfectly, though, because everything is in the control of the individual user. Each member of the target audience controls whether he or she is subscribed to the list. The user also controls whether the list should distribute every separate contribution to the discussion—as individual email messages—or whether the contributions should be collected first, then sent to the user's mail box as a compiled digest.

The listowner, on the other hand, has fairly complete control over what kind of content reaches the target audience. The listowner can set up the list to be:

- Announcements only—no replies are forwarded to the list as a whole.
- Moderated—the listowner monitors traffic to make sure that everything is on-topic and that certain netiquette breaches (such as advertising or personal attacks) are not redistributed to the entire list.
- Unmoderated—the only time the listowner interferes with the flow of traffic, if ever at all, is when the technology generates bad postings (duplicates, unsubscribe notices, etc.).

The only thing that's really important in setting yourself up as a listowner is making sure your audience *knows* what type of list it is. If the list is unmoderated, any attempt to censor content (even personal attacks) will be perceived as outside the rules of the game. Moderated groups—especially those run as part of a for-profit operation—are sometimes mistrusted, since the opportunity for a conflict of interest in censoring critical content is obvious (especially if there is a marketing aspect to this effort). For this reason, many moderated lists try to err on the side of airing anything that even *appears* to contain substantive criticism. The only thing that holds a moderated discussion together is the trust that all sides are being heard—any breach of that trust will likely be revealed

9 Not only do you have to worry more about security breaches, but you also have a stronger obligation to support users who have questions about using your software.

immediately, with disastrous effect on the discussion group. Announcement-only groups may be shameless public-relations constructs, but at least their purpose is obvious. No one is tricked into thinking that this will be a discussion group or that posts to the list will reach the rest of the users. (Of course, no one should be tricked into believing everything they get from an announcements-only list, anyway.)

Another feature that can be a key enhancement to a listserv list is a mechanism for reaching the list archives. Some listserv handlers have a built-in capability for accessing old discussions, but those capabilities tend to be weak, crude, and poorly understood by the users themselves. As an e-publisher, you might want to build a separate ftp server, or web server, to store the files containing those old discussions. Ideally, you could pull together some of the more frequently asked questions in those discussions and create a group of FAQ files where list newcomers can go without bothering the group at large.

You might start a listserv list as a spin-off from another list. Or perhaps as a follow-up to a conference or a meeting. Certainly, a client list represents a key opportunity. But you need to know your audience well enough to gauge how they would perceive this activity.

Preferably, your initial listserv list would come from people who voluntarily give you their email addresses for the express purpose of joining a particular list. Whether they gave you their addresses by signing a sheet of paper, or by subscribing in response to an invitation—the self-determination principle is maintained. Another option is to send just an announcement of the list (and an invitation to subscribe) to people who you think might be interested in that type of information.

If you decide to simply create a mailing list (i.e., unilaterally and without express permission)—*especially if it's your own clients*—you should be certain they won't mind. (And you should make sure the first note shows them just how easy it is to UNSUBSCRIBE from the list.)

This is different from regular mail—where if you sent out promotional brochures to your entire client list, you probably wouldn't raise a single eyebrow about the appropriateness of using a mailer for such a purpose. Junk mail is so common that the risk of having a client get *annoyed* about receiving your brochure is comparatively low. But on the Internet, junk email is completely unusual and sending it can cast you in a very poor light.

By the way, if you do start up a successful listserv group, make sure that you keep that list confidential. The contents of a listserv list—because it is so readily targeted for marketing purposes—are generally considered confidential and off limits. Handing that list to someone else (and especially selling that list to someone else) is considered a grievous breach of trust.

Newsgroups

Newsgroups are one of the most intuitively appealing services for the would-be e-publisher. But they are probably the least effective and the most dangerous.

The newsgroup community is arguably the most zealously anti-commercial group within the Internet, and they are not above breaking a few rules to defend what they think of as their particular patch of e-frontier turf.

One of the reasons is completely fundamental: Even though there may be newsgroups whose participants are the same people who make up your target audience, that doesn't mean that your announcement or advertisement is welcome. It goes back to self-determination. Unless the group specifically says that they are interested in receiving advertisements and junk email (and I know of none that do), then they are not. The participants join a group, quite frequently, to get *away* from the commercial interests that have a financial stake in a particular position. They want a truly open forum. If commercial vendors participate, they should be answering questions—or expressing opinions only when they are clearly labeled as such.[10] Some vendors, showing a close-but-no-cigar understanding of netiquette and the Internet ethic, have targeted their advertising spam at newsgroups where the subject matter of the newsgroup and the product line of the vendor "match." This shows more restraint than the Green Card lawyers did, but it still misses the point. Newsgroups, for the most part, are not interested in receiving a direct advertising pitch—even if it happens to hit the "right" audience. If the advertiser is selling bird-watching equipment and posts the ad in the just the bird-watching newsgroup and nowhere else, it's *still* considered spam. Hitting the right audience doesn't change the fact that you've interrupted discussions among a special-interest group with an advertisement.[11]

A second reason the newsgroups are so sensitive about this is that they're an especially easy target. Each newsgroup represents a pre-existing mailing list, divided conveniently by topic and interest area, that can be accessed simply by posting a message. And instead of forcing the would-be advertiser to send out thousands and millions of separate email messages, the newsgroup capability distributes that posting automatically—at the cost (to the advertiser) of just

[10] "If I wanted to hear Exxon talk about how much it's doing to save the environment," one reader explained it to me, "I would turn on the television. We go to the newsgroups to get away from the PR flacks." Having a financial stake in the outcome of a subject being discussed is generally considered enough to disqualify you from the discussion. (Unless, of course, you're the one being discussed.)

[11] One might argue that matched advertising *is* on-topic. And that particular argument might make for some interesting discussion among groups that follow the Internet ethic and netiquette. But it doesn't change the users' expectations—that advertisers should keep their spam out of newsgroups. And—as they would no doubt volunteer with no provocation whatsoever—*that goes double for lawyers.*

a single posting. Of course, the cost to the thousands and millions of newsgroup readers is much more than that. Indeed, the newsgroup version of junk email differs from the listserv version because this junk mail comes with postage due.

This, of course, is where the Green Card Incident occurred. The response, of course, was a torrent of vigilante justice—starting with vitriolic "flames" and email bombs, then escalating to threats and destructive hacking—clearly intended to try to intimidate the lawyers. Then it culminated with the cancel-bots that seem to have shut this particular activity down. It's remarkable to me that anyone would think this was a model to emulate.

Here's *my* advice. Don't.

If you want to advertise on the net, there are much better ways to do it. There are hundreds of ways to use the net—effectively—to announce skills and availability (in much more detail than any pamphlet or mailing could hope to cover), but without violating the practices and standards of the network. And without inspiring a violent backlash. Listservs, gophers, web sites[12] (look in the other sections of this chapter)—you might not generate the same level of bad publicity and tabloid-esque notoriety that has preceded you, but of course that's not the objective.

If you want to participate in the newsgroups, participate as an individual. If something that you have a financial stake in comes up in discussion, feel free to comment on it, but make sure you state your affiliations clearly.[13] Even if you've been lurking for several months and haven't seen anyone chime in with a conflict-of-interest disclaimer, include it anyway if it applies. It's not unusual for a disclaimer to go unneeded for months at a time, but when it's needed, people expect it to be there.

Occasionally, you might see an advertisement or announcement posted in a newsgroup—but those are almost always grabbed from some other source (gopher, announcement lists, etc.) and usually posted as an item for discussion. If the posting seems unnecessarily long, it will likely be suspected of being posted by a shill.

Which brings me to the last newsgroup-related item: Yes, some vendors participate in these discussions without revealing their

[12] Siskind and Susser, an immigration and nationality law firm in Nashville, Tennessee, for example, set up a web page that includes their firm newsletter and a detailed FAQ describing the U.S. Green Card lottery. It shows us the exact opposite end of the spectrum from the Green Card Incident. You can visit the Siskind and Susser site at http://www.telalink.net/siskind.

[13] For example, it's not unusual to see an advertiser speak up—quite forthrightly—when his or her product line is challenged. Similarly, when a newsgroup participant asks an easy question like, "Geez! How come *no one offers a service that can help me?*", the vendor is allowed (even expected) to jump in at that point with an informative answer and maybe even a little gratuitous puffing. But only if the answer is directed at a specific question or comment (i.e., within the immediate context of the discussion), and only if the answerer clearly identifies his or her affiliation.

identity or interests in the matter. Others try to convince friends or acquaintances to be shills—to post comments that would be discredited if the true source of the comment was known. Don't do it. It's just plain dishonest.

Menu-Based Browsing—Gopher Sites

The network information retrieval browsers represent another major category of services that can be used to good effect by would-be e-publishers.

Gopher sites, in particular, represent a special quandary—a compromise of good and bad.

Gopher is strictly a menu-based tool. That means it works in a completely text-based environment, which is good from a lowest-common-denominator perspective. But without the images, the formatting, or the point-and-click interface of the web, it's not exactly exciting or compelling. It's simplistic. Some web sites can be operated in an all-text environment as well, but the text-only interface is somewhat more difficult to grasp, and text-only webs lose the strength of the graphics-oriented web interface.

Gopher sites can be accessed using web client software, but web sites can't be accessed using gopher clients.[14] Gopher sites are a bit more efficient than web sites and are easier to set up. But as the web technology becomes more and more popular, most of the new developments are happening there—rather than in gopher-related technologies.

Ideally, you would set up *both* a web and a gopher site. But failing that, you'll just have to choose between the better user interface or the more ubiquitous accessibility.

Full-Graphics Browsing—Web Sites

This is the second of the Big Two Internet services for would-be e-publishers.

Web sites seem to be the most popular of the browser services available in today's Internet services market. (To be fair, gopher held that top spot for quite some time until the web browser software—like Mosaic and Netscape—became widely distributed.) Will web survive another few months? Another few years? Or will it be taken over by the next bandwagon fad?

Whatever its future, the web is the key

14 Ironically, this produces a Meinecke Muffler paradox. In the market for installing automobile mufflers, Midas Muffler had captured the market's attention with a lifetime warranty on a product (automobile mufflers) that have an inherently short lifetime. In an attempt to grab some of that market share, Meinecke offered a lifetime warranty with a plus—they would honor Midas warranties as well as their own. The paradox is that no matter how much you liked Meinecke, this policy encouraged you to buy your muffler from Midas: Because if you bought from Meinecke, your warranty would be covered *only* by Meinecke; but if you bought from Midas, your warranty would be covered by *both* Midas and Meinecke. Web software lets you access both web sites and gopher sites. Gopher software lets you access only gopher software. No matter how much you like the web software, if your only interest is reaching the highest number of people, and if you can only set up one site (and not both), then gopher should be your Meinecke Muffler choice.

technology for most Internet e-publishers right now. Some of the features are just plain fun—neat graphics, links to other applications like movies or sound, even pixel-by-pixel point-and-click operations that let users click on a particular part of a picture (such as a map or a group photograph) to go to the relevant hypertext link. But the meat of this technology is the hypertext linking itself. It supports the many different kinds of multimedia files, linked from relevant portions of both menus and context, in a manner that delivers a high-quality graphical user interface and is driven by an efficient technology that uses simple ASCII text files for command structures.

Here's how it works. You set up a web site, running WWW server software, with a file that contains the initial set of text and links that the users will see when they first attach to the server. The file is a plain-text file, but it contains certain embedded comments in the text—linking and formatting tags in standard HyperText Markup Language (HTML) format. HTML is a simple syntax for specifying how text files will be presented on a WWW display, and for specifying which pieces of text (or pictures) will link the user to other files or locations. None of the fancy graphical user interface is programmed by the person running the web site. All of that is handled by the web browser software.

For example, I might build an HTML file that says "<H1>Welcome to My Home Page</H1>". With the H1 tags, I've told the user's web browser to display that text as a top-level heading. I don't send any fonts or graphics or instructions on special formatting—instead I just put that string of text in the file and the browser software will choose what font and what formatting to apply. Mosaic might show an H1 heading in 36-point Times; Netscape might show it as 24-point Helvetica; a hundred other web browsers might show it a hundred different ways. As an e-publisher, I don't worry about that—the users get to choose whatever web browsers they prefer.

I can use HTML to specify bulleted or numbered lists, and display italics, bold, or fixed-width character displays. I can use it to embed bitmapped graphics and to do some basic alignments. But the list of tags is pretty elementary. The power of this tool is that it's *not* another C programming language—it's relatively simple and straightforward. But the most important part of HTML are the tags that pass control to another file. If I build an HTML file that includes the line "click <a ref="map.html">here</a> to see a map of the complex", the word *here* will be highlighted, and when the user clicks on it, control will pass to map.html (another HTML file). Using this basic construct, the e-publisher can build a complete network of linked documents. If the linked file is a graphics file, then the software will display it. If the linked file is another of several special kinds of files, then the user's machine will download the file, start up the required software, and open the downloaded file—all with no special programming on the server side. The e-publisher can focus on the one thing that will make a difference between one web site and the next—content, content, content.

Content and Advertising

If you build it, they will come.

Regardless of what Internet service you provide, the users will come for just one thing—content.[15] If some of that content is going to be advertising or purely commercial in nature, you need to follow a couple of key guidelines.

The first is that if you're going to advertise on the net, you need to make sure that your advertising is nonintrusive and in a place where it "belongs."

Frequently, this means setting up a server of some kind—where users can log on and get information about your firm and its services. You can put whatever you want there, and you can track which files people are actually using. Unlike most other forms of advertising, there's no per-page distribution cost of adding additional material—it's just a few more files on the disk.[16] And there's no "boredom" cost associated with putting too much information or too much detail in a mailer or brochure. Mailers need to be quick, concise, and to the point. Unfortunately, that usually prevents any substantive depth of information or detail—readers quickly tire of wading through mounds of material. The point of the mailer is to get the reader to *call* for more information. But on the net, the server can *be the place* to get more information. If you have 200 M-bytes of information about your firm and its services, none of that depth has to weigh down the opening home page.

But that server needs to deliver information on demand—not broadcast it to the world. Given the browser technologies available today, one of the more effective tools will be a simple link that identifies your server and provides the necessary link. When the user arrives, he or she can decide for themselves exactly what additional information to look for.

The second interesting challenge is to figure out how to advertise your link—either by telling people so they'll know how to find it when they need it—or by putting the link in a place where people will find it.

Talk to your Internet service provider about making sure that you are accessible through all of the appropriate resource discovery tools (such as finger, whois, netfind, archie, veronica, etc.). Make sure that any mailings you send out give people specific directions on how to access your Internet service.

[15] Actually, that applies only to the e-flatland settlers. The explorers will show up just to see what you've got. Usually, though, if you're trying to be an information provider on this net, it's the settlers that you're trying to reach, not the explorers.

[16] There *is* a cost associated with those files—the cost of *developing* the content and keeping those files up-to-date. But it's not a significant *distribution* cost—such as you would incur with a standard mailing.

In addition to the straightforward approaches, you might want to consider adding your link to one of the burgeoning business yellow pages on the net. Certainly the best known of these services is O'Reilly and Associates' GNN (Global Network Navigator). GNN will sell you—using a price *structure* not unlike that of traditional yellow pages advertising—a page on their GNN web service. You might use your GNN page to link to your own server, or you might set up that GNN page as your *only* server. Many law firms are doing just that—they may have nothing more than an email address and a contract with GNN, but to the net.connected potential client, they show up with an information web page and a pointer to a name, office, email address, and telephone number. Other business yellow pages services are coming into the market. Also look into Erik Heels's *Legal List* and the Yahoo server at Stanford University (see #4 and #14 in "Burge's Bookmarks"). Each includes pointers and URL references to servers operated by law firms.

Of course, the latest development in announcing your server is true upfront advertising. No, not the kind of advertising you see on the sides of large blimps floating over football games, but a new type of advertising in which the early days of television meet the early days of Internet—the Milton Berle effect that we discussed earlier. The problem with advertiser servers, of course, is that the content—while it might be useful when you're actually searching for a lawyer—tends to make for rather dull browsing. If early television had decided to do nothing more than documentaries explaining the products and services offered by its advertisers, viewers would have stayed away in droves. But to draw the viewers, television had to give us *content* that we wanted (or a reasonable facsimile thereof). Viewers didn't want to see a catalog of vendor products—they wanted to see Milton Berle. So Uncle Miltie is what they got. And the advertisers jumped at the chance to have their names plastered at the beginning-end-and-middle of the shows that drew viewers. Now log onto the always-popular NCSA What's New page. It's not popular because it's chockfull of product listings—it's popular because it's fun, because that's where the action is, because if you're interested in what this net is all about, that's the place to see it first. And when you log onto that page—which is now being taken over by GNN—notice that there's this little blurb that tells you "This week's NCSA What's New Page is brought to you by" some advertiser.

Content draws viewers. And viewers draw advertisers. It doesn't have to be intrusive. And the content doesn't have to be related. All it's gotta do is point interested prospects to your home page. (Ain't commerce great?)

A third key to being an effective e-publisher—and the most important—is figuring out what kind of added-value content you can provide.[17]

Think about things that might be useful for *you*. Then think about things that your target audience might be interested in as well. In a couple of minutes, you ought to be able to rattle off ten good ideas. Here's a few you might want to consider as just *starter* ideas:

- Develop a hypertext-annotated section of your state's code (in your field of law).
- Sponsor a local law school to develop an HTML version of a key part of the code.
- Help your local bar association set up a public-access Internet site.
- Help your local library set up a legal-research web server starting point.
- Develop and maintain a list of *local* net.connected legal sources.
- Develop and maintain a nationwide list of net.connected experts in your field.
- Build a FAQ for your local or state courts.
- Write and e-publish a FAQ for your field of law.
- Build a list of government agencies and other sources that clients in your field need to know about.
- Look through your files with an eye to lists and information that your clients ask you for regularly. If you've got something that you're handing out freely anyway—and clients find it useful—making it available online is an obvious choice.

Some of these won't work, some of them might not really help anyone, and some will be impractical. Think up your own—*you're* the one who knows what would be useful for you. Give up the content—publish what you know your clients are looking for.

Content, content, content.

But be sure to do something that's useful for *you*—and consider e-publication as a potentially beneficial side effect. If you spend a huge amount of time producing something that *you* can't use but that you *guess* would be useful for others, and if your guess turns out to be wrong (or the users just don't show up), then your effort will be effectively wasted.

Don't be concerned about "giving away" the store[18]—the users are out there looking for content; substantive content will let you show up in the mainstream of Internet-accessible

17 The content doesn't *necessarily* have to be law-related, but you probably have a better chance to provide quality law-related content than you do to provide quality non-law-related content. I mean, well heck, if you can build the definitive web site describing biking trails through the southwest deserts—and it attracts viewers—then by all means go ahead and do it. It might not be *especially* effective in attracting labor relations work, and you might want to consider that before expending the effort, but the point here is that it's hard enough to find some good, attractive content. Do what you can, and do it well.

18 I've never liked the game of hide-the-puck, and as Technical Editor for *Law Practice Management*, I've always been annoyed by articles that imply a subject is so complex that you need to hire the author to help you solve the problems. Personally, I figure that if I can accidentally "give away" everything I know in a half-hour speech, or in a five-page article, then I've got other more serious problems to deal with.

"resources" and the prospective clients can identify you as someone who knows the field. It may work or it may not, but remember it's the content that draws viewers. And that's what you've got to deliver.

Where to Go for How-To Details and More

In the Reference section, I've listed several books that provide detailed next-steps for the would-be Internet service provider.

Here are some highlights:

- Cronin-Reinhold's *Doing Business on the Internet* and Resnick-Taylor's *The Internet Business Guide* are both good guides to the pure-business aspects of using the Internet for traditional business research and customer relations.

- *Managing Internet Information Services*—yet another O'Reilly and Associates book—is one of the first books I've seen that's devoted to the specifics of how to set up Internet servers. Jason Manger's *The World Wide Web, Mosaic and More* is focused entirely on World Wide Web servers and is targeted at novices.

- Susan Estrada's *Connecting to the Internet* describes some of the specific features you might need to look for if you're going to run a full-time Internet server site (obviously, your computer will need to be connected full time, rather than just when you need to dial in).

- Cheswick-Bellovin's *Firewalls and Internet Security* covers the important aspect of security for the would-be information provider. Specifically, if you're going to put up a full-time connection to the net and invite strangers to log onto your machine, you need to make sure your machine is protected.

Chapter 13

The Internal Internet

I feel I've saved the best for last.

That's because the software that's been developed for use on the Internet—especially gopher, WAIS, and WWW—represents a strategically viable alternative to commercial products as a front-end for distributing and browsing through internal databases and resources.

If you take nothing else away from this book, let it be that adding TCP/IP to your office network environment will enable you to take advantage of this type of network information retrieval (NIR) software, and that the NIR software can be an effective part of your office's information infrastructure—right now.

Network Information Retrieval (NIR) Software in the Marketplace

No, you haven't seen gopher and Mosaic evaluated in the usual trade journal product comparisons, and it's rare to see it mentioned in the context of Information Technology architectures. Mostly, that's because the Internet's NIR software tools represent a fundamental shift in both the software and in the mechanisms for bringing that software to the market. Just as the traditional data processing departments were unprepared for the influx of personal computers in the early 1980s—because it represented a fundamentally new way of doing things—the traditional Information Technology marketplace is unprepared for the adoption of NIR tools, and uncomfortable with the way they are being implemented.

The NIR tools also would likely fare poorly in the types of product evaluations that are generally found in the trade press. That's because most check-the-box product evaluations favor feature-itis products that try to do everything for everyone (the more features you have, the better). Most NIR products, however, have very few features—they're simple. Almost simplistic. They do one thing and they do it well. But the real strength of the NIR tools isn't any one particular feature or technical strength, it's in that intangible factor that trade-press product comparisons are loathe to evaluate—third-party support.

If you've been choosing and using software for any length of time, you've undoubtedly run into this particular analysis: Someone walks in and says "I've just seen the best <whatever it is> on the market! It walks, it talks, it washes windows! It has the highest rating of any product of its kind! How can we live in the dark ages with that old <whatever you've got> for even one more day?" Well, comes the practiced reply, the reason we stick with the standard is because it's the standard. Market share, market share, market share. Your product might be able to run circles around the standard, but what do we do when the secretary is out sick? No one knows how to use the greatest thing since sliced bread, but every temp agency in town has people who know how to use the industry standard. I can hire consultants who will write programs for it, I can buy add-ons that do what *I* need, and the user groups and trade press are paying attention to our product, not yours. And what do I do next year when there's yet another Best Product? Do I switch and switch and switch? Always trying to keep up with that moving target called the leading edge? No thanks. I'll stick with what the rest of the planet is using, if for no other reason than the third-party support for the standard will always be better and easier to find than for the breakthroughs.[1]

This is what the Internet's NIR software has more of than any competing products on the market: third-party support. There are millions of users, and thousands of developers—all working feverishly to promote the best out of a brutally *laissez faire* system of open standards where only the strong survive.

To be fair, the NIR software is not fully matured. It is not so popular that every kid at the corner computer store is a burgeoning HTML coders. (Not yet.) But its characteristics are mainstream and compelling.

Let's look at the details.

NIR Applications

The sole purpose of NIR software is to make information available to users.

It's best at ad hoc requests for dipping into reference materials. Most intranets start out with simple query systems—a client phone book, a list of file numbers, policy manuals. But with a little imagination, these graphics-and-sound enabled,

1 This is the reasoning of a true flatlander. This argument should be made with pride—not shame. Let the explorers tout what they've found. Let them skin their knees and wander around the dead-end canyons. Eventually (they can't help it, you know) they'll come back and tell us what they've found. And the best part is, they'll only tell us what works! Showing no sense of Little-Red-Hen bitterness (and almost no sense of humor), they never seem to come back and tell us to follow a path that takes us right off a cliff.

point-and-click hypertext systems can realize a lot of potential. Conflicts-of-interest checking, client billing status, search and retrieval of internal workproduct. Almost any reference material is a legitimate candidate.

Without a single line of C code (and without having to buy into some sophisticated proprietary package), you can link your client phone book to selected billing reports, then to receivables reports, client matter listings, docket tracking output, and other selected reports that your clients tend to ask you about frequently. If it turns out to work well enough, you might add more and more interesting things—the client's spouse's name, the teenager's high school, other things from your copious Rolodex, maybe the date the client last called, maybe a photograph of the client. Get carried away. Live a little. Think a little. What would it help you to have readily available whenever a client called? How come American Express has your entire history online the minute you give them your account number, but your own clients have to wait while someone runs down the hall to grab the file? It's not because they have mainframes and hordes of programmers. (Well, actually, of course, they do.) But the technology is readily available through first-level implementations of standard NIR technologies.

Of course, it's easy to get carried away. It's easy to think of things you need to be able to put your hands on. But the hardest part of the problem isn't the technology. It's the content. It's not enough to figure out *what* you need—the challenge is to make it available electronically and to keep it up-to-date. (It's easy enough to scan in one client photo and make it available, but how are you going to make sure you get everyone's picture and make sure that your system stays up-to-date?) The technology won't do the hard work for you.

What NIR software does that most other query systems don't is make the process at least *somewhat* easier, and capable of supporting output from many existing systems, even if they come from vastly different proprietary products and platforms.

Most NIR software runs from straight ASCII text files. (You can *distribute* binary files and software. But for general-purpose reference applications, the reference files are almost always straight text.) HTML files are straight text, with the tags and links information added in. Browsers can be set to change their menus dynamically—depending on what happens to be in the target directory at the moment. And WAIS servers—while a little more sophisticated because they're running full-text search operations—use standard indexes built from the files to be searched.

Most existing applications—billing systems, accounting systems, electronic Rolodexes, file tracking, conflicts checking, whatever you've got as your current source of electronic information—can be set up to produce straight ASCII text files as output. Most databases (even spreadsheets and word processors) can be programmed to dump the needed information—preformatted in either text or HTML format—for *automatic* inclusion in the appropriate web page. Many of those systems can be set up to run automatically—overnight—to prepare the formatted text files and put them in a directory where the web browser can reach them.

Because NIR uses straight text files as a lowest common denominator for communicating with other applications, the software is well positioned to be a reasonable front-end for several different applications, from several different products. Also, because the developers of this software are not interested in captive user bases and world domination, there are no hidden tricks to "encourage" you to stay within a vendor's proprietary product line.

Commercial Product Alternatives

It's entirely true that other products can do much of what the NIR software can be used for. They can and they do—often with good results. The problem is that most of the commercial vendor products either put you on a steep learning curve or they lock you into a particular product line.

To compare the different approaches of non-NIR software, you need to go back to the basic objective: to support ad hoc requests from reference materials and information. How does the user find that information, and how does the e-publisher make it available?

Traditional databases make that information available by either having the user know enough about the database structure and language to run his or her own queries, or, hiring a programmer who will write an information retrieval program. Not only do you need specific skills to get this set up, but once it's set up, you need to make sure that every machine in your network has a copy of the necessary software—which is often expensive, and inevitably ties you to that particular vendor (and to the particular user interface as well). Even with some of the newer, more user-friendly data browsers and data dippers, you might have to do less programming, but you're still stuck with a proprietary choose-one-vendor approach.

Traditional commercial and custom-written applications can do wondrous things—*if* you find the product or *if* you've got the programmer to build exactly what you need. Usually, a custom-written program doesn't force you to buy a particular vendor's product for every machine on the net, but the programmer's services are usually expensive. And although you're not locked into a commercial vendor, you may be effectively locked into using that one programmer or at least that programmer's approach.

NIR software, on the other hand, is zealously open—in its standards and in its interoperability.

There's nothing mysterious or terribly impossible about setting up the networks and software within your own firm or office to establish an internal Internet. It's the exact same software that runs on the Internet—the exact same functionality—with the only differences being that it's available constantly and you don't have to dial-in to your Internet service provider to reach it. Frankly, there's not a lot of rocket science in this. The elegance of these systems is that they're *comparatively* simple—they *lessen* the need for programming skills, and they work with multiple products instead of forcing you to stick with just one.

Gopher and WWW are plug-and-play technologies that install and operate using TCP/IP networks—an existing and ubiquitous networking infrastructure.[2] They're relatively easy to set up and easy to use. Based on a menu or point-and-click user interface (that even a managing partner could learn), the NIR tools take the user from menu to menu, or page to page, looking at files or starting searches—grabbing whatever information is needed. Double-click on the search icon, and it asks you what words you want to search for. (WAIS is frequently the search engine—it builds an index of words found in each document to be made searchable. The resulting searches are actually quite fast.)

The server software is reasonably effective, but the real strengths of the NIR technologies are found on the client side of this client/server technology.

The Effect of Open Standards in NIR Technologies

There are gopher and web clients for virtually every hardware platform and operating system on the market. Even if your office suffers from a harrowing mix of machines that stubbornly refuse to work with one another, they all should be able to reach the web server. Also, for the more popular NIR services, there tend to be multiple clients for most major environments. Because they're so emphatically standards-based, if you don't like how one client works, you can choose another. And if two people in the office want to use different clients, that's fine, too. The entire office doesn't have to settle on a single product. Interoperability means that you *can* have different browsers—indeed, different servers if that's what you'd like. And they still work together.

This is a key characteristic that differentiates Internet-based NIR software from the proprietary products available from commercial vendors. It's not the features—it's the future.

2 No, they don't run on Novell's IPX. But TCP/IP can run together with IPX on the exact same wire, using the exact same Ethernet network adapters and interface units. The TCP/IP network drivers need to be added to the start-up processes for whatever machines on the network will use it.

The strength of the NIR software is that it's supported by an enormous global community capable of producing products and services that no single vendor could possibly hope to match.[3] When a service becomes popular, literally thousands of programmers begin working on their own custom versions of the supporting software. These are very bright people—often working on their "own time." And because of the community ethic, they tend to share their software rather than keep it to themselves. The result is a development environment that fiercely *relies* on open standards (though it sometimes focuses more on the "open" than on the "standards"). The result is a system in which developers tend to build on what others have done—making things better, making things faster, or maybe making something completely new. The *end* result tends to be reliably interoperable software products (particularly for the more popular services) in which there's usually a version of the software for virtually every platform and operating system on the planet—often as freeware or shareware. If a service is *very* popular, you'll usually find several alternatives to choose from, most of which operate with one another just fine. It's this uncompromising zeal for interoperability that establishes and enforces standards—not some vendor wielding a licensing agreement or a look-and-feel copyright lawsuit. No single commercial vendor can hope to match the output, alternatives, or prices of the Internet's software development community. And while this cooperative spirit persists, no vendor has the clout to challenge these emerging standards.

A lot of commercial products can do what the NIR software does—and in many cases, better. But few can match the breadth of machines supported. Nor the flexibility of choices. Nor the purchase price of public-domain software.

Of course there are disadvantages.

NIR Constraints

To run these services, you *do* need to be running TCP/IP—which is different from Novell Netware's IPX. To take advantage of NIR software, you first have to set up your office machines with TCP/IP network drivers.[4] They shouldn't conflict with Novell, and they should use the exact same hardware and wiring you've already got installed. But it is something different.

A second constraint is that the NIR products *are* rather simplistic. If you need something with a lot more horsepower to deliver a key mission critical application, if does-one-thing-and-does-

3 Not Microsoft. Not IBM. Not the telephone companies. And those information superhypeway wannabes—the cable TV companies, the entertainment combines, and the permanently perplexed Regional Bell Operating Companies—aren't even in the same town with a chance.

4 It's at least interesting to note that Microsoft is positioning itself to operate in a TCP/IP environment, IBM is building TCP/IP support into its OS/2 product line, and Novell—the inventors and proprietors of IPX, TCP/IP's most widely installed network protocol competition—is making a version of Novell Netware that runs on top of TCP/IP.

it-well doesn't match your needs, then a simple NIR package could be out-gunned. These are simple tools—nothing more. If what you need is a fortress, then you'd better go get what you need.

Finally, you need to recognize that the NIR software and standards are primarily the product of a rather loosely organized academic and computer-industry community. For the most part, the software is written by college students, researchers, and programmers who volunteer their time to make incremental improvements to products that they're interested in. There is no real "central source" of either software or documentation, and it has to be considered at least a challenge (perhaps an intellectual leap of faith) to entrust your information infrastructure to a software package that was written by a student who graduates-next-year-and-will-be-gone-to-who-knows-where.

There's no one to call when something goes wrong. There are no service stations on the Internet. (OK, so maybe it *is* a frontier.)

Some of the NIR products, as you might guess, are graduating from share-ware distribution into full-scale commercial operations. As long as they stick with the net's open standards, these can be extremely helpful. Not only do they give you the documentation and tutorials that the all-geek shareware editions often lack, but they should give you a technical support phone number as well.

My Least-Favorite Intranet Object Lesson

Not too long ago I sat through a new-product demo by a vendor with a "breakthrough" product that offered internal "electronic publishing"—elegant, programmable, and a graphical point-and-click interface into common reference files. And next year they hoped to come out with hypertext linking. Price? About twelve grand for a starter package for about five users. At the end of a very pleasant presentation, I asked how this differed from gopher. Or Mosaic. "From what?" came the reply. (Uh oh.) That's right—for the last three years, this company of heads-down programmers labored to create a nearly functional facsimile of what thousands of programmers had collaborated to produce on the Internet. As sad I was for these programmers, I was sadder still for their customers who had shelled out twelve grand for a product with less functionality than a simple freeware web browser.

By way of contrast, here's what it takes to turn a Macintosh into a gopher server:

1. Download a copy of MacGopher.
2. Double-click on the MacGopher application.

That's it. You're up and running.

Now you need to spend some time working on the *content* of that gopher site. You need to set up the text files so that they give the user something useful. You need to set up the subdirectories so that the content is well organized. You have a lot of work ahead of you. But notice that the work is where it *should* be: On the content. *Not* on the technology.

Where to Go for How-To Details

If you want to find out more about setting up servers that you can use internally, look for the following how-to books. Frankly, there aren't a lot of books on this topic just yet, but once again the ubiquitous O'Reilly and Associates is leading the way:

- *Managing Internet Information Services* (Liu, Peek and Jones, O'Reilly and Associates) is a good how-to guide for setting up servers for most of the basic Internet services. It focuses on external Internet services, but the instructions apply equally to setting up internal services. The book covers a wide range of NIR technologies.
- *The World Wide Web, Mosaic and More* (Jason Manger, McGraw-Hill) is focused almost entirely on web servers, and its target audience is novices. An excellent choice for someone who is just starting out.
- *WorldWideWeb Unleashed* (SAMS Publishing, can be hard to find sometimes) is a monster 1,058-page tome on just the web. Obviously, it's not really intended for beginners, but if you start doing a lot, this might be just the too-thick desk reference you need.

Of course, online, you should be able to find pointers to several developers who are making NIR software available. Most of the basics (ftp and telnet, for example) should be included with whatever TCP/IP network drivers you get. But for information on others, you should try the appropriate newsgroups and FAQ files. For pointers to the sites for major NIR software tools, see John December's *internet-tools* and *internet-cmc* guides—#15 in "Burge's Bookmarks."

Where to Go for More

Despite all of the e-library spectacles and fancy marketing opportunities that the Internet may tempt you with, this is the one part of the Internet that may have the best chance of providing a real and tangible benefit—immediately.

I said at the beginning of the book that if there is one profession that can take immediate advantage of the Internet, it is the legal profession. Of course that assessment focuses on the e-library materials that are *more likely* to be of practical use to lawyers—generally speaking—than to any *other* profession.

But in the intranet—in this unheralded use of the Internet—in the back office, quietly, with no fanfare, just trying to invent better ways to do what we've always been trying to do—I believe the NIR technologies offer their most immediate payback. And a significant long-term payback as well.

This is one area in which the traditional PC and software vendors have failed to deliver on the promise of the PC revolution. We find ourselves locked in a Tower of Babel in which the vendors seem determined to sell us the best language money can buy—thereby ensuring that our simple needs for inter-operability and cross-platform compatibility will go ever unheeded.

Finally, we have a new set of tools. These *are* paleotechnologies. They're new, and crude, and just getting started. But they have the right foundation. These are the tools of the e-flatland settlers—who are trying to husband the natural resources of the e-landscape they've been stuck in.

Think global and act local?

Exactly. But let's put a *reluctant* pioneer's take on this: We're "thinking global" because that's where the answers are coming from—our local prob-lem-solvers just aren't getting the job done. And we're "acting local" because that's where our problems are. Right here.

I'm no explorer. But if people are inventing long-term answers that apply to *my* long-term problems—even if the tools are crude—I'd be a fool not to listen. I've got too much work to do. And not enough time.

Innovation? Sure, you can call it that if you want to. But the way I see it, I'm just grabbing the *easy stuff* 'cause I can't afford not to.

Sure I'm an e-flatland settler. And mighty proud to be one.

References

Learning More

Chapter 14

Book Reviews

So how can the curious law office get started? Where can you find a good road map to the information highway? Exit ramps? Service stations? Restaurants that serve rapidly prepared food? (Or how about a guidebook to shamelessly extended highway metaphors?)

For specific details and how-to's (as a user, as a provider, or internally), there are just Way Too Many books on the Internet at your local book store. For better or worse, the sudden interest in the Internet has generated a flood of new books—of shall we say—uneven quality. As we've already noted, you can download a list of Internet book reviews by Kevin Savetz (see #21 in "Burge's Bookmarks"), but here are my favorites:

Connecting to the Internet—An O'Reilly Buyer's Guide, Susan Estrada, O'Reilly and Associates, ISBN 1-56592-061-9. This is the definitive guide for reaching the Internet. Hardware, software, networking connectivity—this book spells it all out: for beginners who just want to dial-in without spending any money, up through corporations who need to set up dedicated leased lines for 24-hour high-speed connectivity. O'Reilly published Ed Krol's original intro- to-Internet classic just as the Internet was becoming popular (see next listing). Now they've done it again with a how-to book that no one else offers—just as the masses are trying to get connected.

The Whole Internet User's Guide & Catalog—2nd ed., Ed Krol, O'Reilly and Associates, ISBN: 1-56592-063-5. This is the classic. Well written and thorough, it covers all of the basic (and not-so-basic) utilities and services that you can use in working on the net. Then it treats you to a high-quality assessment of specific Internet resources. Frankly, although there are a lot of excellent Internet books available online, none of them measure up to Krol's *Whole Internet*.

Be sure to look for the latest edition (even to the point of contacting O'Reilly about impending plans). The reference-desk nature of this book makes it an important book to have—for any actively practicing *Internaut*; but because the information is so specific it goes out-of-date more quickly than many other books.[1] The first edition was *the* definitive Internet book—but it lost relevancy before O'Reilly got it updated. This book *needs* to be updated regularly.

Internet Starter Kit for Macintosh, Adam Engst, Hayden Books, ISBN 1-56830-064-6, with software, and **Internet Starter Kit for Windows,** Adam Engst, with Corwin Low and Michael Simon, Hayden Books, ISBN 1-56830-094-8, with software. These are just what they say they are: starter kits—everything you need to get on the Internet: software, free-trial Internet accounts, and step-by-step instructions that take you well beyond the initial tasks of dialing in and logging on. These books stand above the rest—despite the growing number of getting-started wannabes (including the highly touted *Internet in a Box* series). They cover the basics of what's available and they offer good advice on finding your way around. But what sets them apart from the rest is their clear, uncompromising focus on the task at hand—not just dialing in and logging on, but actually learning enough and doing enough to become effective, i.e., getting "started." The tutorials on how to get connected are comprehensive and platform specific. They even include a temporarily complete listing of Internet service providers. They're well written, thorough, and provide a good introduction for beginners (without patronizing) as well as substantive information for more experienced net.denizens.

Honorable mentions in the PC category go to **The Complete Idiot's Guide to the Internet,** Peter Kent, Alpha Books, ISBN 1-56761-414-0, and **The Internet Roadmap,** Bennett Falk, Sybex, ISBN 0-7821-1365-6. The *Idiot's Guide* is well organized and provides plenty of how-to-use-the-Internet detail. It's weaker on how to get connected, but it includes special deals and coupons for trial accounts with many Internet service providers whose *job it is* to get you connected. *Roadmap* is another good how-to-use-the-Internet guide. It covers the basics (not the fancy stuff), doesn't wander around too much, and gets down to the business of teaching you what you need to know—as quickly as it can. *Idiot's Guide* is a best-seller (deservedly) and *Roadmap* looks like it could become very popular.

[1] Not that the information becomes wrong. But for a detailed how-to reference guide, the absence of suddenly popular technologies becomes almost painful.

Doing Business on the Internet, Mary Cronin, Van Nostrand Reinhold, ISBN 0-442-01770-7, and **The Internet Business Guide: Riding the Information Superhighway to Profit,** Rosalind Resnick and Dave Taylor, SAMS Publishing, ISBN: 0-672-30530-5. If you're interested in hearing how other businesses are planning to make commercial use of the net, these two guides give you a good, solid capitalist's view. They focus on the traditional foundations of business enterprise: marketing, research, customer contacts, targeted advertising—all within the context of the Internet and the Internet ethic.

Firewalls and Internet Security, Cheswick/Bellovin, Addison-Wesley, ISBN 0-201-63357-4. If you're serious about putting up a real full-time connection to the Internet from your office, you need to address the security concerns of living on the net. This book explains the details of *how* to set up the necessary protections—keeping out unauthorized users, curiosity seekers, determined hackers, as well as worms and viruses that range from accidental to intentionally destructive. It's the best book on the subject, but it's not for beginners.

Managing Internet Information Services, Liu, Peek and Jones, O'Reilly and Associates, ISBN 1-56592-062-7. This is a wide-ranging how-to guide for setting up servers for most of the basic Internet services—especially gopher and web servers. This is useful whether you're interested in becoming an information provider on the net, or just want to use the NIR software internally. There aren't many books on this topic, but the ubiquitous O'Reilly and Associates is here to fill another gap.

The World Wide Web, Mosaic and More, Jason Manger, McGraw-Hill, ISBN 0-07-709132-9. The title is misleading because it's *not* much more. World Wide Web is the name—and that's what it covers. This guide to setting up web servers—again, for external or internal access—is targeted more at novices than the O'Reilly book. By contrast, SAMS Publishing's new web-specific book, **WorldWideWeb Unleashed,** is a 1,058-page heavyweight. It's complete (1,058 pages on *just the web?*), but it can be a bit intimidating.

Let me close with two books that don't deal with the Internet, per se, but which I keep on my own Internet bookshelf as object lessons on the continuing need for computer systems security. *Not* as how-to guides. Both are nonfiction horror stories.

Secrets of a Super Hacker, pseudonym The Knightmare, Loompanics Unlimited (Box 1197, Port Townsend, WA), ISBN 1-55950-106-5. The sophomoric writing style and 8½-by-11 laser-printed format might lead you to dismiss the author as a self-aggrandizing teenaged braggart. But it's exactly these qualities that should chill you to the bone. The author has written 200 pages of detailed how-to instructions for breaking into computer systems, and the descriptions are obviously based on firsthand experience. This isn't the work of an academic security specialist; this is the work of just one denizen of the information superbackalleyway—one of many (presumably) who wander around the neighborhood trying electronic doorknobs. If you've got a network, you should read this book. Most of his tricks can be foiled easily—but only if you know what the tricks are.

Information Warfare: Chaos on the Electronic Superhighway, Winn Schwartau, Thunder's Mouth Press. This is a more mainstream tale of hacking in today's e-business environment. Schwartau describes systematic attacks on each of the electronic tools used in today's common office environment. He goes beyond the subject of simple hacking into computer systems, to describe tools and techniques for intercepting faxes, breaking into cellular phone calls, cracking voice mail, installing physical taps on networks, stealing passwords, and actually attacking a competitor's data network. He takes you a little bit further than Knightmare does—out past the edge of paranoia. And frankly, most of the described attacks are extremely difficult to defend against. This book is better at telling you what not to trust, rather than telling you what to do about it.

And Magazines

Wired, Wired Ventures, ISSN 1059-1028. If you decide to spend any money at all trying to keep up with the latest Internet events, buy this magazine. No other publication comes close to capturing the flavor, the spirit, and the energy of what's happening on the Internet. (It also happens to have more advertising by Internet service providers[2] than any other publication on the planet, but that's not really the point.) It truly is a bellwether for the new-geek generation—disaffected, radical, and possessed of boundless energy to make things work that the rest of us are just buying clues about. Go to the newsstand and buy a copy.[3] Trust me. What goes on in its pages makes the bleeding edge of technology look positively pathetic. It's the MTV generation graduating from Nintendo to client/server. (This thing frightens me *every single time I open it up.*) And it's popular. Every issue, they keep printing more copies, and they keep selling 'em all.[4] And I *don't* think they're selling those copies to you and me. I think they're selling 'em to the hordes of kids who grew up with computers—kids who have probably *never even seen a typewriter.*

2 If you want something right away that will tell you which Internet service providers are hungry, advertising, and looking to help you connect to the net today, the ads in this magazine do exactly that. *Wired* may be the most up-to-date source for commercial Internet-related services.

3 Or subscribe. Either call 1-800-769-4733 with a credit card, or mailto:subscriptions@wired.com with the message "help." They'll send you an email format for subscribing.

4 If you can't find a copy on the newsstand, you can download it from gopher://gopher.wired.com. But it's really not the same as the real thing. Ironically, I take some comfort in the fact that the print version is scarier than the online versions. As Marshall McLuhan taught us Way Too Long ago, the medium is the message.

Internet Service Providers

This is just a straight listing of a few selected Internet service providers, for use—if you just *have to*—with the chapter titled "Getting Started" (in The User's Internet section of this book). My recommendation, though, is that you try to get a copy of the latest Internet service provider lists—either online (OK, I know it's a circular instruction), or through one of many books on the subject.

Even if you can't find an up-to-date listing, here are my two much-preferred recommendations for finding a good access provider and getting connected:

- Get a copy of Susan Estrada's book on connecting to the net, *Connecting to the Internet—An O'Reilly Buyer's Guide* (O'Reilly and Associates, ISBN 1-56592-061-9). This guide is simple and elegant. It only does one thing, and it does it better than any other. And it covers a complete range of possible Internet connections—from simple freenet dialins up to open-channel full-bore surgical implants.[1]
- Buy a copy of *Wired* magazine. Once in a while, some of the popular PC magazines (such as, oh say, *PC Magazine*) will try to do a "buyers' guide" on this subject, but you have to wait for that particular issue to come out, and you have to deal with the fact that the vendors change the products faster than the magazines can print their reviews. *Wired* magazine is where most of the Internet service providers do their most aggressive advertising. Don't expect *Wired* to do a feature-by-feature comparison—it's just one of the better places to look when you're trying to find a vendor.

> **1** OK, OK, I lied about the implants.

The list is by no means comprehensive. (That's the job of other people and other lists.) These are just a few of the providers that—in *my* opinion—appear to have developed some level of reputation and stability over the years.

I've divided the list into several parts depending on the principal characteristics of the providers.

Full-Service Providers

These providers not only offer all Internet services—usually including shell account, SLIP/PPP account, and LAN connectivity—but they also offer the important service of being able to register a domain name for you. Almost all can give you an 800 number for using the service. Prices vary, of course. UUnet and PSINet may be the market leaders in this class, but they're also some of the more expensive. Netcom can be a good choice, too.

AlterNet—UUnet Technologies
voice:703-204-8000
mailto:alternet-info@uunet.uu.net

CERFnet (Western U.S.)
voice:619-455-3900
mailto:help@cerf.net

NEARnet (Northeast U.S.)
voice:617-873-8730
mailto:nearnet-join@nic.near.net

NETCOM
voice:408-554-8649
mailto:info@netcom.com

PSINet
voice:703-709-0300
mailto:interramp-info@psi.com
mailto:all-info@psi.com

SURAnet (Southeast U.S.)
voice:301-982-4600
mailto:marketing@sura.net

No-Fee Access Providers

You've got to pay for the long distance phone call if one of these is not in your area, and the type of service can be fairly limited, but these can be just about the quickest way to get started. Talk to local sources to find freenets in your calling area.

Prairienet Freenet
voice:217-244-1962
dialup://visitor@217-255-9000
mailto:jayg@uiuc.edu

M-Net Public Access Unix
dialup://313-994-6333

Nyx (University of Denver)
dialup://new@303-871-3324
mailto:aburt@nyx.cs.du.edu

Other Internet-Access Providers

These are some of the most prolific of advertisers, and they seem to be among the most interested in making this process easy for you. They are usually shell account and SLIP/PPP providers. Pipeline and Netcom (a full-service provider) are fairly common choices, and probably a good easy choice if you're starting out completely from scratch.

NovaLink
voice:800-274-2814
dialup://WRD94A@800-937-7644
mailto:info@novalink.com

NVN (U.S. Videotel)
voice:800-336-9096
dialup://W194WW@800-336-9092
mailto:info@nvn.com

Pipeline
voice:212-267-3636
mailto:info@pipeline.com

Special Law-Related Networks

Most of these aren't really Internet service providers,[2] but they have special applicability to the legal community and are included. Each is very different from its neighbors.

ABA/net[3]
voice:800-242-6005

Law Journal Extra
voice:212-545-6199

[2] Law Journal Extra, however, *does* provide a meaningful access path to the Internet—Extra is provided through the commercial Internet service provider, Pipeline.

[3] Contact the American Bar Association for information about other online services—including Internet-related services—that it is planning to announce shortly. Details were not available as this book was being written, but the ABA's Internet-related initiatives are being given a very high priority. To be fair, most of the other law-related networks are also considering updates and revisions to their online network offerings.

LAW/Net
voice:800-940-1402

LEXIS Counsel Connect
voice:800-955-5291

Commercial Online Service Vendors

Most of these give you gateways rather than the Internet itself, but they're promising great things. If you're looking for true Internet access, you might consider what these vendors are offering—but be very careful to find out the details behind advertised "features." Many gateways are advertised as the features themselves. To be fair, these folks are the most likely to get you up and running the fastest. They have the biggest budgets, the biggest computers, and the biggest technical support staffs. Some novices start with these, get familiar with the technologies, and then move up to full Internet access after they've gotten comfortable with the basics. Compuserve is certainly the biggest, America Online is probably the best all-around service, and Delphi tries to deliver the most extensive list of Internet services (albeit with a more cumbersome user interface than most of its competitors).

America Online
voice:800-827-6364
mailto:aohotline@aol.com

Compuserve Information System
voice:800-848-8990
mailto:postmaster@csi.compuserve.com

Delphi
voice:800-695-4005
dialup://JOINDELPHI:WRD949@800-365-4636
mailto:info@delphi.com

GEnie
voice:800-638-9636

MCI
voice:800-444-6245

NOTE: MCI has announced a new Internet-related service that may move them from the email gateway business into a significant presence on the Internet.

Chapter 16

Fun with Statistics: Internet Growth

Research, education, entertainment—content providers are swarming to the net in droves. And of course, the users are there as well. Based on the most recent count, more than 4.8 million host computers are attached to the net. (And just *one* of those "host computers" is *all of Compuserve*. Another is all of America Online.) The trade press argues about whether there are really twenty-five million different users that have access to the net (at least through email), and how much turnover there is. But by any count, it's A Lot. And the number of hosts still *doubles* every year.

Well not exactly doubles, but pretty darn close.

How close?

Glad you asked.[1]

Infinite Growth

Since 1968, the rate of growth for the Internet is infinite. There were zero computers connected to the net, because it didn't exist, so the growth rate is infinity percent. Move that initial data point up to 1969, though, and the annual rate of growth drops to a barely whopping 72.3 percent, per year, compounded, every year, since the first four computers were connected.

If you're trying to look at somewhat more meaningful growth trends for the net, there seem to have been three distinct phases.

- 1969 to 1982—annual growth 36.8 percent. In the first thirteen years of the net, it was primarily a closed community of Department of Defense installations and related research

[1] **Are you sure you want to ask this question?**

173

facilities. It grew from the first four sites to just 235 over the course of thirteen years.

- 1982 to 1991—annual growth 135.1 percent. In the eighties, the Defense Department relinquished its hold on the net, opening it up and allowing other agencies and Internet service providers to establish access points for universities, commercial organizations, and other early adopters. In just about nine years, the number of sites grew from 235 to 313,000.

- 1991 to 1995—annual growth 88.2 percent. In the early nineties, growth "leveled off" at an annual rate of about 80 to 90 percent. Skeptics keep announcing that the rate just can't continue. There aren't enough human beings on the planet; there aren't that many computers; somehow, somewhere, someway, this growth has to stop.[2] Maybe it does, but they predicted that in 1992. And 1993. And 1994. But for now at least, year after year, the rate seems to keep running pretty steadily in that 80 to 90 percent range.

Want to see specifics? The Internet Domain Survey comes out every three months[3]—reporting the latest statistics on whatever Internet-connection statistics it can readily measure. They can't really count the total number of users or even the number of computers that are connected occasionally or indirectly to the net (such as those having email-only access through AOL or Compuserve). But they can count the number of *host* computers that are directly connected to the Internet (as well as networks and registered domains) and so they do. The table of Internet-Connected Hosts, Networks and Domains gives you historical raw numbers from the Internet surveys. Remember that in these statistics, a single host computer may have thousands or even millions of users.

Ever wonder where all these computers are located? What countries? What types of institutions? Hey, you want data? We got data. The table of Country Host Statistics shows we got *more than enough* to go around.

My very favorite charts of Internet growth are the ones that try to show

2 Don't believe 'em. We've got *plenty* of people—heck at this rate, the net won't even hit the billion mark until sometime during 2003. Of course, this rate *does* project that we'll pass the total number of human beings on the planet in the year 2006. Not feeling constrained by such analog-imposed limits, my calculator tells me that we'll still hit the 10 billion mark in 2007 and the 100 billion mark in 2010. We'll need a trillion superhighway Internauts by the year 2014 to keep this rate going. Computers to feed all those information-starved netters? No sweat—we can make as many chips as you need. "Eat all you want. We'll make more."

3 The Internet Domain Survey is run by Mark Lottor at Network Wizards. Every time the Survey results are released, the Internet Society—ISOC—uses them to compile and publicize Internet-related growth statistics. Therefore, if you're one of those people who look at the fine-print "source" citations on graphs and tables, you'll find that some will show ISOC as the source and others will show Network Wizards. Regardless of where the chart or graphic came from, the source is almost always the same: the Internet Domain Survey run by Mark Lottor.

Internet-Connected Hosts, Networks, and Domains

Date	Hosts	Networks	Domains
1969	4		
04/71	23		
06/74	62		
03/77	111		
08/81	213		
05/82	235		
08/83	562		
10/84	1,024		
10/85	1,961		
02/86	2,308		
11/86	5,089		
12/87	28,174		
07/88	33,000		
10/88	56,000		
01/89	80,000		
07/89	130,000		3,900
10/89	159,000		
10/90	313,000		9,300
01/91	376,000		
07/91	535,000		16,000
10/91	617,000		18,000
01/92	727,000		
04/92	890,000		20,000
07/92	992,000	6,569	16,300
10/92	1,136,000	7,505	18,100
01/93	1,313,000	8,258	21,000
04/93	1,486,000	9,722	22,000
07/93	1,776,000	13,767	26,000
10/93	2,056,000	16,533	28,000
01/94	2,217,000	20,539	30,000
07/94	3,212,000	25,210	46,000
10/94	3,864,000	37,022	56,000
01/95	4,852,000	39,410	71,000

Source: January 1995 Quarterly Internet Domain Survey, by Mark K. Lottor at Network Wizards. For more information on this survey or other information concerning their products and services, contact Network Wizards at PO Box 343, Menlo Park CA 94026, USA (415-326-2060), mailto:info@nw.com, or visit its home page at http://www.nw.com. (Data source: ftp://ftp.nw.com/zone/WWW/report.html.)

Country Host Statistics

Country	Domain	Hosts	Percent of Total
U.S.—Commercial	com	1,316,966	27%
U.S.—Educational	edu	1,133,502	23%
U.S.—Government	gov	209,345	4%
U.S.—Defense	mil	175,961	4%
U.S.—Non-Profit	org	154,578	3%
U.S.—Network Operator	net	150,299	3%
U.S.—Local	us	37,615	<1%
U.S. TOTAL		**3,178,266**	**66%**
United Kingdom	uk	241,191	5%
Germany	de	207,717	4%
Canada	ca	186,722	4%
Australia	au	161,166	3%
Japan	jp	96,632	2%
France	fr	93,041	2%
Netherlands	nl	89,227	2%
Sweden	se	77,594	2%
Finland	fi	71,372	1%
Switzerland	ch	51,512	1%
Norway	no	49,725	1%
New Zealand	nz	31,215	<1%
Italy	it	30,697	<1%
Austria	at	29,705	<1%
Spain	es	28,446	<1%
South Africa	za	27,040	<1%
Denmark	dk	25,935	<1%
Belgium	be	18,699	<1%
Korea	kr	18,049	<1%
Taiwan	tw	14,618	<1%
Israel	il	13,251	<1%
Hong Kong	hk	12,437	<1%
Czech Republic	cz	11,580	<1%
Poland	pl	11,477	<1%
Hungary	hu	8,506	<1%

Country Host Statistics

Country	Domain	Hosts	Percent of Total
Mexico	mx	6,656	<1%
Ireland	ie	6,219	<1%
Portugal	pt	5,999	<1%
Singapore	sg	5,252	<1%
Russian Fed.	su	4,963	<1%
Iceland	is	4,735	<1%
Greece	gr	4,000	<1%
Chile	cl	3,054	<1%
Turkey	tr	2,643	<1%
Russian Fed.	ru	1,849	<1%
Slovenia	si	1,773	<1%
Thailand	th	1,728	<1%
Malaysia	my	1,606	<1%
Slovakia	sk	1,414	<1%
Estonia	ee	1,396	<1%
Argentina	ar	1,262	<1%
Colombia	co	1,127	<1%
Croatia (Hrvatska)	hr	1,090	<1%
Int'l Organizations	int	904	<1%
Brazil	br	800	<1%
Costa Rica	cr	798	<1%
Luxembourg	lu	614	<1%
Latvia	lv	612	<1%
Romania	ro	597	<1%
Ukraine	ua	574	<1%
China	cn	569	<1%
Venezuela	ve	529	<1%
Bermuda	bm	474	<1%
India	in	359	<1%
Philippines	ph	334	<1%
Ecuador	ec	325	<1%
Kuwait	kw	220	<1%
Indonesia	id	177	<1%
Uruguay	uy	172	<1%
Peru	pe	171	<1%

Country Host Statistics

Country	Domain	Hosts	Percent of Total
Egypt	eg	161	<1%
Bulgaria	bg	144	<1%
Lithuania	lt	121	<1%
Cyprus	cy	88	<1%
Puerto Rico	pr	82	<1%
Jamaica	jm	76	<1%
Zambia	zm	69	<1%
Tunisia	tn	57	<1%
Nicaragua	ni	49	<1%
Liechtenstein	li	27	<1%
United Kingdom	gb	27	<1%
Armenia	am	19	<1%
Zimbabwe	zw	19	<1%
Iran	ir	18	<1%
Panama	pa	17	<1%
Macau	mo	12	<1%
Algeria	dz	10	<1%
Kazakhstan	kz	7	<1%
Fiji	fj	5	<1%
Antarctica	aq	4	<1%
Faroe Islands	fo	3	<1%
Greenland	gl	3	<1%
Moldova	md	3	<1%
Belarus	by	2	<1%
Guinea	gn	2	<1%
Saudi Arabia	sa	2	<1%
Azerbaijan	az	1	<1%
Non-US TOTAL		**1,673,577**	**34%**
TOTAL		**4,851,843**	

Source: January 1995 Quarterly Internet Domain Survey, by Mark K. Lottor at Network Wizards. For more information on this survey or other information concerning their products and services, contact Network Wizards at PO Box 343, Menlo Park CA 94026, USA (415-326-2060), mailto:info@nw.com, or visit its home page at http://www.nw.com. (Data source: ftp://ftp.nw.com/zone/WWW/dist-bynum.)

Internet Growth, 1969–95

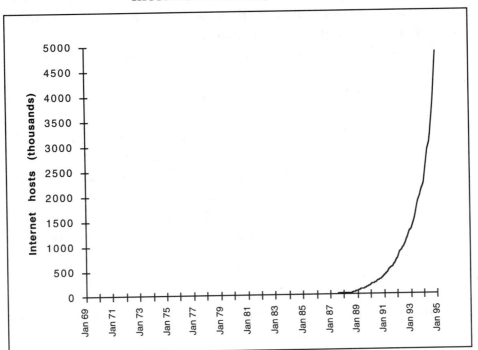

Source: January 1995 Quarterly Internet Domain Survey, by Mark K. Lottor at Network Wizards. For more information on this survey or other information concerning their products and services, contact Network Wizards at PO Box 343, Menlo Park CA 94026, USA (415-326-2060), mailto:info@nw.com, or visit its home page at http://www.nw.com. (Data source: ftp://ftp.nw.com/zone/WWW/report.html.)

growth on a regular scale of zero to however-many-million. No matter what time period you choose to make the chart cover, the only pieces of the chart that actually show anything are just the last few years. When we take the hosts count from the Internet Domain Survey and plot them on a chart (see the Internet Growth chart showing 1969–95), the first time the numbers even register on the scale is in the last year or two of the 1980s.

No matter what you do, no matter what time period you choose, the only numbers that even *show on the chart* are the most recent numbers. If you re-scale the chart to show just the growth through 1989, sure enough, the only numbers that register on the scale start in 1985. *Any* numeric series that keeps doubling like this will defy a straight-line scale to show a significant number of years. Of course, on a logarithmic scale you get to see all the data points, but that's not half as much fun.

Tools Too Big Fer Their Britches

Web? Gopher? WAIS? WAIS and gopher grew spectacularly, then the rate of growth trailed off. The World Wide Web has had the same kind of start, but it seems to be fueled by something a little different. I don't know what it is about the web growth, but it doesn't have the same feel as the gopher explosion.[4] Let's see if we can look at some poor estimates:

- Web growth? They say it's running at a rate of some 341,000 percent annually.[5]

- Gopher growth? Trailing off to a lousy growth rate of under 1,000 percent per year.

- WAIS? Sorry. It fell off the charts. Sure, it's still growing. But on this scale of measurements, mere double-digit growth rates barely register. And if you're flirting with single-digit growth, that's practically dead.

The problem with all of these estimates is that there is no way to count the number of network information retrieval (NIR) sites. We don't know how many sites there are now, and we don't know how many there were in the past.[6] The NIR sites are so easy to put up and take down that it's impossible to just go looking one day and try to find them all (although some of the insatiably curious have built network-crawling automatons that try to do just that). Also, there's no mandatory central registration. Therefore, virtually all of the counts of NIR sites are simply estimates—ostensibly conservative estimates based on the observations of developers and system administrators who preface each estimate with something like, "I'm sure I haven't counted all of them, but I have a list that includes *n* sites." That would suggest the estimates are low. On the other hand, a lot of the sites are empty shells—showing nothing but the phrase "under construction." And a lot of the counted sites just aren't there any more—empty URLs that have been dismantled after a failed Internet experiment, or after it was moved somewhere else. All of these arguments suggest the numbers are meaningless. Which is what they probably are. But, hey, that's why they're called *estimates*. Also, we're not doing anything serious with these numbers— we're just havin' a little fun.

Here's a chart based on the volume of traffic that passed

4 Seat of the pants statistics? A "feel" for growth? Hey—sometimes you've gotta gauge popularity and growth *not* by some attempt to count things that you can't really count, but by what you're seeing in the day-to-day activities on the net. I was there during the WAIS growth and I was there during the gopher growth. They were wildly popular, but nothing compared to what's going on with the web. Not at least in terms of discussion, questions, interest level, or desperation-by-new-users-who-want-to-get-involved. Call it seat of the pants or subjective. *I* think it's got a different feel.

5 At first, I thought this number was *just* a function of measuring from a too-early start date. For example, If Kellogg sells 100,000 boxes of Cap'n Draper cereal in its first year of introduction, it will have gone from sales of 1 to 100,000 in just one year—a tidy little ten million percent annual growth rate derived entirely by choosing a too-short time for measurement. But we've gone past the too-short-time-period start up and this thing is *still* growing at a ridiculous pace.

6 Except to the extent that before they were invented, the number was zero. Yup, we got ourselves a pretty good fix on *that starting point*.

WWW and Gopher Traffic Growth, Dec 92-Nov 94

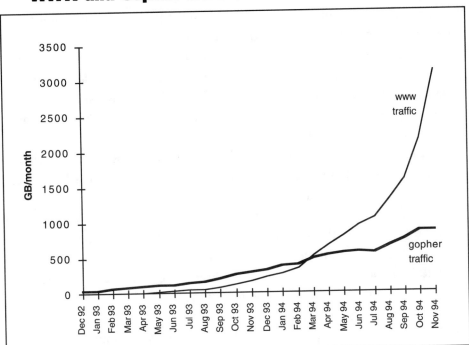

Source: November 1994 monthly NSFNET usage statistics, by Merit Network Information Center Services, a nonprofit consortium of state-supported universities in Michigan which provides backbone services for NSFNET in a cooperative agreement with the National Science Foundation. For more information about Merit Network and the NSFNET project, contact Merit/NSFNET Information Services, 2901 Hubbard, Pod G, Ann Arbor MI 48105, USA (313-936-3000), mailto:NSFNET-Info@merit.edu. (Data source: ftp://NIC.MERIT.EDU/nsfnet/statistics.)

over the NSF Internet backbone. (Since we don't have a good way to count what we want, we revert to counting the things we *can* count—then we try to figure out whether any of those numbers are interesting.) The NSF backbone traffic doesn't show the number of sites for each NIR service, but it should do a good job of showing the *relative* usage and growth of the different services. The actual statistic is how much data associated with each service—expressed as gigabytes, or billions of characters—passed over the NSF backbone each month. Of course, the NSF backbone is just one part of the net, so the actual volume of traffic would be much higher. Oh, and if you're looking for WAIS traffic, it's not there. On this scale of gigabytes per month, WAIS doesn't even register.

Gosh, that was almost a lot of fun. Is there anything even *marginally* useful we can get out of this chapter?

I don't know. Maybe a little bit of insight as to how this is happening, and why now? Well, let's give it a try.

Why Am I Just *Now* Hearing About <Fill in the Blank>?

Why are we just now hearing about the Internet? Why are we just now hearing about the web? And what was the deal with gopher?

One reason—obvious at first, but somehow not really believed by people who like to think they're trying to keep up with these technologies—is that these technologies are *really new*. Some of these things were *just invented*.**⁷**

Another reason is a little less obvious: The supporting technologies have just recently become ubiquitous.

- *Cheap Ethernet.* Back when network interface cards cost $2,000 each and Ethernet was still a fledgling technology, most Internet users had to use dumb terminals connected to large host computers. Now, of course, Ethernet cards are inexpensive enough to put in almost every office computer and by the end of the 1980s, a large number of corporate and university computers were equipped with Ethernet. Even though most office networks run Novell Netware over those Ethernet connections, it's now fairly easy to run the *Internet's* network protocol—TCP/IP—over that same Ethernet network.

- *Cheap hardware.* Of course, the falling price of PC equipment means that there are a lot more computers than there were ten years ago, a lot more computers connected to networks, and a lot more people who are potential Internet users. But another significant development that came with the falling price of hardware was the falling price of communications equipment. Specifically, the cost of routers and bridges—hardware that's used to connect networks together and a key element in developing high-speed links both internally and externally—came down *dramatically* during the early 1990s as well.

- *Cheap Connectivity.* When competition and deregulation hit the communications marketplace, the competition for those services that were perceived as business-oriented services intensified (especially when many of the very large businesses and federal agencies started building their own microwave systems and wide area networks). Eventually, costs for leased high-speed lines came down significantly. With the combination of cheap hardware and cheap communications costs, a lot of providers in the government sector especially found that establishing a full-time connection to the Internet was simply not a major undertaking.

- *Graphical software.* The World Wide Web started out as an interesting exercise in hypertext technolo-

⁷ The first time I saw the web, it was just a few months old. But there were already *hundreds* of web sites up and running—with scores of new sites being added every day. I felt that I was already behind the power curve, when in fact the power curve is so short and so steep that's it's tremendously easy to not-notice some key development. Stick around though. The big ones become obvious pretty quickly.

gy. But the initial text-only implementations required a careful attention to TAB keys and arrow keys, and [noticing] which [words or phrases] were surrounded by [brackets]. Frankly, the interface was just plain ugly. But as more and more machines became graphics-enabled—especially the Windows-based machines[8]—the technology simply cried out for a true graphical web browser. When NCSA brought out Mosaic, that user interface was there. It took a little while for the Internet "publishers" to catch on to the true impact that graphics has in this application, but as soon as they did, the content started showing up. And as I've mentioned about a thousand times before, it's the content that attracts the users. It took a while, but as soon as the graphics-based enabling technologies were in place (WWW, Windows, Mosaic), the explosion of interest was almost inevitable.

As the new content develops, as the new e-publishers reach out for new users and try to draw them with "entertaining" content, and as the would-be e-advertisers try to straddle line between sponsoring catalogs and sponsoring "cool sites," it's entirely feasible that these technologies will continue to grow. And that they'll continue to be replaced by something bigger, better, and faster.

And each time something new comes along, expect to be amazed by new capabilities that make you slap yourself on the forehead and say "You're kidding—it does *that??!*"

I don't know if that'll happen to you, but it happens to me a lot. I think *that's* why my hairline has moved so far away from my forehead.

8 Macintoshes and most of the high-end Unix boxes were already quite adept with graphics and point-and-click interfaces.

Reference Listing
LEGALLIST Excerpts

The Legal List

Law-Related Resources on the Internet and Elsewhere

by Erik J. Heels

info@justice.eliot.me.us

v5.1, 17 Sep 94
Copyright © 1994 Erik J. Heels
Earlier Versions Copyright © 1992, 1993, 1994 Erik J. Heels

With support from
The University of Maine School of Law and
Midnight Networks Inc.

Excerpted for *The Lawyer's Guide to the Internet*

Special Note (February, 1995)

Version 5.1 of Erik Heels' "The Legal List" (dated September 17, 1994) was the most recent version available at the press time for inclusion in "The Lawyer's Guide to the Internet." However, at that time, certain changes were being made that are especially relevant. Erik Heels explains the changes in the question-and-answer session below.

—G. Burgess Allison

First published in 1992—and now in its fifth edition—"The Legal List" is a consolidated guide to all of the law-related resources available on (and off) the Internet. "The Legal List" contains descriptions of law-related resources made available on the Internet (via e-mail, FTP, Telnet, Gopher, WWW, WAIS) and off the Internet (via BBSs and commercial online services) by government organizations, law schools, law firms, and corporations (for-profit, nonprofit, and not-for-profit). I have been self-publishing "The Legal List" since 1992. In the spring of 1995, "The Legal List" will be published exclusively by Lawyers Cooperative Publishing.

Q: Who is Lawyers Cooperative Publishing?

A: Lawyers Cooperative Publishing (LCP), a Thomson Professional Publishing company, is a leading provider of analytical and practice information to the legal profession, offering a cross-referenced system of state and federal statutes, cases, forms, and analysis. LCP's integrated legal library includes hundreds of products and services in both print and electronic form (including USCS, ALR, L.Ed., and Am.Jur.).

Q: Do you work for LCP?

A: Yes. As of January, 1995, I started working for LCP.

Q: Will "The Legal List" still be available "free" on the Internet? Via the listserv lists? Via FTP, Gopher, and WWW servers?

A: All electronic services, including the listserv lists (legal-list and TLL-announce), FTP, Gopher, and WWW servers, will soon be transitioned to LCP. You will still be able to get the ASCII text-only file for "free" via the legal-list listserv list or via Internet Servers (FTP, Gopher, and WWW). Soon, all e-mail from me will be from the domain "lcp.com" rather than the domain "justice.eliot.me.us," and all e-mail regarding "The Legal List" sent to the "justice.eliot.me.us" domain will be auto-forwarded to the "lcp.com" domain. Similarly, the primary Internet Servers for "The Legal List" will reside in the "lcp.com" domain.

Q: How can I get "The Legal List"?

A: See chapter 0.7—Getting and Redistributing "The Legal List"—below. For more information and a more complete list of Frequently Asked Questions, send a blank email message to info@justice.eliot.me.us. This FAQ will soon be updated with ordering information for the version to be published by LCP.

—Erik J. Heels

Summary of Contents

Chapter 0. Introduction to "The Legal List."

The purpose of "The Legal List" is to provide a consolidated list of all of the law-related resources available on the Internet and elsewhere. I have been "on the Internet" since 1984. I initially learned about the Internet by looking over the shoulders of my friends and coworkers (I believe that this is the way most people learn how to navigate the Internet), and then I began exploring the Internet for myself. I spent a great deal of 1992 exploring the Internet in search of law-related resources, and I was frustrated that a comprehensive list of such resources did not exist, so I created my own list. As I discussed what I had been doing with others, they began to request copies of my list. In August, 1992, I released the first version. I called this version "beta.4," because it was (and is) a work in progress. What started as a relatively short list for my own use has grown into the relatively large book you are now reading.

I am committed to providing high-quality information, and as such, I have tried to verify all of the information in "The Legal List." If I have not been able to verify a resource, I have indicated so. I also include resources that are no longer available, so that you need not waste your time responding to an announcement of a so-called "new" resource that has, in fact, been extinct for some time.

But providing high-quality information costs money. "The Legal List" receives no financial support from any organization. (Administrative support in the form of a gopher server [and its disk space] is provided by the University of Maine School of Law. Administrative support in the form of an anonymous FTP server [and its disk space] is provided by Midnight Networks, Inc.) I have invested my own time and money into "The Legal List." As the copyright notice indicates, "The Legal List" is free on the Internet, but it costs if you print it. I believe that this arrangement is consistent with the spirit of providing free information on the Internet, while at the same time allowing me to partially recover the costs of producing "The Legal List." In response to those who say that this arrangement makes those without Internet access subsidize those with such access, I can only say that 1) this arrangement encourages people to get on the Internet to get the free version, and 2) I cannot think of a better solution.

I believe that "The Legal List" is worth the price. It is comprehensive, frequently updated, and "subscribable." Users of "The Legal List" include individuals from courts (including the United States Supreme Court and the United States Court of Appeals for the 9th Circuit), approximately 70 universities (including 49 of the top 50 U.S. law schools), and 15 countries. But do not take my word for it, listen to what others have said (names have been used with permission):

"I cannot wait to explore *The Legal List* further."
 - *06/28/93*

"I am very new to the Internet (and to computers in general) but I am delighted by the quality of information I am receiving."
 - *06/29/93*

"Thanks for recently sending *The Legal List.* It is a marvelous service."
 - *07/02/93*

"*The Legal List* has saved me much searching to compile a list for introducing our academics to the wonders of the Internet."
 - *09/09/93, Janine Cairns, Liaison Law Librarian, University of Technology, Sydney, Australia*

"I have just received a copy of *The Legal List,* and I wanted to congratulate you on a fine piece of work. It is a great document and should be extremely useful to those of us trying to find our way around the legal side of Internet."
 - *09/07/93, Boston attorney*

"A quick note of praise on *The Legal List*. I think it is a great idea, and I have found it useful to get a feel for what is available online in the legal domain."
- *09/23/93*

"Thank you for your assistance, and for your work on this most worthwhile source."
- *01/05/94, Angus M. Gunn*

"I had the pleasure of reading *The Legal List* this morning. I am an attorney and am new to the Internet. *The Legal List* will prove to be a tremendous research tool for me."
- *01/06/94*

"I am one of the facilitators of NELANet, the online service operated by the National Employment Lawyers Association. We have just added the full text of *The Legal List* to our system. This will be an invaluable addition to the information we provide our members."
- *02/05/94, Barry Roseman, chair, computer committee, National Employment Lawyers Association*

"I have got to tell you, however, that I truly appreciate your hard work on *The Legal List*. I have used it to discover an entire new way to conduct research, and, in our profession, research that leads to publishing is critical! Thanks again for the help."
- *03/22/94, Laura B. Pincus, Assistant Professor of Legal Studies and Ethics, DePaul University, Kellstadt Graduate School of Business*

"*The Legal List* is fantastic! I never realized how much was available on the Internet."
- *04/06/94, Ann L. Kalb*

"I downloaded *The Legal List* from CompuServe's Lawsig data libraries 2 or 3 months ago, and I was VERY impressed."
- *04/11/94, Frederic M. Wilf, Elman Wilf & Fried (intellectual property and business law, including computer and biotechnology law), Media, PA, 72300.2061@compuserve.com*

"Thank you for having made our jobs so much easier by putting together *The Legal List*. I work for the *National Law Journal*. We are in the process of bringing up a new online service for the legal community that will, among other things, provide Internet access to lawyers. Your excellent work in assembling and maintaining *The Legal List* has been instrumental in our efforts."
- *05/12/94, Joseph Lamport, lamport@pipeline.com*

"Thanks for creating *The Legal List*. I just FTPed it from MIT and was amazed at your work. It is just great."
- *05/15/94, Richard Anderson*

"I was looking for legal materials and found your invaluable guide. Many thanks for all the work—it is so incredibly useful."
- *05/26/94, Susan Crysler, Librarian, McCarthy Tetrault, Vancouver, B.C. Canada, mccarthy@cyberstore.ca*

"*The Legal List* is all the rage on CompuServe."
- *06/04/94, Jeffrey A. Fuisz*

"*The Legal List* seems like the useful resource on the net I have been looking for (as distinct from the interesting ones)."
- *06/12/94, Ken Nielsen, Sydney, Australia*

"*The Legal List* is a great compilation of legal resources on the net."
- *06/23/94, Jeffrey Flax, National Systems Support Analyst, Office of the Federal Public Defender, Denver, CO, JFLAX@RMII.COM*

"I have just downloaded *The Legal List* and wanted to take a moment to thank you, and to compliment you, on your excellent work in organizing and presenting the material."
- *08/02/94, Dr. Dennis McConnell, Finance Professor, College of Business Administration, Unversity of Maine, MAC@MAINE.MAINE.EDU*

0.7. Getting and Redistributing "The Legal List."

0.7.1. Summary of How To Get "The Legal List."

Please read the following sections carefully. Please do NOT try to access "The Legal List" in a manner that is not described in the following sections. Please read the details below. The purpose of this summary is to describe, in chart format, how to get "The Legal List" and how NOT to get "The Legal List." If you read and follow the directions in the following sections, you will have no problems. This advice applies not only to "The Legal List" but to all of the resources it describes.

SITE	How is "The Legal List" accessible at this site?
ftp.midnight.com	FTP access ONLY. No e-mail, TELNET, or gopher access.
justice.eliot.me.us	E-mail access ONLY (by subscription). I No FTP, TELNET, or gopher access.
gopher.usmacs.maine.edu	Gopher access ONLY. No e-mail, FTP, or TELNET access.
rtfm.mit.edu	E-mail and FTP access. No TELNET or gopher access.

0.7.2. E-mail.

Due to the size of "The Legal List" (and to keep justice.eliot.me.us running as efficiently as possible), I only send the initial release of "The Legal List" via e-mail to those who have subscribed to "The Legal List" (see Section 0.7.2.1). I will NOT be able to send individual copies via e-mail after the initial release. However, you can still get a copy of "The Legal List" e-mailed to you by using FTPMail (see Section 0.7.3) or by using the mail-server at MIT (see Section 0.7.5).

0.7.2.1. Subscriptions.

Two subscription services are available.

1) Full-text delivery via e-mail plus announcements.

If you wish subscribe to "The Legal List," send a message in the following form:

       To: listserv@justice.eliot.me.us
       Body of message: subscribe legal-list "your name" (where "your name" is your real
                         name)

The next version of "The Legal List" (as well as other announcements) will be mailed to those who subscribe. I always like to hear where you learned about "The Legal List," so if you also include this information in the BODY of the message, I would greatly appreciate it! (This service is not a listserv list, but I am considering this option. That is why I have made the subscription method the same as for listserv lists.)

To cancel your subscription to "The Legal List," send a message in the following form:

       To: listserv@justice.eliot.me.us
       Body of message: unsubscribe legal-list

Please allow a day or two for a reply to messages sent to listserv@justice.eliot.me.us. (If you send multiple subscription requests, you will get multiple responses. However, duplicate addresses are removed before any messages are sent to "The Legal List" subscribers, so you should not receive multiple copies of any messages.)

URL: mailto::listserv@justice.eliot.me.us (Erik J. Heels)

2) Announcements only.

If you wish receive only announcements about the next version of "The Legal List," send a message in the following form:

    To: listserv@justice.eliot.me.us
    Body of message: subscribe TLL-announce "your name" (where "your name" is
                              your real name)

TLL-announce subscribes will receive all of the announcements that legal-list subscribers receive, but TLL-announce subscribers will not receive the next version of "The Legal List" via e-mail. I always like to hear where you learned about "The Legal List," so if you also include this information in the BODY of the message, I would greatly appreciate it! (This service is not a listserv list, but I am considering this option. That is why I have made the subscription method the same as for listserv lists.)

To cancel your subscription to TLL-announce, send a message in the following form:

    To: listserv@justice.eliot.me.us
    Body of message: unsubscribe TLL-announce

Please allow a day or two for a reply to messages sent to listserv@justice.eliot.me.us. (If you send multiple subscription requests, you will get multiple responses. However, duplicate addresses are removed before any messages are sent to "The Legal List" subscribers, so you should not receive multiple copies of any messages.)

URL: mailto::listserv@justice.eliot.me.us (Erik J. Heels)

0.7.2.2. Updates.

Updates, additions, and corrections to "The Legal List" should be sent to legal-list@justice.eliot.me.us.

URL: mailto::legal-list@justice.eliot.me.us (Erik J. Heels)

0.7.3. Anonymous FTP.

"The Legal List" is available via anonymous FTP:

URL: ftp://ftp.midnight.com/pub/LegalList/legallist.txt

You may connect to ftp.midnight.com by anonymous FTP ONLY. (Please do NOT TELNET to ftp.midnight.com.) Your FTP session should look something like the following:

```
220-Welcome, archive user! This is an experimental FTP server.
220-If you have any unusual problems, please report them via e-mail
220-to admin@midnight.com. Sessions are logged, if you don't like
220-it, don't use it. Have a nice day :-)
220-
220-If you do have problems, please try using a dash (-) as the first
220-character of your password—this will turn off the continuation
220-messages that may be confusing your ftp client.
220-
```

220-midnight FTP server (Version wu-2.1b(5) Mon Aug 2 18:12:50
220-EDT 1993) ready.

USER (identify yourself to the host): anonymous
331 Guest login ok, send your complete e-mail address as password.

Password:
>>>PASS ********
230 Guest login ok, access restrictions apply.

Command: cd /pub/LegalList
>>>CWD /pub/LegalList
250 CWD command successful.

Command: ls
>>>PORT 130,111,130,4,16,152
200 PORT command successful.
>>>NLST
150 Opening ASCII mode data connection for file list.
README
Whois_Midnight.txt
legallist.txt
226 Transfer complete.

Command: get README
>>>PORT 130,111,130,4,16,166
200 PORT command successful.
>>>RETR README
150 Opening ASCII mode data connection for README (34328 bytes).
226 Transfer complete.
35133 bytes transferred. Transfer rate 23.47 Kbytes/sec.

Command: get legallist.txt
>>>PORT 130,111,130,4,16,180
200 PORT command successful.
>>>RETR legallist.txt
150 Opening ASCII mode data connection for legallist.txt (165063 bytes).
226 Transfer complete.
170151 bytes transferred. Transfer rate 46.66 Kbytes/sec.

Command: get Whois_Midnight.txt
>>>PORT 130,111,130,4,16,188
200 PORT command successful.
>>>RETR Whois_Midnight.txt
150 Opening ASCII mode data connection for Whois_Midnight.txt (3737 bytes).
226 Transfer complete.
3828 bytes transferred. Transfer rate 6.82 Kbytes/sec.

Command: quit
>>>QUIT
221 Goodbye.

0.7.3.1. Internet Resource Guide - Directory of Directories.

"The Legal List" is one of many resources officially documented by the InterNIC Directory and Database Services maintained by the NSF Network Systems Center (NNSC) under a

contract with AT&T. The "Internet Resource Guide" (IRG) (formerly compiled and maintained by BBN, Inc., for the NNSC) has been moved to the "Directory of Directories" provided by the InterNIC Directory and Database Services. In previous versions of "The Legal List," I wrote "[t]he [IRG] is invaluable, and everyone with a serious interest in the Internet should maintain a copy. The NNSC's stated goal is 'to expose users to those facilities that will help them do their work better.' (Internet Resource Guide, Introduction, dated 16 Apr 90.) I wholeheartedly agree with this goal." Although the IRG in its 1990-form is being discontinued, the entries have been incorporated into the NNSC's new "Directory of Directories." The "Directory of Directories" should prove to be an invaluable resource.

For more information, contact:

> The InterNIC Directory and Database Services Administrator
> AT&T
> 5000 Hadley Road Room 1B13
> South Plainfield, NJ 07080
> Phone: 1-800-862-0677
> E-mail: admin@ds.internic.net

URL: mailto::admin@ds.internic.net (AT&T InterNIC Administrator)

0.7.4. Gopher.

"The Legal List" is available via gopher from the University Maine School of Law gopher site.

URL: gopher://gopher.usmacs.maine.edu/11e%3a/usm/law

0.7.4.1. Adding "The Legal List" to Your Gopher Site.

You are encouraged to add "The Legal List" to your Gopher site. If you choose to do so, please include the words "The Legal List" in the gopher menu. (See the title page for copyright restrictions.) In order to have your gopher site automatically updated, you can link it to the anonymous FTP site at ftp.midnight.com:

URL: ftp://ftp.midnight.com/pub/LegalList/legallist.txt

0.7.4.2. Other Gopher Sites.

"The Legal List" has been posted many gopher sites, including the following:

> URL: gopher://ftp.sunet.se
> URL: gopher://gopher.nic.ad.jp
> URL: gopher://infoserver.ciesin.org
> URL: gopher://is.internic.net
> URL: gopher://jupiter.willamette.edu
> URL: gopher://liberty.uc.wlu.edu
> URL: gopher://miles.library.arizona.edu
> URL: gopher://sluava.slu.edu
> URL: gopher://una.hh.lib.umich.edu

Do a Veronica search of "Legal List" to find other sites. (This is why it is important to include the words "The Legal List" when you add "The Legal List" to your gopher site.)

0.7.5. Usenet FAQ.

"The Legal List" is periodically posted as a FAQ (a file of Frequently Asked Questions) to misc.legal, misc.legal.computing, misc.answers, and news.answers. It is also available via anonymous FTP from rtfm.mit.edu in /pub/usenet/news.answers/law/net-resources/ as files part1-part3. To obtain a copy via e-mail from MIT, send a message to mail-server@rtfm.mit.edu with the following lines in it:

```
send usenet/news.answers/law/net-resources/part1
send usenet/news.answers/law/net-resources/part2
send usenet/news.answers/law/net-resources/part3
send usenet/news.answers/law/net-resources/part4
quit
```

URL: mailto::mail-server@rtfm.mit.edu (with the above text in the body of the message) (MIT's Usenet mail-server)

URL: ftp://rtfm.mit.edu/pub/usenet/news.answers/law/net-resources/part1
URL: ftp://rtfm.mit.edu/pub/usenet/news.answers/law/net-resources/part2
URL: ftp://rtfm.mit.edu/pub/usenet/news.answers/law/net-resources/part3
URL: ftp://rtfm.mit.edu/pub/usenet/news.answers/law/net-resources/part4

0.7.6. Elsewhere.

You are encouraged to add "The Legal List" to any other electronic storage or computer system. "The Legal List" has been posted to CompuServe, PeaceNet, and others. (See the title page for copyright restrictions.)

0.7.7. Paperback Copies.

Paperback copies of "The Legal List" are also available. The paperback copies are superior in quality to the text-only versions distributed on the Internet (e.g. multiple fonts are used). The price for each copy is $29.95. The shipping and handling for each copy is $3 U.S., $4 Canada or Mexico, and $10 for all other countries. To receive a hard copy of "The Legal List," please send a purchase order, or a check or money order payable to "Erik J. Heels," to:

Erik J. Heels
The Legal List
39 Main St.
Eliot, ME 03903-2234
USA

Orders may also be faxed to (207) 439-8647. Please allow four to six weeks for delivery via United States Postal Services mail.

Chapter 1. Corporations and Organizations.

This chapter describes law-related resources made available by for-profit, nonprofit, and not-for-profit corporations and organizations. An organization in this chapter would most likely have a domain name ending in ".com" (commercial) or ".org" (organization). Law firms are listed separately—sorted by the state (or country) of their main office.

One of the best ways to find the e-mail address for a particular individual is to call that individual. If you choose to contact the individuals listed below via e-mail, please keep your e-mail message short and to-the-point.

1.2.00. Other Organizations.

1.2.01. ABA Law Practice Management Section.

American Bar Association
Law Practice Management Section
750 North Lake Shore Drive
Chicago, IL 60611
E-mail: FITZGERALDR@ATTMAIL.COM (Robin Fitzgerald)
E-mail: STEWARTS@ATTMAIL.COM (Susan Stewart)

1.2.02. ABA Legal Technology Resource Center.

The ABA's Legal Technology Resource Center provides a number of services to ABA members and the legal profession dealing with how automation is applied in the practice of law.

For more information, contact the director of the Center:
E-mail: DHAMBOURGER@ATTMAIL.COM (David Hambourger)

1.2.03. ABA Science and Technology Section.

American Bar Association
Section of Science and Technology
750 North Lake Shore Drive
Chicago, IL 60611-4497

1.2.04. ABA Section of Intellectual Property Law.

American Bar Association
Section of Intellectual Property Law
750 North Lake Shore Drive
Chicago, IL 60611

1.2.05. Action for Blind People.

URL: gopher://able.afbp.org:70/1

1.2.06. American Civil Liberties Union, Free Reading Room.

URL: gopher://aclu.org:6601/1
The main menu looks something like the following:

About the ACLU Free Reading Room
The ACLU: The Voice of Liberty for 75 Years

Civil Liberties: Our Membership Newsletter
ACLU Newsroom
The ACLU Speaks: Op-eds, Speeches, Letters to the Editor (coming soon)
Publications and Reports
Legislative Alerts (still under construction—more coming soon)
The ACLU in Court: Supreme Court and Other Filings (coming soon)
Spotlight on Civil Liberties Issues (coming soon)
Seeking Help from the ACLU
Ordering ACLU Publications and Merchandise
Join the ACLU

1.2.07. American Political Science Association.

URL: gopher://APSA.TRENTON.EDU:70/1

1.2.08. ATLA BBS.

The Association of Trial Lawyers of America (ATLA). You must be an ATLA member to use this BBS.

BBS Phone: (202) 337-4509

1.2.09. Butterworth Legal Publishers.

Bibliographic and order information.

URL: gopher://gopher.infor.COM:4800/1

1.2.10. CALI - The Center for Computer-Assisted Legal Instruction.

URL: gopher://cali.law.umn.edu:70/1

1.2.11. Center for Computer-Aided Legal Instruction.

The Center for Computer-Aided Legal Instruction (CALI), a non-profit institute based at the Chicago-Kent College of Law, maintains a library of computer-aided legal instruction software. CALI was formed in 1982. For more information, contact:

Phone: (312) 906-5308

1.2.12. Center for Computer/Law, The.

The Center for Computer/Law holds an annual computer law writing competition. For more information, contact:

> The Center for Computer/Law
> PO Box 3549
> Manhattan Beach, CA 90266

1.2.13. Center for Study of Responsive Law.

Center for Study of Responsive Law
PO Box 19367
Washington, DC 20036

1.2.14. China News Digest.

URL: gopher://cnd.org:70/1

1.2.15. CIESIN Global Change Information Gateway.

The Consortium for International Earth Science Information Network (CIESIN). This contains a selection of international legal instruments and documents related to the 1992 United Nations Conference on the Environment and Development (UNCED).

URL: gopher://gopher.ciesin.org (select "exploring Human Dimensions of Global Change/ Policy&Political Systems" and "Environmental Internet Catalog/Law")

1.2.16. Clinton Watch.

URL: gopher://dolphin.gulf.net:3000/1

1.2.17. Coalition for Networked Information.

The Coalition for Networked Information, a joint project of the Association of Research Libraries, CAUSE, and EDUCOM, promotes the creation of and access to information resources in networked environments in order to enrich scholarship and to enhance intellectual productivity. To see a membership list, you can send the following message to listserv@cni.org:

get CNI-info CNIMembers

URL: mailto::listserv@cni.org (with the above line in the body of the message) (Coalition for Networked Information)

1.2.18. Committees of Correspondence (U.S. Socialist Organization).

URL: gopher://garnet.berkeley.edu:2000/1

1.2.19. Computer Professionals for Social Responsibility.

The mission of CPSR is to provide the public and policymakers with realistic assessments of the power, promise, and problems of information technology. As concerned citizens, CPSR members work to direct public attention to critical choices concerning the applications of information technology and how those choices affect society. Founded in 1981 by a group of computer scientists concerned about the use of computers in nuclear weapons systems, CPSR has grown into a national public-interest alliance of information technology professionals and other people.

For more information, contact:

Computer Professionals for Social Responsibility
PO Box 717
Palo Alto, CA 94301
E-mail: cpsr@cpsr.org

URL: mailto::cpsr@cpsr.org

CPSR also maintains a number of listserv lists that focus on various issues and projects. To find out what lists are available, send an e-mail message containing the message LIST to listserv@cpsr.org.

URL: mailto::listserv@cpsr.org (with "list" in the body of the message)

Gopher:

Internet Library.

URL: gopher://gopher.cpsr.org:70/1

1.2.20. Computer Systems Policy Project.

The Computer Systems Policy Project (CSPP) is an affiliation of Chief Executive Officers of American computer companies that develop, build, and market information processing systems and related software and services. CSPP was formed in 1988 to provide the CEOs of the industry with a forum to discuss, develop, and advocate public policy positions on trade and technology issues critical to the computer systems industry and county.

For more information, contact:

> The Computer Systems Policy Project
> 1735 New York Ave. NW, Suite 500
> Washington, DC 20006

1.2.21. Computers, Freedom, and Privacy Conference.

CFP-94 was held 3/22-25/94 in Chicago. CFP-93 was held in San Francisco. A Report on the Second Conference on Computers, Freedom, and Privacy (CFP-92), March 18-20, 1992, Washington, DC, sponsored by the Association for Computing Machinery, thirteen co-spo sors, and a wide variety of advocacy groups, is available via anonymous FTP:

URL: ftp://ftp.apple.com/alug/rights/cfp2

1.2.22. Congressional Human Rights Foundation.

Congressional Human Rights Foundation
1056 Thomas Jefferson Circle
Washington, DC 20007
E-mail: Steele@GDN.ORG (Jeff Steele)

1.2.23. Congressional Quarterly, Inc.

Congressional Quarterly, Inc.
1414 22nd St. NW
Washington, DC 20037
E-mail: fisher@CQALERT.COM (John Fischer)

Gopher:

URL: gopher://gopher.cqalert.com:70/1

1.2.24. Contraxx BBS, The.

Federal contracting and procurement issues.

BBS Phone: (703) 573-5255

For more information, contact:

> E-mail: stephen.walter@contraxx.com

URL: mailto::stephen.walter@contraxx.com

1.2.25. Copyright Clearance Center.

Copyright Clearance Center
222 Rosewood Dr.
Danvers, MA 01923
E-mail: wjohnson@CCC.ORG (Woody Johnson)

1.2.26. Counterpoint - Federal Register Index.

This company provides a daily index of entries in the *Federal Register;* to get the actual text, you must subscribe.

URL: gopher://gopher.counterpoint.com:2002

1.2.27. Crime Online.

Crime Online
36468 U.S. Hwy. 19 North
Palm Harbor, FL 34684

1.2.28. Dialog.

Dialog is accessible by TELNET from dialog.com.

URL: telnet://dialog.com

For more information, contact:

Dialog Information Services
3460 Hillview Avenue
PO Box 10010
Palo Alto, CA 94303-0993

1.2.29. Electronic Frontier Foundation - Archives.

The Electronic Frontier Foundation (EFF) was founded in July 1990 to ensure that the principles embodied in the Constitution and the Bill of Rights are protected as new communications technologies emerge. The archives of the EFF are available via anonymous FTP:

URL: ftp://ftp.eff.org/pub/EFF/legal-issues/Index
URL: ftp://ftp.eff.org/pub/EFF/eff.about

For more information, contact:

E-mail: ask@eff.org (The Electronic Frontier Foundation)

URL: mailto::ask@eff.org (The Electronic Frontier Foundation)

Gopher:

URL: gopher://gopher.eff.org:70/1

1.2.30. Electronic Newstand, The.

International law-related journals such as *International Legal Materials* and the *American Journal of International Law* are available at this site.

URL: gopher://gopher.Internet.com

1.2.31. FatherNet BBS.

The National Organization for Men Inc. This BBS includes conferences on New York practice, federal practice, child custody and visitation, child support, and civil rights.

BBS Phone: (718) 494-1719

For more information, contact:

Phone: (718) 494-2250

1.2.32. Federal Info. Exchange (FEDIX).

This gopher site is apparently under construction.

URL: gopher://fedix.fie.com:70/1

1.2.33. First Texas Lawyer's BBS.

Includes information about Paralegal Services International and Internet research.

BBS Phone: (512) 206-0802

For more information, contact:

> Valerie Atkinson
> PO Box 12763
> Austin, TX 78711
> E-mail: valerie@bga.com

URL: mailto::valerie@bga.com (Valerie Atkinson)

1.2.34. Frolic and Detour BBS.

The Frolic and Detour BBS is run by Electronic Law Publishing Company for the purpose of supporting the products it makes available to lawyers. Its principal product is an electronic practice support system known as RESPA Resolver, a series of computer programs designed to facilitate the production of the HUD1 A&B "Settlement Statement" and other related documents used in real estate transfers.

BBS Phone: (919) 893-5206

For more information, contact:

> Electronic Law Publishing Company
> PO Box 1119
> Buies Creek, NC 27506-1119

1.2.35. HandsNet.

Legal services and human services BBSs. A subsection, the Juvenile Justice Folder, is sponsored in part by the ABA and the National Association of Child Advocates.

E-mail: HN0009@handsnet.org (Jan Sola)
E-mail: HN3377@handsnet.org (Juvenile Justice Folder)

1.2.36. Illuminati Online, Steve Jackson Games.

The lawsuit involving Steve Jackson Games lead to the formation of the Electronic Frontier Foundation (EFF).

URL: gopher://io.com:70/1

1.2.37. Inforonics, Inc.

URL: gopher://gopher.infor.com/

The main menu looks something like the following:

> About the TitleBank Internet Catalog and Inforonics, Inc.
> American Chemical Society - Publications
> Butterworth Legal Publishers
> Co-operative Internet Catalog

E.J. Brill - Publications
Facts On File - Publications
Insurance Information Institute - Publications
MIT Press - Publications
Oceana - Publications

1.2.38. Inherent Technologies, Inc.

Inherent Technologies is a legal information systems technology company. Inherent provides custom software development (Windows-NT and NEXTSTEP), Internet consulting, and distributed network computing design for the legal profession. Inherent technical staff are formally trained in computer science and are also lawyers. They have a combined total of over 50 years' direct experience with the Internet and networking technology. Inherent may have been the first company to produce an electronic seminar for lawyers and legal professionals new to the Internet.

For more information, contact:

Gregory A. Miller, J.D., President/CEO
Inherent Technologies, Inc.
2130 SW Jefferson Street, Suite 300
Portland, OR 97201
E-mail: info@inherent.com
WWW: http://www.inherent.com

1.2.39. Institute for Global Communication.

URL: gopher://gopher.igc.apc.org/11/gov

The main menu looks something like the following:

U.S. Executive Branch: Agencies and Departments
U.S. Legislative Branch
U.S. Judiciary Branch (via Library of Congress)
Academic Servers with U.S. Government Information
United States Bureau of the Census
U.S. Government related information from NGOs
Political Parties
Gophers with California Legislative Information
List of U.S. Government Information on the Internet
American Political Science Association
State Governments on the Internet
National Telecommunications & Information Administration (telnet)
Voter Information Services (VIS)
Law

1.2.40. International Law Institute.

International Law Institute
1615 New Hampshire Ave., N.W.
Washington, DC 20009
E-mail: kerr@ILI.ORG (Stuart Kerr)

1.2.41. Internet Company, The.

URL: gopher://gopher.internet.com/

The main menu looks something like the following:

> Information about this Service
> The Internet Company
> Counterpoint Publishing
> The Electronic Newsstand(tm)
> The Nautical Bookshelf
> Dern's Internet Info, News and Views
> The Civic Network (civic.net)
> Information Resources of and about the Global Internet

1.2.42. InterNIC, Internet Network Information Center.

URL: gopher://rs.internic.net:70/1

1.2.43. Kentucky Capital Litigation Resource Center, The.

The Kentucky Capital Litigation Resource Center is engaged in the representation of persons sentenced to death in the State of Kentucky in their collateral appeals.

For more information, contact:

> The Kentucky Capital Litigation Resource Center
> Department of Public Advocay
> 100 Fair Oaks, Suite 301
> Frankfort, KY 40601
> E-mail: resource@advocate.pa.state.ky.us

URL: mailto::resource@advocate.pa.state.ky.us

1.2.44. Law Companies Group, Inc.

Law Companies Group, Inc.
1000 Abernathy Road, N.E.
Atlanta, GA 30328

1.2.45. Law & Economics Consulting Group, Inc.

Law & Economics Consulting Group, Inc.
2000 Powell Street, Suite 600
Emeryville, CA 94608
E-mail: Ken_K._Lim@LECG.COM (Ken K. Lim)

1.2.46. Law Manager, Inc.

Law Manager, Inc. writes software for law firms, corporate legal departments and government agencies. It has been in existence for 10 years and has been dedicated exclusively to serving the legal profession for the past 5 years. LMI has several products used by the legal profession collectively referred to as Law Manager 4.0. This is a modularized suite of applications centered around providing Case/Matter Management, Calender/Docketing Management, Litigation Support, Telephone Integration, and a Telephone/Address Book.

For more information, contact:

> Bill Swank, Controller/Project Manager
> Law Manager, Inc.
> 443 Germantown Pike, Suite 300
> Lafayette Hill, PA 19444
> E-mail: bill@lmi.com

1.2.47. Law MUG BBS.

Started in 1983 by Paul Bernstein, this may be the first lawyer-run BBS in the U.S. The goal of the BBS is to explore how this technology could be used by lawyers to serve the legal needs of the public.

BBS Phone: (312) 661-1740

For more information, contact:

Paul Bernstein
E-mail: 72466.3137@compuserve.com

URL: mailto::72466.3137@compuserve.com (Paul Bernstein, Esq.)

1.2.48. Law School Admission Services.

Law School Admission Services
661 Penn Street
Newtown, PA 18940
E-mail: JJaffee@LSAS.ORG (Janice Jaffee)

1.2.49. Lawyers' Committee for Civil Rights Under Law, The.

This free BBS includes opinions, briefs, complaints, and other information about civil-rights related issues. The Lawyers' Committee was formed in 1963 at the request of President Kennedy, which he made at the White House to about 200 leading members of the established bar. At that time, Governor Wallace was trying to block the integration of the University of Alabama, and the response was to try to uphold the rule of law by forming an organization to provide free legal representation to blacks in the South. The committee has since become national in scope, handling cases on behalf of women and Hispanics in addition to blacks and frequently working with established law firms in the representation of its clients.

BBS Phone: (202) 783-0854,0855,0856

For more information, contact:

Richard Seymour, Sysop
The Lawyers' Committee or Civil Rights Under Law
1450 G Street, N.W., Suite 400
Washington, DC 20005

1.2.50. Lawyers Cooperative Publishing.

Lawyers Cooperative Publishing
50 Broad St.
Rochester, NY 14694
E-mail: postmaster@LCP.COM

URL: mailto::postmaster@LCP.COM

1.2.51. Legal Advisor BBS, The.

Legal advice regarding credit, tax, and contract issues.

BBS Phone: (510) 685-1280

1.2.52. Legi-Slate.

Legi-Slate is an online service covering Congress and federal regulations. This prototype gopher site contains information about sample bills and resolutions from the current Congress and *Federal Register* documents from 1993.

URL: gopher://mudhoney.micro.umn.edu:7000/1

For more information, contact:

> Legi-Slate
> 777 North Capitol Street
> Washington, DC 20002
> E-mail: legislate@mudhoney.micro.umn.edu

URL: mailto::legislate@mudhoney.micro.umn.edu

1.2.53. LERN.

The LERN service is offered by the LEgal Research Network (LERN). It is intended to network attorneys with each other and with expert witnesses. LERN is primarily intended for attorneys engaged in product liability, personal injury, medical malpractice, property damage, and family law (although other fields, such as environmental law, are encouraged). Several database services are offered including a product literature database, a deposition exchange, OSHA standards, files of expert resumes, and a catalog of professional materials (such as audio tapes and books for professional development). LERN permits Internet e-mail and imports selected Usenet newsgroups and Internet mailing lists.

BBS Phone: (508) 829-9564

For more information, contact:

> The Legal Research Network
> PO Box 528
> Holden, MA 01562
> E-mail: System.Operator@lern.dmc.com
> E-mail: bill.dobson@lern.dmc.com

URL: mailto::System.Operator@lern.dmc.com (LERN BBS sysop)
URL: mailto::bill.dobson@lern.dmc.com (LERN BBS sysop)

1.2.54. Lexis/Nexis.

The LEXIS/NEXIS Communication Center is under construction. The Center will provide, via WWW, bulletins, newsletters, e-mail points of contact, and other information. LEXIS/NEXIS is also available via TELNET.

URL: http://www.meaddata.com

URL: mailto::webmaster@meaddata.com.

URL: telnet://lex.meaddata.com
URL: telnet://hermes.merit.edu (enter "lexis" at the "Which Host?" prompt)

For more information, contact:

> Mead Data Central
> PO Box 933
> Dayton, OH 45401
> E-mail: help@meaddata.com (customer service)
> E-mail: sales@meaddata.com (sales)

1.2.55. Libertarian BBS.

News and information regarding the Libertarian Party.

BBS Phone: (203) 257-1960

1.2.56. Master-McNeil, Inc.

Master-McNeil is a naming consulting firm, and they have made information on trade-marks at this site. Currently, the international trademark classes are available.

URL: http://www.naming.com/naming.html

URL: http://www.human.com/naming.html

For more information, contact:

> Master-McNeil, Inc.
> 2030 Addison Street, Suite 620
> Berkeley, CA 94704
> E-mail: info@naming.com

URL: mailto::info@naming.com

1.2.57. Mike's Online Tavern.

Among other things, this free BBS includes the Clinton economic and health plans.

BBS Phone: (203) 269-2135

1.2.58. National Association of Criminal Defense Lawyers (NACDL).

A criminal law BBS operated by E.X. Martin, a criminal defense lawyer practicing in Dallas, TX.

BBS Phone: (214) 340-8120

1.2.59. National Center for State Courts.

National Center for State Courts
300 Newport Avenue
Williamsburg, VA
E-mail: ehh@NCSC.DNI.US (Hank Heidt)

1.2.60. National Clearinghouse for Legal Services.

National Clearinghouse for Legal Services
205 West Monroe, 2nd Floor
Chicago, IL 60606-5013
E-mail: ncls@interaccess.com

1.2.61. National Employment Lawyers Association.

NELANet is the online service operated by the National Employment Lawyers Association (NELA). NELANet is operated through the IGC's LaborNet. NELA is an organization of some 1,800 members who represent plaintiffs in employment and labor matters.

For more information, contact:

National Employment Lawyers Association (NELA)
600 Harrison Street, Suite 535
San Francisco, CA 94107
E-mail: nelahq@igc.apc.org

1.2.62. National Public Telecomputing Network.

The National Public Telecomputing Network (NPTN) exists to make free public access to computerized communications and information services a reality, just as free books were made available to the by the public library system in previous generations. The NPTN is an Ohio nonprofit corporation, and has received 501(c)(3) tax-exempt status. While the NPTN has its origins at Case Western Reserve University (specifically, when Dr. Tom Grundner, then of CWRU's Department of Family Medicine, started the Cleveland Free-Net, first as a BBS and then as a larger Internet-based system), the two are separate entities. A basic guide to the NPTN is available via anonymous FTP:

URL: ftp://nptn.org/pub/nptn/nptn.info/basic.guide.txt

The following are some of the NPTN-sponsored freenets:

Computer Systems	Community	Modem Number
Big Sky Telegraph	Dillon, Montana	(406) 683-7680
Buffalo Free-Net	Buffalo, New York	(716) 645-6128
Cleveland Free-Net	Cleveland, Ohio	(216) 368-3888
COIN	Columbia, Missouri	(314) 884-7000
Denver Free-Net	Denver, Colorado	(303) 270-4865
Heartland Free-Net	Peoria, Illinois	(309) 674-1100
Lorain County Free-Net	Elyria, Ohio	(216) 366-9721
Medina County Free-Net	Medina, Ohio	(216) 723-6732
National Capital Free-Net	Ottawa, Canada	(613) 780-3733
Tallahassee Free-Net	Tallahassee, Florida	(904) 576-6330
Tristate Online	Cincinnati, Ohio	(513) 579-1990
Victoria Free-Net	Victoria, British Columbia, Canada	(604) 595-2300
Wellington Citynet	Wellington, New Zealand	64-4-801-3060
Youngstown Free-Net	Youngstown, Ohio	(216) 742-3072

For more information, contact:

National Public Telecomputing Network
PO Box 1987
Cleveland, OH 44106
E-mail: info@nptn.org

1.2.63. New York Law Publishing Company.

New York Law Publishing Company
345 Park Avenue South
New York, NY 10010
E-mail: finson@NLJ.COM (Larry Finson)

URL: mailto::finson@NLJ.COM (Larry Finson)

1.2.64. NOLO Press.

Self-help legal books and software.

NOLO Press
950 Parker St.
Berkeley, CA 94710
E-mail: nolonews@aol.com

URL: mailto::nolonews@aol.com

1.2.65. Paradigm Legal & Printing Technologies.

This free BBS is run by a company that provides legal software, hardware, and services.

BBS Phone: (516) 694-2318

1.2.66. Paralegal Services International.

This is a small information brokerage, translation, and paralegal referral business. Services include patent searching and research, online searches, and translation of legal and business correspondence, especially in relation to NAFTA-related enterprises (primarily Spanish to English with other language combinations available through referrals). The Firm also has a TELNET site for subscribers.

For more information, contact:

Valerie J. Atkinson
Paralegal Services International
PO Box 12763
Austin, TX 78711
Phone: (512) 452-4288
Fax: (512) 406-3915
BBS Phone: (512) 206-0802
E-mail: valerie@bga.com, valerie@spring.com

URL: telnet://spring.com (for subscribers only)

1.2.67. PeaceNet World News Service.

The PeaceNet World News service (PWN) is an e-mail news publication sponsored by the Institute for Global Change (ICG). Subscribers receive, each day, a single e-mail news digest with a table of contents and international stories. Subscribers choose from several issue- and region-oriented digests.

For more information, contact:

E-mail: PWN-info@igc.apc.org

URL: mailto::PWN-info@igc.apc.org (PeaceNet World News Service)

1.2.68. Pluto Press - Critical Law and Legal Studies Books.

URL: http://www.demon.co.uk/bookshop/

1.2.69. Republican BBS.

News and information regarding the Republican Party.

BBS Phone: (408) 247-3229

1.2.70. Safe 'n' Secure BBS.

For professionals in the fields of safety, law enforcement, emergency disaster management, and occupational health. This free BBS includes graphics files of missing children distributed by the National Center For Missing and Exploited Children Arlington, VA. Verification of professional status by telephone is required.

BBS Phone: (602) 870-6004

For more information, contact:

Wayne Church
Director of Safety and Security
John C. Lincoln Hospital
Phoenix, AZ

1.2.71. Smithsonian Institution, Natural History.

URL: gopher://nmnhgoph.si.edu:70/1

1.2.72. Society for the Advancement of Scandinavian Study, The.

URL: gopher://sass.byu.edu:70/1

1.2.73. Software Patent Institute.

Founded by Apple Computer, Inc., Digital Equipment Corp., IBM Corp., Industrial Technology Institute, Lotus Development Corp., Michigan Strategic Fund, Microsoft Corp., and the University of Michigan, the Software Patent Institute was formed to provide the US Patent and Trademark Office (and those who practice before it) with a database of software to be used as prior art for potential software patents.

For more information, contact:

Software Patent Institute
PO Box 1485
Ann Arbor, MI 48106-1485
E-mail: spi@iti.org

1.2.74. Software Publishers Association.

The Software Publishers Association (SPA) is a consortium of software manufacturers dedicated to eliminating illegal software copying. SPA offers a variety of educational and monitoring tools.

Software Publishers Association
1730 M St. N.W., Suite 700
Washington, DC 20036

1.2.75. Source Resources.

A company providing business, legal, and investigative information.

BBS Phone: (615) 537-6996 (log in as "new")

For more information, contact:

Source Resources
PO Box 88
Cookeville, TN 38503
E-mail: 73330.2734@compuserve.com

URL: mailto::73330.2734@compuserve.com

1.2.76. TogetherNet.

The Together Foundation, located in Burlington, VT, was incorporated in 1989 with the idea of fostering global unity and promoting world peace. Its main project has been the development of the TogetherNet, an on-line information and communication network for use by individuals and organizations working toward a sustainable future for the planet.

URL: gopher://gopher.together.uvm.edu/

For more information, contact:

> Together Foundation
> 130 South Willard Street
> Burlington, VT 05401

1.2.77. UNA-USA BBS.

United Nations Association.

BBS Phone: (910) 722-5164

1.2.78. UNitek Research BBS.

United Nations news.

BBS Phone: (201) 678-1367

1.2.79. University Microfilms International (UMI).

URL: gopher://gopher.umi.com:70/1U

1.2.80. Volunteers in Technical Assistance (VITA).

URL: gopher://lan.vita.org:70/1

1.2.81. Voorhees Reports - "Information Law Alert."

"Information Law Alert" began publishing as a print newsletter in May 1993 and in electronic form in January 1994. Is is published 20 times a year and covers court disputes, legal developments, and major regulatory battles that affect the development of the telecommunications and information technology. It focuses especially on wireless communications, intellectual property, and battles between the cable and telephone industries.

URL: gopher://marketplace.com/00/ila/

For more information, contact:

> Voorhees Reports
> 411 First Street
> Brooklyn, NY 11215-2507
> E-mail: markvoor@phantom.com

URL: mailto::markvoor@phantom.com

1.2.82. Voter Information Services (VIS).

URL: gopher://ftp.std.com:70/11/periodicals/voteinfo

1.2.83. West Publishing Company.

WestLaw.

WestLaw is available via TELNET.

URL: telnet://hermes.merit.edu (enter "westlaw" at the "Which Host?" prompt)

For more information, contact:

West Publishing Company
620 Opperman Drive
PO Box 64526
St. Paul, MN 55164-0526

West's Legal Directory.

West's Legal Directory (WLD) contains over 675,000 profiles of law firms, branch offices, and biographical records of attorneys from all fifty states, the District of Columbia, Puerto Rico, the Virgin Islands, and Guam. The WAIS database is available via TELNET and gopher:

URL: telnet://wais:wld@wld.westlaw.com
URL: gopher://wld.westlaw.com:70/1.dir/wld

1.2.84. Wiretap.

A great deal of international law documents (most in English) are available via the Wiretap gopher:

URL: gopher://wiretap.spies.com (under Government Docs.../World Constitutions)

The following are some of the available documents:

Australian documents
Basic Law of Germany, 1949
Basic Law of Hong Kong 1990
Canada Constitution Act, 1867
Canadian documents
Chinese Declaration of Human Rights 1992
Constitution of Italy (in Italian)
Constitution of Macedonia (in former Yugoslavia)
Constitution of Peru, in Spanish
Constitution of the Iroquois Nations
Constitution of the People's Republic of China 1982
Constitution of the Republic of Hungary
Constitution of the Slovak Republic 1991
Draft Constitution of Romania 1991
Draft Constitution of the Estonian Republic 1992
English Bill of Rights 1689
Hamas Covenant (Islamic Resistance) 1988
Hong Kong Bill of Rights Ordinance 1991
Maastricht Treaty
Magna Carta, John at Runnymede
NAFTA
NATO Press Releases
UN resolutions and treaties (selected)
United States Articles of Confederation 1781
United States Constitution 1789

Chapter 2. Government Organizations.

This chapter describes law-related resources made available by U.S. government organizations. An organization in this chapter would most likely have a domain name ending in ".gov" (government). This chapter is divided into four subsections: 1) U.S. Federal Executive Branch, 2) U.S. Federal Judicial Branch, 3) U.S. Federal Legislative Branch, and 4) U.S. State Government Organizations.

One of the best ways to find the e-mail address for a particular individual is to call that individual. If you choose to contact the individuals listed below via e-mail, please keep your e-mail message short and to the point.

2.0. Government Organizations.

2.1.00. U.S. Federal Government - Executive Branch.

2.1.01. Agency for International Development (USAID).
URL: gopher://gopher.info.usaid.gov:70/1

2.1.02. Department of Agriculture, Children Youth Family Education Research Network (CYFER-net).
A report on human rights practices of various nations is available from this site.

URL: gopher://cyfer.esusda.gov

2.1.03. Department of Commerce.
URL: gopher://GOPHER.ESA.DOC.GOV:70/1

2.1.04. Department of Commerce - Economic Conversion Information Exchange.
URL: gopher://ecix.doc.gov:70/1

2.1.05. Department of Commerce - Economics and Statistics Administration.
URL: gopher://gopher.stat-usa.gov:70/1

2.1.06. Department of Justice.
URL: gopher://gopher.usdoj.gov:70/1

2.1.07. Environmental Protection Agency - Future Studies.
URL: gopher://futures.wic.epa.gov:70/1

2.1.08. Environmental Protection Agency.
URL: gopher://gopher.epa.gov:70/1

2.1.09. Federal Communications Commission.
The FCC has been on the Internet since 02/15/94. The following is the directory structure of this site:

Daily_Business/
Daily_Digest/
Events/
News_Releases/
    Cable/
    Common_Carrier/
    Engineering_Technology/
    Mass_Media/
    Miscellaneous/
    Private_Radio/
Notices/
Orders/
    Cable/
    Common_Carrier/
    Engineering_Technology/
    Mass_Media/
    Miscellaneous/
    Private_Radio/
Panel_Discussions/
Public_Notices/
    Cable/
    Common_Carrier/
    Engineering_Technology/
    Mass_Media/
    Miscellaneous/
    Private_Radio/
Reports/
Speeches/

For more information, see the following:

    URL: ftp://ftp.fcc.gov/README

2.1.10. FedWorld.

FedWorld(TM) is a pilot project, set up by the National Technical Information Service (NTIS), that allows users to connect electronically to many Federal departments and agencies. From FedWorld, you can access more than 100 BBSs operated by the U.S. government including JAG-NET, OASH-BBS, Library of Congress News Service, and the National Criminal Justice Reference System. FedWorld is also available via TELNET:

URL: telnet://fedworld.gov
BBS Phone: (703) 321-8020

For more information, contact:

    Ken Royer, Systems Mgr & Developer
    Phone: (703) 487-4608
    or:
    Bob Bunge, Business Manager
    Phone: (703) 487-4648

2.1.11. Food and Drug Administration, National Center for Toxicological Research.

URL: gopher://gopher.nctr.fda.gov:70/1

2.1.12. National Archives.

URL: gopher://gopher.nara.gov:70/1

2.1.13. Occupational Safety & Health Administration.

URL: gopher://ginfo.cs.fit.edu:70/1

2.1.14. Patent and Trademark Office.

URL: http://www.uspto.gov

2.1.15. Securities and Exchange Commission - EDGAR Filings.

The Internet EDGAR Dissemination project is a research project to investigate how such large data archives can be made easily available to the general public. The Internet EDGAR Dissemination project allows you to receive any 1994 filings to the Securities and Exchange Commission (SEC) that are available to the public. The data in this project consists of electronic filings by corporations to the SEC. Not all corporations currently file electronically, but those that do participate in the EDGAR filing system. Because this is a research project, you should expect the data formats and access methods to change. The information is available via e-mail, FTP, gopher, and WWW:

URL: mailto::mail@town.hall.org (with "HELP" in the body of the message)
URL: ftp://ftp.town.hall.org
URL: gopher://gopher.town.hall.org
URL: http://www.town.hall.org

For, more information, see the following file:

URL: ftp://town.hall.org/edgar/general.txt

2.1.16. White House Publications.

For information on how to get White House publications via e-mail, send a message to Publications@WhiteHouse.GOV with "send info" in the body of the message.

URL: mailto::Publications@WhiteHouse.GOV (with "send info" in the body of the message)

White House Publications are available via anonymous FTP from numerous organizations, including the Computer Professionals for Social Responsibility.

URL: ftp://cpsr.org /cpsr/clinton/

2.1.17. White House, The.

The White House has several e-mail addresses including 75300.3115@compuserve.com, MCI Mail "White House," president@whitehouse.gov, and vice-president@whitehouse.gov. The ".gov" addresses were created in June 93 and appear to be the best. Also, a service based on the Clinton volunteer e-mail campaign still exists. For more information send a message to clinton-info@campaign92.org with "help" as the subject.

URL: mailto::75300.3115@compuserve.com (President Bill Clinton)
URL: mailto::president@whitehouse.gov (President Bill Clinton)
URL: mailto::vice-president@whitehouse.gov (Vice President Al Gore)
URL: mailto::clinton-info@campaign92.org (with "help" as the subject) (Bill Clinton campaign)

2.2.0. U.S. Federal Government - Judicial Branch.

2.2.1. Supreme Court Decisions - Project Hermes.

U.S. Supreme Court decisions are available online as part of "Project Hermes." On May 11th, 1990, the United States Supreme Court announced that it was beginning a two-year experimental program with the objective to rapidly provide copies of the Court's opinions in electronic form to as wide an audience as possible. One of the twelve participants is a noncommercial, nonprofit, consortium composed of Case Western Reserve University (CWRU), EDUCOM, and the National Public Telecomputing Network (NPTN). You can electronically receive the full text of the Court's opinions within minutes of their release—free.

The consortium grants permission to download, reproduce, or repost any of the Supreme Court opinion files PROVIDED NO CHANGES OR EDITING ARE MADE TO THE SUBJECT MATERIAL. The consortium would greatly appreciate it if source credit were given to CWRU, EDUCOM, and the National Public Telecomputing Network if these files are used.

The following are two of the anonymous FTP sites that maintain Supreme Court rulings:

URL: ftp://ftp.cwru.edu/hermes/
URL: ftp://ftp.uu.net/government/usa/supreme-court/Index

2.3.00. U.S. Federal Government - Legislative Branch.

2.3.01. Congressional Budget Office.

Congressional Budget Office
2nd & D Streets, S.W.
Ford Office Building #2, Room 486
Washington, DC 20515
E-mail: stacy.sdru@CBO.GOV (Stacy Newman)

URL: mailto::stacy.sdru@CBO.GOV (Stacy Newman)

2.3.02. Federal Bulletin Board, The.

The Federal Bulletin Board is a service of the U.S. Government Printing Office, Office of Electronic Information Dissemination Services (EIDS), Washington, D.C., 2040l. The BBS enables Federal agencies to provide the public immediate, self-service access to Federal information in electronic form at reasonable rates.

BBS Phone: (202) 512-1387

For more information, contact:

   Phone: (202) 512-1524

2.3.03. Government Printing Office.

In compliance with the Electronic Information Access Enhancement Act of 1993 (PL 103-40), the Government Printing Office has made the Federal Register, the *Congressional Record,* and other documents available (for a fee) via WAIS.

telnet://wais.access.gpo.gov (enter "wais" at the first prompt, "newuser" at the second)

For more information, contact:

   GPO Access Registration
   U.S. Government Printing Office
   PO Box 37082
   Washington DC 20013-7082
   E-mail: help@eids05.eids.gpo

URL: mailto::help@eids05.eids.gpo

2.3.04. Library Catalogs.

Many library catalogs are available online. These are described in detail in The Internet Resource Guide/Directory of Directories (see Section 0.7.3.1). Access to The Library of Congress Information System (LOCIS) is also described in The Internet Resource Guide/Directory of Directories. To access the system, TELNET to locis.loc.gov.

URL: telnet://locis.loc.gov

Data Research Associates, Inc., also maintains a database that contains all the cataloging records as distributed by the Library of Congress Cataloging Distribution Service (as part of their "Complete Service"), but this database is not the same as the Library of Congress Catalog.

URL: telnet://dra.com

2.3.05. Library of Congress.

URL: gopher://marvel.loc.gov:70/1

2.3.06 U.S. House of Representatives.

In June 1993, the House of Representatives' Committee on House Administration announced a pilot program called the Constituent Electronic Mail System. E-mail addresses are available for individual representatives and for House committees. So far, however, only a few representatives have signed up for e-mail.

The organizers of the pilot program kindly request that constituents send a letter or postcard (that includes the sender's name, address, and Internet e-mail address) by U.S. mail to their representative so that the representatives will be able to verify the incoming e-mail is from an actual constituent. The organizers also note that representatives may reply to e-mail messages via USPS mail.

For more information, contact:

   E-mail: congress@HR.house.gov

URL: mailto::congress@HR.house.gov (US House of Representatives)

Comments about the program can be e-mailed to:

   E-mail: COMMENTS@HR.HOUSE.GOV

URL: mailto::COMMENTS@HR.HOUSE.GOV

The following Representative are on the Internet:
[list omitted]

2.3.07. U.S. House of Representatives.

URL: gopher://gopher.house.gov:70/1

2.3.08. U.S. House of Representatives, 103rd Congress Phone and Fax Numbers.

From U.S. Congress Yellow Book, January 1993, with some updates and corrections as of March 1994.

```
p   st   representative                 phone            fax
=   ==   =====================          ==============   ==============
[list omitted]
```

Chapter 3. Educational Institutions.

This chapter describes law-related resources made available by U.S. educational institutions. An organization in this chapter would most likely have a domain name ending in ".edu" (education). This chapter is divided into two subsections: 1) U.S. law schools, 2) other U.S. educational institutions.

One of the best ways to find the e-mail address for a particular individual is to call that individual. If you choose to contact the individuals listed below via e-mail, please keep your e-mail message short and to-the-point.

3.1.00. Law Schools - Introduction.

ABA-approved U.S. and Puerto Rico law schools, with their Internet domain, are listed below. Non-ABA-approved law schools that are on the Internet are also listed. For schools that do not have an e-mail address listed, information should be available via e-mail at postmaster@domain.name, where "domain.name" is the domain shown below. For example, information about Samford University should be available via e-mail from postmaster@samford.edu. Some schools have made information available via a generic e-mail address, usually in the form of info@law.domain.name, which is set up to automatically reply to e-mail messages. I believe that the use of this type of "info" e-mail address combined with a "law" subdomain is a good idea, one that I hope to see catch on as a *de facto* standard.

Gopher main menus and submenus are shown for some of the more well-known law school gopher sites. Note how the following law schools have addressed some of the issues facing gopher administrators in trying to make their gopher sites easily accessible and user friendly: Case Western Reserve University (see Section 3.1.35.02) distinguishes, in part, between those resources that are hosted locally (for which it is primarily responsible) and links to resources hosted remotely (for which it is not primarily responsible). Cornell University (see Section 3.1.32.04) provides a means for giving feedback to the gopher administrators and groups its resources into several categories, including U.S. primary law, non-U.S. law, and U.S. administrative information. Temple University (see Section 3.1.38.03) provides date and file size information for its resources. Villanova University (see Section 3.1.38.06) has perhaps the most readable main menu, provides a means for giving feedback to the gopher administrators and groups its resources into several categories, including U.S. state government information, U.S. federal government information, and European/Canadian government information. Note also how some gopher sites (e.g. Chicago-Kent College of Law, see Section 3.1.13.02) are accessible as top-level sites at the University of Minnesota (and hence are easier to locate) while others are several submenus lower in the hierarchy.

3.1.13.00 Illinois.

3.1.13.02. Illinois Institute of Technology, Chicago-Kent College of Law.

Illinois Institute of Technology
Chicago-Kent College of Law
565 West Adams St.
Chicago, IL 60661-3691
Domain: mail.kentlaw.edu
E-mail: info@chicagokent.kentlaw.edu

Faculty and students all have e-mail addresses in the form of username@mail.kentlaw.edu, where "username" consists of someone's first initial followed by the first 7 characters of their last name.

Gopher:

URL: gopher://chicagokent.kentlaw.edu/1

The main menu looks something like the following:

> About The Chicago-Kent Gopher
> IIT Administrative Gopher
> IIT Student Gopher
> CALI - The Center for Computer-Assisted Legal Instruction
> Chicago-Kent Services and Information
> Access to Human Rights Decisions - A Chicago-Kent Special Project
> Internet Help and Information
> Internet Services
> Search all menus on this gopher
> WHAT'S NEW ON THIS GOPHER SERVER!

The Legal Domain Network.

Access to Usenet articles from the following Usenet newsgroups:

> law - The Exclusive Law Domain Network in USENET
> bit.listserv - Substantive law-related discussions on BITNET
> alt.dear.whitehouse - Discussions and letters to the White House
> alt.freedom.of.information.act - FOIA Discussions
> alt.motherjones - Mother Jones magazine
> alt.politics - Political discussions
> comp.org.eff - The Electronic Frontier Foundation
> misc.activism.progressive - Information for Progressive activists
> (Moderated)
> misc.int-property - Discussion of intellectual property rights
> misc.legal - Substantive law-related discussions on Usenet
> misc.taxes - Tax laws and advice
> talk - Various political and activist discussions

URL: http://www.kentlaw.edu/lawnet/lawnet.html

For more information, contact:

> E-mail: webmaster@chicagokent.kentlaw.edu

URL: mailto::webmaster@chicagokent.kentlaw.edu

3.1.14.00. Indiana.

3.1.14.01. Indiana University, Bloomington.

Indiana University, Bloomington
School of Law
Law Building Rm. 203
Bloomington, IN 47405-1001
Domain: indiana.edu, law.indiana.edu

Gopher:

The Federal Communications Law Journal, published jointly by the Indiana University School of Law, Bloomington, and the Federal Communications Bar Association is available from this site.

URL: http://www.law.indiana.edu:80/fclj/fclj.html

URL: telnet://www@www.law.indiana.edu
WWW:

Information available at this site includes the *Global Legal Studies Journal,* the *Federal Communications Law Journal,* environmental law information, and "LawTalk" (radio broadcasts containing general legal information).

URL: http://www.law.indiana.edu:80

URL: telnet://www@www.law.indiana.edu

For more information, contact:

Will Sadler
IU School of Law, Bloomington
E-mail: will@polecat.law.indiana.edu

URL: mailto::will@polecat.law.indiana.edu (Will Sadler)

3.1.16.00. Kansas.

3.1.16.02. Washburn University.

Washburn University
School of Law
17th and MacVicar
Topeka, KS 66621
Domain: wuacc.edu
E-mail: zzchri@acc.wuacc.edu (John Christensen)
Telnet:

AALNet.

AALNet is the American Association of Law Libraries Information System. AALNet uses the Lynx program (copyright 1993 University of Kansas, Lou Montulli, montulli@ukanaix .cc.ukans.edu).

URL: telnet://lawnet@acc.wuacc.edu

For more information, contact:

E-mail: zzfolm@acc.wuacc.edu (Mark Folmsbee)

URL: mailto::zzfolm@acc.wuacc.edu (Mark Folmsbee)

WashLaw.

WashLaw is Washington University's general law-related information system.

URL: telnet://washlaw@acc.wuacc.edu

The main menu will look something like the following:

[1]Catalog (Washburn Law Library and Mabee Library)
[2]About Washlaw/What's new?
[3]About Washburn Law Library

[4]About Washburn University School of Law
[5]Directories-Email/Phone (national and local)
[6]Law Systems (Gophers/Hytelnet/WWW/WAIS/Freenet/Usenet/FTP Sites)
[7]Campus and Other Information Systems (National and Local)
[8]Other Law Library Catalogs
[9]LEXIS/NEXIS Communication Center- Beware, Construction in Progress
[10]Clinical Legal Education Information System (AALS)
[11]Holocaust Information System
[12]Legal Writing and Research Info Sys (TULSA)
[13]Oil and Gas Law Information System
[14]Telejurist
[15]Information Network of Kansas (INK)-Password Needed
[16]The "Virtual" Law Reference Desk
[17]Foreign Law and United Nations Materials
[18]U.S. Law
[19]Federal Government Information
[20]Law Library Related Files that may be sent to you by Email

For more information, contact:

E-mail: zzfolm@acc.wuacc.edu (Mark Folmsbee)

URL: mailto::zzfolm@acc.wuacc.edu (Mark Folmsbee)

3.1.19.00. Maine.

3.1.19.01. University of Maine.

University of Maine
School of Law
246 Deering Ave.
Portland, ME 04102
Domain: maine.edu
E-mail: USMLAW@maine.maine.edu

Gopher:

One of the original homes of "The Legal List."

URL: gopher://gopher.usmacs.maine.edu/11e%3a/usm/law

WWW:

URL: http://bettyj.caps.maine.edu

For more information, contact:

E-mail: bettyj@maine.maine.edu

URL: mailto::bettyj@maine.maine.edu

3.1.25.00. Missouri.

3.1.25.01. Saint Louis University.

Saint Louis University
School of Law
3700 Lindell Blvd.
St. Louis, MO 63108

Domain: slu.edu
E-mail: millesjg@sluvca.slu.edu (Jim Milles, Law Library)

Gopher:

The listing under "Law-Related Gophers and Information Servers" is one of the most comprehensive.

URL: gopher://sluava.slu.edu/11gopher$root%3a%5bdata21._library_services._lawlib%5d

The main menu looks something like the following:

> About This Gopher
> SLU Law Library Info
> SLU Law School Info
> MAALL (Mid-America Association of Law Libraries) Info
> Law-Related Gophers and Information Servers
> Health Law Resources
> Human Rights and International Law Resources
> Other Specialized Gophers and Information Servers
> Discussion Lists: Information and Archives
> Electronic Texts
> Internet Training and Access Info
> Library Catalogs
> Library of Congress
> Other Useful Resources
> Wide Area Information Server (WAIS)
> World-Wide Web (WWW)
> Fun stuff

WWW:

URL: http://lawlib.slu.edu/home.htm

For more information, contact:

> Jim Milles
> Head of Computer Services
> Saint Louis University Law Library
> E-mail: millesjg@sluvca.slu.edu

URL: mailto::millesjg@sluvca.slu.edu

3.1.32.00. New York.

3.1.32.04. Cornell University.

Cornell University
Law School
Myron Taylor Hall
Ithaca, NY 14853
Domain: cornell.edu
E-mail: trb2@cornell.edu (Tom Bruce)

Telnet:

Most portions of the current copyright law have been made available by Cornell University. It also includes access to the Berne Convention. The following will allow you to use the World Wide-Web software to navigate the copyright law.

URL: telnet://www@fatty.law.cornell.edu:8210

Gopher:

Cornell Law School, through its wholly owned subsidiary the Legal Information Institute, operates a gopher server on fatty.law.cornell.edu (port 70). It is focused largely on legal information. Teknoids is archived there in searchable form, and LAW-LIB soon will be. If you do not have a gopher client, you can TELNET to fatty and log in as "gopher"; you will be placed in the UNIX gopher client.

URL: gopher://fatty.law.cornell.edu:70

URL: telnet://gopher@fatty.law.cornell.edu

The main menu looks something like the following:

    Cornell Law School Information
    Directory of Legal Academia
    Discussions and Listserv Archives
    U.S. Law: Primary Documents and Commentary
    Foreign and International Law: Primary Documents and Commentary
    Other References Useful in Legal Education and Research
    Government (U.S.) and Agency Information
    Information Services: Academic Institutions
    Library Resources (online catalogs)
    Periodicals, News, and Journals
    Other Gophers and Information Services
    WAIS-based information
    Internet (FTP sources, Archie, listserv directory)
    Locators (where to find people and things)
    Miscellaneous
    Other Internet Law Sites
    +---+ Please give us feedback! +---+

The Directory of Legal Academia is accessible via gopher (main menu), TELNET, and electronic mail. To use the TELNET version, telnet to fatty.law.cornell.edu and login as "lookup". Simple instructions are provided on the opening screen.

URL: telnet://lookup@fatty.law.cornell.edu

To use the mail version, send mail to lookup@fatty.law.cornell.edu. Somewhere in the body of the mail message, you may place one or more queries in one of two forms:

    query name=Somebody
    query department=Somewhere

The "query name" form looks up someone by name; the "query department" form looks up someone by location, e.g.:

    query name=Bruce

returns five entries, including Thomas Bruce and Bruce Kennedy.

    query department=Harvard

returns entries for all personnel at the Harvard Law School. There are about 1,000 names of legal academics and law librarians currently in the database; Cornell is looking for more.

URL: mailto::lookup@fatty.law.cornell.edu (with the text as illustrated above in the text of the message) (Legal Information Institute at Cornell Law School, Directory of Legal Academia)

To add or change information, send appropriate mail to change-request@fatty.law .cornell.edu.

URL: mailto::change-request@fatty.law.cornell.edu (Legal Information Institute at Cornell Law School, Directory of Legal Academia)

For more information, contact:

E-mail: tom@law.mail.cornell.edu

URL: mailto::tom@law.mail.cornell.edu (Thomas R. Bruce)WWW:

This WWW server integrates both the gopher-based and the WWW-based offerings of the Legal Information Institute (LII), Cornell Law School. All Internet hypertext publications of the LII are available, with links to other relevant legal materials on the LII's gopher server and elsewhere on the Internet. This server offers the LII's hypertext front-end to recent Supreme Court decisions (which are distributed on the day of decision under Project Hermes) and the LII's e-mail address directory of faculty and staff of U.S. law schools. It is also host to the *NASDAQ Financial Executive Journal.* Also included is information about Cello.

URL: http://www.law.cornell.edu

3.1.32.04.1. Legal Information Institute - E-bulletin.

The Legal Information Institute (LII) at Cornell Law School provides an e-mail bulletin and an e-mail full-text delivery service of U.S. Supreme Court Decisions. E-mail bulletin subscribers will receive the syllabi of decisions of the Supreme Court as they are placed on the Internet. To subscribe to the e-mail bulletin, send the following message (all on one line) to listserv@fatty.law.cornell.edu:

subscribe liibulletin name, address, telephone number

URL: mailto::listserv@fatty.law.cornell.edu (with the above text in the body of the message) (Legal Information Institute at Cornell Law School, Supreme Court opinion syllabi delivery via e-mail)

To have the full text of a decision e-mailed to you, send the following message to liideliver@fatty.law.cornell.edu:

request docket number

URL: mailto::liideliver@fatty.law.cornell.edu (with the above text in the body of the message) (Legal Information Institute at Cornell Law School, Supreme Court full text opinion delivery via e-mail)

where docket number is the docket number of the case you want sent ("request 91-611" is the proper format for a request). You can request several decisions at once by putting the docket numbers on separate lines.

Full-text decisions are also available via anonymous FTP:

URL: ftp://ftp.cwru.edu/U.S.Supreme.Court/

via LII's gopher server:

URL: gopher://gopher.law.cornell.edu

or via LII's WWW server:

URL: http://www.law.cornell.edu

To access the gopher server via TELNET, telnet to gopher.law.cornell.edu and log in as gopher.

URL: telnet://gopher@gopher.law.cornell.edu

To access the WWW server via Telnet, Telnet to www.law.cornell.edu and log in as www.

URL: telnet://www@www.law.cornell.edu

3.1.35.00. Ohio.

3.1.35.02. Case Western Reserve University.

Case Western Reserve University
School of Law
11075 East Boulevard
Cleveland, OH 44106
Domain: cwru.edu

FTP:

Ohio Court Decisions.

URL: ftp://ftp.cwru.edu/OH.Appeals.8th.dist/

Gopher:

URL: gopher://holmes.law.cwru.edu/1

The main menu looks something like the following:

> Welcome to the CWRU Law Gopher
> Basic help on the Internet
> Case Western Reserve University Law School Information
> Case Western Reserve University Law Library Information
> Law Services on the Internet
> Law and Medicine References (UNDER CONSTRUCTION)
> Legal Documents at Case Western Reserve University
> Legal Documents on the Internet
> Internet Law Related Libraries
> Other Law School Gophers
> Women and The Law (UNDER CONSTRUCTION)

3.1.38.00. Pennsylvania.

3.1.38.03. Temple University.

Temple University
School of Law
1719 North Broad St.
Philadelphia, PA 19122
Domain: temple.edu
Gopher:

URL: gopher://astro.ocis.temple.edu/11/Temple%20Law%20School%20Gopher

The main menu looks something like the following:

> About Temple Law Gopher [16Jul93, 1kb]
> Temple Law School Information
> Important Law School Phone Numbers [16Jul93, 1kb]
> Area Libraries
> Other Gophers

Other Law School Gophers
Court Futures Studies
Faculty
Gophers by Subject
Internet Resources
Miscellanea
Search Gopherspace using Veronica

3.1.38.06. Villanova University.

Villanova University
School of Law
Garey Hall
Villanova, PA 19085
Domain: vill.edu
Gopher:

The Villanova Center for Information Law and Policy, with support from the National Center for Automated Information Research (NCAIR), administers this site. The server has information likely to be of interest to practicing lawyers and accountants and to law professors and law students, including papers on tax law and policy issues written by graduate students in taxation at various institutions, papers on legal utomation and computer law written by JD candidates at Villanova, articles on legal automation and computer law written by law faculty at Villanova and elsewhere, full text material on labor and employment law, including the Americans With Disabilities Act, with additions planned in the labor and employment, and tax areas.

URL: gopher://ming.law.vill.edu/11

This gopher site is one of the most well organized for law-related information. The main menu looks something like the following:

About this Gopher Server
Villanova University School of Law - Information Directory
National Center for Automated Information Research (NCAIR)
The Villanova Information Law Chronicle
The Villanova Tax Law Compendium
Information Law Papers
Phone books
- - - AVAILABLE LEGAL INFORMATION - - - - - - - - - -
State Government Information
Federal Government Information
European/Canadian Government Information
- - - AVAILABLE SERVICES - - - - - - - - - - - - - -
INTERNET - Server Services (Gopher, WAIS, World-Wide Web)
FTP - File Transfer Protocol sites
LISTSERV - Mailing Lists Archive Directories
- - - OTHER SERVICES - - - - - - - - - - - - - - - -
Internet Questionnaire for Law Firms
~~~~Feedback on Villanova Law School Gopher~~~~~

For more information, contact:

Henry H. Perritt, Jr.
Professor of Law
Villanova Law School
E-mail: perritt@ucis.vill.edu

URL: mailto::perritt@ucis.vill.edu (Prof. Henry H. Perritt, Jr.)

See also "The Legal Domain Network" listed under the Illinois Institute of Technology, Chicago-Kent College of Law..

3.1.47.00. Virginia.

3.1.47.06. Washington and Lee University.
Washington and Lee University
School of Law
Lewis Hall
Lexington, VA 24450
Domain: wlu.edu, fs.law.wlu.edu

Telnet:

There is a great deal of law-related information available at this gopher site:

URL: telnet://lawlib@liberty.uc.wlu.edu

Gopher:

The Washington & Lee archives are also accessible via Gopher.

URL: gopher://liberty.uc.wlu.edu/1

3.2.00. Other Educational Institutions.

3.2.01. Carnegie-Mellon University - EnviroGopher.
URL: gopher://envirolink.hss.cmu.edu:70/1

3.2.02. Texas A&M University.
URL: gopher://gopher.tamu.edu/11/.dir/law.dir

3.2.03. Tufts University - Multilaterals Project.
The Multilaterals Project is an experimental program begun at the Fletcher School of Law and Diplomacy in Medford, MA, to make available to the Internet community the text of a wide variety of multilateral conventions. The conventions are available via anonymous FTP and WWW.

URL: ftp://ftp.fletcher.tufts.edu/pub/diplomacy/ (The home location for these materials.)

URL: ftp://ftp.fletcher.tufts.edu/pub/diplomacy/A.INDEX (New users should consult this file.)

URL: ftp://ftp.fletcher.tufts.edu/pub/diplomacy/A.README (New users should consult this file.)

URL: ftp://ftp.fletcher.tufts.edu/pub/diplomacy/new/ (Copies of the most recent postings are placed here for a short time.)

URL: ftp://ftp.fletcher.tufts.edu/pub/diplomacy/historical/ (A small number of older documents.)

URL: http://www.tufts.edu/departments/fletcher/multilaterals.html

For more information, contact:

Peter Stott, Director
Multilaterals Project
Fletcher School of Law & Diplomacy
E-mail: pstott@emerald.tufts.edu

URL: mailto::pstott@emerald.tufts.edu (Peter Stott)

3.2.04. University of California, Davis.

This experimental server was created in conjunction with an undergraduate class in international environmental law

URL: http://www.ucdavis.edu (under Spring Quarter 1994 Class Home Pages/Pointers to Spring 1994 Class Home Pages/Political Science 122—International Law)

For more information, contact:

krweiss@ucdavis.edu (Ken Weiss)
safaith@ucdavis.edu (Steve Faith)

3.2.05. University of California, Irvine - U.S. Government Gophers.

This site maintains one of the most comprehensive listings of U.S. government gopher sites.

URL: gopher://peg.cwis.uci.edu:7000/11/gopher.welcome/peg/GOPHERS/gov

This menu looks something like the following:

Call for assistance...
POLITICS and GOVERNMENT
What's new in the listing?
Definition of a "United States Government Gopher"
Federal Government Information (via Library of Congress)
AVES: Bird Related Information
Americans Communicating Electronically
Arkansas-Red River Forecast Center (NOAA)
AskERIC - (Educational Resources Information Center)
CYFERNet USDA Children Youth Family Education Research Network
Catalog of Federal Domestic Assistance
Co-operative Human Linkage Center (CHLC) Gopher
Comprehensive Epidemiological Data Resource (CEDR) Gopher
Consumer Product Safety Commission Gopher
Defense Nuclear Facilities Safety Board
Defense Technical Information Center Public Gopher
ERIC Clearinghouse for Science, Math, Environmental (OSU)
ERIC Clearinghouse on Assessment and Evaluation
ERIC Clearinghouses (via Syracuse)
ESnet Information Services Gopher
Electronic Government Information Service
Environment, Safety & Health (USDE) Gopher
Environmental Protection Agency
Environmental Protection Agency Futures Group
Environmental Protection Agency Great Lakes National Program Office
Gopher
Extension Service, USDA

FedWorld (NTIS) - 100+ electronic government bulletin boards
Federal Communications Commission Gopher
Federal Deposit Insurance Corporation Gopher (via SURA.net)
Federal Info Exchange (FEDIX)
Federal Networking Council Advisory Committee
Federal Register - Sample access
Federal Reserve Board (via town.hall.org)
FinanceNet (National Performance Review)
GrainGenes (USDA) Gopher
Information Infrastructure Task Force (DoC) Gopher
InterNIC: Internet Network Information Center Gopher
LANL Advanced Computing Laboratory
LANL Gopher Gateway
LANL Nonlinear Science Information Service
LANL Physics Information Service
LANL T-2 Nuclear Information Service Gopher
LEGI-SLATE Gopher Service (via UMN)/
LTERnet (Long-Term Ecological Research Network)
Lawrence Berkeley Laboratory (LBL)
Library of Congress MARVEL Information System
Los Alamos National Laboratory
NASA Network Application and Information Center (NAIC)
NASA Center for Computational Sciences
NASA Goddard Space Flight Center
NASA High Energy Astrophysics Science Archive Research Center
NASA Information Sources TELNET (compiled by MSU)
NASA K-12 NREN Gopher
NASA Laboratory for Terrestrial Physics Gopher
NASA Langley Research Center
NASA Lewis Research Center (LeRC)
NASA Mid-Continent Technology Transfer Center
NASA Minority University Space Interdisciplinary Network
NASA Office of Life and Microgravity Sciences and Applications
NASA Scientific and Technical Information
NASA Shuttle Small Payloads Information
NASA Space Mechanisms Information Gopher
NIST Computer Security
NOAA Environmental Services Gopher
NOAA National Geophysical Data Center (NGDC)
NOAA National Oceanographic Data Center (NODC) Gopher
NOAA Online Data and Information Systems
NTIS FedWorld - 100+ electronic government bulletin boards
National Agricultural Library Genome Gopher
National Archives Gopher
National Cancer Institute
National Center for Atmospheric Research (NCAR) Gopher
National Center for Biotechnology Information (NCBI) Gopher
National Center for Education Statistics
National Center for Research on Evaluation, Standards
National Center for Supercomputing Applications
National Center for Toxicological Research
National Coordination Office for High Performance Computing and Communications

National Geophysical Data Center (NOAA)
National Heart, Lung, and Blood Institute (NHLBI) Gopher
National Institute of Allergy and Infectious Disease (NIAID)
National Institute of Environmental Health Sciences (NIEHS) Gopher
National Institute of Mental Health (NIMH) Gopher
National Institute of Standards and Technology (NIST)
National Institute of Standards and Technology Gopher
National Institutes of Health (NIH)
National Library of Medicine
National Library of Medicine TOXNET Gopher
National Oceanographic Data Center (NODC) Gopher
National Renewable Energy Laboratory
National Science Foundation (STIS)
National Science Foundation Center for Biological Timing
National Science Foundation Metacenter
National Telecommunication and Information Administration (NTIS) Gopher
National Toxicology Program (NTP) NIEHS-NIH
National Trade Data Bank
National Weather Service Telecommunication Gateway Gopher
Naval Ocean System Center (NRaD) Gopher
Naval Research Laboratory
Naval Research Laboratory Central Computing Facility
Oak Ridge National Laboratory Center for Computational Sciences
Oak Ridge National Laboratory ESD Gopher
Protein Data Bank - Brookhaven National Lab
Public Broadcasting Service (PBS) Gopher
STIS (Science and Technology Information System-NSF)
Securities and Exchange Commission "EDGAR" Gopher
Smithsonian Institution Natural History Gopher
Social Security Administration
U.S. Agency for International Development Gopher
U.S. Bureau of Mines Gopher
U.S. Bureau of the Census Gopher
U.S. Consumer Product Safety Commission Gopher
U.S. Dept Agriculture ARS GRIN National Genetic Resources Program
U.S. Dept Agriculture Children Youth Family Education Research Network
U.S. Dept Agriculture Economics and Statistics
U.S. Dept Agriculture Extension Service
U.S. Dept Agriculture Food and Nutrition Information Center
U.S. Dept Agriculture National Agricultural Library Plant Genome
U.S. Dept Commerce Information Infrastructure Task Force
U.S. Dept Commerce Economic Conversion Information Exchange
U.S. Dept Commerce Economics and Statistics Administration
U.S. Dept Education
U.S. Dept Energy
U.S. Dept Energy Environment, Safety & Health Gopher
U.S. Dept Energy Office of Nuclear Safety
U.S. Dept Health and Human Services
U.S. Dept Justice Gopher
U.S. Dept Transportation
U.S. Environmental Protection Agency
U.S. Environmental Protection Agency Futures Group

U.S. Environmental Protection Agency Great Lakes National Program Office Gopher
U.S. Geological Survey (USGS)
U.S. Geological Survey Atlantic Marine Geology
U.S. House of Representatives Gopher
U.S. Military Academy Gopher
U.S. National Information Service for Earthquake Engineering
U.S. Naval Observatory Satellite Information
U.S. Navy Naval Ocean System Center NRaD Gopher
U.S. Patent and Trademark Office Information (via town.hall.org)
U.S. Securities and Exchange Commission "EDGAR" Gopher
U.S. Senate Gopher
Voice of America (Radio)
\PEG, a Peripatetic, Eclectic Gopher

3.2.06. University of California, Santa Cruz.

This site has a very good listing of U.S. government-related information.

URL: gopher://gopher.ucsc.edu/11/ (under The Community/Guide to Government...)

This menu looks something like the following:

Americans Communicating Electronically (ACE)
CQ Congressional Quarterly Gopher
California Department of Education Gopher
California Elections Gopher Server
California Legislative Information
Public Utilities Commission
Clinton's Inaugural Address
Congressional Directory 103rd
Congressional Directory 103rd (searchable)
Congressional Electronic Mail Access
Congressional Information from Library of Congress
Copyright Information from Library of Congress
Elected Representatives for the Santa Cruz Region
Electronic Government Information Service (Syracuse Univ.)
Executive Branch Addresses
FEDWORLD Bulletin Board (NTIS)
Federal Government Information from Library of Congress
Legi-Slate Gopher Information Service
National Health Care Reform Information
National Performance Review (NPR) Documents
US Budget 1993-94 (By Section)
US Budget 1993-94 (searchable)
US Budget 1995
US Bureau of the Census Gopher
US Government Agencies via Gopher
US House Gopher Information Service
US Presidential Campaign '92 Documents
US Senate Gopher Information Service
White House Electronic Mail Access
White House Electronic Publications and Public Access Email
White House Information Service

3.2.07. University of Georgia, The Regents' Global Center.

Resources related to Eastern Europe and the newly independent states, including political information, economic data, trade leads, databases, scholarly papers, grant information, and current news.

URL: gopher://gopher.peachnet.edu

URL: telnet://info:info@info.peachnet.edu

3.2.08. University of Illinois at Urbana-Champaign - Project Gutenberg.

Project Gutenberg was started in 1971. Its goal is to release 10,000 books, whose U.S. copyrights have expired, by the year 2001. Project Gutenberg requests that you check your own copyright laws for using a file outside the United States. Files are released monthly in ASCII text format. An electronic newsletter is also available. For more information contact:

> Michael S. Hart
> Director, Project Gutenberg
> 405 West Elm St.
> Urbana, IL 61801
> E-mail: hart@vmd.cso.uiuc.edu

URL: mailto::hart@vmd.cso.uiuc.edu (Michael S. Hart)

or the Director of Communications:

E-mail: dircompg@ux1.cso.uiuc.edu

URL: mailto::dircompg@ux1.cso.uiuc.edu (Project Gutenberg, Director of Communications)

Project Gutenberg requests that the following FTP sites not be used from 10a.m. to 6p.m. Central Standard Time (Daylight in summer) as this is peak usage.

URL: ftp://mrcnext.cso.uiuc.edu/etext/ (the home location)

URL: ftp://mrcnext.cso.uiuc.edu/README (introductory information)

URL: ftp://mrcnext.cso.uiuc.edu/etext/etext91/README (introductory information about 1991 postings)

URL: ftp://mrcnext.cso.uiuc.edu/etext/etext91/feder15.txt (*The Federalist Papers*)

URL: ftp://mrcnext.cso.uiuc.edu/etext/etext93/civil10.txt (*Civil Disobedience*, Thoreau)

URL: ftp://mrcnext.cso.uiuc.edu/etext/articles/ (newsletters)

3.2.09. University of Massachusetts.

URL: gopher://gopher.ucs.umass.edu/11/academic/law

3.2.10. University of Michigan - The Clearinghouse.

The goal of the Clearinghouse is to make available Internet subject-oriented resource guides. The guides made available by the Clearinghouse have been created by various individuals in the Internet community, including students in a course co-taught by the administrator of the Clearinghouse at the University of Michigan, School of Information and Library Studies. Well over 100 guides (including "The Legal List") are maintained at this site. Of particular interest to those interested in foreign affairs is Sam Sternberg's "Daily News - Free Internet Sources & Information About the Daily News Media Globally." The "Daily News" gives instructions for accessing news from abroad (e.g. Eastern Europe, Germany, Italy, Finland, Denmark, China, Brazil) via the Internet.

The guides are available via anonymous FTP:

> URL: ftp://una.hh.lib.umich.edu/inetdirsstacks/

The guides are also available via Gopher:

> URL: gopher://una.hh.lib.umich.edu/11/inetdirs

Gopher path information:

> Minnesota's list of Gophers ->
> Michigan ->
> Clearinghouse of Subject-Oriented Internet Resource Guides

For more information, contact:

> Lou Rosenfeld
> University of Michigan
> School of Information and Library Studies
> 403B West Engineering
> Ann Arbor, MI 48109-1092
> E-mail: lou@umich.edu

URL: mailto::lou@umich.edu (Lou Rosenfeld)

3.2.11. University of Virginia - Copyright Law.

A good collection of U.S. copyright laws.

URL: gopher://orion.lib.virginia.edu/11/alpha/copyright

This menu looks something like the following:

> About These Resources
> U.S. 1976 Copyright Act, Section 107 (Fair Use)
> U.S. 1976 Copyright Act, Section 108 (Libraries)
> Copyright Law, Libraries & Universities, by Kenneth D. Crews (ASCII)
> Copyright Law, Libraries & Universities, by Kenneth D. Crews (PS)
> Copyright Law, Libraries & Universities, by Kenneth D. Crews (Word)
> Copyright Law, Libraries & Universities, by Kenneth D. Crews (WP5.1)
> TEXACO - Summary of Leval, by Ritchie Thomas
> TEXACO brief, March 1993 (ASCII)
> TEXACO brief, March 1993 (PS)
> TEXACO reply brief, May 1993 (ASCII)
> TEXACO reply brief, May 1993 (PS)
> TEXACO - ARL etc. Joint AMICUS (ASCII)
> TEXACO - ARL etc. Joint AMICUS (WP5.1)
> TEXACO - ALA AMICUS 3/93 (ASCII)
> TEXACO - ALA AMICUS 3/93 (PS)
> TEXACO - Association of American Publishers Brief 4/93 (ASCII)
> TEXACO - Association of American Publishers Brief 4/93 (PS)
> Copyright FAQ, part 1
> Copyright FAQ, part 2
> Copyright FAQ, part 3
> Copyright FAQ, part 4

Copyright FAQ, part 5
Copyright FAQ, part 6

3.2.12. University of Virginia - EcoGopher.

Ecological and environmental information.

URL: gopher://ecosys.drdr.virginia.edu/1

Back Cover.

The Legal List, Law-Related Resources on the Internet and Elsewhere

The first Internet reference book for those in the legal profession

Erik J. Heels has been writing about law and technology since 1992 (when "The Legal List" was first released) and is starting his second decade on the Internet. His first started when he entered the Massachusetts Institute of Technology in 1984. He graduated from MIT in 1988 with a degree in electrical engineering. In the years following MIT, he spent four years as a United States Air Force officer and worked for various high-tech firms in the Route 128 region of Boston. His interest in law and technology led him to the University of Maine School of Law in Portland, Maine, where he is now a third-year student and from where he will be graduating in December 1994. Before entering the Air Force, Erik spent some time working as an engineer in Finland. While in Finland, he met Pirjo, whom he married three years later. Erik and Pirjo and their five-month-old son, Samuel, now live in Eliot, Maine.
USA $29.95

ISBN 0-9643637-0-4

Reference Listing
LAWLISTS

Law Lists
(as of 12 February 1995)

by Lyonette Louis-Jacques
Copyright © 1995

Below are lists related to law on the Internet with instructions for subscribing to them included, followed by a list of law-related Usenet newsgroups. "Lists" here are electronic mailing lists which include discussion groups, announcements-only lists, electronic journals, newsletters or news digests, etc., on the Internet where mail is sent to a group of people. Lists on CompuServe, ABA/net, Lexis Counsel Connect, and other such services have been omitted.

To subscribe to a list, send the following form of request:

    subscribe listname Your Name

to LISTSERV or LISTSERVER or LISTPROC or [list-name]-REQUEST as indicated, and replace "Your Name", "firstname lastname", etc., with your real name; leave the subject line blank, and only include the single line subscription request in the body of the message (do not include any other information in the message, not even your .sig, unless otherwise instructed). Note that for lists run by MAJORDOMO or MAILSERV, you normally omit your name, and MAILBASE lists use "join" instead of "subscribe". These standard protocols for subscribing to lists may be used, unless otherwise indicated by the instructions.

For instance, if Worf Rozhenko wanted to subscribe to the INT-LAW@VM1.SPCS .UMN.EDU list, he'd send the following message/command to LISTSERV@VM1.SPCS .UMN.EDU (and *not* to INT-LAW@VM1.SPCS.UMN.EDU): subscribe int-law Worf Rozhenko

    Example:
    To: listserv@vm1.spcs.umn.edu
    Cc:
    Subject:
    Message:
    subscribe int-law Worf Rozhenko

He'd get back a message from the LISTSERV software running INT-LAW telling him that he has successfully subscribed to the INT-LAW list, and giving him instructions for unsubscribing/signing off, reviewing a list of the subscribers to the list, etc. Once the LISTSERV software has processed his subscription command, he can then send to and receive messages directly from INT-LAW subscribers.

It is very easy to subscribe to most lists, and very easy to sign off if you find out that a list is not for you (unless the list is manually run or otherwise requires human intervention, instead of a computer to unsubscribe you; then there might be some delay in getting unsubscribed). For a few lists, subscription is not automatic. Some lists require approval by the owner in order to subscribe, are by invitation-only, or are "closed" (private), not "open" and "public" lists available for automatic subscription. I have indicated herein when a list is "closed" or restricted. So, for the purposes of the "Law

Lists", a "closed" list is one that has restrictions on subscription, not one that is defunct. I have also indicated when a list is "defunct" or likely no longer in operation. (Some lists have so little traffic, they may seem "defunct", but are not).

It is important to retain instructions for unsubscribing from a list or temporarily postponing (setting to "nomail") receipt of list messages while on vacation or unable to read your e-mail for any reason; otherwise, unwanted mail piles up, a very frustrating experience!

Most lists allow you to unsubscribe or signoff the same way you subscribed with one major difference—you leave off your name. So, to get off a list, you'd send the following form of message/command to LISTSERV, LISTPROC, MAJORDOMO, or whatever name the software running the list has:

    unsubscribe listname

Some lists also use "signoff" or "unsub". That is if you used "subscribe" to sign on to the list in the first place. If you used "join" as with MAILBASE lists, you use the command "leave" in order to unsubscribe. On one list, "add" is used to subscribe and "delete" to unsubscribe. But "unsubscribe" and "signoff" are the most popular ways, but send the message to the software that runs the list and *not* to the list itself (e.g. to LISTSERV and not to INT-LAW). So, if Worf Rozhenko wanted to get off the INT-LAW@VM1.SPCS.UMN.EDU list, he'd send the following message to LISTSERV@VM1.SPCS.UMN.EDU: unsubscribe int-law

    Example:
    To: listserv@vm1.spcs.umn.edu
    Cc:
    Subject:
    Message:
    unsubscribe int-law

(note that once again, she leaves the subject line blank, includes no other text in the body of the message, but this time, because he's unsubscribing from a LISTSERV list, leaves off his name)

But, as lists do have variations in how to unsubscribe, keep the instructions you got upon subscribing handy!

As the number of law-related lists increases, the need to choose lists well and manage the flow of information increases. Some lists enable you to receive a "digest" of list messages; this is useful for "heavy traffic" lists with a large amount of messages each day. You get the messages with a list of topics covered first, followed by the full text of messages with the bulk of the routing/queueing information stripped out, as one message (reduces length and number of messages received). Another way to handle the information load is to subscribe to moderated lists (tend to have fewer messages posted and more messages relevant to the topic of the list as messages are screened by the moderator first usually) or lists that have restricted memberships or that do not allow non-subscribers to post (reduces postings of irrelevant messages to the list). An alternative is to subscribe instead to the Usenet newsgroup for a list (some of the lists below have Usenet gateways; ask your local computer guru for help in identifying listservs that are also Usenet newsgroups). Also, the Legal Domain Network at Chicago-Kent Law School provides a listserv-to-Usenet gateway for reading selected law lists. The URL is:

http://www.kentlaw.edu/lawnet/lawnet.html

There are also gopher archives for selected law-related lists, some with WAIS text search capability, for instance at the Cornell University Law School gopher with the URL:

gopher://gopher.law.cornell.edu:70/11/listservs

and at the University of Chicago Law School gopher with the URL:

gopher://lawnext.uchicago.edu:70/11/.internet/.lists

I maintain the most current version of "Law Lists" at the U of C gopher at the following URL:

gopher://lawnext.uchicago.edu:70/00/.internetfiles/lawlists

(some older versions are available at other sites - for instance, the 29 November 1994 version is at ftp://sluaxa.slu.edu/pub/millesjg/lawlists.txt)

Also, there are lists that allow non-subscribers to post messages, so you don't have to subscribe to that list in order to post your question on it (you're not getting unwanted messages in the meantime). The downside to this is that the non-subscriber who posts a question does not receive responses to the question that are directed to the list. When posting to lists you don't belong to, always indicate that, and instruct subscribers to send replies directly to your e-mail address and not to the list. Sharing responsibility for monitoring lists is another good way to manage e-mail (your colleague on another list can forward messages of interest to you and you can do likewise for the lists that you are on for them). The type of mail reader you use can also help in managing messages from lists. And, of course, you can always unsubscribe from lists that have more "noise" than relevant information.

Note that you should avoid adding to the "noise"/irrelevant information content of lists by choosing carefully the list(s) to post to and what to post. Mass mailings ("spamming") of a message to multiple law-related lists can be very annoying especially if the message is irrelevant to the topic of the list, is an advertisement for a product, is a long one, etc. Mass mailings cause disk space problems, and are particularly annoying to people who belong to multiple lists. So, if you must post your message to more than one list, post to as few lists as possible based on subject matter of your message, the number of subscribers to the list, the types of subscribers on the list, etc.

Make sure that messages that you post originally or forward to a list are relevant to the list and not off-topic. Verify information, consult your local computer gurus, get authoritative opinions, think twice before forwarding messages to lists that might have netwide repercussions (be especially leery of messages that urge you to forward the message to X number of persons, any interested persons, a particular e-mail address; messages that are not signed or include vague information about the original sender; messages that promote a product or company, that include items for sale, etc.). Keep in mind that messages sent or forwarded to lists or an e-mail address in a short space of time by thousands of people, even if well-meaning/for good purposes, can still have the same effect as mass mailings or "spam" - they generate e-mail in response (sometimes angry ones) and they slow down net traffic, among other things. Beware of hoax virus warnings, "Good Luck" chain letters, business scams, requests to send business cards, letters, e-mail to a particular postal or e-mail address for charitable purposes, etc. And post to as few lists as possible!

There are several resources for finding out more about lists generally and new lists. Basic information about LISTSERV lists is available from the LISTSERV home page at http://www.clark.net/pub/listserv/listserv.html. Lurking on support lists for software that run lists helps: LSTOWN-L@SEARN.SUNET.SE; UNIX-LISTPROC@AVS.COM; MAJOR DOMO-USERS@GREATCIRCLE.COM; LIST-MANAGERS@GREATCIRCLE.COM; and on the Usenet newsgroups: comp.mail.misc; comp.mail.list-admin.software; and comp.mail .list-admin.policy. LSTOWN-L is for owners of LISTSERV lists; there is LEGAL-LIST OWNERS for managers and owners of law-related lists and newsgroups. Jim Milles has compiled a short guide to various software for running electronic mailing lists and their features called "Discussion Lists: Mail Server Commands". It is available as follows:

E-mail: Send a message containing only the line
GET MAILSER CMD NETTRAIN F=MAIL
to LISTSERV@UBVM.cc.buffalo.edu

FTP: Anonymous ftp to ubvm.cc.buffalo.edu
cd /nettrain
get mailser.cmd

or

Anonymous ftp to SLUAXA.SLU.EDU
cd /nettrain
get mailser.cmd

Announcements of new lists are posted on NEW-LIST@VM1.NODAK.EDU (mainly LISTSERV lists) and NEW-LISTS@MAILBASE.AC.UK (for new mailbase lists), NET-HAPPENINGS@is.internic.net (comp.internet.net-happenings), and SCOUT-REPORT @is.internic .net, but most law-related lists are announced on LAWSRC-L, TEKNOIDS, LAW-LIB, LAWPROF, or other lists where potential subscribers might be.

You can also find lists by looking through the guides at the University of Michigan's "Clearinghouse for Subject-Oriented Internet Resource Guides" (gopher://una.hh.lib .umich.edu:70/00/inetdirs/ or http://http2.sils.umich.edu/~lou /chhome.html), the Info-Magnet (http://www.clark.net/pub/listserv/listserv.html), the Association of Research Libraries' _Directory of Electronic Journals, Newsletters and Academic Discussion Lists_ (gopher://arl.cni.org:70/11/scomm/edir/edir94), Steve Bonario & Ann Thornton's " Library-Oriented Lists and Electronic Serials" (gopher:/ /una.hh.lib.umich.edu:70/00/ inetdirsstacks/library:bailey), and the Political Science List of Lists (gopher://ilstu .edu:70/depts/polisci/listof). A quick way to find a list on any topic is to send the following message to LISTSERV@VM1.NODAK.EDU:

list global/[keyword]

(e.g. list global/history)

To learn about other lists of lists, read Marty Hoag's "Some Lists of Lists" (send the following message to LISTSERV@VM1.NODAK.EDU: get listsof lists) and Arno Wouters' "How to Find an Interesting Mailing List" (send the following message to LISTSERV @VM1.NODAK.EDU: get new-list wouters). If a list does not exist on your topic of interest, you can start one. Guides for starting and managing lists can be retrieved as follows: 1) send the following message to LISTSERV@VM1.NODAK.EDU: get new-list create 2) send the following message to LISTSERV@UHUPVM1.UH.EDU: get kovacs prv2n1 f=mail 3) send the following message to LISTSERV@BITNIC.CREN.NET: get listserv tips f=mail.

I started compiling the "Law Lists" to facilitate networking among persons involved in law-related work worldwide and to make the study, teaching, and research of the law easier. The "Law Lists" is intended to foster global legal information exchange. Hopefully the law-related electronic mailing lists below will be useful for your work. Happy networking!

Permission for electronic dissemination of "Law Lists" is granted. Reproduction of "Law Lists" in hardcopy/print format for educational/non-commercial purposes or by non-profit organizations such as libraries and law schools is permitted. For questions and requests related to the use of "Law Lists", or to send announcements of new or defunct lists, corrections, comments, suggestions, please contact Lyonette Louis-Jacques, Internet: LLOU@midway.uchicago.edu, Telephone: 312/702-9612, Telefax: 312/702-2889.

187-L@cmsa.berkeley.edu (Resisting and Organizing Against Prop 187; list for discussion of California Proposition 187 related to illegal immigrants)
    Send the following message to listserv@cmsa.berkeley.edu or listserv@ucbcmsa.bitnet:
    subscribe 187-l Your Name

AAASHRAN@gwuvm.gwu.edu (Human Rights Action Network of the American Association for the Advancement of Science)
    Send the following message to listserv@gwuvm.gwu.edu or listserv@gwuvm.bitnet:
    subscribe aaashran Your Name

AALSMIN-L@ube.ubalt.edu (restricted list for members of the Association of American Law Schools Section on Minority Groups)
    Send the following message to listserv@ube.UBALT.edu or listserv@ube.bitnet:
    subscribe AALSMIN-L yourname (your institution)

ABA-UNIX-LIST@austin.onu.edu (American Bar Association Law Practice Management Section Unix Interest Group; mainly practicing lawyers; subscription subject to approval by owner)
    Send the following message to listserv@austin.onu.edu:
    subscribe aba-unix-list Your Full Name

ABAINTINV@cali.kentlaw.edu (The Internet Listserv Discussion Group of the American Bar Association Section on International Law & Practice - Committee on International Investment and Development)
    Send the following message to listserver@CALI.kentlaw.edu:
    subscribe abaintinv <your name and position and institution here>

ABUSE-L@ubvm.cc.buffalo.edu (Professional Forum for Child Abuse Issues)
    Send the following message to listserv@ubvm.cc.buffalo.edu or listserv@ubvm.bitnet:
    subscribe ABUSE-L Your Name

ACADEME THIS WEEK (summaries of the articles from the _Chronicle of Higher Education_)
    URL=http://chronicle.merit.edu/

ACALI-L@sulaw.law.su.oz.au (Innovative methods of teaching law; conference on computer assisted learning in law; mostly Australian/New Zealand subscribers)
    Send the following message to listserv@SULAW.LAW.su.oz.au:
    subscribe ACALI-L YourFirstName YourLastName

ACRL-AAMES@mcfeeley.cc.utexas.edu (Asian, African, and Middle Eastern Section of the Association of College and Research Libraries list)
> Send the following message to listproc@mcfeeley.cc.utexas.edu:
> subscribe acrl-aames Your Name

ACTION@eff.org (ACTIvism ONline mailing list; forum and resource hosted by the Electronic Frontier Foundation; includes discussion of public access to government representatives and information, plus news releases and action alerts; formerly EFF-activists list)
> Send the following message to listserv@eff.org:
> subscribe action

ACTIV-L@mizzou1.missouri.edu (Activists Mailing List; peace, human rights, justice)
> Send the following message to listserv@MIZZOU1.missouri.edu
> or listserv@MIZZOU1.bitnet:
> subscribe ACTIV-L Your Name
> (see also Usenet newsgroups, alt.activism.d and
> misc.activism.progressive)

ADA-LAW@vm1.nodak.edu (for discussion of the Americans with Disabilities Act and other disability-related legislation worldwide)
> Send the following message to listserv@VM1.nodak.edu or
> listserv@NDSUVM1.bitnet:
> subscribe ada-law Your Name
> (bit.listserv.ada-law and ABLE-LAW on Fidonet)

ADLAW@webcom.com (Advertising and Marketing Law Internet Site Mailing List)
> Send the following message to majordomo@webcom.com:
> subscribe adlaw

ADMIN-TECHTRANS@mailbase.ac.uk (for discussion of all aspects of technology transfer, including posting of technology offers)
> Send the following message to mailbase@mailbase.ac.uk:
> join admin-techtrans firstname(s) lastname
> The JANET address is mailbase@uk.ac.mailbase

ADMINLAW@cali.kentlaw.edu (Administrative Law Professors & Lecturers list)
> Send the following message to listserver@CALI.kentlaw.edu:
> subscribe adminlaw your name here

ADMLPROF (Admiralty Law Faculty Discussion)
> Contact Lyonette Louis-Jacques, llou@midway.uchicago.edu, for
> subscription information

ADOPTION@listserv.law.cornell.edu (Adoption list)
> Send the following message to listserv@listserv.law.cornell.edu:
> subscribe adoption Your Name

AFRICA-N (Africa News & Information Service)
> Send the following message to listserv@vm.utcc.utoronto.ca or
> listserv@utoronto.bitnet:
> subscribe africa-n <full name>

AGLAW-L@lawlib.wuacc.edu (Agricultural Law list)
> Send the following message to listserv@lawlib.wuacc.edu:
> subscribe AGLAW-L Your Name

AIL-L@austin.onu.edu (Artificial Intelligence and Law)
> Send the following message to listserv@austin.onu.edu:
> subscribe AIL-L Your Name

ALAOIF@uicvm.uic.edu (American Library Association Office for Intellectual Freedom; discussion of censorship and intellectual freedom issues)
> Send the following message to listserv@uicvm.uic.edu or listserv@uicvm.bitnet:
> sub alaoif Your Name

ALAWON/ALA-WO (American Library Association Washington Office Newsline/Update)
> Send the following message to listserv@uicvm.uic.edu or listserv@uicvm.bitnet:
> subscribe ala-wo Your Name

ALAWORLD@uicvm.uic.edu (American Library Association International Relations Discussion Forum)
> Send the following message to listserv@uicvm.uic.edu or listserv@uicvm.bitnet:
> subscribe alaworld Your Name

ALL-OF-ELSA@jus.uio.no (European Law Students Association list)
> Send your e-mail address and subscription request to the list moderator, Arild Kvanvik-Joergensen, akj@jus.uio.no

ALSBNEWS (Academy of Legal Studies in Business (ALSB) News)
> Send the following message to listserv@miamiu.acs.muohio.edu or listserv@miamiu.bitnet:
> subscribe ALSBNEWS Your Name
> (also ALSBTALK limited to ALSB members)

AMEND1-L@uafsysb.uark.edu (Free Speech Discussion list sponsored by the American Communication Association; freedom of expression, constitutional interpretation, communication policy, privacy, censorship, etc., both in the U.S. and elsewhere)
> Send the following message to listserv@uafsysb.uark.edu or listserv@uafsysb.bitnet:
> sub AMEND1-L your name

AMEND2-DISCUSS@cs.colorado.edu (Colorado Constitutional Amendment 2 list; discussions of the amendment banning legislation providing civil rights protection for homosexuals)
> Send the following message to majordomo@cs.colorado.edu:
> subscribe amend2-discuss

AMEND2-INFO@cs.colorado.edu (Colorado Constitutional Amendment 2 information list)
> Send the following message to majordomo@cs.colorado.edu:
> subscribe amend2-info

AMNESTY@suvm.syr.edu (Syracuse University Amnesty International list for SU members communication)
> Send the following message to listserv@suvm.syr.edu or listserv@suvm.bitnet:
> subscribe amnesty Your Name

ANZ-LAW-LIBRARIANS-ONE@uow.edu.au (Australia & New Zealand Law Librarians list)
> Send the following message to majordomo@uow.edu.au:
> subscribe anz-law-librarians-one

APINESS-L@massey.ac.nz (Asia-Pacific Information Network for the Social Sciences; administered by the New Zealand Social Research Data Archives; restricted?)
> Send the following message to majordomo@massey.ac.nz:
> subscribe APINESS-L

AR-ALERTS@ny.neavs.com (Animal Rights Alerts list; postings of informational items such as press releases, official statements, action alerts, articles, etc.)
> Send the following message to majordomo@ny.neavs.com or listserv@ny.neavs.com:
> subscribe ar-alerts

AR-NEWS@cygnus.com (Animal Rights public news wire)
> Send the following message to ar-news-request@cygnus.com:
> subscribe ar-news Your Name

AR-SFBAY@mellers1.psych.berkeley.edu (Animal rights and vegan/vegetarian issues and events in the San Francisco Bay Area)
> Send the following message to listproc@MELLERS1.psych.berkeley.edu:
> subscribe ar-sfbay <your name here>

AR-TALK@cygnus.com (Animal Rights/Welfare open discussion forum)
> Send the following message to ar-talk-request@cygnus.com:
> subscribe ar-talk Your Name

ARIZONA@asuvm.inre.asu.edu (Arizona State Public Information Network)
> Send the following message to listserv@asuvm.inre.asu.edu or listserv@asuacad.bitnet:
> subscribe arizona Your Name

ARKNET-L@uafsysb.uark.edu (Arkansas State Network Discussions)
> Send the following message to listserv@uafsysb.uark.edu or listserv@uafsysb.bitnet:
> subscribe arknet-L Your Name

ARMS-L@buacca.bu.edu (Mailing list for discussions of policy issues related to peace, war, national security, weapons, the arms race, etc.)
> Send the following message to listserv@buacca.bu.edu or listserv@buacca.bitnet:
> subscribe ARMS-L Your Name

ASC-L@beach1.csulb.edu (Consenting Academics for Sexual Equity (CASE) Academic Sexual Correctness list; discussion of all aspects of campus sexual control issues including harassment, consent, speech, content of course materials, discrimination, privacy, academic freedom, etc.)
> To subscribe or for more information, contact moderator, Barry Dank, at request@BEACH1.CSULB.edu

ASIA-PACIFIC-SECURITY-L@coombs.anu.edu.au (subscription must be approved)
> Send the following message to majordomo@coombs.anu.edu.au:
> subscribe asia-pacific-security-L <your e-mail address>

Asian American Law Librarians Caucus of the American Association of Law Libraries mailing list (forthcoming on listserv@lawlib.wuacc.edu)

ASILIELG@cali.kentlaw.edu (American Society of International Law list for members of the International Economic Law Group)
> Send the following message to listserver@CALI.kentlaw.edu:
> subscribe ASILIELG <your name, position and institution here>

ASP-L@chicagokent.kentlaw.edu (restricted discussion list for people supervising, developing and teaching academic support programs at law schools)
> Send the following message to listserver@chicagokent.kentlaw.edu:
> subscribe asp-L Your full name, Your position

ASSOC-L@ukanvm.cc.ukans.edu ("Associates: The Electronic Library Support Staff Journal")
> Send the following message to listserv@ukanvm.cc.ukans.edu or listserv@ukanvm.bitnet:
> subscribe assoc-L Your Name

ASYLUM-L@ufsia.ac.be (Legal Aspects of Asylum and Refugee Status)
> Send the following message to majordomo@ufsia.ac.be:
> subscribe asylum-L

AUSTRAL-POLSCI-L@coombs.anu.edu.au (Australian political science list)
> Send the following message to majordomo@coombs.anu.edu.au:
> subscribe AUSTRAL-POLSCI-L <your e-mail address>

AUTOCAT@ubvm.cc.buffalo.edu (Library Cataloging and Authorities Discussion Group)
> Send the following message to listserv@ubvm.cc.buffalo.edu or listserv@ubvm.bitnet:
> subscribe autocat Your Name

AWD@counterpoint.com (Americans With Disabilities list; moderated forum for discussion related to the Americans with Disabilities Act (ADA), and other laws and legal decisions related to people with disabilities)
> Send the following message to majordomo@counterpoint.com:
> subscribe awd your_e-mail_address

AZPOLIT@asu.edu (discussion of political issues related to Arizona)
> Send the following message to listserv@asu.edu:
> subscribe AZPOLIT Firstname Lastname
> (az.politics)

BALT-L@ubvm.cc.buffalo.edu (Baltic Republics Discussion List; includes discussions of constitutional and citizenship law issues)
> Send the following message to listserv@ubvm.cc.buffalo.edu or listserv@ubvm.bitnet:
> subscribe BALT-L Your Name

BANKRLAW@polecat.law.indiana.edu (list for discussion of legal and financial aspects of bankruptcy and financial distress, domestic (U.S.) or foreign; theory, practice, teaching of bankruptcy and commercial law, and related topics, such as business aspects of turnarounds and bankruptcy; academics, lawyers, students)
> Send the following message to listproc@polecat.law.indiana.edu:
> subscribe bankrlaw <your name>

BAYOUDOC@vm.cc.latech.edu (Bayou Area (Louisiana) Government Documents)
> Send the following message to listserv@vm.cc.LATECH.edu:
> sub BayouDoc your name

BELL (list for regular updates on telecommunications reform legislation)
> Send the following message to listserver@bell.com:
> subscribe bell firstname lastname

BIBLIO-FR@caen1.unicaen.fr (moderated list for discussions in French of Internet resources)
> Send the following message to listserv@univ-RENNES1.fr or listserv@CAEN1.unicaen.fr:
> subscribe biblio-fr Your Name
> (or sub biblio-fr <Votre_prenom> <Votre_Nom>...:-); there's also
> BIBLIO-FR-A, for French accents; archived at gopher.univ-rennes1.fr)

BIOETHICSLAW-L@lawlib.wuacc.edu (Bioethics Law list)
Send the following message to listserv@lawlib.wuacc.edu:
subscribe bioethicslaw-L your firstname lastname

BIOMED-L@vm1.nodak.edu (Biomedical Ethics list)
Send the following message to listserv@VM1.nodak.edu or
listserv@NDSUVM1.bitnet:
subscribe biomed-L Your Name

BIZLAW-L@umab.umd.edu (Association of American Law Schools Section on Business
Associations list for law faculty & practitioner discussions of academic aspects of business
organizations and securities; scholarship and teaching)
Send the following message to listserv@umab.umd.edu or
listserv@umab.bitnet:
sub BIZLAW-L Firstname Lastname

BOSNET (BosNet distributes international press, radio & TV news related to events
in/about the Republic of Bosnia-Hercegovina; in English); see BOSNEWS

BOSNEWS
Send the following message to listproc@doc.ic.ac.uk:
subscribe bosnews Your Name
(also available via the Usenet newsgroups misc.news.bosnia,
bit.listserv.bosnet, and soc.culture.bosna-herzgvna; in Bosnian
from bosnet-request@gnu.ai.mit.edu)

BUDDIES-LIST (closed list)

BUSLIB-L@idbsu.idbsu.edu (Business Libraries List)
Send the following message to listserv@idbsu.idbsu.edu or
listserv@idbsu.bitnet:
subscribe buslib-L Your Name

C-NEWS (Conservative news and politics)
Send the following message to majordomo@world.std.com:
subscribe c-news

CA-FIREARMS@shell.portal.com (announcement and discussion of California firearms
legislation and related statewide issues)
Send the following message to majordomo@shell.portal.com:
subscribe ca-firearms

CABLEREG-L (Cable Regulation Digest; free, weekly newsletter summarizing regulatory
news from Multichannel News)
Send the following message to listserv@netcom.com:
subscribe cablereg-L

CALDOC-L@fullerton.edu (California Document Librarians)
Send the following message to listserv@fullerton.edu:
subscribe CalDoc-L Your Name

CALGOVINFO@cpsr.org (California Electronic Government Information)
Send the following message to listserv@cpsr.org:
subscribe calgovinfo Your Name

CALI-L@cali.kentlaw.edu (US-based Computer-Assisted Legal Instruction list)
Send the following message to listserver@CALI.kentlaw.edu:
subscribe CALI-L your name, your position, your institution

CALL-L@unb.ca (Canadian Academic Law Libraries list)
    Send the following message to listserv@unb.ca or
    listserv@UNBVM1.bitnet:
    subscribe CALL-L Your Name

The Canter & Siegel Report
    ftp://ftp.armory.com:pub/user/leavitt/html/cands.report.Z (compressed)

CAVEAT-L@fhs.mcmaster.ca (Canada-based list of the Citizens Against Violence
Everywhere Advocating its Termination)
    Send the following message to listproc@fhs.mcmaster.ca:
    subscribe caveat-L yourfirstname yourlastname

CCIJLEX@uchcecvm.cec.uchile.cl (Foro de Informatica Juridica; legal informatics list)
    Send the following message to listserv@uchcecvm.cec.uchile.CL or
    listserv@uchcecvm.bitnet:
    subscribe ccijlex Your Name

CCOAR (Coalition of Campus Organizations Address Rape's moderated discussion list for
activists, educators, and researchers working against rape)

CDN-FIREARMS@skatter.usask.ca (moderated list for distribution of information about
firearm laws, regulations, and related issues affecting Canadians)
    Send the following message to listproc@skatter.usask.ca:
    subscribe cdn-firearms your_name_here

CDN-NUCL-L@mcmaster.ca (Canadian Nuclear Info List)
    Send the following message to listproc@mcmaster.ca:
    subscribe cdn-NUCL-L Your Name

CEI (Competitive Enterprise Institute op-ed list; free market and limited government,
economic rights and the law)
    Send subscription request to listowner, Alexander "Sasha" Volokh,
    VOLOKH@netcom.com

CELLO-L@listserv.law.cornell.edu (Cello web browser list; developed by Tom Bruce at
Cornell Law School)
    Send the following message to listserv@listserv.law.cornell.edu:
    subscribe CELLO-L Your Full Name

CENTAM-L@ubvm.cc.buffalo.edu (Central America Discussion List; includes news in English
and Spanish about Latin American human rights)
    Send the following message to listserv@ubvm.cc.buffalo.edu or
    listserv@ubvm.bitnet:
    subscribe centam-L Your Name

CENTRAL-ASIA-STUDIES-L@coombs.anu.edu.au (Australian National University forum for
communications re Central Asia's history, politics, economics, etc.)
    Send the following message to majordomo@coombs.anu.edu.au:
    subscribe central-asia-studies-L youre-mailaddress

CERRO-L@aearn.edvz.univie.ac.at (Central European Regional Research Organization)
    Send the following message to listserv@aearn.edvz.univie.ac.at or
    listserv@aearn.bitnet:
    subscribe cerro-L Your Name

CERT-ADVISORY@listas.unam.mx (Security discussion group)
    Send the following message to listproc@listas.unam.mx:
    subscribe cert-advisory Your Name
    (see also comp.security.announce = cert-advisory@cert.org)

CET-ONLINE (Central Europe Today News Service; daily political, economic and business news in English)
>   Send the following message to cet-online-request@eunet.cz:
>   subscribe

CFO-LAW@email.unc.edu (Law School Chief Financial Officers list; was @gibbs.oit.unc.edu)
>   Send the following message to listproc@email.unc.edu:
>   subscribe cfo-law Your Name

CHECHNYA@plearn.edu.pl (list for discussion of the current situation in Chechnya, including news of recent developments, human rights and humanitarian aid issues)
>   Send the following message to listserv@PLEARN.edu.PL or
>   listserv@plearn.bitnet:
>   sub chechnya firstname lastname

CHIAPAS-L@listas.unam.mx (list for discussion of the conflict in the State of Chiapas, Mexico; discussion primarily in Spanish, but English accepted)
>   Send the following message to listproc@listas.unam.mx:
>   sub chiapas-L yourfirstname yourlastname

CHIFEMS (private discussion list for legal feminists in the professions)

CHILDRI-@nic.surfnet.nl (Discussion on the United Nations Convention on the Rights of the Child; especially the right to information)
>   Send the following message to listserv@nic.surfnet.NL or
>   listserv@hearn.bitnet:
>   subscribe childri- Your Name
>   (note that there is no "L" after "CHILDRI-")

CHINA-ND (China News Digest - U.S. News)
>   Send the following message to listserv@kentvm.kent.edu or
>   listserv@kentvm.bitnet:
>   subscribe china-nd Your Name
>   (for more information about accessing the Global Service or from
>   outside the U.S., send a blank message to cnd-info@cnd.org; also
>   available via gopher at cnd.org or web at http://www.cnd.org:80/)

CHOICE-NET (California Abortion and Reproductive Rights Action League - North weekly newsletter)
>   Send the following message to dtv@well.com:
>   subscribe choice-net

CIRCPLUS@idbsu.idbsu.edu (Circulation Discussion List)
>   Send the following message to listserv@idbsu.idbsu.edu or
>   listserv@idsu.bitnet:
>   subscribe circplus Your Name

CIRLNET@rutvm1.rutgers.edu (Community of Industrial Relations Librarians)
>   Send the following message to listserv@RUTVM1.rutgers.edu or
>   listserv@RUTVM1.bitnet:
>   subscribe CIRLNET Your Name

CIVIC-VALUES
>   Send the following message to majordomo@civic.net:
>   subscribe civic-values

CIVILRTS@chicagokent.kentlaw.edu (Civil Rights and Civil Liberties Discussion Group for law professors and others working in the field)
>   Send the following message to listserv@chicagokent.kentlaw.edu:
>   subscribe CivilRts Your Name, Position, Institution

CIVILSOC (Civil Society News and Resources for the former USSR; Center for Civil Society International list for news and resources, electronic and print, of interest to individuals and organizations engaged in civil society institution-building projects in the NIS)
Send the following message to listproc@SOLAR.rtd.utk.edu:
subscribe CivilSoc firstname lastname

CJMOVIES (Journal of Criminal Justice and Popular Culture; film reviews and original essays)
Send the following message to listserv@albany.edu, listserv@ALBNYVM1.bitnet or listserv@albany.bitnet:
sub cjmovies Yourfirstname Yourlastname

CJUST-L@cunyvm.cuny.edu (Criminal Justice Discussion List)
Send the following message to listserv@cunyvm.cuny.edu or listserv@cunyvm.bitnet:
subscribe cjust-L Your Name

CLIPPER@vector.casti.com (Clipper Chip *announcements-only* list)
Send the following message to majordomo@vector.casti.com:
subscribe clipper

CLNET@u.washington.edu (The Chinese Law Net; an electronic discussion group on the modern law of the People's Republic of China; postings related to other Chinese jurisdictions or to Chinese legal history are also welcome; was CHINALAW)
Send the following message to listproc@u.washington.edu:
subscribe CLNET Firstname Lastname

CNI-COPYRIGHT@cni.org (Coalition for Networked Information's Copyright & Intellectual Property Forum)
Send the following message to listproc@cni.org or listserv@cni.org:
subscribe cni-copyright Yourfirstname Yourlastname

CNI-LEGISLATION@cni.org (Coalition for Networked Information's Working Group on Legislation, Codes, Policies, and Practices)
Send the following message to listproc@cni.org or listserv@cni.org:
subscribe cni-legislation Yourfirstname Yourlastname

CNI-MODERNIZATION@cni.org (Coalition for Networked Information's Modernization of Scholarly Publication Working Group)
Send the following message to listproc@cni.org:
subscribe cni-modernization Yourfirstname Yourlastname

CNI-PUBINFO@cni.org (Coalition for Networked Information's Access to Public Information Working Group; includes discussion of access to information collected by the United States government via electronic networks)
Send the following message to listproc@cni.org or listserv@cni.org:
subscribe cni-pubinfo Yourfirstname Yourlastname

CNI-TRANSFORMATION@cni.org (Coalition for Networked Information's Transformation of Scholarly Communication Working Group)
Send the following message to listproc@cni.org:
subscribe cni-transformation Yourfirstname Yourlastname

COGOPUB-L@lists.colorado.edu (Colorado Government Documents list)
Send the following message to listserv@lists.colorado.edu:
subscribe CoGoPub-L Your Name

COLLBARG@cms.cc.wayne.edu (Collective Bargaining and Librarians)
Send the following message to listserv@cms.cc.wayne.edu:
subscribe collbarg Your Name

COM-PRIV@psi.com (Commercialization of the Internet)
     Send the following message to com-priv-request@psi.com:
     subscribe com-priv Your Name

COMLAW-L@lawlib.wuacc.edu (list for discussion of communications law issues sponsored by the Section on Mass Communications Law of the Association of American Law Schools; was list of the Washburn Communications Law Society; "TELEJURIST" e-journal distributed herein)
     Send the following message to listserv@lawlib.wuacc.edu:
     sub comlaw-L Yourfirstname Yourlastname

COMLAW-L@vm.ucs.ualberta.ca (Computers and Legal Education)
     Send the following message to listserv@vm.ucs.ualberta.ca or listserv@ualtavm.bitnet:
     subscribe comlaw-L Your Name

COMMERCIAL-REALESTATE@syncomm.com (Commercial Real Estate list; for professionals involved in sales, acquisitions, management and development of commercial property)
     Send the following message to listserv@syncomm.com:
     sub commercial-realestate Your-Internet-address/name

COMMUNET@uvmvm.uvm.edu (Community & Civic Networks)
     Send the following message to listserv@uvmvm.uvm.edu or listserv@uvmvm.bitnet:
     subscribe communet Your Name

COMMUNITY-PROPERTY@uidaho.edu (moderated list for lawyers and legal educators to discuss substantive issues of community property law)
     Send the following message to majordomo@uidaho.edu:
     subscribe community-property youre-mailaddress

COMMUNITYDEVELOPMENTBANKING-L@cornell.edu (list for practitioners of community reinvestment: community development (CD) credit unions, CD banks, CD loan funds, CDCs, and support organizations)
     Send the following message to listproc@CORNELL.edu:
     subscribe CommunityDevelopmentBanking-L Your Name

COMP-ACADEMIC-FREEDOM-ABSTRACTS@eff.org (weekly summary of the Usenet newsgroup, alt.comp.acad-freedom.talk, and its listserv equivalent, comp-academic-freedom-talk@eff.org; there is also a weekly digest called CAF-News, available as Usenet newsgroup, alt.comp.acad-freedom.news)
     Send the following message to listserv@eff.org:
     add comp-academic-freedom-abstracts
     ("subscribe" may work also)

COMP-ACADEMIC-FREEDOM-TALK@eff.org (academic freedom and computers and networks list of the Electronic Frontier Foundation)
     Send the following message to listserv@eff.org:
     add comp-academic-freedom-talk
     ("subscribe" may work also)

COMP-PRIVACY (Computer Privacy Digest; effect of technology on privacy)
     Send the following message to comp-privacy-request@uwm.edu:
     subscribe comp-privacy Your Name

COMPCONS@uofrlaw.urich.edu (Constitutions & Constitutionalism Around the World; comparative constitutions list sponsored by the Center for the Study of Constitutionalism in Eastern Europe at the University of Chicago and the University of Richmond)
     Send the following message to listserv@UofRLaw.URich.edu:
     subscribe compcons Your Name

COMPUTER UNDERGROUND DIGEST (CuD; weekly newsletter on legal, ethical, social and other issues concerning computerized information and communications)
> Send the following message to listserv@vmd.cso.uiuc.edu or listserv@uiucvmd.bitnet:
> sub cudigest Your Name
> (also comp.society.cu-digest)

COMPUTERSUPPORT-LAW-SCHOOLS@mailbase.ac.uk (U.K.-based Computer Support in Law Schools list)
> Send the following message to mailbase@mailbase.ac.uk:
> join computersupport-law-schools Your Name
> The JANET address is mailbase@uk.ac.mailbase

*ConflictNet (see Institute for Global Communications Networks)

CONG-REFORM@essential.org (Congressional Reform Briefings)
> Send the following message to listproc@essential.org:
> subscribe cong-reform your name

CONSTPARTY@tomahawk.welch.jhu.edu (Constitution Party News and Information; forum for discussion of the Constitution Party platform to protect the Constitution and to return the U.S. federal government to a Constitutionally-based government)
> Send the following message to constparty-request@tomahawk.WELCH.jhu.edu:
> subscribe youre-mailaddress

CONTRACTS@austin.onu.edu (Teaching and Application of Contract Law)
> Send the following message to listserv@austin.onu.edu:
> subscribe contracts YourFullName

COSELL-L@alpha.acast.nova.edu (Consortium of Southeastern Law Libraries)
> Send the following message to listserv@alpha.acast.nova.edu:
> subscribe COSELL-L Your Name

COUNTERSERVE@counterpoint.com (Counterpoint Publishing Company's moderated list for discussion of their law-related CD-ROMs and other products)
> Send the following message to majordomo@counterpoint.com:
> subscribe counterserve

COVICO-L (Committee on Viable Constitutionalism; closed list)

CPAE@catfish.valdosta.peachnet.edu (Center for Professional and Applied Ethics list, including computing, law, and business ethics)
> Send the following message to listserv@catfish.VALDOSTA.peachnet.edu:
> subscribe cpae Your Name

CPS-L@nic.surfnet.nl (Centre for Pacific Studies list)
> Send the following message to listserv@nic.surfnet.NL or listserv@hearn.bitnet:
> subscribe cps-L Your Name
> (can also send request to U211610@HNYKUN11.urc.kun.NL?)

CPSR ALERT (Computer Professionals for Social Responsibility e-journal)
> Send the following message to listserv@cpsr.org:
> subscribe cpsr-announce <your name>
> (=comp.org.cpsr.announce; see also comp.org.cpsr.talk)

CPSR-GLOBAL@cpsr.org (worldwide discussions of the USA's National Information Infrastructure or NII, the emerging Global Information Infrastructure or GII, and related international issues of security, privacy, computer law, "cultural pollution", national identity, communication, computer development and design, language, etc.)
    Send the following message to listserv@cpsr.org or listserv@sunnyside.com:
    subscribe cpsr-global Firstname Lastname
    (digests posted on comp.org.cpsr.talk)

CRIM-L@sulaw.law.su.oz.au (Australian Criminal Justice and Criminology Mailing List; also called CrimNet)
    Send the following message to listserv@SULAW.LAW.su.oz.au:
    subscribe crim-L Yourfirstname Yourlastname

CRIMPROF@chicagokent.kentlaw.edu (Criminal Law/Procedure Professors; private list for law professors who teach or write in the areas of Criminal Law, Criminal Procedure, and related courses)
    Send the following message to listserv@chicagokent.kentlaw.edu:
    subscribe crimprof <your name>, <your title>, <your institution>

CROATIAN-NEWS (Croatian News in English; also HRVATSKI-VJESNIK in Croatian)
    Send the following message to listserver@carnet.hr:
    subscribe croatian-news <your name>

CSPPLIST@weber.ucsd.edu (list for Critical Discussion of Crime, Society, and the Politics of Punishment)
    Send the following message to listproc@weber.ucsd.edu:
    subscribe cspplist Your First and Last Name
    At the same time, send a brief letter of introduction to the
    moderator, Tristan Riley (triley@weber.ucsd.edu), containing your
    name, interests in crime and punishment, and related work or projects

CTI-LAW@mailbase.ac.uk (UK-based list on use of information technology in law teaching; Warwick Law Technology Centre list)
    Send the following message to mailbase@mailbase.ac.uk:
    join cti-law firstname lastname
    The JANET address is mailbase@uk.ac.mailbase

CWD-L (Brock Meeks' CyberWire Dispatch news)
    Send the following message to majordomo@cyberwerks.com:
    subscribe cwd-L

CYBERIA-L@birds.wm.edu (The Law and Policy of Computer Networks; formerly CYBERLAW, then briefly CYBERLAW-L)
    Send the following message to listserv@listserv.cc.wm.edu
    or listserver@eagle.birds.wm.edu:
    subscribe cyberia-L Your Name

CYPHERPUNKS@toad.com (cryptography/encryption, digital cash & electronic banking, etc.)
    Send the following message to cypherpunks-request@toad.com:
    subscribe cypherpunks Your Name

CYPHERPUNKS-DIGEST@vorlon.mankato.msus.edu (cryptography/encryption and privacy)
    Send the following message to majordomo@VORLON.mankato.msus.edu:
    subscribe cypherpunks-digest

CYPHERWONKS@lists.eunet.fi (splinter group from CYPHERPUNKS also interested in promoting and implementing crytographic techniques to ensure privacy and anonymity)
    Send the following message to majordomo@lists.EUnet.fi:
    subscribe cypherwonks
    (send the message "info cypherwonks" for more information)

DAILY (Statistics Canada daily release of data and publications information)
Send the following message to listproc@statcan.ca:
subscribe daily Your Name

Danish News (see NYHEDS-LISTEN)

DATA-PROTECTION@mailbase.ac.uk (UK data protection law list)
Send the following message to mailbase@mailbase.ac.uk:
join data-protection Yourfirstname Yourlastname
The JANET address is mailbase@uk.ac.mailbase

DECONSTI-L@ulima.edu.pe (Lista de Derecho Constitucional Latinoamericano = Latin American Constitutional Law List; e-journal posted therein, "REDECO: Revista Electronica de Derecho Constitucional Latinoamericano")
Send the following message to listserv@ULIMA.edu.pe:
add youre-mailaddress deconsti-L

DEM-NET@netcom.com (Discussion List of the Democratic Party; including electoral politics)
Send the following message to listserv@netcom.com:
subscribe dem-net youremailaddress

DERECHO (conference for distribution of electronic bulletin on legal topics; in Spanish)
Send subscription request to dpto.derecho@upsa.bo

DERHUMAN@rcp.net.pe (Derechos Humanos = Human Rights; Peru-based list in Spanish)
Send the following message to listasrcp@rcp.net.pe:
add youre-mailaddress derhuman

DEVEL-L@american.edu (Technology Transfer in International Development)
Send the following message to listserv@american.edu or
listserv@auvm.bitnet:
subscribe DEVEL-L Your Name

DIRCON95@law.uark.edu (short-term list for Legal Research & Writing directors interested in conference to be held in summer of 1995)
Send the following message to listserv@LAW.uark.edu:
subscribe dircon95

DISARM-L@uacsc2.albany.edu (Disarmament Discussion List)
Send the following message to listserv@uacsc2.albany.edu or
listserv@ALBNYVM1.bitnet:
subscribe disarm-L Your Name
(bit.listserv.disarm-l)

DISC-EVIDENCE (see EVIDENCE)

DISPUTE-RES@listserv.law.cornell.edu (Dispute Resolution list for teachers and practitioners)
Send the following message to listserv@listserv.law.cornell.edu:
subscribe dispute-res yourfirstname yourlastname

DNSLIST@cali.kentlaw.edu (The Internet Listserv for Law School Associate and Assistant Deans)
Send the following message to listserv@CALI.kentlaw.edu:
subscribe DNSLIST <Your name, position, and institution>

DOMESTIC@cs.cmu.edu (Domestic Partners Benefits discussion list)
Send the following message to domestic-request@cs.cmu.edu:
subscribe domestic Your Name

DOT (Departments of Transportation Discussion List)
Send the command SUB in the subject field to dot%t3ew@dot.ca.gov

DOXNJ@rutvm1.rutgers.edu (New Jersey Government Documents Forum)
    Send the following message to listserv@RUTVM1.rutgers.edu or
    listserv@RUTVM1.bitnet:
    subscribe DoxNJ Your Name

DRUGABUS@umab.umd.edu (Drug Abuse list)
    Send the following message to listserv@umab.umd.edu or
    listserv@umab.bitnet:
    subscribe drugabus Your Name

DUAL-USE@netcom.com (U.S. defense conversion programs list)
    Send the following message to listserv@netcom.com or
    majordomo@netcom.com:
    subscribe DUAL-use

E-EUROPE@pucc.princeton.edu (Eastern Europe Business Network)
    Send the following message to listserv@pucc.princeton.edu or
    listserv@pucc.bitnet:
    subscribe e-europe Your Name

E LAW (see ELAW-J)

EASMNT-L@vm.ucs.ualberta.ca (An Electronic Forum Discussing Issues of Property Law and Trusts)
    Send the following message to listserv@vm.ucs.UALBERTA.ca or
    listserv@UALTAVM.bitnet:
    subscribe easmnt-L Your Name

EC (see EU)

ECA-L@gsuvm1.gsu.edu (Eastern Europe & the Former Soviet Union list of the Regents' Global Center Institute for EastWest Studies in Georgia)
    Send the following message to listserv@GSUVM1.gsu.edu or
    listserv@GSUVM1.bitnet:
    subscribe eca-L Your Name

ECOJUSTICE@econet.apc.org (list for discussion of environmental justice, environmental racism, toxic hazards in communities of color, and related topics; based at the EcoNet computer network)
    Send the following message to majordomo@econet.apc.org:
    subscribe ecojustice

ECOL-ECON@csf.colorado.edu (Ecological Economics, including discussions of free trade, multinational economic institutions and the environment)
    Send the following message to listserv@csf.colorado.edu:
    subscribe ecol-econ Your Name

*EcoNet (see Institute for Global Communications Networks)

ECONLAW@gmu.edu (US-based Economic Analysis of Law list for academics)
    Send the following message to listproc@gmu.edu:
    subscribe econlaw [your name]

ECPR-PILOT@mailbase.ac.uk (European Consortium for Political Research; development of research and teaching in political science in Europe)
    Send the following message to mailbase@mailbase.ac.uk:
    join ecpr-pilot Your Name
    The JANET address is mailbase@uk.ac.mailbase

EDI-L@uccvma.ucop.edu (Electronic Data Interchange Issues)
> Send the following message to listserv@uccvma.ucop.edu:
> subscribe edi-L Your Name

EDLAW@ukcc.uky.edu (Law and Education)
> Send the following message to listserv@ukcc.uky.edu or
> listserv@ukcc.bitnet:
> subscribe edlaw Your Name

EDPOL-D@scholastic.com (Education Policy Digest from Scholastic, Inc.)
> Send the following message to listproc@scholastic.com:
> subscribe edpol-d Your Name

EDUPAGE@educom.edu (twice-weekly summary of news items on information
technology, including related federal government action; electronic newsletter of
EDUCOM, a consortium of colleges and universities seeking to transform education
through the use of information technology)
> Send the following message to listproc@educom.edu or
> listproc@ivory.educom.edu:
> sub edupage yourfirstname yourlastname

EEECON-L@cep.polisci.yale.edu (Economic Transition in Eastern Europe)
> Send a blank message to listserv@cep.polisci.yale.edu with the
> following in the _subject_ line: sub eeecon-l Your Name

EEHED-L@yalevm.cis.yale.edu (Eastern Europe Higher Education List of the Civic Education
Project)
> Send the following message to listserv@yalevm.cis.yale.edu:
> sub eehed-L <your full name here>

EEJH@beacon.bryant.edu (Eastern European Jewish History and Khazar Studies List)
> Send the following message to majordomo@beacon.bryant.edu:
> subscribe eejh

EELAW-L@cep.polisci.yale.edu (Legal Reform in Eastern Europe; forum for discussion of
legal reform in the countries of Eastern Europe, Russia, and the Newly Independent
States (NIS))
> Send a blank message to listserv@cep.polisci.yale.edu with the
> following in the _subject_ line: sub eelaw-l Your Name

EEWOMEN-L@cep.polisci.yale.edu (Women's Issues in Eastern European)
> Send a blank message to listserv@cep.polisci.yale.edu with the
> following in the _subject_ line: sub eewomen-l Your Name

EFA@iinet.com.au (Electronic Frontiers Australia list; temporary mailing list for
establishing an Electronic Frontier Foundation-like organization in Australia for
computers and civil liberties issues; gated to the Usenet newsgroup aus.org.efa)
> Send the following message to efa-request@iinet.com.au:
> subscribe

EFC-ANNOUNCE (Electronic Frontier Canada announcements list)
> Send the following message to efc-announce-request@insight.mcmaster.ca:
> subscribe efc-announce Your Name

EFC-TALK@insight.mcmaster.ca (Electronic Frontier Canada discussion list)
> Send the following message to efc-talk-request@insight.mcmaster.ca:
> subscribe efc-talk Your Name

EFF-Activists (see ACTION)

EFF-News@eff.org (Electronic Frontier Foundation's News list)
   Send the following message to listserv@eff.org:
   subscribe comp-org-eff-news

EFF-Talk@eff.org (list for discussion of Electronic Frontier Foundation policy, cyberspace legal issues, the "data superhighway", networking and activism, etc.)
   Send the following message to listserv@eff.org:
   subscribe comp-org-eff-talk
   (EFF's "Online Activism Resource List" is available via ftp at
   the following URL:
   ftp://ftp.eff.org/pub/EFF/Issues/Activism/activ_resource.faq

EFFector-Online (US-based Electronic Frontier Foundation's biweekly newsletter covering privacy rights, freedom of speech in digital media, intellectual property, and other issues related to computer-based communications media)
   Send the following message to listserv@eff.org:
   subscribe effector-online

EFI-ANNOUNCE (Electronic Frontier Ireland)
   Send e-mail to EFI@EFI.IE with the subject "subscribe efi-announce"

EFI-TALK (Electronic Frontier Ireland)
   Send e-mail to EFI@EFI.IE with the subject "subscribe efi-talk"

EFJ@twics.com (Electronic Frontiers Japan)
   Send the following message to efj-request@twics.com:
   subscribe your name

EFN@oslonett.no (Electronic Frontier Norway; mailing list?; FAQ at http://www.ii.uib.no/efn/)

EJINTVIO (Electronic Journal of Intimate Violence)
   Send the following message to listserv@uriacc.uri.edu or
   listserv@uriacc.bitnet:
   subscribe ejintvio Your Name

ELAW-J (E Law - Murdoch University Electronic Journal of Law)
   Send the following message to majordomo@CLEO.murdoch.edu.au:
   subscribe elaw-j

ELAW.PUBLIC.INTEREST (Public communications area/"conference" on EcoNet, a network of the Assocation of Progressive Communications, sponsored by the Environmental Law Alliance Worldwide, for discussing the development of assistance to grassroots environmental lawyers and their clients around the world; for more info, contact apc-info@igc.apc.org or igc-info@igc.apc.org)

Electronic Green Journal (international environmental issues)
   Send the following message to majordomo@uidaho.edu:
   subscribe egj your_email_address
   (archived at URL=gopher://gopher.uidaho.edu/1/UI_gopher/library/egj/)

ENV.SEASHEPHERD (Sea Shepherd Conservation Society; discussion of international conservation law & related environmental topics)
   Send name, postal & e-mail address to owner, Nick Voth at
   dcasmedic@aol.com or nvoth@igc.apc.org

ENVCEE-L@rec.hu (Environment in Central and Eastern Europe)
   Send the following message to listserv@rec.hu:
   subscribe envcee-L Your Name

ENVIROLAW@oregon.uoregon.edu (list for environmental law students around the world)
Send the following message to mailserv@oregon.uoregon.edu:
subscribe envirolaw

Environmental Health Briefing (weekly bulletin summarizing U.K. and European environmental health legislation; free?)
Contact postmaster@ehas.demon.co.uk for more information

ENVLAWPROFS@oregon.uoregon.edu (list for teachers of environmental law around the world)
Send the following message to mailserv@oregon.uoregon.edu:
subscribe envlawprofs

EPA-PRESS (U.S. Environmental Protection Agency press releases)
Send the following message to listserver@unixmail.rtpnc.epa.gov:
subscribe epa-press Your Name

EPAFR-CONTENTS (U.S. Environmental Protection Agency's list for daily distribution via e-mail of the table of contents of the _Federal Register_ - a publication which includes the texts of federal agency administrative rules, regulations, and notices; includes entire _Federal Register_, not just EPA section, table of contents)
Send the following message to listserver@UNIXMAIL.rtpnc.epa.gov:
subscribe epafr-contents your first and last name
(other lists on the listserver include epa-air, epa-general,
epa-impact, epa-meetings, epa-pest, epa-sab, epa-species, epa-tax,
epa-tri, epa-tri, epa-waste, epa-water)

EPIC ALERT (Electronic Privacy Information Center)
Send the following message to listserv@cpsr.org or
listserv@snyside.sunnyside.com:
subscribe cpsr-announce your name
(also alert@epic.org)

ESAPRESS (European Space Agency official press releases)
Send the following message to listserv@esoc.bitnet:
sub esapress your name

ESBDC-L@IST01.ferris.edu (Small Business Development Center list)
Send the following message to listserv@IST01.ferris.edu:
sub esbdc-L

ESTPLAN-L@netcom.com (Discussion of Estate Planning, including tax and non-tax issues; for professionals)
Send the following message to listserv@netcom.com:
subscribe estplan-l

EU@knidos.cc.metu.edu.tr (European Union)
Send the following message to listproc@knidos.cc.metu.edu.tr or
listserv@listserv.metu.edu.tr:
sub eu Your Name
(was the EC or European Community list)

EU-DB@fgr.wu-wien.ac.at (EUropean DataBases list; European Documentation Centres (EDCs) in Austria)
Send the following message to listserv@fgr.wu-wien.ac.at:
subscribe eu-db

EU-TALK@phoenix.oulu.fi (forum for discussing European Union-related matters, mainly from the ordinary citizen's point of view)
> Send the following message to majordomo@phoenix.OULU.fi:
> subscribe eu-talk <your e-mail address>

EURO-LEX@vm.gmd.de (All EUROpean Legal Information EXchange; includes discussion of European Community/European Union & European country legal information sources; exchange of and mutual assistance with legal information research in all European countries; intended to be multilingual)
> Send the following message to listserv@vm.gmd.de or
> listserv@dearn.bitnet:
> subscribe euro-lex Your Name

EURODOC@durham.ac.uk (U.K.-based list for librarians running European Documentation Centres)
> Send request to register to R.I.CADDEL@durham.ac.uk (or to
> R.I.CADDEL@uk.ac.durham)

EVIDENCE@chicagokent.kentlaw.edu (forum in which scholars and teachers of evidence law can discuss topics in their field; was DISC-EVIDENCE)
> Send the following message to listserver@chicagokent.kentlaw.edu:
> subscribe evidence yourname yourschool

EXLIBRIS@rutvm1.rutgers.edu (Rare Books and Special Collections Forum)
> Send the following message to listserv@RUTVM1.rutgers.edu or
> listserv@RUTVM1.bitnet:
> subscribe exlibris Your Name

EXPERT-L@lern.mv.com (Expert Witnesses list; for expert witnesses or persons considering being expert witnesses, and those in the legal profession who use expert witnesses)
> Send e-mail to expert-L@LERN.mv.com with the word "subscribe"
> in the subject header

EYE-ON-GOVERNMENT (Eye-On-Government newsletter)
> Send the following message to listproc@einet.net:
> subscribe eye-on-government Your Name

FAIRNESS@mainstream.com (monitors issues of "fairness" with respect to government)
> Send the following message to fairness-request@mainstream.com:
> subscribe fairness Your Name

FAMILYLAW-L@lawlib.wuacc.edu (US-based Family Law list)
> Send the following message to listserv@lawlib.wuacc.edu:
> subscribe familylaw-L Your Name

FAST@gitvm1.gatech.edu (Fight Against Sexist Tyranny list; open, moderated forum; per owner, forum will not contain Gay issues as there are other lists for such discussions)
> Send the following message to listserv@GITVM1.gatech.edu or
> listserv@GITVM1.bitnet:
> subscribe fast your-first-name your-last-name

FEAR-LIST@svpal.org (Forfeiture Endangers American Rights list; sponsored by the national civil asset forfeiture reform organization, F.E.A.R.; for victims of civil asset forfeiture, lawyers, and reform advocates)
> Send the following message to listproc@SVPAL.org:
> subscribe fear-list yourfirstname yourlastname

Federal Communications Law Journal
> URL=http://www.law.indiana.edu:80/fclj/fclj.html

FEDJOBS@dartcms1.dartmouth.edu (Federal Job Bulletin Board)
>   Send the following message to listserv@DARTCMS1.dartmouth.edu or
>   listserv@dartmouth.edu or listserv@DARTCMS1.bitnet:
>   sub fedjobs "your name"

FEDLIB-L@sun7.loc.gov (Federal Library and Information Center Committee (FLICC)'s
FEDLINK Library Network News; announcements only)
>   Send the following message to listserv@sun7.LOC.gov:
>   subscribe fedlib-L Your Name

FEDTAX-L@shsu.edu (US-based Federal Taxation and Accounting Discussion List)
>   Send the following message to listserv@shsu.edu or
>   listserv@shsu.bitnet:
>   subscribe fedtax-L Your Name
>   (gatewayed to misc.taxes)

FEMISA@csf.colorado.edu (list of the Feminist Theory and Gender Studies Section of the
International Studies Association; for scholarly discussions of feminism and international
political economy, global politics, international relations, etc.)
>   Send the following message to listserv@csf.colorado.edu or
>   listproc@csf.colorado.edu:
>   subscribe femisa Your Name

FEMJUR@suvm.syr.edu (Discussions & Information about Feminist Legal Issues)
>   Send the following message to listserv@suvm.syr.edu or
>   listserv@suvm.bitnet:
>   subscribe femjur Your Name

FEN (FINANCIAL ECONOMICS NETWORK: publishes electronically the Journal of Financial
Abstracts; from Social Science Electronic Publishing, Inc.; contact Paul Hopper for
application form at Paul_Hopper@ssep.com or (803) 653-5516 (phone and fax); for more
info, see http://www.crimson.com/ssep/ssephome.html)

FINANCENET (U.S. federal government's financial management network; for information
about the e-mail lists available via FinanceNet, send a blank e-mail message to
email-info@financenet.gov; for general information, send a blank e-mail message to
info@financenet.gov)

FIREARMS-ALERT@shell.portal.com (Firearms list)
>   Send the following message to majordomo@shell.portal.com:
>   subscribe firearms-alert

FIREARMS-POLITICS@tut.cis.ohio-state.edu (list for discussion of firearms legislation and
general talk about rights and current trends related to the Second Amendment of the
U.S. Constitution)
>   Send the following message to
>   firearms-politics-request@tut.cis.ohio-state.edu:
>   subscribe firearms-politics
>   (also on majordomo@world.std.com)

FL-LIST (see FORENSIC-LINGUISTICS)

FLADOCS@nervm.nerdc.ufl.edu (Southeast Document Librarians)
>   Send the following message to listserv@nervm.nerdc.UFL.edu or
>   listserv@nervm.bitnet:
>   subscribe fladocs Your Name

FOI-L@suvm.acs.syr.edu (State and Local Freedom of Information Issues)
    Send the following message to listserv@suvm.acs.syr.edu or
    listserv@suvm.bitnet:
    subscribe FOI-L Your Name

FOIDAY@mtn.org (list for discussion of Freedom of Information Day, March 16, 1995, in
Minnesota, including issues of access to electronic information; archived by the
Minneapolis Telecommunications Network)
    Send the following message to listproc@mtn.org:
    subscribe FoIDay yourfirstname yourlastname

FOOD-LAW@vm1.spcs.umn.edu (Laws Dealing with Food Science)
    Send the following message to listserv@VM1.spcs.umn.edu or
    listserv@UMINN1.bitnet:
    subscribe food-law Your Name

FORCED-MIGRATION@mailbase.ac.uk (Discussion of Refugees and Involuntary Resettlement)
    Send the following message to mailbase@mailbase.ac.uk:
    join forced-migration Your Name
    The JANET address is mailbase@uk.ac.mailbase

FORENS-L@acc.fau.edu (Forensic Medicine and Science list)
    Send the following message to mailserv@acc.fau.edu or
    mailserv@fauvax.bitnet:
    subscribe forens-L Your Name

FORENSIC-LINGUISTICS@mailbase.ac.uk (Language and the Law; list to discuss the use of
linguistic evidence in court, features of courtroom and legal discourse including court
interpreting, and other aspects of the relationship between language and the law; was
FL-LIST)
    Send the following message to mailbase@mailbase.ac.uk:
    join forensic_linguistics Your_first_name(s) Your_last_name
    The JANET address is mailbase@uk.ac.mailbase

FORENSIC-PSYCHIATRY@mailbase.ac.uk (scholarly discussion of forensic psychiatry)
    Send the following message to mailbase@mailbase.ac.uk:
    join forensic-psychiatry Your Name
    The JANET address is mailbase@uk.ac.mailbase

FORENSICECONOMICS-L@acc.wuacc.edu (Forensic Economics list for academics, lawyers,
expert witnesses)
    Send the following message to listserv@acc.wuacc.edu:
    subscribe forensiceconomics-L <first name> <last name>

FREE-L@indycms.iupui.edu (Fathers' Rights and Equality Exchange)
    Send the following message to listserv@indycms.iupui.edu or
    listserv@indycms.bitnet:
    subscribe free-L Your Name

FREEDOM@idbsu.idbsu.edu (list for organizing against the Idaho Citizens Alliance
anti-gay ballot initiative)
    Send the following message to listserv@idbsu.idbsu.edu or
    listserv@idbsu.bitnet:
    subscribe freedom Your Name

FROG-FARM@blizzard.lcs.mit.edu (claiming, exercising and defending rights in America;
restricted membership at discretion of moderator)
    Send the following message to
    frog-farm-request@blizzard.LCS.mit.edu:
    add Frog-Farm Your Name

FSU@sovset.org (Developments in the Former Soviet Union; discussion of economic and political reform movements, nuclear weapons, regional conflicts and environmental concerns)
> Send the following message to fsu-request@sovset.org:
> subscribe fsu Your Name

FUTUREL@vm.temple.edu (Futures Studies for Court Systems)
> Private list; send the following message to listserv@vm.temple.edu or listserv@templevm.bitnet:
> sub FUTUREL (first name) (last name)
> If there are problems, contact Richard B. Klein at V5441E@templevm.bitnet or v5441e@vm.temple.edu

GANGOF10 (closed list for law library directors)

GANGTM@dhvx20.csudh.edu (Open Talk About Gangs)
> Send the following message to listserv@dhvx20.csudh.edu:
> subscribe gangtm
> or to gangtm-request@dhvx20.csudh.edu:
> subscribe

GAYLAW (The National Journal of Sexual Orientation Law; electronic journal devoted to legal issues affecting lesbians, gay men and bisexuals)
> Send the following message to listserv@unc.edu:
> subscribe gaylaw [YOUR FIRST NAME] [YOUR LAST NAME]

GAYNET@queernet.org (GayNet mailing list; gay, lesbian, bisexual political action, AIDS education, etc.)
> Send the following message majordomo@queernet.org:
> subscribe gaynet
> or to listserv@queernet.org:
> sub gaynet <FULL NAME>
> (also GAYNET-DIGEST; for a list of related lists (159K), send the following message to listserv@umdd.umd.edu: get LESBIGAY lists)

GDSIS@polecat.law.indiana.edu (Government Documents Special Interest Section of the American Association of Law Libraries)
> Send the following message to listproc@polecat.law.indiana.edu:
> subscribe gdsis Your Name

German-American Law Journal
> URL=gopher://gal.umd.edu:72/11/

GERMNEWS (German News)
> Send the following message to listserv@vm.gmd.de or listserv@dearn.bitnet:
> subscribe germnews Your Name

GILS@cni.org (Coalition for Networked Information forum for discussion of the Government Information Locator Service initiative)
> Send the following message to listproc@cni.org:
> subscribe gils Your Name

GLB-NEWS@brownvm.brown.edu (Information Repository for News of Interest to GLB* Folk; gay, lesbian, bisexual news)
> Send the following message to listserv@brownvm.brown.edu or listserv@brownvm.bitnet:
> subscribe GLB-news Your Name

Global Legal Studies Journal
    URL=http://www.law.indiana.edu/glsj/glsj.html

GOVACCESS (Government Technology news list)
    Send request to be added to the GovAccess list to Jim Warren,
    jwarren@WELL.com

GOVDOC-L@psuvm.psu.edu (Discussion of Government Document Issues; U.S. based)
    Send the following message to listserv@psuvm.psu.edu or
    listserv@psuvm.bitnet:
    subscribe govdoc-L Your Name

Government Information in Canada = _Information Gouvernementale au Canada_
(quarterly e-journal; contact govinfo@usask.ca.edu for more info)
    URL=http://www.usask.ca/library/gic/index.html

GOVMANAG@list.nih.gov (Management and Leadership in Government)
    Send the following message to listserv@list.nih.gov:
    sub govmanag Firstname Lastname

GPLLA-L@hslc.org (Greater Philadelphia Law Library Association list)
    Send the following message to listserv@HSLC.org:
    subscribe GPLLA-L Your Name

GROEN-LINKS@nic.surfnet.nl (discussion list for members of the Dutch political party,
GroenLinks - protection of the environment and fairer distribution of wealth)
    Send the following message to listserv@nic.surfnet.NL or
    listserv@hearn.bitnet:
    subscribe groen-links yourfirstname yourlastname

GUTNBERG@vdm.cso.uiuc.edu (Project Gutenberg list; electronic texts)
    Send the following message to listserv@vdm.cso.uiuc.edu:
    sub gutnberg

H-DIPLO@uicvm.uic.edu (diplomatic history, foreign affairs & international relations list)
    Send the following message to listserv@uicvm.uic.edu or
    listserv@uicvm.bitnet:
    sub h-diplo Firstname Surname, Yourschool

H-ETHNIC@uicvm.uic.edu (American ethnic & immigration history)
    Send the following message to listserv@uicvm.uic.edu or
    listserv@uicvm.bitnet:
    sub h-ethnic Firstname Surname, Yourschool

H-LAW@uicvm.uic.edu (Legal History list, including U.S. constitutional history)
    Send the following message to listserv@uicvm.uic.edu or
    listserv@uicvm.bitnet:
    sub h-law Firstname Lastname, School

HATE-HOTLINE@jerusalem1.datasrv.co.il (list for reporting hate crimes)
    Send the following message to listserv@JERUSALEM1.datasrv.co.IL:
    subscribe hate-hotline Your Name

HEALTHLAW-L@lawlib.wuacc.edu (Health Law list)
    Send the following message to listserv@lawlib.wuacc.edu:
    subscribe healthlaw-L Your Name

HEALTHPLAN (White House Health List Online; health-reform announcements)
    Send a message to sfreedkin@igc.apc.org in the following exact format:
    Subject: SUBSCRIBE LIST.HEALTHPLAN

In the BODY: ADD:
>   your-electronic-address-here (your real name in parentheses)
>   Your real name here
>   Your postal address (optional)
>   City, State
>   Profession
>   Profession interest in health care (if any)
>   Institutional affiliation, if relevant

HEALTHRE@ukcc.uky.edu (Health Care Reform)
>   Send the following message to listserv@ukcc.uky.edu or
>   listserv@ukcc.bitnet:
>   subscribe healthre Your Name

HISLAW-L@ulkyvm.louisville.edu (History of Law: Feudal, Common, Canon)
>   Send the following message to listserv@ULKYVM.louisville.edu or
>   listserv@ULKYVM.bitnet:
>   subscribe hislaw-L Your Name

HOA-LIST@netcom.com (Home Owner Associations; for owners and associations, as well as attorneys, accountants, and managers working with HOA)
>   For guidelines and instructions for subscribing, send the
>   following message to hoa-list-request@netcom.com: help
>   (ftp://ftp.netcom.com/pub/jr/jraphael/hoa.html)

HOLOCAUS@uicvm.uic.edu (Holocaust studies, anti-semitism)
>   Send the following message to listserv@uicvm.uic.edu or
>   listserv@uicvm.bitnet:
>   sub holocaus Firstname Surname, Yourschool

HOME-ED@mainstream.com (all aspects of home education)
>   Send the following message to listproc@mainstream.com:
>   sub home-ed firstname lastname

HOME-ED-POLITICS@mainstream.com (discussion of political issues related to home education; government intrusion into families, state and federal legislation, public schooling as it influences home education)
>   Send the following message to listproc@mainstream.com:
>   sub home-ed-politics firstname lastname

HOMEHLTH@usa.net (Home Health Care Management issues list)
>   Send the following message to listserv@usa.net:
>   subscribe homehlth Your Name

Homeschool_train_up_a_child@mainstream.com

HOTLINE (newsletter of the U.S. climate action network)
>   Send subscription request to Lelani Arris (larris@igc.apc.org)

HRS-L@bingvmb.cc.binghamton.edu (Systematic Studies of Human Rights)
>   Send the following message to listserv@bingvmb.cc.binghamton.edu or
>   listserv@bingvmb.bitnet:
>   sub hrs-L Your Name

HUMANRIGHTS-L@lawlib.wuacc.edu (International Human Rights Law list)
>   Send the following message to listserv@lawlib.wuacc.edu:
>   subscribe humanrights-L Your Name
>   (was on listserv@acc.wuacc.edu)

IFLA-L@silverplatter.com (International Federation of Library Associations & Institutions list)
> Send the following message to listserv@silverplatter.com:
> subscribe IFLA-L <Your First Name Your Last Name>

IFREEDOM@snoopy.ucis.dal.ca (Forum on Censorship and Intellectual Freedom Issues in Canada)
> Send the following message to listserv@snoopy.ucis.DAL.ca:
> sub ifreedom <FULL NAME>

IGLHRC@igc.apc.org (International Gay and Lesbian Human Rights Commission list)
> Send the following message to IGLHRC@igc.apc.org:
> subscribe IGLHRC Your Name

IIAIPO (see Information Policy Online)

ILL-L@uvmvm.uvm.edu (Interlibrary Loan Discussion Group)
> Send the following message to listserv@uvmvm.uvm.edu or
> listserv@uvmvm.bitnet:
> subscribe ILL-L Your Name

ILSA-L@chicagokent.kentlaw.edu (International Law Students Association list)
> Send the following message to listserv@chicagokent.kentlaw.edu:
> subscribe ILSA-L Your Name

INDKNOW@uwavm.u.washington.edu (Indigenous Knowledge Systems list; cultural property and indigenous peoples)
> Send the following message to listserv@uwavm.u.washington.edu or
> listserv@uwavm.bitnet:
> subscribe indknow <Your Name>

INET-MARKETING@einet.net (Marketing on the Internet list?)
> Send the following message to listproc@einet.net:
> info inet-marketing

INETBIB (German Internet use in libraries list)

INFO-EUROPA@iluso.ci.uv.es (Boletin Informativo sobre la Union Europa; weekly bulletin on the process of European integration published by the Centro de Documentacion Europea in Spain)
> Send the following message to listserv@listserv.uv.es or
> listproc@ILUSO.ci.uv.es:
> subscribe info-europa Your Name

INFO-LAW (defunct Computers in Law list; see TECH-LAW)

INFO-PGP@lucpul.it.luc.edu (Pretty Good Privacy)
> Send the following message to Info-PGP-Request@LUCPUL.it.LUC.edu:
> subscribe info-pgp Your Name

INFOJUR-L (Informatica Juridica = Legal Informatics)

INFOLAW (Information Law Alert; newsletter covering telecommunications, wireless technology, and intellectual property; free trial from 9 September to 11 November 1994; ordinarily 2x/mo. at $195/yr.)
> Send the following message to infolaw-request@his.com:
> join
> (or send free trial request to majordomo@marketplace.com)
> (use "drop" or "unsubscribe" to leave the free trial)

INFOPRO (Information Professionals List; private law related list for professional public record researchers, document & court filings retrieval specialists, private investigators, law and business librarians with investigative duties, certain litigation support professionals with investigative or information retrieval duties, investigative reporters, commercial intelligence analysts, news librarians, etc.)
> For application to join InfoPro, send an email to James Cook
> at jcook@netcom.com

Information Policy Online (Information Industry Association news covering legislation regarding government restriction on information, including privacy issues)
> Send to iiaipo-request@his.com:
> subscribe Your Name

INFOTERRA@pan.cedar.univie.ac.at (global discussion of environmental topics, including the United Nations Environment Programme)
> Send the following message to listproc@pan.cedar.univie.ac.at:
> subscribe InfoTerra Your Name

INMAGIC-ONLINE@knowledgeware.com (InMagic discussion list)
> Send the following message to listserv@knowledgeware.com:
> subscribe inmagic-online firstname lastname

*Institute for Global Communications/Association for Progressive Communications Networks—PeaceNet, EcoNet, ConflictNet, and LaborNet—contain conferences on human rights, conflict resolution, environmental law, women, labor, etc.; unlike the Internet, there is a cost to accessing these networks for academics—after a $15 sign-up fee, the monthly subscription is $10; to find out more information about these networks, use the Institute for Global Communications' gopher (gopher igc.org) or contact support@igc.apc.org (outside of the U.S., use apc-info@apc.org); for information about the PeaceNet World News Service, contact pwn-info@igc.apc.org.

INT-LAW@vm1.spcs.umn.edu (Foreign and International Law Librarians list; includes discussion of foreign & international legal print, electronic, & "people" resources; advanced table of contents posted for _International Legal Materials_ & the _American Journal of International Law_)
> Send the following message to listserv@VM1.spcs.umn.edu or
> listserv@UMINN1.bitnet:
> subscribe int-law Your Name

INT-REL-NAT-SOVEREIGNTY@mailbase.ac.uk (International Relations - National Sovereignty list)
> Send the following message to mailbase@mailbase.ac.uk:
> join int-rel-nat-sovereignty Your Name
> The JANET address is mailbase@uk.ac.mailbase

INT-TRADE-RESEARCH@mailbase.ac.uk (International Trade Research list)
> Send the following message to mailbase@mailbase.ac.uk:
> join int-trade-research Your Name
> The JANET address is mailbase@uk.ac.mailbase

INTCAR-L@american.edu (Internationally-Oriented Computer-Assisted Reporting List; wordwide electronic news & sources)
> Send the following message to listserv@american.edu or
> listserv@auvm.bitnet:
> subscribe intcar-L Your Name

International Trade & Commerce (discussions of international trade, commerce and the global economy, incudes postings of company profiles, trade leads and topics pertaining to entrepreneurial ventures)
> Send subscription request to info-request@tradent.wimsey.bc.ca

INTVIO-L@uriacc.uri.edu (Intimate Violence Research and Practice Issues)
   Send the following message to listserv@uriacc.uri.edu or
   listserv@uriacc.bitnet:
   subscribe intvio-L Your Name

IPE@csf.colorado.edu (International Political Economy)
   Send the following message to listproc@csf.colorado.edu:
   sub ipe yourname
   (contact Lev Gonick, LGONICK@MACH1.WLU.ca, if there are problems
   with subscribing)

IPR-SCIENCE@mailbase.ac.uk (Intellectual Property in Science, including sociological/
ethical/legal analyses)
   Send the following message to mailbase@mailbase.ac.uk:
   join IPR-Science Your Name

IRE-L?

IRISHLAW@irlearn.ucd.ie (Irish Law - Ireland and Northern Ireland)
   Send the following message to listserv@IRLEARN.ucd.ie or
   listserv@listserv.ucd.ie or listserv@IRLEARN.bitnet:
   subscribe IrishLaw Yourfirstname Yourlastname

IRL-POL@rutvm1.rutgers.edu (Irish Politics)
   Send the following message to listserv@RUTVM1.rutgers.edu or
   listserv@RUTVM1.bitnet:
   subscribe IRL-POL Your Name

ISAFP@csf.colorado.edu (International Studies Association Foreign Policy list)
   Send the following message to listproc@csf.colorado.edu:
   subscribe isafp Your Name

ISCNEWS (News Releases and Fact Sheets by the Communications Canada portion of
Industry and Science Canada; communications policy)
   Send the following message to listserv@debra.dgbt.doc.ca:
   subscribe iscnews Firstname Lastname
   (http://debra.dgbt.doc.ca/isc/isc.html)

ISRAELINE (Israel news list from the Israeli Consulate in New York)
   Send the following message to listserv@vm.tau.ac.IL:
   subscribe israeline Your Name
   (called ISRALINE by the listserv)

JAI@israel.nysernet.org (Jewish Activism Initiative; a closed list)
   Send the following message to listproc@israel.nysernet.org:
   subscribe jai Your Name

JAPAN@pucc.princeton.edu (Japan Business and Economics Network)
   Send the following message to listserv@pucc.princeton.edu or
   listserv@pucc.bitnet:
   subscribe japan Your Name

JEDDI-L (a closed list on electronic filings in courts, including discussion of a uniform
non-proprietary legal citation system; also JEDDI-DATA-L)

JEWISHLAWPROF-L@lawlib.wuacc.edu (Jewish Law Professors list)
   Send the following message to listserv@lawlib.wuacc.edu:
   subscribe jewishlawprof-L Your Name

JLS@austin.onu.edu (The Jewish Law Students List; including Jewish law professors interested in assisting students & organizations)
> Send the following message to listserv@austin.onu.edu:
> subscribe JLS [your name]

JPOL@shamash.nysernet.org (Jewish Political Discussion Mailing List)
> Send the following message to listproc@shamash.nysernet.org:
> subscribe jpol Your Name

JUDAFF-L@bingvmb.cc.binghamton.edu (Student Judicial Affairs Discussion List)
> Send the following message to listserv@bingvmb.cc.binghamton.edu or
> listserv@bingvmb.bitnet:
> subscribe judaff-L Your Name

JUDAISME-L@jerusalem1.datasrv.co.il (discussion of Judaism in French)
> Send the following message to listserv@JERUSALEM1.datasrv.co.IL:
> subscribe judaisme-L Your Name

JUDGES-L@ubvm.cc.buffalo.edu ("judges" who cancel posts to Usenet newsgroups that threaten to overload Net News/Usenet)
> Send the following message to listserv@ubvm.cc.buffalo.edu or
> listserv@ubvm.bitnet:
> subscribe judges-L Your Name

JURIST-L@nic.surfnet.nl (Lawyers inform Lawyers on networking=Juristen informeren juristen over netwerkgebruik; discussion is in Dutch)
> Send the following message to listserv@nic.surfnet.NL or
> listserv@hearn.bitnet:
> subscribe jurist-L Yourfirstname Yourlastname

JURIX@nic.surfnet.nl (Discussielijst van stichting juridische kennissystemen)
> Send the following message to listserv@nic.surfnet.NL or
> listserv@hearn.bitnet:
> subscribe jurix Your Name

JUSTINFO (Justice Information Electronic Mailing List; electronic newsletter of the National Criminal Justice Reference Service; designed for criminal justice professionals to obtain accurate, current, and useful criminal justice-related information)
> Send the following message to listproc@ncjrs.aspensys.com:
> subscribe justinfo yourname

KANSASATTORNEYS-L@lawlib.wuacc.edu (Kansas Attorneys list)
> Send the following message to listserv@lawlib.wuacc.edu:
> subscribe kansasattorneys-L Your Name

KSGOV-L@ukanvm.cc.ukans.edu (Kansas Government Forum)
> Send the followning message to listserv@ukanvm.cc.ukans.edu or
> listserv@ukanvm.bitnet:
> subscribe ksgov-L Your Name

LABOR-L@vm1.yorku.ca (Forum on Labor in the Western Hemisphere)
> Send the following message to listserv@VM1.yorku.ca or
> listserv@YORKVM1.bitnet:
> subscribe labor-L Your Name

*LaborNet (see Institute for Global Communications Networks)

Law and Religion list (see LAWREL-L)

LAW-ECONOMICS@mailbase.ac.uk (UK-based Law and Economics list)
Send the following message to mailbase@mailbase.ac.uk:
join law-economics Your Name
The JANET address is mailbase@uk.ac.mailbase

LAW-EUROPE@mailbase.ac.uk (UK-based European Law list)
Send the following message to mailbase@mailbase.ac.uk:
join law-europe Your Name
The JANET address is mailbase@uk.ac.mailbase

LAW-FAMILY@mailbase.ac.uk (UK-based Family Law list)
Send the following message to mailbase@mailbase.ac.uk:
join law-family Your Name
The JANET address is mailbase@uk.ac.mailbase

LAW-LIB@ucdavis.edu (US-based Law Library Mailing List)
Send the following message to listproc@ucdavis.edu:
subscribe law-lib firstname lastname

LAW NOTES (Moncton, New Brunswick, Canada-based Murphy Collette Murphy law firm
bi-monthly publication available electronically about 30 days after hardcopy)
Send subscription request to Hank Murphy at murco@nbnet.nb.ca
(URL=http://www.mps.ohio-state.edu/cgi-bin/hpp?MurCo.html)xyzz2hrtLAW-PUBLIC
@mailbase.ac.uk (UK-based Public/Constitutional Law list)
Send the following message to mailbase@mailbase.ac.uk:
join law-public Your Name
The JANET address is mailbase@uk.ac.mailbase

LAWAID@rutvm1.rutgers.edu (Law School Financial Aid Directors & Officers List; restricted
to Law School personnel working in Financial Aid, Admissions, Administration)
Send the following message to listserv@RUTVM1.rutgers.edu or
listserv@RUTVM1.bitnet:
subscribe lawaid Your Name

LAWAND@polecat.law.indiana.edu (Law and Society list; for interdisciplinary
communication between scholars researching related issues)
Send the following message to listproc@polecat.law.indiana.edu:
subscribe lawand your name

LAWARIEL-L@lawlib.wuacc.edu (Ariel project discussion list; document delivery)
Send the following message to listserv@lawlib.wuacc.edu:
subscribe LAWARIEL-L Your Name

LAWCLINIC@lawlib.wuacc.edu (Clinical Law Teachers discussion group)
Send the following message to listserv@lawlib.wuacc.edu:
subscribe lawclinic your firstname lastname

LAWCONTINUINGED-L@lawlib.wuacc.edu (Law Continuing Education list)
Send the following message to listserv@lawlib.wuacc.edu:
subscribe lawcontinuinged-L your firstname lastname

LAWDEANS-L@lawlib.wuacc.edu (moderated list for Deans of Law Schools (or
representatives); sponsored by the Association of American Law Schools and Washburn
University School of Law)
Send subscription request to Mark Folmsbee, zzfolm@acc.wuacc.edu,
including complete mailing address and title; the information
will be verified in the current AALS _Directory_

LAWDEVEL-L@law.uoregon.edu (list for law school development officers)
    Send the following message to mailserv@law.uoregon.edu:
    subscribe LAWDEVEL-L

LAWFIRMADMIN-L@lawlib.wuacc.edu (Law Firm Administration discussion list)
    Send the following message to listserv@lawlib.wuacc.edu:
    subscribe lawfirmadmin-L Your Name

LAWJOBS-L@lawlib.wuacc.edu (Law Jobs list; job announcements/openings in any
law-related profession may be posted; NO RESUMES)
    Send the following message to listserv@lawlib.wuacc.edu:
    subscribe lawjobs-L Your Name

LAWJOURNAL-L@lawlib.wuacc.edu (list for Law School Law Review and Law Journal staffs)
    Send the following message to listserv@lawlib.wuacc.edu:
    subscribe lawjournal-L Your Name

LAWLIBDIR-L@lawlib.wuacc.edu (Academic Law Library Directors)
    Send the following message to listserv@lawlib.wuacc.edu:
    subscribe lawlibdir-L Your Name

LAWLIBREF-L@lawlib.wuacc.edu (list for Legal Reference Librarians)
    Send the following message to listserv@lawlib.wuacc.edu:
    subscribe lawlibref-L your firstname lastname

LAWPROF@chicagokent.kentlaw.edu (Law Professors & Lecturers list)
    Send the following message to
    listserv@chicagokent.kentlaw.edu:
    subscribe lawprof Your name, Position, Institution

LAWREL@ualr.edu (electronic discussion list of Law & Religion class at the University of
Arkansas at Little Rock School of Law)
    Send the following message to mailser@ualr.edu:
    subscribe lawrel {your full name}

LAWREL-L@lists.cua.edu (list of the Association of American Law Schools Section on Law
and Religion)
    Send the following message to mailserv@lists.cua.edu:
    subscribe LAWREL-L

LAWSCH-L@american.edu (US-based Law School Discussion List; mainly law students)
    Send the following message to listserv@american.edu or
    listserv@listserv.american.edu or listserv@auvm.bitnet:
    subscribe lawsch-L Your Name

LAWSOC-L@cc.umanitoba.ca (Canadian Law and Society list)
    Send the following message to lawsoc-L-request@cc.umanitoba.ca:
    subscribe lawsoc-L Your Name

LAWSRC-L@listserv.law.cornell.edu (Internet Law Sources list; for exchange of information
about Internet resources for law teachers, librarians, and practitioners)
    Send the following message to listserv@listserv.law.cornell.edu:
    subscribe lawsrc-L Your full name

LAWSUIT (MTV v. Adam Curry)
    Send the following message to lawsuit-request@mtv.com:
    subscribe LAWSUIT Your Name

LEFT-L@cmsa.berkeley.edu (forum for activist discussion of building the democratic left in the U.S. and in the world)
>Send the following message to listserv@cmsa.berkeley.edu:
>subscribe LEFT-L <your full name>

LEGAL BYTES (quarterly newsletter from the Texas law firm of George, Donaldson & Ford; intellectual property, copyright, computer communications and related topics)
>Send the following message to legal-bytes-request@io.com:
>subscribe legal-bytes
>(archived at http://www.eff.org/pub/Publications/
>E-Journals/Legal_Bytes/)

LEGALETHICS-L@lawlib.wuacc.edu (Legal Ethics list)
>Send the following message to listserv@lawlib.wuacc.edu:
>subscribe legalethics-L Your Name

LEGALINK (Small, Craig & Werkenthin, P.C., monthly electronic newsletter summarizing current legal developments of interest to high tech businesses)
>Send the message with "subscribe" in the subject field and in the
>body of the message to legalink-request@tpoint.net; also archived at
>the tpoint.net gopher & via web at http://www.hal.com/~markg/LegaLink/)

LEGALINT-L@sunbird.usd.edu (Legal Internships list; discussion of locating and obtaining legal internships)
>Send the following message to listproc@sunbird.usd.edu:
>subscribe LEGALINT-L Your Name

THE LEGAL LIST (_The Legal List: Law-Related Resources on the Internet and Elsewhere_ by Erik J. Heels)
>Send the following message to listserv@justice.eliot.me.us:
>subscribe legal-list yourname
>(this will put you on the list to receive via e-mail
>announcements re, plus the full text, of new versions of
>the _Legal List_ book; to receive announcements only via
>e-mail, see TLL-ANNOUNCE below)
>(the most recent version is accessible via the URL:
>ftp://ftp.midnight.com/pub/LegalList/legallist.txt;
>for more information, send a request to info@justice.eliot.me.us)

LEGAL-LISTOWNERS@listserv.law.cornell.edu (list for owners and managers of electronic mailing lists and Usenet newsgroups)
>Send the following message to listserv@listserv.law.cornell.edu:
>subscribe legal-listowners Your Name

LEGAL-WEBMASTERS@listserv.law.cornell.edu (support list for legal web developers)
>Send the following message to listserv@listserv.law.cornell.edu:
>subscribe legal-webmasters Your Name

LEGALSTUDIES@listserv.law.cornell.edu (list for undergraduate level legal educators)
>Send the following message to listserv@listserv.law.cornell.edu:
>subscribe legalstudies yourfirstname yourlastname

LEGALTEN@world.std.com (Topical Evaluation Network on Issues in Mental Health Care and Law; legal and forensic issues in mental health)
>Send the following message to majordomo@world.std.com:
>subscribe legalten
>(or subscribe legalten-digest)

LEGISLATE-L@lists.colorado.edu (list for discussion of the LEGI-SLATE U.S. federal documents database)
    Send the following message to listserv@lists.colorado.edu:
    subscribe legislate-L <your full name>

LEGWRI-L@chicagokent.kentlaw.edu (Legal Writing Instructors list)
    Send the following message to listserv@chicagokent.kentlaw.edu:
    subscribe legwri-L Your Name

LEXISUSER-L@lawlib.wuacc.edu (list for law student discussion of the LEXIS legal database; the list is not formally affiliated with LEXIS-NEXIS company)
    Send the following message to listserv@lawlib.wuacc.edu:
    subscribe lexisuser-L Your Name

LIBADMIN@umab.bitnet

LIBER-PILOT@mailbase.ac.uk (European Research Libraries)
    Send the following message to mailbase@mailbase.ac.uk:
    join liber-pilot Your Name
    The JANET address is mailbase@uk.ac.mailbase

LIBERNET@dartmouth.edu (Libertarian mailing list)
    Send the following message to libernet-request@dartmouth.edu:
    subscribe libernet Your Name

LIBSUP-L@u.washington.edu (Library Support Staff List)
    Send the following message to listproc@u.washington.edu:
    subscribe LIBSUP-L Your Name

LICENSE@uga.cc.uga.edu (Software Licensing list)
    Send the following message to listserv@uga.cc.uga.edu or
    listserv@uga.bitnet:
    subscribe license Your Name
    (also on listserv@bitnic.bitnet, @dearn.bitnet, @marist.bitnet)

LIFEINS-L@netcom.com (Discussion of Life Insurance; for life insurance agents)
    Send the following message to listserv@netcom.com:
    subscribe lifeins-l

LIIBULLETIN (Cornell Legal Information Institute e-bulletin containing syllabi of U.S. Supreme Court decisions)
    Send the following message to listserv@listserv.law.cornell.edu:
    subscribe LIIBULLETIN Name, Address, Telephone Number
    [all on one line, i.e. without carriage return]

LINUX-LAW@law.uark.edu (discussion of Linux-Law related issues such as setting up Linux server or workstations)
    Send the following message to listserv@law.uark.edu:
    subscribe linux-law
    (archived at http://law.uark.edu/arklaw/listserv.htm)

LIS-LAW@mailbase.ac.uk (UK-based legal information & law libraries list)
    Send the following message to mailbase@mailbase.ac.uk:
    join lis-law firstname lastname
    The JANET address is mailbase@uk.ac.mailbase

LLSDC@gmu.edu (Law Librarians' Society of Washington, D.C. list)
    Send the following message to listproc@gmu.edu:
    sub llsdc Your Name

LNET-LLC@usa.net (Limited Liability Company Net: LLCNET; Limited Liability Companies and Partnerships conference)
> Send the following message to listserv@usa.net:
> sub LNET-LLC [first name] [last name]

LNN (Legal Net Newsletter; defunct e-journal was at fergp@sytex.com; see ftp://tstc.edu/legal-net-news/)

LOANSTAR@twu.edu (Library Resource Sharing in Texas)
> Send the following message to listserv@venus.twu.edu or listserv@twu.edu:
> subscribe LoanStar <your name>

LONGMAN (list for notification of new publications of Longman Asia)
> Send a message to RLOWE@net.super.hk with the SUBJECT:
> subscribe longman

LPBR-L (Law and Politics Book Review)
> Send the following message to listserv@listserv.acns.nwu.edu:
> subscribe LPBR-L Your Name

LPSS-L@lists.acs.ohio-state.edu (Law and Political Science Section of the Association of College and Research Libraries; forum for the exchange of information in the broad areas of law and political science)
> Send the following message to listserver@lists.acs.ohio-state.edu:
> subscribe LPSS-L Firstname Lastname

LSE@cms.cc.wayne.edu (Legal Studies Education)
> Send the following message to listserv@cms.cc.wayne.edu or listserv@WAYNEST1.bitnet:
> subscribe LSE Your Name

MAALL@wuvmd.wustl.edu (Mid-America Association of Law Libraries list)
> Send the following message to listserv@wuvmd.WUSTL.edu or listserv@wuvmd.bitnet:
> sub MAALL Firstname Lastname

MAK-NEWS (Macedonian News)
> Send the following message to listserv@ubvm.cc.buffalo.edu or listserv@ubvm.bitnet:
> subscribe maknws-L Your Name

MANAGED-BEHAVIOURAL-HEALTHCARE@mailbase.ac.uk (international discussion of behavioural health care including impact of health care reform in the U.S.)
> Send the following message to mailbase@mailbase.ac.uk:
> join managed-behavioural-healthcare Your Name
> The JANET address is mailbase@uk.ac.mailbase

MEHR-JUS@fgr.wu-wien.ac.at (Mehr-Jus; Austria-based law list; discussion in German)
> Send the following message to listserv@fgr.wu-wien.ac.at:
> sub mehr-jus Your Name
> (at.mail.mehr-jus)

MIGRA-LIST@cc.utah.edu (International Migration list)
> Send the following message to migra-list-request@cc.utah.edu:
> subscribe migra-list Your Name

MIGRATION NEWS (summaries of current immigration and integration developments; archived at the dual.ucdavis.edu gopher)
> To subscribe, send e-mail address to migrant@primal.ucdavis.edu

MN-DEBATE@mr.net (Minnesota moderated list for first electronic mail gubernatorial and U.S. Senate debate; will not accept messages, but public can view debate without comment)
> Send the following message to majordomo@mr.net:
> subscribe mn-debate

MN-GOVT (list of the Information Policy Office of the Minnesota Department of Administration for distribution of "Access Minnesota Update", e-bulletin concerning public electronic access to Minnesota government documents)
> Send the following message to listserv@VM1.spcs.umn.edu or
> listserv@UMINN1.bitnet:
> subscribe mn-govt Your Name

MN-POLITICS@MR.NET (Minnesota Politics and Public Policy Electronic-Mail Forum of the Minnesota E-Democracy Project)
> Send the following message to majordomo@mr.net:
> subscribe mn-politics

MODELUN@indycms.iupui.edu (Model United Nations Bulletin)
> Send the following message to listserv@indycms.iupui.edu or
> listserv@indycms.bitnet:
> subscribe modelun Your Name

MUNINET@financenet.gov (FinanceNet's List for City Managers; coordinated by the International Institute of Municipal Clerks; issues relating to financial accountability and stewardship of municipalities, towns and townships within larger geopolitical jurisdictions)
> Send the following message to listproc@financenet.gov:
> subscribe MuniNet yourfirstname yourlastname

NAFTA@mexnet.org (list of the Mexico Business Network)
> Send the following message to listserv@mexnet.org:
> subscribe nafta Your Name

NASA DAILY (U.S. NASA & other space news)
> Send to pds-listserver@space.mit.edu:
> subscribe your name

The National Journal of Sexual Orientation Law (see GAYLAW)

NATIVE-L@tamvm1.tamu.edu (Issues Pertaining to Aboriginal Peoples)
> Send the following message to listserv@TAMVM1.tamu.edu or
> listserv@TAMVM1.bitnet:
> subscribe native-L <Your Full Name>

NATODATA (North Atlantic Treaty Organization press releases, speeches, articles, communiques, NATO REVIEW, fact sheets, etc.)
> Send the following message to listserv@CC1.KULEUVEN.ac.be or
> listserv@BLEKUL11.bitnet:
> subscribe natodata Firstname Lastname

NATRESLIB-L@cc.usu.edu (Natural Resources Librarians and Information Specialists)
> Send subscription request to annhed@cc.usu.edu or
> annhed@library.lib.usu.edu

NAVNEWS (Navy News Service - official news service of the Department of the Navy of the United States of America)
> Send an e-mail message to navnews-request@ncts.navy.MIL with the
> single word in the subject line: subscribe
> (you can leave the body of the message blank; for more
> information, check the web site at URL=
> http://www.navy.mil/navpalib/news/navnews/Nnsmail.txt

NCLSMTG@gwuvm.gwu.edu (National Conference of Lawyers and Scientists)
Send the following message to listserv@gwuvm.gwu.edu or
listserv@gwuvm.bitnet:
subscribe NCLSMTG Your Name

NCS-L@umdd.umd.edu (National Crime Survey Discussion)
Send the following message to listserv@umdd.umd.edu or
listserv@umdd.bitnet:
subscribe ncs-L Your Name

NEA (Nuclear Energy Agency Monthly Update; news of new files added to NEA FTP site,
including the _Nuclear Law Bulletin_ and agreements)
Send a blank message to listserv@nea.fr with the subject: sub
(see also web at http://www.nea.fr/)

NET-LAWYERS@webcom.com (Lawyers and the Internet; moderated list for lawyers,
librarians, law professors, paralegals, law students, and others interested in law to
discuss issues related to the use of the Internet in the study, practice, development, and
marketing of law)
Send the following message to net-lawyers-request@webcom.com:
subscribe
(also NET-LAWYERS-DIGEST)

NETTRAIN@ubvm.cc.buffalo.edu (Internet/BITNET Network Trainers Discussion List; *not
for beginners* ; HELP-NET at LISTSERV@TEMPLEVM.BITNET or LISTSERV@VM.TEMPLE.EDU
or the Usenet newsgroup, bit.listserv.help-net, is for beginning users of the Internet; the
NETTRAIN list for people who train others on how to use the Internet was started by Jim
Milles at Saint Louis University Law Library)
Send the following message to listserv@ubvm.cc.buffalo.edu or
listserv@ubvm.bitnet:
subscribe nettrain Your Name

NETWORK2D-L@austin.onu.edu (American Bar Association list for discussion of issues
raised in _Network 2d_, the quarterly newsletter on using technology in law offices and
in the courts)
Send the following message to listserv@austin.onu.edu:
subscribe network2d-L Your Name
(include your occupation in the subject line)

NEWJURIS-L (closed list)

NEWLAWBOOKS-L@lawlib.wuacc.edu (New Law Books list)
Send the following message to listserv@lawlib.wuacc.edu:
subscribe newlawbooks-L Your Name

NEWS (U.S. FinanceNet National Performance Review News; list for general government
financial management documents, news, announcements and notices)
Send the following message to listproc@financenet.gov:
subscribe news Your Name

NHCTEN@world.std.com (National Health Care Reform Topical Evaluation Network -
impact on delivery of mental health care and drug abuse treatment services at the state
and local level)
Send the following message to majordomo@world.std.com:
subscribe nhcten
or subscribe nhcten-digest

NIL-L@austin.onu.edu (NeXT-In-Law discussion list; official electronic forum for JuriNUG, the NeXT Legal Users Group; not affiliated with NeXT Inc.)
Send the following message to listserv@austin.onu.edu:
subscribe NIL-L Your Name

NOCALL-LIST@netcom.com (Northern California Association of Law Libraries, a regional chapter of the American Association of Law Libraries)
Send the following message to listserv@netcom.com:
subscribe NOCALL-LIST

NORML-L@tamvm1.tamu.edu (National Organization for the Reform of Marijuana Laws, Texas)
Send the following message to listserv@TAMVM1.tamu.edu or listserv@TAMVM1.bitnet:
subscribe NORML-L Your Name

NORWAVES (Royal Ministry of Foreign Affairs' weekly news about Norway in English)
Send the following message to listserv@nki.no:
subscribe norwaves Your Name

NOTISLAW@listserv.law.cornell.edu (NOTIS Law Users' Group)
Send the following message to listserv@listserv.law.cornell.edu:
subscribe notislaw your name

NRCH@usa.net (National Report on Computers and Health's Hospital Information Systems Issues list; open discussion of management, operations, and technical issues facing health care information systems executives)
Send the following message to listserv@usa.net:
subscribe nrch yourfirstname yourlastname

NREN-DISCUSS@psi.com (National Research and Education Network discussion list)
Send the following message to nren-discuss-request@psi.com:
subscribe nren-discuss Your Name

NYCOMNET@ubvm.cc.buffalo.edu (New York State Community Networks and Free-Nets List)
Send the following message to listserv@ubvm.cc.buffalo.edu or listserv@ubvm.bitnet:
sub nycomnet your name

NYHEDS-LISTEN (Danske Nyheder = Danish News)
Send subscription request to nyheder-request@sysadmin.com
(archived at gopher.denet.dk)

OFFSHORE (a free e-mail newsletter on offshore company and trust formations, private annuities, limited liability companies & creation of asset protection strategies)
Send a blank message to offshore@dnai.com with the subject: sub

OILGASLAW-L@lawlib.wuacc.edu (Oil & Gas Law list)
Send the following message to listserv@lawlib.wuacc.edu:
subscribe oilgaslaw-L Your Name

OMRI-L (Daily Digest of the Open Media Research Institute; compilation of news concerning the former Soviet Union and East-Central and Southeastern Europe; continues the RFE/RL Daily Report; public-private venture of the Open Society Institute and the U.S. Board for International Broadcasting)
Send the following message to listserv@ubvm.cc.buffalo.edu:
subscribe omri-l (your name)

OTANEWS (U.S. Office of Technology Assessment news list)
   Send the following message to listserv@ota.gov:
   subscribe otanews [your name]

PACLIB-L@info.anu.edu.au (Asia Pacific Special Interest Group of the Australian Library
and Information Association list for discussion of Pacific Island materials and the
development of Pacific collections and networks)
   Send the following message to majordomo@info.anu.edu.au:
   subscribe paclib-L

PACS-L@uhupvm1.uh.edu (Public Access Computer Systems Forum)
   Send the following message to listserv@UHUPVM1.uh.edu:
   subscribe pacs-L Your Name

PARALEGAL-L@lawlib.wuacc.edu (Paralegal/Legal Assistant discussion list)
   Send the following message to listserv@lawlib.wuacc.edu:
   subscribe PARALEGAL-L Your Name

PATENTS@world.std.com (Internet Patent News Service)
   To subscribe, send the message "help" to patents@world.std.com

*PeaceNet (see Institute for Global Communications Networks)

PGP-PUBLIC-KEYS@c2.org (list to distribute PGP public keys; gated to alt.security.pgp;
questions or problems with PGP are posted on alt.security.pgp)
   Send the following message to majordomo@c2.org:
   subscribe pgp-public-keys
   (contact owner, Samuel Kaplin, skaplin@skypoint.com, for further info)

PITTSBURGH95-L@lawlib.wuacc.edu (American Association of Law Libraries list for
discussion of the July 1995 Annual Convention)
   Send the following message to listserv@lawlib.wuacc.edu:
   subscribe pittsburg95-L Your Name

PJAL@utxvm.cc.utexas.edu (The Progressive Jewish Activism List; for peace and social
justice discussions)
   Send the following message to listserv@utxvm.cc.utexas.edu or
   listserv@utxvm.bitnet:
   subscribe pjal Your Name

PJML@israel.nysernet.org (The Progressive Jewish Mailing List)
   Send the following message to listserver@israel.nysernet.org:
   subscribe pjml Your Name

POL-ECON@shsu.edu (Political Economy)
   Send the following message to listserv@shsu.edu or
   listserv@shsu.bitnet:
   subscribe pol-econ Your Name

POLI-SCI@rutvm1.rutgers.edu (Political Science Digest)
   Send the following message to listserv@rutvm1.rutgers.edu or
   listserv@RUTVM1.bitnet:
   subscribe poli-sci Your Name

POLICE-L@cunyvm.cuny.edu (The Police Discussion List; restricted to sworn law
enforcement officers (LEOs))
   Send the following message to listserv@cunyvm.cuny.edu or
   listserv@cunyvm.bitnet:
   sub police-L yourfirstname yourlastname

POLICY@sovset.org (Russian Foreign Policy)
    Send the following message to policy-request@sovset.org:
    subscribe policy Your Name

POLITICS@sovset.org (Political and Economic Change in Russia)
    Send the following message to politics-request@sovset.org:
    subscribe politics Your Name

POLITICS@ibm.ucis.vill.edu (Forum for the Discussion of Politics)
    Send the following message to listserv@ibm.ucis.VILL.edu or
    listserv@VILLVM.bitnet:
    subscribe politics Your Name

POS302-L@ilstu.edu (Race/Ethnicity Book Review List; for Race, Ethnicity and Social Inequality seminar, Political Science 302, at Illinois State University, expanded to include "virtual" participants; subscription open to all faculty and students at any university or college)
    Send the following message to to listserv@ILSTU.edu:
    subscribe pos302-L Your Full Name, Institution
    For further information, contact Gary Klass, GMKLASS@ILSTU.edu

POSCIM@vm.gmd.de (POlitical SCIences Mailinglist)
    Send the following message to listserv@vm.gmd.de or
    listserv@dearn.bitnet:
    subscribe poscim Your Name

PRELAW-L@vax1.elon.edu (Prelaw Advisor's Discussion List)
    Send the following message to PRELAW-L-request@VAX1.ELON.edu:
    subscribe your_name

PRELAW-STUDENTS@lawlib.wuacc.edu (forum for pre-law students who wish to discuss law school and career issues)
    Send the following message to listserv@lawlib.wuacc.edu:
    subscribe prelaw-students Your Name

PRESS-RELEASE (National Rifle Association of America press releases)
    Send the following message to press-release-request@nra.org:
    subscribe press-release Your Name

PRIVACY@vortex.com (Privacy Forum digest)
    Send the following message to privacy-request@vortex.com:
    subscribe privacy <your full name>

PRIVACY101@c2.org (online seminar beginning 1 September 1994)
    Send the following message to majordomo@c2.org:
    subscribe PRIVACY101

PRIVATELAWLIB-L@lawlib.wuacc.edu (Private Law Libraries list)
    Send the following message to listserv@lawlib.wuacc.edu:
    subscribe privatelawlib-L your firstname lastname

PSRT-L@mizzou1.missouri.edu (Political Science Research and Teaching list; has the Law and Politics Book Review e-journal)
    Send the following message to listserv@MIZZOU1.missouri.edu or
    listserv@MIZZOU1.bitnet:
    subscribe psrt-L Your Name

PSYLAW-L@utepvm.ep.utexas.edu (Psychology & Law, International Discussion list)
    Send the following message to listserv@utepvm.ep.utexas.edu or
    listserv@utepa.bitnet:
    subscribe psylaw-L Your Name

PUBADM-L@vm.marist.edu (Teaching Public Administration)
Send the following message to listserv@vm.marist.edu or
listserv@marist.bitnet:
subscribe pubadm-L Your Name

PUBLABOR@relay.adp.wisc.edu (Public Sector Unionism)
Send the following message to listserver@relay.adp.wisc.edu:
subscribe publabor <your name>

PUBPOL-L@vm1.spcs.umn.edu (Public Policy Graduate Studies Network)
Send the following message to listserv@VM1.spcs.umn.edu or
listserv@UMINN1.bitnet:
subscribe pubpol-L Your Name
(or subscribe pubpol-d Your Name, for Public Policy Open
Discussion list)

QUEERLAW@qrd.org (list for discussion, analysis and promulgation of queer legal theory
and all other aspects of sexual orientation and the law; for law professors, students, and
others interested in how the law affects, and is affected by, sexual minorities)
Send the following message to majordomo@qrd.org or
majordomo@abacus.oxy.edu:
subscribe queerlaw

QUEERPLANET@qrd.org (list for organizing the International Lesbian and Gay Assocation
conference in 1994, to improve nondiscrimination on the basis of sexual orientation
worldwide, to discuss immigration issues affecting homosexuals)
Send the following message to majordomo@abacus.oxy.edu
or majordomo@oxy.edu or majordomo@qrd.org:
subscribe queerplanet
(was on majordomo@vector.casti.com)

QUOTE-PAGE (list containing daily ranges of a number of commodity futures; lists most
actively traded commodities in the U.S.)
Send the following message to listserv@pitstar.com:
sub quote-page youre-mailaddress

RARE-LAWBOOKS@netcom.com (Meyer Boswell Books, American Antiquarian Bookshop,
searchable electronic catalogue of about 6,000 rare law books in its inventory)
For more information about the database and for searching
instructions, send to rare-lawbooks@netcom.com, the message:
help
with the subject:
help

REGS-L@albnydh2.bitnet (Title 10 Rules and Regulations)
Send the following message to listserv@ALBNYDH2.bitnet:
subscribe regs-L Your Name

RELIGIONLAW@grizzly.ucla.edu (Religion and the Law —U.S.-based list for discussion of
free exercise, the Establishment Clause, Religious Freedom Restoration Act, equal
protection, religious discrimination and religious harassment under Title VII, etc.; for law
professors and lawyers who practice in the area; a listproc list)
Send the following message to listserv@GRIZZLY.UCLA.edu:
subscribe ReligionLaw yourfirstname yourlastname

RESIDENTIAL-REALESTATE@property.com (list restricted to full-time real estate brokers,
investors, management companies, developers, or institutions; networking/dealmaking
forum)
Send the following message to listserv@property.com:
subscribe residential-realestate [Your Internet Name/Address]

REVS@csf.colorado.edu (Racial-Religious-Ethno-Nationalist Violence Studies list; news and discussion of collective violence based on racial, religious, ethnic discrimination)
>   Send the following message to listserv@csf.colorado.edu:
>   sub revs Your Name

RFERL-L@ubvm.cc.buffalo.edu (Radio Free Europe/Radio Liberty Research Institute Daily Report; daily digest of the latest developments in Russia, Transcaucasia and Central Asia, and Central and Eastern Europe)
>   Send the following message to listserv@ubvm.cc.buffalo.edu or
>   listserv@ubvm.bitnet:
>   subscribe RFERL-L Your Name
>   (continued by OMRI-L list?)

RIGHTS-L@american.edu (Rights and Responsibilities list)
>   Send the following message to listserv@american.edu or
>   listserv@auvm.bitnet:
>   subscribe rights-L Your Name

RISKNET@mcfeeley.cc.utexas.edu (Discussion of Risk and Insurance Issues)
>   Send the following message to listproc@mcfeeley.cc.utexas.edu:
>   subscribe risknet <your real name>
>   For more information, contact James R. Garven
>   (jgarven@MCL.cc.utexas.edu)

RISKS@uga.bitnet (RFD: RISKS Forum Digest - risks to the public in computers and related systsems; ACM Committee on Computers and Public Policy)
>   Send the following message to listserv@uga.bitnet:
>   subscribe risks
>   (reading RISKS as a newsgroup, comp.risks, is preferred;
>   if the above methods don't work, contact
>   risks-request@CSL.SRI.COM, a non-automated address)

RKBA-ALERT (National Rifle Association of America announcements)
>   Send the following message to rkba-alert-request@nra.org:
>   subscribe rkba-alert Your Name

RLGLAW-L@lyra.stanford.edu (Research Libraries Group Law Library list; beginning 4 November 1994, unmoderated closed listproc list that focuses on matters of particular interest to the law library community; open to any staff working in an RLG member institution; new subscriptions are added by RLG staff upon request; for more information, contact Win-Shin Stella Chiang at BL.wsc@RLG.standford.edu; was @VM1.spcs.umn.edu)

ROGUELIB (Law Librarians Association of Wisconsin (LLAW) list; defunct)
>   Contact Lyonette Louis-Jacques, llou@midway.uchicago.edu, for
>   subscription information for replacement list

ROUNDTABLE@cni.org (Telecommunications Policy Roundtable Forum)
>   Send the following message to listproc@cni.org:
>   subscribe roundtable Your Name

RPG-COPYRIGHT@vorlon.mankato.msus.edu (state of the role-playing industry with regard to the copyright concerns raised by T&R, Inc.)
>   Send the following message to majordomo@VORLON.mankato.msus.edu:
>   subscribe rpg-copyright

RRE@weber.ucsd.edu (Red Rock Eaters list)
>   Send the following message to rre-maintainers@weber.ucsd.edu:
>   subscribe rre Your Name
>   or to rre-request@weber.ucsd.edu with the subject:
>   subscribe firstname lastname

RSAREF-DEV-L@consensus.com (discussion list for software developers interested in RSAREF - a cryptography source code toolkit)
> Send the following message to listproc@consensus.com:
> subscribe rsaref-dev-L Your Name

RUNEBERG-LIST@lysator.liu.se (Project Runeberg list; effort to make available on the Internet all the publications (including laws) of the Scandinavian languages and Finnish, plus Estonian)
> Send the following message to runeberg-LIST-request@LYSATOR.LIU.se:
> subscribe runeberg-LIST your name

RURALNET-L@musom01.mu.wvnet.edu (Rural Health Care Discussion List)
> Send the following message to listserv@MUSOM01.mu.wvnet.edu:
> subscribe RuralNet-L Your Name

RUSHTALK@ohionet.org (Conservative Politics with the Views of Rush Limbaugh)
> Send the following message with the subject "subscribe" to
> rushtalk-request@ohionet.org:
> subscribe

RVDM-L@nic.surfnet.nl (De Rechten van de Mens Lijst = Human Rights List; initiative of the Maastricht Centrum voor de Rechten van de Mens, the Netherlands; in Dutch)
> Send the following message to listserv@nic.surfnet.nl:
> subscribe rvdm-l Uwvoornaam Uwachternaam

SAGE@lyman.stanford.edu (moderated forum of the Students Against GEnocide (SAGE) - Project Bosnia)
> Send the following message to mailserv@lyman.stanford.edu:
> subscribe sage Firstname Lastname

SAMSBEST@zilker.net (read-only "patriotic" movement list; postings from related postings on other lists and newsgroups; contact tsjwr@ACAD1.alaska.edu for more information)
> Send the following message to majordomo@ZILKER.net:
> subscribe samsbest

SASH-L@asuvm.inre.asu.edu (Sociologists Against Sexual Harassment)
> Send the following message to listserv@asuvm.inre.asu.edu or
> listserv@asuacad.bitnet:
> subscribe sash-L Your Name
> (or contact Phoebe M. Stambaugh, azpxs@asuacad.bitnet or
> azpxs@asuvm.inre.asu.edu)

SCALL-LIST@netcom.com (Southern California Association of Law Libraries)
> Send the following message to listserv@netcom.com:
> subscribe SCALL-LIST

SEA-10035@sea.org (New York-based Society for Electronic Access' list for discussion of bill on access to legislative information in New York)
> Send to sea-10035-request@sea.org message with "subscribe" as the
> subject

SEA-LEGAL@sea.org (New York-based Society for Electronic Access Legal Watch; list for discussion of legislators, bills/laws, cases pending, regulations and regulatory infrastructure relating to online civil liberties and access issues either of national scope or relevant to NYC)
> Send the following message to sea-legal-request@sea.org:
> subscribe sea-legal Your Name

SEATTLE94-L@acc.wuacc.edu (list to discuss the July 1994 American Association of Law Libraries convention in Seattle, Washington)
>   Send the following message to listserv@acc.wuacc.edu:
>   subscribe seattle94-L Your Name
>   (defunct)

SENATE-NEWS@sen.ca.gov (California State Senate bill status updating service)
>   For information about the service and how to subscribe to it,
>   send the following message to senate-news@sen.ca.gov:
>   help

SERIALST@uvmvm.uvm.edu (Serials in Libraries)
>   Send the following message to listserv@uvmvm.uvm.edu or
>   listserv@uvmvm.bitnet:
>   subscribe SERIALST Your Name

SLABF-L@psuvm.psu.edu (Business and Finance Division of the Special Library Association)
>   Send the following message to listserv@psuvm.psu.edu or
>   listserv@psuvm.bitnet:
>   subscribe SLABF-L Your Name

SLAVLIBS (Slavic Librarians list)
>   Subscription limited to persons who actively work with Slavic
>   materials; contact Lyonette Louis-Jacques, llou@midway.uchicago.edu,
>   for subscription information

SOC-SUMMIT@confer.edc.org (United Nations Development Programme list for discussion of issues of the World Summit on Social Development in 1995)
>   Send the following message to majordomo@confer.edc.org or
>   listserv@confer.edc.org:
>   subscribe soc-summit

SOCPOL-L@vmd.cso.uiuc.edu (Social Politics: Gender, State and Society list; discussions of gender and social policy, citizenship, and the role to the state in the family, workplace, and society)
>   Send the following message to listserv@vmd.cso.uiuc.edu or
>   listserv@uiucvmd.bitnet:
>   sub socpol-L Your Name

SOFTPATS@uvmvm.uvm.edu (Software Patents and related issues, including legality and desirability of software patents)
>   Send the following message to listserv@uvmvm.uvm.edu or
>   listserv@uvmvm.bitnet:
>   subscribe SoftPats Your Name
>   (apparently defunct)

SOUTH-ASIA-STUDIES-L@coombs.anu.edu.au
>   Send the following message to majordomo@coombs.anu.edu.au:
>   subscribe south-asia-studies-L <your e-mail address>

SPORTLAW@cmsuvmb.cmsu.edu (Sport Law)
>   Send the following message to listserv@cmsuvmb.cmsu.edu or
>   listserv@cmsuvmb.bitnet:
>   subscribe sportlaw Your Name

STATEPOL@umab.umd.edu (Politics in the American States)
>   Send the following message to listserv@umab.umd.edu or
>   listserv@umab.bitnet:
>   subscribe statepol Your Name

STONEWALL25@queernet.org (List for discussion and planning of "Stonewall 25", international gay/lesbian/bi rights march in New York City on June 26, 1994)
> Send the following message to stonewall25-request@queernet.org:
> subscribe stonewall25 Your Name

STOPRAPE@brownvm.brown.edu (Sexual Assault Activist List)
> Send the following message to listserv@brownvm.brown.edu or listserv@brownvm.bitnet:
> subscribe stoprape Your Name

STUDENTLAWTECH@listserv.law.cornell.edu (Students of Law and Technology; forum for law students interested in issues related to law and technology)
> Send the following message to listserv@listserv.law.cornell.edu:
> subscribe StudentLawTech yourname

STUMPERS-L@crf.cuis.edu (Difficult Reference Questions)
> Send the following message to mailserv@crf.cuis.edu:
> subscribe STUMPERS-L youre-mailaddress

SUSTAINABLE-DEVELOPMENT@world.std.com (Sustainable Development list)
> Send the following message to majordomo@world.std.com:
> subscribe sustainable-development

SWALL-L@Post-Office.UH.EDU (Southwestern Association of Law Libraries, regional chapter of the American Association of Law Libraries)
> Send the following message to mailserv@post-office.uh.edu:
> subscribe SWALL-L

T'SQUARED (official newsletter of the Technology Transfer Society; also _Journal of Technology Transfer_)
> Archived at the gopher at technology.tamu.edu

TAP-INFO (Taxpayer Assets Project - Information Policy Note; TAP was founded by Ralph Nader to monitor management of government property; TAP-INFO reports on TAP activities regarding federal information policy, including summaries of news, legislation, U.S. agency action, etc. related to information; a listproc list)
> Send the following message to listproc@tap.org:
> subscribe tap-info Your Name

TAP-RESOURCES (distribution list for information about management of publicly-owned natural resources)
> Send the following message to listproc@tap.org or listserver@essential.org:
> subscribe tap-resources Your Name

TaxDigest: A Tax Newsletter (via TaxDigest@aol.com?)

TEALE-TALES (list set up to replace the Usenet newsgroup, alt.fan.karla-homolka)
> Send the following message to teale-tales-request@io.com:
> subscribe teale-tales youre-mailaddress
> (send the message "info teale-tales" for more detail re the list)

TECH-LAW@techlaw.com (Marger Johnson McCollom & Stolowitz Internet E-Mail Discussion List on Technology and the Law; was INFO-LAW@BRL.MIL; a majordomo list)
> Send the following message to listserver@techlaw.com:
> subscribe tech-law

TECHNOLOGY-TRANSFER-LIST@sei.cmu.edu (Technology Transfer and related topics; sponsored by the Technology Applications Group of the Software Engineering Institute)
>   Send the following message to
>   technology-transfer-request-list@sei.cmu.edu:
>   subscribe technology-transfer-list Your Name
>   (defunct?)

TEKNOIDS@listserv.law.cornell.edu (US-based list for law school technical support personnel)
>   Send the following message to listserv@listserv.law.cornell.edu:
>   subscribe teknoids Your Full Name

TELECOM-TECH@zygot.ati.com (forum for discussion of technical aspects of telecommnications, including legislation and regulations)
>   Send the following message to teletech-request@zygot.ati.com:
>   subscribe telecom-tech Your Name

TELECOMDOCS@relay.adp.wisc.edu (moderated forum for the distribution of telecommunications rules, regulations and other official communications)
>   Send the following message to listserver@relay.adp.wisc.edu:
>   subscribe telecomdocs <your name>

TELECOMREG@relay.adp.wisc.edu (Telecommunications Regulation list; "Cable Regulation Digest", formerly posted herein, now at CABLEREG-L)
>   Send the following message to listserver@relay.adp.wisc.edu:
>   subscribe telecomreg Your Name

THE LEGAL LIST (see the _Legal List_ above)

The Week in Germany (German Information Center newsletter)
>   URL=ftp://langlab.uta.edu/pub/GIC/TWIG/

THRACE@vm3090.ege.edu.tr (West Thracian Discussion List; open, unmoderated discussion list on Greek West Thracian (A Province of Greece) Turking Minority issues)
>   Send the following message to listserv@vm3090.ege.edu.tr or
>   listserv@trearn.bitnet:
>   sub thrace yourfirstname yoursecondname

THRDWRLD@gsuvm1.bitnet (Association of Third World Studies list)
>   Send the following message to listserv@GSUVM1.bitnet:
>   subscribe thrdwrld Your Name

TI_FORUM@kabissa.com (Transparency International—coalition against corruption in international business transactions; includes info re banks and bankers)
>   Send the following message to listserv@kabissa.com:
>   sub TI_FORUM name

TI_PRESS (Transparency International news)
>   Send the following message to listserv@kabissa.com:
>   sub TI_PRESS name

TLL-ANNOUNCE (_The Legal List_ *announcements-only* list)
>   Send the following message to listserv@justice.eliot.me.us:
>   Subscribe TLL-announce yourname

TLTP-LAW@mailbase.ac.uk (UK-based list on creating & using legal computer- based learning materials; Law Courseware Consortium list)
>   Send the following message to mailbase@mailbase.ac.uk:
>   join tltp-law firstname lastname
>   The JANET address is mailbase@uk.ac.mailbase

TLTP-LAWOFSCOTLAND@mailbase.ac.uk (Scottish Law Courseware Consortium Project)
Send the following message to mailbase@mailbase.ac.uk:
join TLTP-LawOfScotland firstname lastname
The JANET address is mailbase@uk.ac.mailbase

TORTPROF@chicagokent.kentlaw.edu (Association of American Law Schools Section on Torts and Compensations Systems; private list limited to teachers of tort law and those with related interests at law schools and graduate schools)
Send the following message to listserv@chicagokent.kentlaw.edu:
subscribe tortprof your name, your position, your school

TORTSLAW (Law of Torts discussion list; now defunct)

TPR-NE@mitvma.mit.edu (Telecomm Policy Roundtable - Northeast)
Send the following message to listserv@mitvma.mit.edu or
listserv@mitvma.bitnet:
subscribe tpr-ne Your Name

TRADE@csf.colorado.edu (International Trade Policy list)
Send the following message to listproc@csf.colorado.edu:
subscribe trade Your Name

TRADE-LIBRARY (documents from the Institute for Agriculture and Trade Policy in Minneapolis, Minnesota)
Send the following message to majordomo@igc.apc.org:
subscribe trade-library

TRADE-NEWS (includes weekly bulletins, _NAFTA Monitor_, _Trade Week_, and _GATT Alert_ from the Institute for Agriculture and Trade Policy)
Send the following message to majordomo@igc.apc.org:
subscribe trade-news

TRADE-STRATEGY (trade issues; Institute for Agriculture and Trade Policy)
Send the following message to majordomo@igc.apc.org:
subscribe trade-strategy

TRAVEL-ADVISORIES (U.S. Department of State Consular Information Sheets and Travel Warnings)
Send the following message to travel-advisories-request@stolaf.edu:
subscribe travel-advisories Your Name

TX-FIREARMS@frontier.lonestar.org (list for discussion of Texas firearms laws, hunting seasons and regulations, etc.)
Send the following message to tx-firearms-request@frontier.lonestar.org:
subscribe tx-firearms Your Name

TXDXN-L@uhupvm1.uh.edu (Texas Documents Information Network)
Send the following message to listserv@UHUPVM1.uh.edu:
subscribe txdxn-L Your Name

UK-MOTSS@pyra.co.uk (UK-based forum for discussions of political and social issues related to gays, lesbians and bisexuals)
Send the following message to uk-motss-request@pyra.co.uk or
uk-motss-request@dircon.co.uk:
subscribe uk-motss Your Name

UKLEGAL@cck.coventry.ac.uk (English and Scottish law list)
Mail to Graham Wilson (LSG001@cck.coventry.ac.uk)
the following message with uklegal as the subject header:
join uklegal Your Name, Your full Internet e-mail address
The JANET address for contacting Graham Wilson is
LSG001@uk.ac.coventry.cck

UN-LIB@irmfao01.bitnet (Electronic Bulletin Board of United Nations Libraries)
Send the following message to listserv@IRMFAO01.bitnet:
subscribe un-lib Your Name

UN-NEWS (Weekly United Nations News; list not open for automatic subscription)
Send the following message to listserv@unmvma.unm.edu or
listserv@unmvma.bitnet:
subscribe un-news Your Name
(defunct or local list?)

UNCJIN-L@uacsc2.albany.edu (United Nations Criminal Justice Information Network)
Send the following message to listserv@uacsc2.ALBANY.edu or
listserv@ALBNYVM1.bitnet:
subscribe uncjin-L Your Name

UNCOVER@uhccvm.uhcc.hawaii.edu (UnCover Database and Document Delivery Users list)
Send the following message to listserv@uhccvm.uhcc.hawaii.edu or
listserv@uhccvm.bitnet:
subscribe UnCover Your Name

UNJUST@phoenix.oise.on.ca (Miscarriages of Justice list)
Send the following message to unjust-request@phoenix.oise.on.ca:
subscribe unjust Your Name

USA-GREENCARDLOTTERY (moderated list on the annual U.S.A. Green Card Lottery
Proram; from the law office of Mark Carmel; was USAGREENCARD, then USA-
IMMIGRATION at uslawyer@inforamp.com)
Send the following message to uslawyer@inforamp.net:
subscribe usa-greencardlottery your first name your last name

USAID_PRESS_RELEASE (United States Agency for International Development press
release)
Send the following message to listproc@info.usaid.gov:
sub USAID_Press_Release YOUR FULL NAME

USNONPROFIT-L@rain.org (Issues facing nonprofit organizations and the people they
serve—the poor, homeless, disabled, abused, etc.)
Send the following message to majordomo@coyote.rain.org:
subscribe usnonprofit-L

USNONPROFIT-L-DIGEST@rain.org (digest of the USNONPROFIT-L list)
Send the following message to majordomo@coyote.rain.org:
subscribe usnonprofit-L-digest

VENUE-L (short-term list for discussion on jurisdiction and venue questions in
cyberspace/on the Internet; spin-off from CYBERIA-L discussion)

VIACON-L@uacsc2.albany.edu (Discussion of Issues Related to Viability of Democratic
Constitutionalism)
Send the following message to listserv@uacsc2.ALBANY.edu or
listserv@ALBNYVM1.bitnet:
subscribe viacon-L Your Name

VIOLEN-L@bruspvm.bitnet (Violence Discussion Forum)
Send the following message to listserv@bruspvm.bitnet:
subscribe violen-L Your Name
(difficult to unsubscribe from)

VLAJUR@belnet.be (Discussielijst voor Vlaamse juristen = Discussion List for Flemish Lawyers; Belgium-based)
Send the following message to majordomo@BELNET.be:
subscribe VLAJUR

VTW-ANNOUNCE@vtw.org (Voters Telecomm Watch (in New York City) announcements list)
Send the following message to VTW-ANNOUNCE-reques@vtw.org:
subscribe VTW-ANNOUNCE Your Name

VTW-LIST@vtw.org (Voters Telecomm Watch; lobbying efforts for privacy, networking, NII issues; active participation in democratic and legislative processes to promote civil liberties in telecommunications)
Send the following message to VTW-LIST-request@vtw.org:
subscribe VTW-LIST Your Name

WALLSTREET-DIRECT-LIST/WSD-LIST (discussion of trading and investing services and products, on and off the Internet)
Send the following message to wallstreet-direct-list-request@cts.com:
sub wsd-list yourfirstname yourlastname
(also WSD-DIGEST)

WESTLAWUSER-L@lawlib.wuacc.edu (list for law student discussion of the West Publishing Company's WESTLAW legal database; the list is not formally affiliated with West Publishing Company)
Send the following message to listserv@lawlib.wuacc.edu:
subscribe westlawuser-L Your Name

WESTPAC-L@willamette.edu (Western Pacific chapter of the American Association of Law Libraries; issues related to law librarianship in the Western United States and Canada)
Send the following message to listproc@WILLAMETTE.edu:
<sub westpac-L your name>

WEU (Western European Union and Assembly)
Send the following message to listserv@CC1.KULEUVEN.ac.be or listserv@BLEKUL11.bitnet:
subscribe weu Your Name

WH-SUMMARY (White House Summaries; press releases)
Send the following message to almanac@esusda.gov:
subscribe wh-summary

WireD (for more information, contact info@wired.com)
URL=http://www.wired.com/

WORLDGOV?

WPS-FORUM (electronic bulletin board for information re Worker Protection Standard for Agricultural Pesticide)
Send the following message to listproc@are.berkeley.edu:
subscribe wps-forum Your Name

WSL@cc.wwu.edu (Washington Student Lobby Discussion list)
Send the following message to listproc@cc.wwu.edu:
subscribe WSL Your Name

XXandLaw (closed list for women law students)

Y-RIGHTS@sjuvm.stjohns.edu (Kid/Teen Rights Discussion Group)
    Send the following message to listserv@sjuvm.stjohns.edu or
    listserv@sjuvm.bitnet:
    subscribe y-rights Your Name

YLOPEARL@suvm.syr.edu (Asian Pacific American Law Professors Discussion Group;
unrestricted list by and for Asian American law professors)
    Send the following message to listserv@suvm.syr.edu:
    sub ylopearl@suvm.syr.edu [your name]

USENET NEWSGROUPS

alt.activism
alt.activism.d
alt.activism.death-penalty
alt.atheism
alt.business.misc
alt.business.multi-level
alt.censorship
alt.child-support
alt.comp.acad-freedom.news
alt.comp.acad-freedom.talk
alt.current-events.bosnia
alt.current-events.korean-crisis (defunct?)
alt.current-events.net-abuse
alt.cyberpunk.*
alt.cyberspace
alt.dads-rights
alt.dear.whitehouse
alt.desert-storm
alt.discrimination
alt.drugs
alt.fan.oj-simpson
alt.feminism
alt.flame.canter-and-siegel
alt.freedom.of.information.act
alt.guns
alt.hacker
alt.law-enforcement
alt.mens-rights
alt.mock.the.court
alt.motherjones
alt.politics.british
alt.politics.clinton
alt.politics.correct
alt.politics.datahighway
alt.politics.ec
alt.politics.economics
alt.politics.elections
alt.politics.europe.misc
alt.politics.european.misc (defunct?)
alt.politics.greens
alt.politics.homosexuality

alt.politics.libertarian
alt.politics.media
alt.politics.org.misc
alt.politics.org.nsa
alt.politics.org.un
alt.politics.nationalism.white
alt.politics.radical-left
alt.politics.reform
alt.politics.usa.constitution
alt.politics.usa.misc
alt.politics.usa.republican
alt.president.clinton
alt.privacy
alt.privacy.anon-server
alt.privacy.clipper
alt.religion
alt.revisionism
alt.revolution.counter
alt.rush-limbaugh
alt.security
alt.security.pgp
alt.skinheads
alt.society.civil-liberty
alt.society.conservatism
alt.society.labor-unions
alt.society.resistance
alt.stop.spamming
alt.visa.us (removed)
alt.war.*
alt.wired
alt.women.attitudes
aus.legal
aus.org.efa
aus.politics
bit.listserv.* (Usenet gateways to various
    LISTSERV e-mail lists)
bit.org.peace-corps
ca.govt-bulletins
can.infohighway
can.legal
can.politics

can.talk.guns
clari.news.politics
clari.news.politics.people
comp.org.cpsr.announce
comp.org.cpsr.talk
comp.org.eff.news
comp.org.eff.talk
comp.patents
comp.risks
comp.security.announce (CERT advisory)
comp.security.unix
comp.society
comp.society.cu-digest
comp.society.futures
comp.society.privacy
de.soc.politik
de.soc.recht
eunet.politics
info.firearms
info.firearms.politics
jp.soc.human-rights
jp.soc.law
misc.activism.progressive
misc.consumers
misc.education.home-school.christian
misc.education.home-school.misc
misc.guns
misc.headlines
misc.immigration.canada
misc.immigration.misc
misc.immigration.usa
misc.int-property
misc.invest.*
misc.legal
misc.legal.computing
misc.legal.moderated
misc.news.bosnia

misc.news.east-europe.rferl
misc.news.southasia
misc.taxes
rec.guns
relcom.comp.law (political and legal
    aspects of computers)
relcom.comp.security (computer data
    security discussion)
relcom.jusinf (information on laws by
    "Justicinform" (moderated))
sci.crypt
soc.culture.* (various countries, cultures,
    religions)
soc.feminism
soc.history.*
soc.men
soc.motss
soc.org.nonprofit
soc.politics
soc.politics.arms-d
soc.religion.*
soc.rights.human
soc.women
talk.abortion
talk.environment
talk.politics.animals
talk.politics.china
talk.politics.crypto
talk.politics.drugs
talk.politics.guns
talk.politics.libertarian
talk.politics.medicine
talk.politics.mideast
talk.politics.misc
talk.politics.soviet
uk.legal
uk.politics

Lyonette Louis-Jacques
Foreign and International Law
Librarian and Lecturer in Law
D'Angelo Law Library
University of Chicago Law School

Internet: llou@midway.uchicago.edu
Phone: 312-702-9612
Fax: 312-702-2889 or 702-0730
"Oh the sweet delight, to sing with
all my might!" — Minnie Riperton

Reference Listing
GOVDOCS

Govdocs

Government Sources of Business and Economic Information on the Internet

Terese Austin   *tmurphy@sils.umich.edu*
Kim Tsang   *kimtsang@sils.umich.edu*

....

NOTICE: THIS GUIDE IS APPROXIMATELY 122 K
Date of last update: February 18, 1994

....

Introduction

How this guide is organized:

This guide is divided into four main parts: A table of contents followed by a long body of descriptions and addresses; miscellaneous items including non-governmental sources; explanatory material discussing decisions we made about guide organization and information about how to use it along with resources to check for help; and a comprehensive index. This index is an important part of the guide. It is an alphabetical list of the specific contents cross-referenced to the broad resources in the guide.

Access (caveats):

It has been frequently noted that information on the Internet is in constant flux. Government sources are relatively more stable, reliable, and plentiful than information in many subject areas. Still, users need to maintain a dispassionate attitude and a critical eye toward what is available.

The Internet's constant ebb and flow mean that what exists one moment may disappear the next; and that, happily, what does not exist one moment may appear the next. Evaluating currency is a constant challenge and is something users need to undertake themselves.

Due to the web-like interconnectivity of Internet resources, there are almost always several pathways to any specific source of information. In our guide, we have tried to choose the least complicated, most direct path that works. Where feasible, we give alternative paths. Many of the sources in this guide are on gophers. Please remember gopher menus change at the whim of the gophermeister; chances are the same information is there under a different title.

TABLE OF CONTENTS

(Note: Contents are arranged alphabetically by subject or by agency. We have chosen to use "see" references to improve access and to collate sources that belong together.)

1. AGRICULTURE

1.1 Extension Service USDA Gopher

AGENCY: U.S. Department of Agriculture
ADDRESS1: gopher esusda.gov
ADDRESS2: gopher riceinfo.rice.edu/Information by Subject/Government, Political Science and Law/Other Government Gophers (Rice University, Texas)
URL: gopher://esusda.gov/1
CONTACT: gopher-admin@esusda.gov
COMMENTS: Under USDA Agency Information, contains Current Reports from the Economic Research Service, including export, wheat, cotton, etc. summaries; Research Reports on many agricultural products and economic indicators of the agricultural sector; and Situation and Outlook Reports for individual agricultural products including export summaries. From the main menu, also contains an option for Communities in Economic Transition, which has background information, White House briefings, and USDA materials for the Rural Empowerment Zones program.

1.2 USDA Economics and Statistics Gopher

AGENCY: U.S. Department of Agriculture, Economic Research Service
ADDRESS1: gopher or telnet usda.mannlib.cornell.edu; userid: <usda>. Ftp also available at same address: userid: <usda>; cd usda. (Cornell University)
URL: gopher://usda.mannlib.cornell.edu/
CONTACT: Access issues: Oya Y. Rieger, Numeric Files Librarian, Albert R. Mann Library, Cornell University: oyrl@cornell.edu Use or interpretation: Data Management Staff, Economic Research Service: jimh@ers.bitnet
COMMENTS: Includes more than 140 agricultural data sets, mostly in Lotus 1-2-3 format. Includes information on Farm Sector Economics, International Agriculture, Rural Affairs (including employment, unemployment, earnings and income statistics), and Trade (including data on U.S. imports and exports classified by 100 economic sectors, for 110 countries, over 10 years—1978-1987). Also, check under General Interest for agricultural data by state. There is a lot of information here. Luckily, there is a lot of user help available. Under the User Guides option, there is information on how to search and save data sets for gopher, TELNET and FTP access. Also provided is the capability to keyword search the README files which are quite useful in providing important indexing information.

2. AREA CODES

AGENCY: N/A
ADDRESS1: gopher or telnet gopher.uoregon.edu; login: <gopher>/Desktop Reference/Geographic and Travel Information/World Telephone Codes (University of Oregon)
URL: gopher://gopher.uoregon.edu/11/Reference/Geographic%20%26%20Travel%Information/phones
CONTACT: cmoore@BRL.MIL
COMMENTS: This database allows users to search for country and area codes in several ways. Entering a country name will pull up a list of regional (sometimes listed by city) area codes. Codes are also listed sequentially with associated state zones. The most extensive source we've found. Very easy to use.

3. BUREAU OF LABOR STATISTICS

see 24. LABOR

4. CENSUS DATA

4.1 U.S. Census Information - Various

AGENCY: U.S. Census Bureau
ADDRESS1:   gopher riceinfo.rice.edu/Information by Subject Area/Census
ADDRESS2:   gopher niord.shsu.edu/Economics (SHSU Network Access Initiative
              Project)/Census Information (Sam Houston State University gopher, Texas)
URL: gopher://riceinfo.rice.edu/11/Subject/census
CONTACT: riceinfo@rice.edu
COMMENTS: The most comprehensive collection of data we've found. Includes census
              summary data for the 1990 U.S. census; historic data from census of pop-
              ulation and housing and governments; and data for selected cities and
              states.

4.2 U.S. Census Information for Lotus

AGENCY: U.S. Census Bureau
ADDRESS: gopher bigcat.missouri.edu/reference center/U.S. and Missouri Census
              Info./U.S. Census Data (COIN - Columbia, MO Online Information
              Network gopher)
URL: gopher://bigcat.missouri.edu/u/reference/census/US
CONTACT: None listed.
COMMENTS: 1990 Basic tables available for Lotus or text files. Includes basic
              demographic trends for the U.S., 1980-1990.

5. COMMERCE

5.1 Commerce Business Daily

AGENCY: Department of Commerce
ADDRESS1:   gopher cscns.com/SPECIAL-Commerce Business Daily
ADDRESS2:   telnet cns.cscns.com
URL: gopher://cscns.com
CONTACT: info@cscns.com
COMMENTS: The *Commerce Business Daily* announces opportunities to bid on propos-
              als requested by the federal government. These pages are provided for
              free by CNS On-line Systems and Softshare Government Information
              Systems. They will, for a fee, set up company profiles and automatically
              mail articles that match the company profile and include information
              about what previous awards have been granted from similar requests.
              Users can search a one day or ten day index by keyword. CBD is updated
              every business day. Keyword searches return a list of CBD entries describ-
              ing the project(s) being requested, amount of funding, and contact peo-
              ple. This site also offers a list of toll free numbers for practically every air-
              line in the world. Search alphabetically. Additionally, users can search the
              Harvard Business Review Index here and get a single, trial copy of the
              Internet Business Journal under the Economics menu (Commerce Business
              Daily is also under the Economics menu and the Enter the CNS Gopher
              menu). This is an interesting site with diverse offerings.

5.2 Economic Bulletin Board

AGENCY: Department of Commerce

ADDRESS1:   telnet ebb.stat-usa.gov; login: <guest>.

ADDRESS2:   telnet link also provided through gopher riceinfo.rice.edu/Information by Subject Area/Government, Political Science and Law/Economic Bulletin Board (Rice University, Texas)

URL: telnet://trial@ebb.stat-usa.gov:23/

COMMENTS: Largely a subscription source. Guests limited to 20 minutes and extremely few choices of files. Guests may access the release dates calendar and search/download a very few guest available files. Guest connection disallows access to GAO reports, TOPs, and the list of basic files. Subscribers to the fee-based version have access to over 700 files updated daily.

Although this is a direct access link, much of the same information is provided (with almost the same currency) through the University of Michigan's gopher which contains many downloaded files from the EBB and which does not limit connection time for guests.

5.3 Economic Bulletin Board - Downloaded Data

ADDRESS1:   telnet or gopher una.hh.lib.umich.edu; login: <gopher>/ebb (University of Michigan Libraries)

URL: gopher://una.hh.lib.umich.edu/11/ebb

CONTACT: Contents: Grace York, Documents Librarian, U. of M. Graduate Library, grace.york@um.cc.umich.edu. Technical: David Barber, Graduate Library, U. of M., dbarber@sansfoy.hh.lib.umich.edu.

COMMENTS: U. of M. gopher downloads information from the Economic Bulletin Board, including Current Business Statistics, Economic Indicators, Employment Statistics, Industry Statistics, Summaries of Current Economic Conditions, etc. More specifically, Durable Goods Shipments and Orders, Housing Starts, Monthly Wholesale Sales, Business Cycle Indicators, Revised Composite Indexes and Indicators, and Summary Text Files for Economic Indicators. The major file areas are arranged alphabetically by topic.

Under the menu choice EBB and Agency Information and Misc. Files find information about the EBB including a list of all EBB files, an overview of the EBB, EBB Technical Help Documentation, pricing changes, registration form, and What's Where on the EBB, etc. Also find here Release Dates Calendar, release dates for Federal Economic Indicators, Government Bulletin Boards, National Trade Data Bank, Telephone Contacts for the Bureau of Labor Statistics, Telephone Directories for the Office of Business Analysis and the Office of Economic Affairs, etc.

Most of these files are presented in table format and are current. The U-M Library says the files are updated daily when possible. This service is provided voluntarily by the University of Michigan. Some of the larger data files are compressed in MS-DOS specific format. Files can be accessed with DOS machines from una.hh.lib.umich.edu in the /bin directory via anonymous ftp.

5.4 Economic Conversion Information Exchange

AGENCY: Department of Commerce

ADDRESS: gopher exic.doc.gov

URL: gopher://ecix.doc.gov/

CONTACT: Amy Williams, awilliams@esa.doc.gov

COMMENTS: This is a valuable resource for anyone interested in defense conversion issues. Menu items include: Economic and Defense Information—information on base closings including remarks by the President; Adjustment Programs and Laws—information on base clean-up, property disposition and a defense conversion bibliography; Contributed Experiences—case studies of Nashua, New Hampshire and St. Louis, Missouri; Defense Technology—information on technology reinvestment; Regional Statistics—divides the U.S. into regions and for each region includes employment by industry and personal income and earnings by major industry. Each region is further divided into individual states, and then cities with information provided on the above categories in addition to transfer payment information. The Economic and Demographic Information folder is currently empty. There is also a feature to keyword search all Economic Conversion Information Exchange documents.

6. CONGRESSIONAL INFORMATION

6.1 Congressional Committee Assignments

AGENCY: Congress
ADDRESS1:   gopher marvel.loc.gov/Federal Government Information/Federal Information Resources/Information by Agency/Legislative Branch/Selected Internet Resources on the US Congress/Committee Assignments (Library of Congress)
URL: gopher://una.hh.lib.umich.edu/11/socsci/poliscilaw/uslegi/congcomm
ADDRESS2:   telnet marvel.loc.gov; login: <marvel>.
URL: telnet://marvel.loc.gov/
CONTACT: comments@hr.house.gov
COMMENTS: House, Senate, and Joint Committee members for the 103rd Congress are searchable by keyword. Very easy to use. Enter a committee name to get a list of committee members, with their state and political affiliations, mailing addresses and phone numbers along with lists of subcommittees and those members' last names. Users can also search for specific members to find out what committees they are on and can search joint, house, or senate committees by topic.

6.2 Congressional Directories

AGENCY: Congress
ADDRESS1:   gopher marvel.loc.gov/Federal Government Information/Federal Information Resources/Information by Agency/Legislative Branch/Congressional Directories (Library of Congress)
URL: gopher://marvel.loc.gov/11/congress/directory
ADDRESS2:   telnet marvel.loc.gov; login: <marvel>
URL: telnet://marvel.loc.gov/
CONTACT: comments@hr.house.gov
COMMENTS: The TELNET address allows only 10 outside users and is often busy; gopher address has no such limitation. Directories include a state-by-state listing of Congresspeople with phone numbers, FAX numbers, political affiliation, state postal code, and Washington, D.C., mailing address. Also, users have the ability to search by phone and fax number and can search the Congressional Directory itself. Very easy to use.

   Information about the pilot project to get Congress on e-mail is at gopher@hr.house.gov.

7. DATA CENTERS

7.1 EconData

AGENCY: None listed.
ADDRESS1: gopher or telnet info.umd.edu/Educational Resources/Economic Data
(University of Maryland gopher)
URL: gopher://info.umd.edu:901/11/inforM/Educational_Resources/Economic_Data
ADDRESS2: ftp info.umd.edu; type <user anonymous> at ftp prompt and follow
above directories.
URL: file://info.umd.edu/inforM/Educational_ Resources/Economic_Data
CONTACT: None listed.
COMMENTS: Several hundred thousand economic time series have been made avail-
able by the University of Maryland. These include national accounts,
labor information, price indices, current business indicators and industrial
production. Certain information that can be updated from Commerce's
Electronic Bulletin Board are updated within a few days of new data
release. These include the National Income and Product Accounts and the
Business Conditions Indicators among others. Other files are updated less
frequently, not less than once a year.

These are data files. The procedures for downloading and reading
them are complicated. In order to use this information effectively, it is
essential to read the README document, and within the Instructions subdirectory, the CONTENTS.DOC and GUIDE.DOC which give a detailed
table of contents and instructions.

7.2 New England Economic Data Center (NEEEDc)

AGENCY: Bureau of Economic Analysis and Federal Reserve Bank of Boston.
ADDRESS: ftp neeedc.umesbs.maine.edu; login <anonymous>; userid: your e-mail
address
URL: Unable to confirm.
CONTACT: James H. Breece, Department of Economics; breece@maine.maine.edu
COMMENTS: This site contains everything from unemployment to housing to energy
statistics going back to 1969, and the data are updated monthly. The
focus is mostly on New England, but many files also include some national data. It also has the gross state product data produced by the Bureau
of Economic Analysis. These files are fully compatible with Lotus 1-2-3
and Quattro. There are problems ftp-ing from this site using the "Fetch"
client. However, regular ftp works fine. Login with "anonymous" and use
your e-mail address as a password. Directories include "bea" for Bureau
of Economic Analysis Data, "fbb" for Federal Reserve Bank of Boston
data. Access the read.me file for information on analyzing data using
Lotus and Quattro.

7.3 Social Security Administration

NAME: Office of Research Services Data Files
AGENCY: Social Security Administration
ADDRESS1: ftp soaf1.ssa.gov; login: <anonymous> (Please note the digit following
soaf is the numeric figure "1")
URL: file://soaf1.ssa.gov/pub
ADDRESS2: gopher fatty.law.cornell.edu/Government Agencies/Social Security
Administration/ORST Databases Via ftp (Cornell Law School gopher)

URL: gopher://fatty.law.cornell.edu/1ftp%3asoaf1.ssa.gov%40/pub/
CONTACT: Joel Packman, jbpackman%ssa.gov@soaf1.ssa.gov
COMMENTS: Many data files whose contents include summary data of persons receiving Social Security payments including payment types, and payment awards by state. Data files are available in different formats. Check the orsindex_txt document for a description of these. This document also includes a table of contents, without which file names are pretty useless.

8. ECONDATA

see 7. DATA CENTERS

9. ECONOMIC BULLETIN BOARD

see 5. COMMERCE

10. ECONOMIC CONDITIONS - SUMMARIES

AGENCY: Department of Commerce
ADDRESS: gopher una.hh.lib.umich.edu/Social Science Resources/Economics/Economic Bulletin Board/Summaries of Current Economic Conditions (University of Michigan Libraries)
URL: gopher://una.hh.lib.umich.edu/11/ebb/summaries
CONTACT: Contents: Grace York, Documents Librarian, U. of M. Graduate Library, grace.york@um.cc.umich.edu. Technical: David Barber, Graduate Library, U. of M., dbarber@sansfoy.hh.lib.umich.edu.
COMMENTS: A subset of the total Economic Bulletin Board information that deserves special mention. Includes summaries of business sales and inventories, construction, durable goods orders, housing starts, personal income, etc. There is often a time lag of several months on this data.

11. ECONOMIC DEVELOPMENT INFORMATION NETWORK (EDIN)

AGENCY: Various
ADDRESS1: gopher psuvm.psu.edu 23
ADDRESS2: gopher info.psu.edu/Information Servers at Penn State/EDIN
ADDRESS3: gopher riceinfo.rice.edu/Information by Subject Area/Economics and Business/EDIN
URL: tn3270://psuvm.psu.edu:23/
CONTACT: Connecting: hotline 814/863-2494 Data Items: Michael Behney 717/9486336.
COMMENTS: Your first time in the system, ignore the "Userid" and "Password" prompts; move arrow key down to "Command" and type "ebb"; select "EDIN" from the menu. Menu options include: Pennsylvania State Data Center in which you can find data for any state in several areas including business, capital resources, government, income, labor force, etc.; demographic and economic database files which allow you to select geographic preferences and then topic areas; procurement leads - in international trade and agriculture; and the Economic Development Directory in which you can design search criteria to select programs or agencies of use. It's easy to lose your way, but online help and tutorials are available. A nice option is that you are allowed to "mark" several items before completing your search and bringing up data on those topics. We found most statistics to be current.

12. ECONOMIC INDICATORS

AGENCY: Department of Commerce
ADDRESS: gopher una.hh.lib.umich.edu/Social Science
               Resources/Economics/Economic Bulletin Board/Economic Indicators
               (University of Michigan Libraries)
URL: gopher://una.hh.lib.umich.edu/11/ebb/indicators
CONTACT: Contents: Grace York, Documents Librarian, U. of M. Graduate Library,
               grace.york@um.cc.umich.edu. Technical: David Barber, Graduate Library,
               U. of M., dbarber@sansfoy.hh.lib.umich.edu.
COMMENTS: A subset of the Economic Bulletin Board information, downloaded by
               and available through gopher. Includes advance retail sales, census con-
               struction review tables, durable goods shipments and orders, earnings,
               new home sales, and new construction. Updated frequently.

13. EDGAR

AGENCY: Securities and Exchange Commission
ADDRESS1:   telnet acc.wuacc.edu/Federal Government Information; login: <washlaw>
               (Washburn University School of Law)
CONTACT: Paul Arrigo, zzarri@acc.wuacc.edu
ADDRESS2:   ftp town.hall.org; login <anonymous>; password <your email address>
ADDRESS3:   email; send mail to mail@town.hall.org; enter "HELP" in the body of the
               message and you will receive instructions.
URL: ftp://town.hall.org:/edgar/
COMMENTS: Indexes include the company index, with company names listed alphabet-
               ically; the master index with entries listed by CIK number; the form index
               which lists entries by form type (no descriptions of form type included).
               WARNING: These indexes are very large—around 347K.
                   Actual filings are listed by CIK number under "Company 10-K
               Reports" in Washburn and in the "data1" subdirectory at town.hall.org.
               To retrieve filings through the ftp site, refer to one of the indexes for a
               file name, which includes CIK, date and file number (e.g. 0000883496-94-
               000002.txt). At the ftp prompt, type "ascii" and return; type "cd data 1"
               and return; and use "get" with the file name. To retrieve a specific file
               using e-mail, type the following message: send edgar/data1/filename.
                   Included at the FTP site, but not through Washburn, is a "feed" sub-
               directory with files available in compressed form. There are plans to
               utilize World-Wide Web in the future, but there is no current hypertext
               capability. Also, although help in navigating the system is scanty, accord-
               ing to the text introduction, this will be improved over time.

14. EDIN

see 11. ECONOMIC DEVELOPMENT INFORMATION NETWORK

15. ENVIRONMENTAL PROTECTION AGENCY (EPA)

15.1. Environmental Futures Gopher

AGENCY: EPA, Office of Strategic Planning and Environmental Data.
ADDRESS: gopher futures.wic.epa.gov
URL: gopher://futures.wic.epa.gov/1
CONTACT: Michael Manning, manning.michael@EPAmail.epa.gov
COMMENTS: Contains bibliographies and reports on industrial ecology, population,

technology (advanced batteries and semiconductors), agriculture (supply and demand and emerging technologies) and sustainable development, among others. The system is under development, and some folders are empty. Also contains an Energygraphics file which must be converted with BinHex 4.0.

15.2. EPA Online Library System

AGENCY: Environmental Protection Agency
ADDRESS1:   telnet epaibm.rtpnc.epa.gov; login: <public>.
ADDRESS2:   gopher riceinfo.rice.edu/Information by Subject/Government, Politics and Law/U.S. EPA Online Library System (Riceinfo gopher)
URL: telnet://epaibm.rtpnc.epa.gov
CONTACT: None listed.
COMMENTS: This is a computerized list of bibliographic citations compiled by the EPA library network. The items listed are not necessarily available in EPA libraries or subject to loan. Not a user-friendly system. Upon entering the system, the patron must choose one of eight databases and type in a command to search by author, title, keyword, or corporate source. This system does not have browsing capabilities.

15.3 Technology Transfer Network

AGENCY: EPA, Office of Air Quality Planning and Standards
ADDRESS1:   telnet ttnbbs.rtpnc.epa.gov
URL: telnet://ttnbbs.rtpnc.epa.gov/
CONTACT: Help line: 919/541-5384
COMMENTS: This network of bulletin boards is available for use 24 hours a day except from 8a.m. to 12p.m. Mondays while it is down for maintenance. Bulletin boards include CAAA—Clean Air Act Amendment; NATICH—National Air Toxics Information Clearinghouse; CTC—Control Technology Center (which offers free engineering assistance); NSR-New Source Review; etc.

          Guests are authorized 30 minutes per login and must register to be allowed full access to all TTN BBS. After registering, users may download software, register for mail, get lists of ongoing projects, review lists of suggested projects, as well as read postings.

          Use is fairly intuitive; users choose letters to go to alternate items. Typing (q)uit lets you go back up a menu, which they don't let you know on each screen. Typing (g)oodbye immediately logs you off, no chance to change your mind.

16. FEDERAL REGISTER

AGENCY: Office of the Federal Register
ADDRESS1:   gopher or telnet gopher.internet.com/Counterpoint Publishing.
ADDRESS2:   gopher niord.shsu.edu/Information by Subject/Government, Political Science & Law/United States Federal Register (Sam Houston State University)
URL: gopher://gopher.netsys.com:2001/11/
CONTACT: fedreg@internet.com
COMMENTS: Most of the information from this source is available only to subscribers. Only the final menu item, "Selected Agencies" is totally open to the public. The agencies included are the Commission on Civil Rights, Copyright Royalty Tribunal, Federal Communications Commission, National

Endowment for the Arts, National Foundation on the Arts and the Humanities, and the Patent and Trademark Office. Entries under these headings are arranged by date, starting with 12/93.

There is also an FAQ with information about Counterpoint's publishing fee schedules and offerings, and the option to search the *Federal Register* by date of issue (starting with volume 58, no. 1), agency, and subject category (from agriculture to transport). Guest users can search the first page of these areas. (Note: The TELNET address has been inordinately slow; we recommend gopher.)

17. FEDWORLD

AGENCY: National Technical Information Service
ADDRESS1: telnet fedworld.gov.
ADDRESS2: gopher riceinfo.rice.edu/Information by Subject Area/Government, Political Science and Law/NTIS's FedWorld (Riceinfo)
URL: telnet://fedworld.gov/
CONTACT: Bob Bunge, bunge@access.digex.net
COMMENTS: A gateway system to over 100 government electronic bulletin boards, including the Consumer Information Center, Export/Import Bank, Department of Labor, Small Business Administration and the FCC daily digest. When you sign on, you will be asked to assign yourself a password. You will need this password every time you subsequently connect to FedWorld.

Connecting is currently a big problem—often all lines are in use. NTIS is currently working on plans to increase the number of lines available. Also, FTP of files is not currently possible, but may be in the future (only from the "Library of Files" directory.

18. FOOD AND DRUG ADMINISTRATION

18.1 FDA Bulletin Board

AGENCY: Food and Drug Administration
ADDRESS1: telnet fdabbs.fda.gov; login: <bbs>
ADDRESS2: telnet or gopher una.hh.lib.umich.edu/Science Resources/Life Sciences/Food and Drug Administration Bulletin Board
URL: telnet://bbs@fdabbs.fda.gov:23/
CONTACT: Technical Support: FDA Parklawn Computer Center, 301/443-7318. If you are looking for a specific report or article, contact Karen Malone in the FDA Press Office, 301/443-3285.
COMMENTS: This system is VERY SLOW. Occasionally I have been timed out before I've gotten anywhere. However, there is a lot of information here, including Drug and Device Product Approval List, current information on AIDS, index and selected articles from *FDA Consumer, FDA Federal Register* summaries by subject and by date of publication. One useful feature is the ability to keyword search FDA documents. The first time you enter the system, you will have to register and assign yourself a password. Write this down as you will need it with each subsequent connection. Some hints for system navigation: type HELP for a list of commands; type MANUAL for online user's manual; type TOPICS for a list of topics; type QUIT to logoff.

19. GENERAL ACCOUNTING OFFICE

19.1 GAO Reports

AGENCY: General Accounting Office
ADDRESS1:   gopher wiretap.spies.com/Government Docs
URL: gopher://wiretap.spies.com/11/Gov/GAO- Reports
ADDRESS2:   gopher dewey.lib.ncsu.edu/NCSU's Library Without Walls/Study
            Carrels/Government and Law/GAO Reports
URL: gopher://dewey.lib.ncsu.edu/11/library/disciplines/government/gao-reports
            (North Carolina State University Library gopher)
ADDRESS3:   gopher info.umd.edu/Educational Resources/United
            States/Government/GAO (University of Maryland gopher)
URL: gopher://info.umd.edu:901/11/info/
CONTACT: gopher@wiretap.spies.com
COMMENTS: The three above sources contain directories for Technical, Transition, and
            High Risk Reports. Useful abstracts provided for High Risk and Technical
            Reports, with an index available for Transition Reports. Technical
            Reports: 10 reports released in the Summer of 1991 on issues such as
            super-computing, computer networks, and HDTV technology. Transition
            Reports: 28 reports released in January 1993 dealing with health care
            reform, financial services, international trade and labor issues among
            others. High risk reports: 17 reports made available by GAO in December
            1992, on subjects including budget, information management and tech-
            nology, and commerce.
ADDRESS4:   ftp.cu.nih.gov
URL: Unable to confirm.
CONTACT: Joe Sokalski, kh3@cu.nih.gov COMMENTS: Ftp site for lists of GAO
            reports released in 1992 and 1993 and test of 56 GAO reports. Includes
            Technical, Transition and High Risk Reports (see above for more info).

20. GEOGRAPHIC NAMES DATABASE (U.S.)

AGENCY: None listed.
ADDRESS1:   telnet or gopher liberty.uc.wlu.edu; login: <guest>/Libraries and
            Information Access/Reference Sources/U.S. Geographic Names Database
            (Washington & Lee University)
URL: gopher://ashpool.micro.umn.edu:4324/1geo
COMMENTS: Searchable by city or zip code. Has geographic coordinates, state loca-
            tion, population, elevation, zip codes and other information for thou-
            sands of places listed on USGS maps. Very easy to use.

21. GLOBAL LAND INFORMATION SYSTEM

AGENCY: U.S. Geological Survey
ADDRESS: telnet glis.cr.usgs.gov; login: <guest>
URL: telnet://glis.cr.usgs.gov/
COMMENTS: This database containing land use maps and graphs, geological informa-
            tion, etc. is mostly for a scientific audience. There is an extensive registra-
            tion process where users must give personal address, phone number,
            Internet address, etc., to be able to fully access the information held here.
                 Organization and hypertext capability make using this information
            confusing. Clients must be able to use arrow keys to select and then
            enter intended choices. Users can examine the data and then choose to

be led through the process of ordering the actual maps. To browse images, users must be connected to GLIS through a DOS compatible PC using PC-GLIS software (information on how to get the software is provided) or via an X-window system. This system is difficult to navigate.

22. GROSS STATE PRODUCTS

AGENCY: Bureau of Economic Analysis

ADDRESS: telnet or gopher una.hh.lib.umich.edu login: <gopher> /Social Science Resources/Economics/Gross State Product Tables From U.S. Bureau of Economic Analysis University of Michigan Libraries)

URL: gopher://una.hh.lib.umich.edu/11/gsp

CONTACT: Content: Grace York, Documents Librarian, University of Michigan Graduate Library, grace.york@um.cc.umich.edu Technical: Lou Rosenfeld, lou@umich.edu

COMMENTS: Menu options for national, regional, and state totals of estimated value of goods and services produced for 61 industries. Each geographic area has separate files for 1977-81, 1982-86 and 1987-89. Updated annually. Note: This information is also available from the New England Electronic Economic Data Center. See DATA CENTERS.

23. HEALTH

23.1 National Health Security Act

AGENCY: Executive Branch

ADDRESS1: gopher calypso.oit.unc.edu/Worlds of SUNSITE/U.S. and World Politics/National Health Security Plan OR telnet to calypso.oit.unc.edu; login as gopher and follow path above. Be sure to enter your terminal type or you will be disconnected. (University of North Carolina Office of Information Technology Gopher)

URL: gopher://calypso.oit.unc.edu/11/sunsite.d/politics.d/health.d

CONTACT: SUNSITE gopher contacts: Darlene Fladager, Darlene_Fladager@unc.edu; and Elizabeth Lyons, Elizabeth_Lyons@unc.edu.

COMMENTS: The best site we've found for accessing this document. Includes entire health security act, in original and formatted versions (original is really screwed up in terms of margins, tabs, etc.). Summaries are available in Word for Windows, WordPerfect and ASCII format. Also includes the President's report on health care, address to joint houses of Congress and the ability to search the text of the National Health Security Act.

ADDRESS2: gopher stellate.health.ufl.edu/Medical Library/Health Care System/National Health Care (University of Florida Space Medicine and Life Sciences gopher)

URL: gopher://stellate.health.ufl.edu/40/Medical%20Library/Health_Care_System/National_Health_Care

CONTACT: Content: Dan Woodward, dan@nasa840.ksc.nasa.gov Software, systems: Tim Cera, cera@cortex.health.ufl.edu

COMMENTS: Entire document available for downloading in hqx.

23.2 Occupational Safety Documents

AGENCY: Occupational Safety and Health Administration

ADDRESS: gopher stellate.health.ufl.edu/OSHA Occupational-Safety (Occupational Safety and Health gopher)

URL: gopher://stellate.health.ufl.edu/11/OSHA
CONTACT: Content: Dan Woodward, dan@nasa840.ksc.nasa.gov Software, systems: Tim Cera, cera@cortex.health.ufl.edu
COMMENTS: Under "Directives" menu option, provides a list of OSHA directives in separate folders based on directive number. Directives in the following subject areas are combined under separate directory headings: Air Contaminates, Asbestos, Blasting Agents, Bloodborne Pathogens, Chemicals, Confined Space Regulations, and Lead. There is also a mechanism to keyword search OSHA documents.

24. LABOR

24.1 Federal Labor Laws

NAME: Federal Labor Laws - Report
AGENCY: Congressional Digest
ADDRESS: gopher garnet.berkeley.edu 1250/Labor Issues/History of Labor Law (Electronic Democracy Information Network - EDIN)
URL: gopher://garnet.berkeley.edu:1250/00/.labor/.labor.law
CONTACT: Gopher contact: newman@garnet.berkeley.edu
COMMENTS: This report is an article reprinted from the *Congressional Digest,* June/July, 1993, detailing the history of federal labor law development.

24.2 Glass Ceiling - Labor Dept. Report

NAME: A Report on the Glass Ceiling Initiative
AGENCY: U.S. Department of Labor
ADDRESS: gopher or telnet info.umd.edu/Educational Resources/Women's Studies/Gender Issues/Glass Ceiling/Department of Labor Information (University of Maryland)
URL: gopher://info.umd.edu:901/11/inforM/Educational_Resources/Womens Studies/GenderIssues/GlassCeiling/LaborDeptInfo
CONTACT: info-editor@umail.umd.edu or Lou Murch, 301/405-2977.
COMMENTS: This report, undated but issued sometime during the Bush presidency, is a study conducted by the Glass Ceiling Commission of the Department of Labor to study barriers to advancement for minorities and women in the corporate world.

24.3 Glass Ceiling - Merit Systems Protection Board Report

NAME: A Question of Equity: Women and the Glass Ceiling in the Federal Government
AGENCY: U.S. Merit Systems Protection Board, Report to the President and the Congress.
ADDRESS: gopher or telnet info.umd.edu/Educational Resources/Women's Studies/Gender Issues/Glass Ceiling/Merit Systems Protection Board Report (University of Maryland)
URL: gopher://info.umd.edu:901/11/inforM/Educational_Resources/Womens Studies/GenderIssues/GlassCeiling/MSPBReport
CONTACT: info-editor@umail.umd.edu or Lou Murch, 301/405-2977.
COMMENTS: Issued in October 1992, this reports studies the imbalance between men and women in higher grades in the U.S. government.

24.4 Labstat

AGENCY: Bureau of Labor Statistics
ADDRESS: ftp stats.bls.gov/pub; login: <anonymous>; password: <your email
address>
URL: ftp://stats.bls.gov/pub
CONTACT: labstat.helpdesk@bls.gov
COMMENTS: This resource contains current and historical data for 25 surveys. Each
database is identified by an abbreviation which can be found in the
pub/doc/overview file. Read this for introductory information. The /pub
directory and its subdirectories contain all the data; the /time.series subdirectories contain the survey-specific historical time series (see the .doc
file in each of these subdirectories for survey description, table structure,
and definitions of data elements).

24.5 Work and Family Needs

NAME: Balancing Work Responsibilities and Family Needs: The Federal Civil
Service Response
AGENCY: U.S. Merit Systems Protection Board, Report to the President and the
Congress.
ADDRESS: gopher or telnet info.umd.edu/Educational Resources/Women's
Studies/Gender Issues/Work and Family Needs (University of Maryland)
URL: gopher://info.umd.edu:901/11/inforM/Educational_Resources/Womens
Studies/GenderIssues/Work%2bFamilyNeeds
CONTACT: gopher contact: infoeditor@umail.umd.edu or Lou Murch, 301/405-2977.
COMMENTS: This report, issued in November 1991, reviews selected employee benefits
which can help civilian federal workers balance their work responsibilities
and personal needs. It covers such areas as child care, elder care, alterna-
tive schedules, and flexiplace among others.

25. LABSTAT
see 24. LABOR

26. LEGAL SOURCES

26.1 Cornell Law School

AGENCY: N/A
ADDRESS: telnet or gopher fatty.law.cornell.edu; login: <gopher> (Cornell Law
School)
URL: gopher://gopher.law.cornell.edu/11/
CONTACT: Thomas R. Bruce, Research Associate, tom@law.mail.cornell.edu
COMMENTS: This extensive and well-organized gopher has a treasure trove of government and economic information as well as legal sources. This site has
numerous law-related resources including discussion groups and archives
of bitnet listservs like Int-Law and Lib-Law. Both of these archives have
information related to business and economics but will require digging
to unearth. Under the Library Resources menu item, users can be connected to and search a variety of other law school library catalogs including Wugate. Among other things, Wugate allows users to search over
300,000 bibliographic citations of the publications of the U.S.
Government Printing Office by title, author, subject, and keyword. The
system is intuitive and easy to use. Type q to quit. Under the U.S. Law

menu item, users can find copyright, patents, trademark, commercial, and Federal Court Decisions legal resources. Important: To access these last items, users need to login as WWW for these are World-Wide Web documents.

26.2 Trademark Law

NAME: Lanham Act
AGENCY: N/A
ADDRESS: telnet or gopher fatty.law.cornell.edu/US Law: Primary Documents and Commentary/Trademark Law/Lanham Act (login: www) (Cornell Law School)
CONTACT: Thomas R. Bruce, Research Associate, tom@law.mail.cornell.edu
URL: http://www.law.cornell.edu/lanham/lanham.table.html
COMMENTS: This World-Wide Web version of the Lanham Act is searchable in hypertext format. Searchable by section, contains full text information on Registration of Trademarks, Service Marks Registrable, Assignment of Mark, Duration of Registration, Renewal of Registration, Opposition, etc. Type q to quit.

26.3 Uniform Commercial Code

AGENCY: N/A
ADDRESS: gopher or telnet fatty.law.cornell.edu; login: <gopher>/US Law: Primary Documents and Commentary/Uniform Commercial Code; login: <www> (Cornell Law School)
URL: http://www.law.cornell.edu/ucc/ucc/table/html
CONTACT: Thomas R. Bruce, Research Associate, tom@law.mail.cornell.edu
COMMENTS: A hypertext searchable document, this WWW version of the Uniform Commercial Code has sections for General Provisions; Title; Creditors, and Good Faith Purchasers; Formation of Contract; Breach; General Obligations, etc. Easy to use. Type q to quit.

27. NATIONAL HEALTH SECURITY REFORM
see 23. HEALTH

28. NATIONAL INSTITUTE OF STANDARDS AND TECHNOLOGY

AGENCY: U.S. Department of Commerce
ADDRESS1: gopher coil.nist.gov
URL: gopher://gopher-server.nist.gov/
ADDRESS2: telnet gopher.nist.gov
URL: telnet://gopher.nist.gov; login: <gopher>
CONTACT: Wo Chang via e-mail wchang@nist.gov for questions on remote access
COMMENTS: This user-friendly gopher has lots of documentation describing NIST's goals and implementations. But before being allowed to read any of NIST's information, users must read the Access Warning. NIST says that under the Clinton administration NIST is being transformed from "primarily a measurement laboratory" to a "full service, technology development, funding, extension, and quality improvement partner for U.S. industry." Along with concrete standards and measures information, NIST offers opportunities for small and medium-sized businesses to get funding for technological advances and for joint research projects on

advanced technologies. In addition, they say that NIST experts are available for consultation on technical problems in a variety of research fields. There is a lot of useful business-related information here.

Under the NIST General Information menu choice, users have the opportunity to search the full text of documents at NIST by keyword, view what NIST has to offer, find a Facilities Index, the NIST Laboratory Programs, the NIST Advanced Technology Program, etc. Useful.

29. NEW ENGLAND ECONOMIC DATA CENTER NEEEDc)

see 7. DATA CENTERS

30. NORTH AMERICAN FREE TRADE AGREEMENT (NAFTA)

AGENCY: The White House
ADDRESS1: Gopher esusda.gov/White House and Congress/North American Free Trade Agreement (USDA Extension Service)
URL: gopher://cyfer.esusda.gov/11/ace/nafta
CONTACT: gopher-admin@esusda.gov.
COMMENTS: The most user-friendly site we've found to browse and obtain this document. It contains a helpful table of contents and is broken up into chapters with informative headings. Also, this is the only site we've found with a 1993 version of the document as well as the 1992 version. Notes from the White House and Press Releases dealing with NAFTA are also available.
ADDRESS2: Gopher calypso.oit.unc.edu/Worlds of SUNSITE/US and World Politics/International Affairs. Telnet to sunsite also available; login as gopher and follow the above path. Sunsite also provides anonymous ftp: use "anonymous" as your name and your e-mail address as a password; cd/pub/academic/economics.
URL: gopher://calypso.oit.unc.edu/11/sunsite.d/politics.d/international.d
CONTACT: Darlene_Fladager@unc.edu Elizabeth_Lyons@unc.edu
COMMENTS: Allows you to keyword search NAFTA, which is useful, but the browsing option gives you an alphabetical list of file names such as anx2usa.txt, which is not very helpful. Check the index.txt file for more clues.
ADDRESS3: Gopher wiretap.spies.com/North American Free Trade Agreement.
URL: gopher://wiretap.spies.com/11/NAFTA
CONTACT: gopher@wiretap.spies.com
COMMENTS: Nice format, with labeled sections, but only has the 1992 version.
ADDRESS4: e-mail: To obtain the most up-to-date version of this document, send mail to nafta@ace.esusda.gov. Do not put any text in the message.

31. OSHA

see 23. HEALTH

32. PATENTS

32.1 Patent Act

AGENCY: None listed.
ADDRESS1: gopher or telnet fatty.law.cornell.edu; login: <gopher> /US Law: Primary Documents and Commentary/Patent Law/Patent Act; login: <www> (Cornell Law School)
URL: http://www.law.cornell.edu/patent/patent.table.html

CONTACT: Thomas R. Bruce, Research Associate, tom@law.mail.cornell.edu
COMMENTS: This World-Wide Web version of the U.S. Patent Act has information in hypertext format on Infringement of Patents; Proceedings in the Patent and Trademark Office; Patent Fees; Patentability of Inventions; Examination of Application; Plant Patents; etc. Intuitive and easy to use.

32.2 Patent Titles Mailing List

AGENCY: Private Source
ADDRESS: patents-request@world.std.com
URL: N/A
CONTACT: Gregory Aharonian patents@world.std.com
COMMENTS: A service to receive e-mail lists of new patents. The provider of this free service asks the following: to subscribe to this service users send a message with their name, postal and e-mail addresses, and the words MECHANICAL, CHEMICAL, ELECTRONIC, OR ALL depending on which files they wish to receive, along with the words ASCII or UUZIP (depending on which format you want - UUZIP means you can receive and UNZIP a uudecoded file). If you want to receive patent news information (PTO announcements, lawsuit outcomes), send the word NEWS. He also requests users send some personal information on their occupation and how they might use this patent information.

33. POSTAL INFORMATION

33.1 U.S. Postal Codes

AGENCY: U.S. Postal Service
ADDRESS: gopher or telnet gopher.uoregon.edu/Desktop Reference/Geographic and Travel Information/U.S. Postal Codes; login: <gopher> (University of Oregon)
URL: gopher://gopher.uoregon.edu/00/Reference /Geographic%20%26%20Information/U.S.%20Postal %20Codes
CONTACT: nethelp@ns.uoregon.edu
COMMENTS: This is an alphabetical arrangement of American states and Canadian provinces with their abbreviations. Extremely simple and easy to use.

33.2. Zip Codes

AGENCY: None listed.
ADDRESS: gopher or telnet gopher.uoregon.edu; login: <gopher> /Desktop Reference/Geographic and Travel Information/Zip Codes (University of Oregon)
URL: gopher://gopher.uoregon.edu/77/Reference/.index/zipcode
CONTACT: None listed.
COMMENTS: Searchable by city name and zip code. Type in a word and a list of city names with that word in it appears together with its associated state and zip code. If your query is more than one word long, the list will contain cities with each name as well as cities with both names.

34. SECURITIES AND EXCHANGE COMMISSION

see 13. EDGAR

35. SOCIAL SECURITY ADMINISTRATION
see 7. DATA CENTERS

36. STATE GOVERNMENT RESOURCES

36.1 Arizona State Economic Development Database

AGENCY: None listed
ADDRESS1:   gopher.isnet.is//Hytelnet/Other Resources/Databases and Bibliographies
            OR All the Gopher Servers in the World/Iceland/Association of Research
            Networks in Iceland/and follow above path.
ADDRESS2:   gopher jupiter.willamette.edu//Library Resources/Topical
            Resources/Economics/Databases
ADDRESS3:   The actual address for this resource is asuvm.inre.asu.edu 23. However, I
            was never able to get through to this address directly, either on gopher
            or using telnet.
URL: tn3270://type helloasu on the asu screen;select2@asuvm.inre.asu.edu:23
CONTACT: The only contact listed for the Arizona State Economic Development
            Database was a toll free number: 1-800-932-2947.
COMMENTS: An easy-to-use interface with a lot of good information, including cli-
            mate; community information; economic indicators (cost of living index
            for Arizona communities; Arizona home sales, retail sales, population
            estimates, etc.); education; labor and employment (Arizona labor force
            by industry, county and state employment/unemployment figures, corpo-
            rate office facility). Unfortunately, most information is not current, with
            some dating back to 1991.

36.2 California Legislative Information

AGENCY: None listed.
ADDRESS1:   gopher svpal.org/Government/California Legislature
URL: gopher://svpal.org/11/Government/CA_Leg
CONTACT: Gopher contact: support@svpal.org; for actual content,
            comments@leginfo.public.ca.gov
ADDRESS2:   ftp leginfo.public.ca.gov; login: <anonymous>, password: <your email
            address>
ADDRESS3:   email; send email to ftpmail@leginfo.public.ca.gov; include ftp
            commands in body of message
URL: ftp://leginfo.public.ca.gov/pub
CONTACT: comments@leginfo.public.ca.gov
COMMENTS: Subdirectories include "dailyfile" which includes a legislative calendar for
            the current session; "bill" which includes subdirectories for the assembly
            and senate which contain bill texts by bill number (these files also include
            indexes with bills listed by author and topic); "code" which contains
            Code text by section; "constitution" which contains the text of the state
            constitution by Article; and "statute" which contains files of the text of
            each statute by chapter. E-mail access is a bit confusing—how to include
            readable FTP commands in an e-mail message is not intuitive, especially if
            you are using email because you don't have access to direct FTP. The fol-
            lowing message was sent, with success:
```
connect
cd pub
get README_FIRST
quit
```

36.3 Hawaii FYI

AGENCY: None listed.
ADDRESS1:   gopher or telnet fyi.uhcc.hawaii.edu 23
URL: telnet://fyi.uhcc.hawaii.edu:23/
ADDRESS2:   liberty.uc.wlu.edu//Explore Internet Resources/Hytelnet/New or Revised Telnet Entries/1030 Hawaii FYI (Washington and Lee University gopher).
URL: gopher://liberty.uc.wlu.edu/11/internet/hytelnet/new_hytelnet/bbs076
COMMENTS: A gateway system to State of Hawaii electronic information servers. Categories include Energy Information; Business and Finance (including economic information from the Department of Business, Economic Development and Tourism); Tax Information Service; Legislative Information Services and Community Services. This system is difficult to navigate and several attempts at connecting to the Department of Business, Economic Development and Tourism BBS failed. Other economic information is meager—a paragraph or two on most subjects. Also, much of the information is dated, from 1989 or 1990.

36.4 Louisiana Contracts

AGENCY: None listed.
ADDRESS: gopher vm.cc.latech.edu/Louisiana State Contracts (Louisiana Tech. University Computing Center Gopher) (There is a theoretical telnet connection; we were never able to get beyond the opening screen.)
URL: gopher://vm.cc.latech.edu/11/lascmain
CONTACT: None listed.
COMMENTS: Provides information on active and pending Louisiana state contracts, listing vendor and pricing information by subject area. Also includes vendor addresses, sorted alphabetically and by vendor number.

36.5 Michigan Census Data

AGENCY: U.S. Census Bureau
ADDRESS: gopher or telnet una.hh.lib.umich.edu/Social Science Resources/1990 Census/Michigan: State, Counties, Cities and Townships (University of Michigan Libraries)
URL: gopher://una.hh.lib.umich.edu/11/census/michigan
CONTACT: ulibrary@umich.edu
COMMENTS: Michigan census data can be retrieved for the state or for separate counties, cities, or townships. Each geographic division is broken up into alphabetical categories which then list the corresponding entities included. Each entry contains population, social characteristics, income and poverty characteristics, and summary and detailed housing data. Also includes a catalog of census variables for data sets—a table of contents giving the standard format for each entity.

36.6 Michigan County Profiles

AGENCY: Michigan Department of Commerce
ADDRESS: gopher or telnet una.hh.lib.umich.edu/Social Science Resources/Economics/Michigan County Profiles (University of Michigan Libraries)
URL: gopher://una.hh.lib.umich.edu/11/business/county
CONTACT: Michigan Department of Commerce: 517/373 4600. Industrial

Development Division of the University of Michigan: 313/7645260.

COMMENTS: Includes an alphabetical list of Michigan counties. Each county profile includes data on population, labor force, principal employers, earning levels, transportation, climate, industrial sites, construction permits, property tax base, municipal services, etc. Updated throughout the year.

This is extremely well organized useful information. System navigation is simple. This type of detailed state information is currently very rare on the Internet.

36.7 Missouri Census Data

AGENCY: U.S. Census Bureau
ADDRESS: gopher bigcat.missouri.edu/Reference Center/United States & Missouri Census Information/Missouri Census Data (COIN Columbia, MO Online Information Center gopher)
URL: gopher://bigcat.missouri.edu/11/reference/census/mo
CONTACT: None listed.
COMMENTS: Includes 1990 Census Basic Tables Descriptions, Basic Census Tables for Missouri, Basic Demographic Trends Report 1980-1990 for Missouri Counties and Historical Census Data for Missouri. Also included is a Missouri State Data Center Reference Manual.

36.8 Missouri Small Business Development Centers

AGENCY: U.S. Small Business Administration
ADDRESS: gopher bigcat.missouri.edu/Reference Center/United States & Missouri Census Information/About the Missouri State Census Data Center Core Agencies/Missouri Small Business Development Centers (COIN Columbia, MO Online Information Center gopher)
URL: gopher://bigcat.missouri.edu/11/reference/census/about/MOSBDC
CONTACT: Terry Maynard, Marketing Specialist
            MO SBDC State Office
            300 University Place University of
            Missouri System Columbia, MO 65211
            Ph. (314) 882-0344
            FAX (314) 884-4297
COMMENTS: Includes information about the development centers, whose mission is to enhance the opportunity for success for Missouri's businesses. Also includes a directory of Center contacts and addresses throughout the state.

36.9 Missouri Rural Opportunities Council

AGENCY: Formed under the National Initiative on Rural Development.
ADDRESS: gopher bigcat.missouri.edu/Government Center/State of Missouri/Missouri Rural Opportunities Council (COIN (Columbia, MO Online Information Center)
URL: gopher://bigcat.missouri.edu/11/govt/state/moroc
CONTACT: None listed.
COMMENTS: The mission of MOROC is to improve the quality of life, enhance opportunities, and help empower citizens and rural communities of Missouri by bringing together a coalition of public and private entities. Includes Meeting Summaries, Calendar of Events, Committee Members, Extension County Program Offices and Resource Inventory.

36.10 New York State Library Gopher

AGENCY: New York State Library/State Archives and Records Administration
ADDRESS: gopher unix2.nysed.gov
URL: gopher://unix2.nysed.gov/
CONTACT: For the entire gopher: david@unix2.nysed.gov; for the Government Information Locator, Robert Trombly, Project Director, rtrombly%sedofis@vm1.nysed.gov.
COMMENTS: This gopher is still under construction, but if it fulfills its mission, will be a valuable resource. One of its stated missions is to assist people in finding what local, county, and state information is available on various topics and with accessing that information. The other is to make available certain of that information. Currently, most of what is available is organizational histories and descriptions of the different agencies, courts, etc., and a compilation of New York State facts in a truly unfortunate format. We are keeping our fingers crossed that this resource lives up to advance billing.

36.11 Texas Marketplace

AGENCY: Texas Department of Commerce
ADDRESS1: telnet texis.tdoc.texas.gov 23
ADDRESS2: gopher riceinfo.rice.edu/Information by Subject Area/Economics and Business/Texas Marketplace
URL: telnet://guest,password:guest@texis.tdoc. texas.gov:23/
CONTACT: None listed.
COMMENTS: Texas information includes Company Directories; Business to Business Texas Product Matching System (products wanted and available in many categories); Waste Exchange; Government Procurement Opportunities; State Licenses and Permit Information; and Small Business Network. Of general interest: the International Trade directory has information on trade leads and U.S. export data by country. Fairly easy system to navigate with good on-screen commands. Some directories allow option for preview, screen/file capture or XModem download. But watch out—some searches bring up screens and screens of information which the user cannot interrupt. The only option is to exit the system. You may do well to begin with a narrow topic to start.

36.12 West Virginia Mountain Gopher

AGENCY: West Virginia Network for Educational Telecomputing
ADDRESS1: gopher or telnet gopher.wvnet.edu
URL: gopher://gopher.wvnet.edu
CONTACT: Jeff Brooks, jeff@wvnvm.wvnet.edu
COMMENTS: The posting announcing this gopher says it is "a central access point for information about West Virginia state higher education, state government, and private industry." So far not all of the information has been loaded yet. There are menu entries entitled 'From the West Virginia State Capitol' which will have news from the governor's office and from the state legislature and another menu entry called 'From the National Capitol' will have information on federal agencies. Most of the useful information to date looks like it is under the WV Private Enterprise menu entry. Although still in the building stages, it looks as though this will be a well-organized gopher with some hard-to-find state information.

37. STATE PRODUCTS

see 22. GROSS STATE PRODUCTS

38. TIMES AROUND THE WORLD

AGENCY: N/A
ADDRESS: gopher esusda.gov/Internet Services and Information/Local Times Around the World (USDA)
URL: gopher://gopher.austin.unimelb.edu.au/11/general/time
CONTACT: gopher-admin@esusda.gov
COMMENTS: This alphabetical listing by country gives the Current Greenwich Mean Time (GMT) and the Universal Coordinated Time for cities around the world. Cities include Ann Arbor, MI; Oslo, Norway; Zagreb, Croatia; Lancaster, UK; Bangkok, Thailand; etc.

39. TRAVEL ADVISORIES

AGENCY: U.S. State Department
ADDRESS: gopher or telnet gopher.stolaf.edu/Internet Resources/US State Department Travel Advisories (St. Olaf College)
URL: gopher://gopher.stolaf.edu/11/Internet%2 0 Resources/US-State-Department-Travel Advisories
CONTACT: gopher@stolaf.edu
COMMENTS: These are current and archived travel advisories arranged by country. Archived information is accessible with FTP, find by date. This keyword searchable data contains information and warnings about nearly every country. Entries include country description, medical facilities, crime information, drug penalties, terrorist activities, entry and registration requirements, and embassy and consulate locations.

Users can also subscribe to travel advisories by sending their e-mail address to travel-advisories request@stolaf.edu.

40. USDA

see 1. AGRICULTURE

41. WEATHER

41.1 University of Illinois Weather Machine

AGENCY: N/A.
ADDRESS: gopher or telnet wx.atmos.uiuc.edu (University of Illinois)
URL: gopher://wx.atmos.uiuc.edu/1
CONTACT: gopher@wx.atmos.uiuc.edu
COMMENTS: Directories are organized by region. Menu choices include /states, with information about road conditions, short-term forecast by city, surface summaries, hourly weather roundup by state, coast guard report, fog advisories; /severe, with flood warnings, all recent severe marine, tornado, thunderstorm, and tropical storm warnings. Probably most impressive are the /images, with pictures and weather maps by region, satellite photos, Hurricane Emily, long-range forecast, etc. These images are in GIF format and require clients have a GIF viewer to be able to see them. These images are very nice. This information is well organized and easy to search.

42. WHITEHOUSE

42.1 Press Releases - Economy

AGENCY: Whitehouse .

ADDRESS: Send e-mail to: ClintonInfo@Campaign92.Org; in the subject line, type RECEIVE ECONOMY. To stop receiving the e-mail, send e-mail to the same address with Subject: REMOVE ECONOMY.

URL: N/A

CONTACT: This is an automatic server and is not set up to answer comments or requests for specific information.

COMMENTS: Information includes press releases, background briefings (e.g. on the American Airlines strike), remarks by the President at selected events, and remarks of senior adminstration officials on topics related to the economy. These documents can be fairly lengthy, so be prepared. Volume is light, an average of about two messages per week.

42.2 Whitehouse e-mail

AGENCY: Whitehouse

ADDRESS: President@Whitehouse.gov Vice-President@Whitehouse.gov

URL: N/A

CONTACT: None listed.

COMMENTS: Supposedly the vice-president alone gets over 60,000 e-mail messages a day. Users can send their message, subject topics will be recorded and an automated response beginning "Dear Friend" and describing the Whitehouse e-mail project will be returned.

MISCELLANEOUS

(Including some non-governmental sources)

A. COMING ATTRACTIONS

A.1 Government Information Locator Service

COMMENTS: This draft document proposes the establishment of a service to help the public locate and use public information resources from the U.S govern-ment. An explanatory message says that GILS will identify information resources, describe the information available in those resources, and pro-vide assistance in how to obtain the information.

   To obtain this document ftp ftp.cni.org; login: anonymous, cd /pub/docs/gils, type get gils1017.txt. Alternately, gopher gopher.cni.org 70/Coalition FTP Archives/Publicly Accessible Documents (pub)/Miscellaneous Documents/Government Information Locator Service.

UPDATE: To obtain the latest version of this document, gopher or telnet marvel.loc.gov, login: <marvel>, follow path Federal Government Information/Federal Information Policy/GILS Proposal. Alternately, ftp from telnet 130.11.48.107 follow path /pub/gils.doc for MS Word for Windows or /pub/gils.txt for ASCII text format.

   This newest version reconfirms the federal government's commitment to making government information available in accessible electronic for-mats, and to providing information about what exists and how taxpayers can get access to it.

B. GOPHERS

B.1 Cornell Law School

ADDRESS: gopher or telnet fatty.law.cornell.edu; login: <gopher>
URL: gopher://gopher.law.cornell.edu/11/
CONTACT: Thomas R. Bruce, Research Associate, tom@law.mail.cornell.edu
COMMENTS: Here is a gopher that has good quality if not exhaustive information. Under Government Agencies from the main menu there are choices for Economics Resources, FEDIX, Federal Register, FDA, FedWorld, GAO reports, Census, US Judges Database, etc. From the Economics Resources option there are choices for EconData, Directory of Economists, Gross State Product Tables, Statistics and Econometrics Collections, etc. The *Federal Register* has options for U.S. Commerce Business Daily, and an experimental version of the Code of Federal Regulations (CFR).

B.2 Riceinfo at Rice University

ADDRESS: gopher riceinfo.rice.edu
URL: gopher://riceinfo.rice.edu/1
CONTACT: riceinfo@rice.edu
COMMENTS: The Rice Subject Information Gopher had one of the most extensive collections of information on practically every subject we could find. From the main menu, under the Government, Political Science, and Law choice alone there are over two hundred entries. These entries range from a Citizen's Guide to Using FOIA to About the Iowa Political Stock Market to How to Use the Government Documents Database to Other U.S. Government Gophers to Search through United States Government Programs to Various U.S. State Laws and on and on. This gopher is worth checking out.

B.3 Sam Houston State University

ADDRESS: gopher niord.shsu.edu
URL: gopher://niord.shsu.edu/1
CONTACT: gopher-mgr@shsu.edu
COMMENTS: Extensive collection of data in three areas especially related to this guide: Economics; Government and Politics; and Internet Resources.
              Find menu choice for Economics (SHSU Network Access Initiative Project) on the main menu for Sam Houston. Under this item live a plethora of economics resources including archives of listservs, proposed budget for 1994, EconBib, Federal Reserve Bank of Boston Data, links to EconData, EBB, Federal Register, NetEc Archive, RiskNet, selected Usenet newsgroups, and many other law, economics, and government gophers.
              Also under the Economics menu choice is the Politics and Government menu (from PEG) item. Here find presidential campaign documents, NAFTA, searchable congressional directories, U.N. links, many government documents like the National Health Security Plan, Technology for America's Economic Growth e-journals, also an FAQ and alternatives for getting information to and from the White House among others. There is also an extensive collection of Internet help resources here. Follow the path from the main menu Network-based Information and References/Internet Tools/Networkin Computers/Internet/Usage of the Internet-End User Guides to find a variety of help resources including the full text of *Zen and the Art of Internet* and Internet Assistance from U

Cal Irvine. The U Cal Irvine link provides all kinds of information on finding e-mail addresses, gopher, FTP, FreeNets, listservs, Veronica, WAIS, World-Wide Web, as well as the Yanoff list and a whole lot of other interesting things.

B.4 United States Government Gophers

ADDRESS: gopher or telnet stis.nsf.gov; login: <public>/Other U.S. Government Gopher Servers (National Science Foundation Gopher)
URL: gopher://stis.nsf.gov/1/Other
CONTACT: stis@nsf.gov
COMMENTS: This is just what it says, a list of links to practically all government gophers. Check the "About this Gopher" document for searching tips.

B.5 University of Michigan Economics Gopher

ADDRESS: gopher alfred.econ.lsa.umich.edu
URL: gopher://gopher.econ.lsa.umich.edu/1
CONTACT: Hal.Varian@umich.edu (313)764-2364
COMMENTS: Here is another good collection of information. Main menu choices include Addresses, Announcements,Bibliographies, Data, Documentation, Economics of Internet, and WWW Server for the U-M Economics Department. Under Data, find Dow Jones averages from 1885-1985, 1952-1990, and 1900-1952. Also find the Social Statistics Research Unit. Under Economics of Internet find choices for Government, Conferences, Working Papers, Accounting, etc.

B.6 USC Gopher

ADDRESS: cwis.usc.edu
URL: gopher://cwis.usc.edu
CONTACT: Mark Brown, mark@usc.edu or gopher-guts@usc.edu
COMMENTS: From the main menu, follow the path Library and Research Information/Research Information/Government Information to find files including the Occupational Outlook Handbook 1992-93, Economic Conversion Information Exchange Database, GAO Reports, U.S. Industrial Outlook-1993, portions of the Federal Register and Commerce Business Daily. There is quite a lot of useful government information here.

B.7 Washington and Lee University

ADDRESS: gopher liberty.uc.wlu.edu; login: <guest>.
URL: gopher://liberty.uc.wlu.edu/11/
COMMENTS: The liberty gopher is not as extensive as some of the others but there is some good quality here. The main menu has an option for keyword searching both local and all menu entries. Following the path from the main menu Libraries and Information Access/Law/Law Related Sources, there are many items that we didn't find elsewhere, including a Copyright FAQ, Cornucopia of Disability Information, Social Security Numbers FAQ, FTP files and a Consumer Credit FAQ and links to many different law schools etc.

There is also a good section of Reference Sources under the Libraries and Information Sources main menu choice. This has options for the American English Dictionary, Dictionary of Acronyms, Internet User's Glossary, Weights and Measures, White House Information, etc.

C. LISTSERVS

C.1 GOVDOC-L

ADDRESS: Send an e-mail message to LISTSERV@psuvm.psu.edu with "Subscribe GOVDOC-L yourfirstname yourlastname" in the message.

URL: N/A

COMMENTS: High volume. As this is a listserv for government document librarians, much of the discussion here relates to the administration of government document collections, with frequent reference questions, conference notices, etc. However, if there is anything new on the Internet in terms of government information, this is one of the first places you'll see it.

D. USENET NEWSGROUPS

(Note: several of the groups with the most current business information are from the clarinet news service. These groups (with the prefix clari.) are subscription—fee-based—sources with current business news, stock market figures, Standard and Poor closing ranges, Dow Jones closing averages, etc. Their inclusion here is not an endorsement, merely a description of what is available.)

*alt.business.misc
- Unmoderated, very few postings, about 10 per month.
- Topics include business opportunities in China, Wal-Mart rumor, availability of jobs (a Russian interpreter).
- Discussion, what there is of it, seems quite informal and chatty. Mostly Q and A, not much in the way of debate.

*alt.business.multi-level
- High traffic, about 240 messages per month.
- Topics include multi-level marketing, equity sharing, quite a bit on Amway, Herbalife, and Visionmedia and dealing with your upline. FAQ posted monthly.
- Discussion is sometimes heated, if you are interested in multi-level marketing don't miss this.

*alt.politics.economics
- Unmoderated, about 120 messages per month.
- Topics include discussion threads concerning capitalism, federal spending and spending policies, negative income tax, money and votes, Panama deception, how Reaganomics worked, etc.
- Discussion is informal, sometimes heated.

*clari.biz.economy
- Moderated, about 120 messages per month.
- Articles, which seem to mostly be from UPI, include the Week in Business, Mortgage Rates Rise, Government to Issue Farm-Price Report, Commerce Issues, Gross Domestic Product, Jobless Rate, U.S. Consumer Price Index.
- Topics seem to be of general interest to the business community. An easy way to pick out business-related items.

*clari.biz.market.amex
- Moderated, about 60 messages per month
- Includes American Exchange stock sales, indexes, active AMEX stocks, weekly report for ASE, AMEX Market Value Index.

*clari.biz.market.dow
- Moderated, about 45 messages per month
- Includes Dow Jones closing stock and bond averages, Dow Jones closing stock and bond ranges.

*clari.biz.market.ny
- Moderated, about 120 messages per month
- Includes widely held NYSE stocks, what the stock market did, the 15 most active NYSE stocks, NYSE stock sales, NYSE closing index, weekly report.

*clari.biz.market.otc
- Moderated, about 40 messages per month
- Includes the most active OTC stocks, trends on OTC market.

*clari.biz.report
- Moderated, about 90 messages per month
- Includes selected mutual funds, volume and trends, Lipper mutual fund reports, stock market index report, Standard and Poor's closing range, Standard and Poor's Daily History.

*clari.news.gov.agency
- Articles, many from UPI, include topics like National Lab Signs Major DNA Research Agreement, Clinton Creates Science and Technology Commission, Hubble Deployment Re-Scheduled, Chicago Consumer Prices Fall.
- This, like the other clari. groups is more a news reader than a discussion group.

*sci.econ
- Unmoderated, quite a bit of traffic, approximately 120 messages per month.
- Topics include cost of environmental regulations, the death of democracy, NAFTA, job announcements, kissing up to oil companies, the health care plan.
- Action is brisk, quite a bit of debate, some flaming and personal attack. In general it seems a productive exchange of opinions by folks knowledgeable in the field.

*sci.econ.research
- Moderated version of the above newsgroup, about half the traffic.
- Topics include one-stage deviation principle, faculty job announcements, fixed and floating exchange rates, genetic algorithms, state policies, correlation matrix bounds.
- Discussion is more sedate and scholarly, no flaming, intellectual discussion about theory and other esoterica of interest to academics.

AFTERWORD

E. Acknowledgements and Explanatory Notes

Description:

This guide is the product of over 3 months of searching/cruising the Internet from September through December of 1993 (with updates through February of 1993). We sought to include any major sources of government-published information that might be of use to anyone interested or involved in business or economics. Before and during this time, several other government and economics guides came out, notably those produced by Blake Gumprecht, Bill Goffe, and Maggie Parhamovich. We are indebted to these individuals and have drawn on their work. We have sought to make our guide as comprehensive a source of government business and economic information as we could and we include a few related useful non-government sources too. Still, there are, no doubt, omissions. We would appreciate suggestions about additions that would be helpful and/or comments with ideas for how this guide could be improved.

In order to provide the most complete access to very broad categories of information, we have found it necessary to list multiple access points. If URLs differ, we have listed all versions we found. Hopefully by sacrificing a bit of brevity we will improve utility.

Who might find this guide useful:

We hope to make the information in this guide useful and accessible to almost anyone with an interest in our subject area. By describing the resources in some detail, a high school student doing a project on the ramifications of NAFTA can find the full text of the proposal as well as comments from the White House on it; a local business person can look up the name and address of her Congress person; an economics professor can find current economic conditions worldwide using the information in this guide.

Accessing this guide:

This guide is available by using the following tools:

anonymous FTP:
    host: una.hh.lib.umich.edu
    path: /inetdiresstacks
    file name: govdocs:tsangaustin

Gopher:
    via U. Minnesota list of gophers (other gophers)
    menus: /North America/USA/Michigan/Clearinghouse
    for Subject-Oriented . . ./All Guides

URL for WorldWideWeb/Mosaic:
    gopher://una.hh.lib.umich.edu/00/inetdirsstacks/govdocs:tsangaustin

F. HELP RESOURCES

F.1 INFORMU Gopher

ADDRESS: gopher mizzou1.missouri.edu:801/How to Access Information via the Internet
URL: gopher://mizzou1.missouri.edu:801/1194453
COMMENTS: The most comprehensive source we found on this topic. Includes the full text of *Zen and the Art of the Internet* as well as sections explaining FTP, TELNET, Archie, gopher, and others.

F.2 University of Minnesota

ADDRESS: ftp boombox.micro.unm.edu; cd/pub/gopher
URL: file://boombox.micro.umn.edu/pub/gopher
COMMENTS: The vast majority of the resources in this guide are available through gopher. This site provides FTP-able public-domain gopher clients. The use of these gopher clients will allow you to download files directly to your computer without having to use FTP.

INDEX

Glossary

anonymous ftp Technically, this is a special case of using ftp to log onto a server where you don't already have an account or password—instead, you use the word *anonymous* as your account name, and the server lets you connect. In practice, though, anonymous ftp is one of the key services for letting users on the Internet exchange documents, software, and other files without having to prearrange user accounts on host computers. There are thousands of anonymous ftp sites that support the exchange of files and data throughout the Internet community.

archie This is a resource discovery system that automatically gathers, indexes, and makes available information about what's on various Internet servers. The first archies provided searchable directories of anonymous ftp servers. Newer archies include collections that are available through other services.

ASCII American Standard Code for Information Interchange. This is a comparatively standard scheme for translating bytes—represented in a computer as a string of ones and zeros—into the characters of an alphabet. It's a lowest-common-denominator standard for exchanging simple text files: for the most part, an ASCII file on a Macintosh will translate perfectly to an ASCII file on a PC, a Unix machine, a VAX, or almost anything else. See *byte*. See also *EBCDIC*. (Better yet, *don't* see EBCDIC—that's an alternative set of codes used primarily on IBM mainframes.)

bandwidth Technically, this is the difference between the highest and lowest frequencies of a data transmission path. But if you ever explain that to someone, they will move away from you (rightfully) and carefully avoid any sudden movements when they're around you in the future. More commonly, bandwidth is used to describe the fastest possible speed that a particular data transmission protocol (e.g., Ethernet, ISDN, T1/T3) can support.

baud Technically, baud and bps (bits per second) aren't really the same but modem manufacturers use the terms as if they were, so the distinction is academic, at best. See *bps*.

bit As a computer stores things, a bit is the smallest possible unit. A bit is set to one or zero (on or off, yes or no, true or false, black or white, yin or yang). A string of eight bits is called a byte. See *byte*. (The word *bit* is abbreviated with a lowercase *b*—e.g., bps represents bits per second, not bytes per second.)

bounce When your email can't be delivered to whoever you addressed it to, it *bounces* and gets sent back to you (usually by a mailer *daemon*). Although this sounds annoying, it's better than if the email gets *munched*—which happens when the email just gets lost. At least when it bounces, you know the recipient didn't get it. The coolest part of bouncing is that it's all done by computers, so if one system bounces an email message to an incorrect address, and that system bounces it back, the process will go on forever—eating up all the network resources it can find—because none of the systems are smart enough to ask "Hey, didn't I bounce that same message about, oh, say sixty thousand times in the last second or two?" This is why email system administrators *earn* their salaries.

bps
Bits per second. This is the basic unit of measure for indicating the speed of a data transfer. Most modems work at very specific predefined speeds: 2400 bps, 9600 bps, 14.4 Kbps (thousands of bits per second), and 28.8 Kbps. However, even though a byte is 8 bits, the translation of bits per second to bytes per second isn't exactly a factor of eight. Instead, because of other things the modem has to do during data transfer, you get a byte transferred after about every ten bits. Roughly therefore, a 2400 bps modem transmits data at about 240 characters, or bytes, per second.

browser
This is the generic term for anything that lets you browse through various Internet service collections. Most frequently though, it's used in the context of a "web browser"—which is the client part of the World Wide Web Internet service. (That's the part that runs on your computer—see *client/server*.) Since the web is fairly standardized (or at least as much as anything on the Internet), you should be able to choose any number of different browsers to wander around the web.

BTW
An abbreviation used in email and postings that means By The Way.

byte
As a computer stores things, a byte is the basic unit for storage. It is made up of 8 bits. See bit. (The word *byte* is abbreviated with an uppercase *B*—e.g., MB represents megabytes, not megabits.) If you are working with ASCII text files, each 8-bit string of ones and zeros is set to represent a specific character (e.g., "01000001" represents the letter "A"). Some communications software transmits only the last seven bits of each byte, instead of the whole thing. That's fine for most ASCII text (which is represented completely with the first bit set to zero), but almost every other file on the planet—including software, image files and simple word processing files—uses all eight bits. That means that if your communication software "strips the eighth bit," then you've either got to be working with straight ASCII (e.g., email messages and newsgroup postings), or you've got to convert the 8-bit file to a 7-bit format.

client
1) *This is who lawyers work for* (of course). And don't ever forget it. 2) In the Internet community, however, "client" is the first half of a mostly meaningless buzzword, *client/server*.

client/server
Client refers to any computer or a program that requests information or support from *another* computer or program—which is called the server. This covers a pretty broad range of topics (hence the meaningless-buzzword status), but it actually becomes useful when you're talking about services that have two parts: the client part of the service that runs on your computer, and the server part of the service that supplies the information you're looking for. Since the service is in two parts, it should be possible for you to use any number of different

client software packages that will work with the right kinds of servers. And each client software package should be able to work with servers that are running different server software packages. That's the heart and soul of standards-based client/server technology. Of course, if someone sells you a proprietary client/server product, the definition stays the same; it's just not as interesting.

communications
software   This is one of many different software programs that you might use to set up a communications link between your computer and the one you're trying to reach. Sometimes communications software will be prettied up to make it look like you're not really using the modem— but you are. In its prettiest forms, you just push some button and the comm software establishes the connection; in its less attractive forms, the comm software lets you talk to your modem, using a somewhat less than intuitive language that includes commands like ATZ and ATDT. Unfortunately, the learning curve for comm software (if you ever have to scratch the surface) typically requires you to learn twice as much as you really need to do a certain task—just so you can understand the terms. Rote memorization is an effective if imprecise weapon against the comm software monster.

Cyberspace   1) A word coined by William Gibson, in his popular science fiction novel *Neuromancer*, to describe the realm and cultural dynamics of people and machines working within the confines of computer-based networks. 2) An entirely meaningless buzzword that *might* have been related to the Gibson term, once, but has since been sucked into the reality distortion field that surrounds Hollywood, Madison Avenue, and pop culture.

Daemon   See *bounce*.

/dev/null   This is Unix-speak for nowhere. Technically, it's a nonexistent device that, not surprisingly, doesn't do anything. If a programmer routes an unwanted print job, for example, to /dev/null then the printer thinks it's sending the print job to a real place, but /dev/null dutifully does nothing with it. (Presumably, the bits from the print job just spill out all over the floor, unless you've got a bit bucket to collect them all.) On the other hand, if an email correspondent tells you to send your comments to /dev/null, they're not exactly giving you a technical sug- gestion.

domain name   This is the last part of an Internet address, such as "abanet.org". The top level of a domain name (i.e., the last part) indicates what kind of organization runs the site: .com is commercial, .edu is educational, .gov is government, .mil is U.S. military, .net is network operations, .org is non-profit, and there are nearly a hundred other top level domains that represent the country of origin. The second level of the domain name (preceding the period) is selected by the organization. (It's first come first served, so register fast.)

dot   When you read an Internet address, a newsgroup name, or just some word that the net.denizens made up to describe something they felt they couldn't express using English, it's Way Cooler to pronounce the embedded periods using the word *dot*. So abanet.org is pronounced A-B-A-net-dot-org, net.denizens is pronounced net-dot-denizens, and alt.barney.die.die.die is pronounced (well, you get the picture). (BTW, you should pronounce all top-level domains as though they were words—but not .edu which is dot-E-D-U, and not the individual country codes, which usually translate into unattractive gutturals anyway.

download
This is the process of copying a file from some other computer to your computer. There are a hundred ways to do this, and the words *other* and *your* are strictly relative. The technology for uploading and downloading is identical—the only difference is your perspective: away from you is up, towards you is down.

EBCDIC
Forget it. See *ASCII*.

email
Electronic mail. These are messages and notes that you send to other people (and that other people send to you). As a popular buzzword, this can be used as a noun, a verb, an adjective, or an expletive.

emoticon
Emotion construct. Only geeks would give such a user hostile name to something intended to convey warm-and-fuzzy emotions in an inherently emotion-free environment. Emoticons run the gamut from the basic-punctuation smiley face :-) to bracket-embedded phrases <grinning and running>. They are appended to electronic communications (such as email and discussion postings) to try to convey the subtleties of language that you otherwise have access to when you're talking F2F (face to face). Of course, emoticons are much better at doing *"exaggerate"* than they are at doing *"subtle."*

Ethernet
A popular standard for local area networks. It has a maximum speed of 10 Mbps (megabits per second). At one time, Ethernet specified a particular type of cabling and topology (coax and bus, respectively), but those details have long since been relaxed—giving in to the mother of invention. Token ring is a competing standard.

FAQ
A frequently asked question, or a file full of FAQs and their answers. Newbies who ask such questions are regularly referred to the FAQ file. Indeed, it makes sense to try to find the FAQ file before sticking your nose into an active discussion group. (Unfortunately, finding the FAQ file isn't always easy. Finding it *should be* the single most common FAQ—if the whole idea weren't so completely recursive.)

finger
This is a standard utility on most Unix systems that lets you find information about individuals—by name—at a particular Internet host computer. Some host computers refuse to accept finger inquiries, but if finger is enabled (so to speak), then this can help track down a person's email address. The finger utility also brings back an individual's .plan file—a file that's supposed to provide descriptive information about the individual. However *some* users, with more time on their hands than they know what to do with, put strange-but-possibly-interesting information in their .plan files. Still others program laboratory test equipment so that it automatically updates the .plan file

every few minutes with selected observations. Thus, some .plan files contain sports results or rotisserie league news. Others tell you the supply levels of vending machines. If you finger the address, it tells you the news.

firewall
This is a special type of gateway that's used to connect an internal network to the Internet. Its purpose is to prevent unauthorized intrusions into the network, which it does by connecting only a "boundary" machine to the Internet, then selectively forwarding only approved types of traffic between the internal network and the boundary machine.

flame
When one person unleashes invective at another—through either email or a discussion-group posting—that message is a flame. Flame is also a verb: I flame, you flame, he, she and it turn the whole thing into a flame war. Occasionally, you can reduce the *personal* nature of the attack by announcing FLAME ON just before the rant (then, presumably, FLAME OFF, when you're done). The intent of labelling the flame is to show that you're just venting your frustration and not expecting real results. But it rarely *does* reduce the personal nature of the attack—it just makes the ranter feel like he or she is playing by the rules.

freenet
These are bulletin board systems (BBSs) that support email gateways, local file exchanges, and, usually, a limited level of connectivity to the Internet. Most freenets are part of NPTN (the National Public Telecomputing Network, based in Cleveland, Ohio). Most are funded and operated by volunteers.

freeware
A software package that the author distributes without charge. This isn't the same as "in the public domain." Freeware authors usually try to preserve their rights to the software so that no one else can sell it.

ftp
File Transfer Protocol. Technically, it's a protocol for letting a user on one computer log onto, review, and transfer files to and from another host computer over a network. Usually, ftp is a standard part of Unix operating systems and other Internet services.

gateway
This is a communications system that passes data from one network to another. Usually a gateway is needed when the two networks run different protocols and can't be connected directly (in which case, you would use a router or a bridge). An *email* gateway refers to a feature usually found on non-Internet systems, to let users of that system send email back and forth to Internet-connected systems.

geek
Webster's defines geek as a carnival performer who performs sensationally morbid or disgusting acts. Personally, I don't think that definition is too far off, but the *intent*, at least, is to fondly invoke the imagery of the pleasant-but-perhaps-overly-focused individual whose knowledge of technology exceeds the limits of what one should expect from a person who otherwise has a life.

gopher
A simple menu-based information service that makes collections of information available across the Internet. It allows gopher clients to

access information from any accessible gopher server, in which connections from one server to the next are handled entirely as background operations—transparent to the user.

HTML

Hypertext Markup Language. When presenting a menu or hyper-linked document, web sites follow the instructions embedded in the appropriate HTML files. The files are usually straight text (i.e., ASCII), but the instructions are expressed in a brief tagging format known as HTML. The tags tell the web site how to display text and images; they identify which items are linked to which other items. See *World Wide Web*.

HTTP

Hypertext Transfer Protocol. If an item on the net is a web site (see *World Wide Web*), then the first part of its URL address (see *URL*) will be the word *http*. HTTP is also the generic term for software running the server part of the World Wide Web Internet service (see *client/server*). If that's not enough cross-references, then see *recursive* as well.

IMHO

An abbreviation used in email and postings that means In My Humble Opinion. Which rarely means humble. (Personally, I prefer to use "IMAO," in which the word *humble* is replaced with the word *arrogant*—a rather honest substitution.)

internet

OK, OK. This is the generic term for any group of networks that have been connected together—usually using bridges and routers, and presumably using whatever network protocols the internet operator has selected (i.e., not necessarily TCP/IP). *The Internet*, on the other hand, is the specific global system that is organized (loosely) under the standards-definition process managed by the international voluntary organization called the Internet Architecture Board. In Kleenex-speak, the Internet would be the Internet-brand internet. (Wow. I'm glad *that's* finally clear.)

Internet

The Internet is a global system for linking other computer networks together, using TCP/IP network protocols as the basis for communications.

ISDN

Integrated Services Digital Network. This is a relatively new technology for delivering high-speed voice and data lines over single telephone lines. Typically, ISDN prices are much less than traditional leased lines, and yet it supports speeds much faster (e.g., from 64 Kbps up to 1.544 Mbps) than you can get with modems and standard dialup phone lines. ISDN is not yet offered everywhere.

jughead

See veronica.

K

Kilo. Usually combined with bytes or bits to represent thousands of bytes or thousands of bits. Depending on your geek quotient and the context within which the measurement is written, K might mean exactly one thousand. But in most computer-related usage, K means 2 to the 10th power—or 1,024.

lurk

The process of regularly reading the contents of a discussion group, but never contributing to it. Since most discussion group technologies don't announce that someone is just-reading, lurkers are virtually invisible to the group. Lurking introduces a curious variation on group dynamics, since a group that's meeting face to face would be able to see any silent attendees in the room. On one hand, lurkers are perceived as eavesdroppers hiding behind a one-way mirror. At the same time, lurking is perceived as the singularly most polite way for a newbie to learn what's going on.

M Mega. Usually combined with bytes or bits to represent millions of bytes or millions of bits. Depending on your geek quotient and the context within which the measurement is written, M might mean exactly one million. But in most computer-related usage, M means 2 to the 20th power—or 1,048,576.

MIME Multipurpose Internet Mail Extensions. This is an email transfer protocol that supports the transfer of 8-bit files (as attachments to email) rather than the 7-bit transfers normally supported by Internet-based email. See also *byte*.

Mosaic Mosaic is the brand name of a particular web browser which was originally written at the National Center for Supercomputing Applications (NCSA). See *World Wide Web*. As it turns out, this was the most popular web browser available during the early growth of the web, and in many circles it became, quite literally, synonymous with the web. See also *Netscape*.

net.denizen Somebody old to the net, or old to a group—sometimes also referred to as a net.veteran or oldbie. (The term *oldbie* seems to be used most frequently by people who have just been referred to as a newbie.)

net.police This is a derisive term for supercilious butt-in-skis who chastise others (usually in a discussion group) for violating what *they* perceive as proper netiquette. Of course, the net.police label is determined entirely by perspective: If you think the complained-of action warranted public censure, then the enforcer is a net.citizen; but if you think the enforcer is a self-appointed censor who is out of line with this complaint, then the individual becomes the net.police. (Especially enthusiastic net.police can evolve into net.nazis; especially enthusiastic net.citizens can evolve into net.vigilantes. Sometimes, it's hard to tell the difference. Unfortunately, most of the time it's not.)

netiquette A set of standards and practices that guide the "proper" behavior of participants on the net. Netiquette is frequently described as common-sense guidelines, but one person's common-sense might be another person's ludicrous constraints. Once in a while, it's hard to tell the difference. Unfortunately, most of the time it's Completely Obvious.

Netscape Netscape is the brand name of a particular web browser that was written by Netscape Communications. See *World Wide Web*. Although Netscape doesn't follow web standards scrupulously, it is dramatically faster than most other web browsers—especially Mosaic (one of the first and most popular browsers). Netscape's speed is especially important to users who are dialing in using modems and standard telephone lines: At normal modem speeds, the images and other graphics used at many web sites can make other browsers prohibitively slow.

Many users report that Netscape makes the difference between being able to use the web and not.

network
: A network may be a local area network or a wide area network, or something in between, or something yet larger. But the common characteristic of a network is that all of the computers and terminals attached to the network have access to wiring and protocols that can put any device on the net in immediate communications with any other device on the net (assuming that both are connected and operating).

newbie
: Somebody new to the net, or new to a group. Newbie isn't always derogatory, but when used in the third person, it almost always is.

newsgroup
: A discussion group that is operated through the Usenet conferencing protocols. These discussion groups are similar to public bulletin boards—in which participants come to a common location to read and post messages. There are newsgroups on thousands of topics. Most of the topics have been carefully screened through a rigorous voting procedure that's intended to make sure that discussion groups are created only on topics where there is sufficient interest. However, there's one entire set of newsgroups—those that start with the preface *alt*—that are specifically available for people who want to set up discussions on entirely frivolous and short-term topics. Hence the name, alt.barney.die.die.die.

nslookup
: This is a standard utility on most Unix systems that lets you find the numeric IP address of a system (e.g., 140.174.72.1) if all you've got is the domain-based Internet address (e.g., wired.com). Nslookup will also tell you the domain address if all you've got are the numbers.

oldbie
: See *newbie*. And see *net.denizen*, too.

posting
: If you are participating in a discussion group—whether it's an email distribution list or a more formal newsgroup—any contribution you make to the discussion is a posting.

PGP
: Pretty Good Privacy, an encryption system that uses private keys and public keys to let people send encrypted messages to one another—without having to exchange secret *decryption* passwords in advance. In the world of cryptography, PGP is only "pretty good." That means you could crack an encrpyted email message in *just a few years* if you had a bazillion supercomputers working on the problem. In *my* world, PGP is GEP—*Good Enough* Privacy.

PPP
: Point-to-Point Protocol. This is a communications software package (usually for a remote computer) that enables you to establish a connection to *any* TCP/IP network—but most apropos to this discussion, to the Internet. If you are in an office with other computers connected to a local area network using Ethernet, you wouldn't need PPP, but if you are trying to link to a network using a modem and a telephone line, this is what you would use. A similar type of protocol is SLIP. Technically, SLIP is faster but less reliable.

protocol	A system of formats and rules that are established to enable two computers to communicate. These can range from very low-level protocols that define how bits are sent across wires, up to high-level protocols that define how communications software packages will exchange files reliably.
recursive	See *recursive*.
RFC	Request For Comments. This curious title is assigned to a series of documents that represent standards and other semi-officially blessed papers that describe various pieces of the Internet. If you see a document referenced by its RFC number, that means that some group of Internet standards boards are treating that document with greater attention than those that don't have RFC numbers.
rot13	This is a trivial encryption technique that's used to hide the contents of newsgroup postings from casual browsers. The encryption technique is completely simplistic—it simply assigns each letter of the alphabet a number, then rotates the numeric assignments by 13—the resulting message looks like garbage to the casual browser, but anyone interested in reading the message simply invokes the rot13 option and the message is automatically shown as originally typed. The purpose of rot13 is to hide the message from browsers who might inadvertently see the message and take offense at foul language or tasteless jokes, or who don't want to see movie reviews or game descriptions that give away all the secrets.
router	See *gateway*.
server	See *client/server*.
shareware	A software package that the author distributes without charge, but for which payment is required if the user decides to keep and use it. This isn't the same as freeware. The author is merely using the enormous software distribution facilities of the system to let prospective users try the software before buying it. Obviously, there is no mechanism that forcibly prevents you from abusing this right-to-try privilege, but you are honor-bound to make the payment if you use it, and the license provisions expressly require you to do so.
.sig file	Many email systems and newsreaders allow you to predefine a particular block of text that should be appended to the end of all your email messages and postings. Ideally, the .sig file lets you skip the process of repeatedly typing in your return address, organizational affiliation, and obligatory disclaimers. More commonly, the .sig file has become a placeholder for nominally-witty sayings, and a digital canvas for what is graciously referred to as ASCII art. (Budding ASCII artists show remarkable-albeit-not-entirely-practical skills in constructing visual images using nothing but slashes, backslashes, and various other combinations of letters and punctuation marks.)
SLIP	Serial Line Internet Protocol. This is another communications software package (usually for a remote computer) that enables you to establish

a connection to *any* TCP/IP network—again apropos to this discussion, including the Internet. See *PPP*.

snail mail

This would be mail of the non electronic kind. You know—paper, envelopes, stamps, postmarks. Not to mention Christmas delays and mountains of mail discovered in the basements of one-or-two-bad-apple Post Office employees. Usually, this is referenced in the context of a *snail mail address*.

spam

Junk mail of the e-frontier kind. Spam is an unsolicited posting—usually off-topic—sent to many discussion groups at once. Arguably, this could be used to describe many overenthusiastic discussion-group contributions, but most spam so thoroughly violates the standards and practices of the net that there's not much room for doubt. Advertisements, get rich quick scams, and political pleas—anything that gets posted to more than a thousand discussion groups qualifies as off-topic and intrusive. Retaliatory e-weapons used by net.vigilantes include the mail bomb and the cancelbot. Whereas spam is *one message* sent to thousands and millions of addresses, a mail bomb sends thousands and millions of messages to *one address* (usually, that's enough to shut down the site that sent the spam). A cancelbot is programmed to check for and cancel out any postings sent from a known spamming site.

sysadmin

System administrator—this is the person (or persons) who runs host computers on the net. These people have more privileges to do cool stuff than you do. *Some* of that cool stuff is really helpful; some of it would fall on the opposite side of that ledger. Be very, very nice to your sysadmins. They can really help you out when things go crunch on the net. But they have to take too much flak from clueless newbies who can't tell the difference between technical support and the sysadmin, and who for some completely bizarre reason think that shouting expletives is the best way to get a sysadmin to come to their aid. It's not. Shouting at your sysadmin is like shouting at your anesthesiologist. Don't.

T1 and T3

These are high-speed leased lines that can be used to connect local area networks and wide area networks to each other, and to the Internet. T1 lines support data transmission speeds of up to 1.544 Mbps; T3 lines support speeds of up to 44.746 Mbps.

TCP/IP

Transmission Control Protocol/Internet Protocol. This refers to a group of protocols and a suite of application-layer services (including ftp, telnet, and the smtp email protocol) that networks connecting to the Internet must use or emulate to be able to communicate.

technical support

These are the people who run the telephone help lines, representing your best chance to learn what has been baffling you for the last several hours. Almost without exception, the people who run the tech support lines know what they're talking about—*flawlessly*. Unfortunately, the people who run the tech support lines also spend eight hours a day taking complaints from unhappy users who have reached a point of total frustration and are completely willing to vent that frustration on whoever answers the phone. If you are polite with them and treat them like the professionals they are, they will take care of you. If you take the time to learn the rules *they* have to work within, and call them before your problem has gotten out of hand, you will find that they can save you a tremendous amount of *your* precious time.

telnet
One of the basic TCP/IP services that lets a user on one computer connect to and operate programs on another computer.

Unix
An operating system that was originally developed by Bell Laboratories—now owned by Unix System Laboratories, a division of Novell. Unix isn't Windows, it isn't OS/2 and it isn't Macintosh. From the perspective of erstwhile Unixoids, those are all *toy* operating systems, while Unix is what you use when you have *real* work to do—"multithreaded and multitasking." The fact is that Unix and its many variants have been around for several decades and it's now fairly ubiquitous on the net. Unfortunately, the command-line Unix interface is among the most hostile anywhere. Such is net.life. (BTW, don't even bother making the obligatory eunuchs jokes. Been there—done that—twenty years ago. They're tired now.)

upload
See download.

URL
Uniform Resource Locator. This is the addressing scheme used to identify the specific *location* of Internet *resources*. (And it's *uniform* because Tim Berners-Lee wrote it down and everyone agreed to use it.) The basic form of most URL addresses is service://hostname/path. That tells you what Internet service you'll need to reach the resource, what computer it's located on, and enough detail so that when you reach that computer, you can find what you're looking for.

Usenet
See newsgroups.

veronica and jughead
These are two resource discovery systems that automatically gather, index and make available information related to gopher servers around the world. You tell 'em what you're looking for; they tell you where it is. (Or at least that's the plan.)

whois
This is a standard utility on most Unix systems that lets you find more detailed information about a particular Internet address. Usually, whois will give you the registered name, snail mail address and organization for the listed host computer.

World Wide Web
A hypertext-based information service that makes collections of information available across the Internet. It allows web browser clients to access information from any accessible web server, in which connections from one server to the next are handled entirely as background operations—transparent to the user. It supports multiple media types, it can be used to invoke other software, and the primary user interface is represented by embedded hypertext links rather than by menus. See *gopher*.

Index

Selected Books From...

THE SECTION OF LAW PRACTICE MANAGEMENT

ABA Guide to International Business Negotiations. A guide to the general, legal, and cultural issues that arise during international negotiations.

ABA Guide to Legal Marketing. A collection of new and innovative marketing ideas and strategies for lawyers and firms.

ACCESS 1994. An updated guidebook to technology resources. Includes practical hints, practical tips, commonly used terms, and resource information.

Becoming Computer Literate. A guide to computer basics for lawyers and other legal professionals.

Beyond the Billable Hour. A collection of 26 articles discussing issues related to alternative billing methods.

Breaking Traditions. A guide to progressive, flexible, and sensible work alternatives for lawyers who want to balance the demand of the legal profession with other commitments. Model policy for childbirth and parenting leave is included.

Changing Jobs, 2nd Ed. A handbook designed to help lawyers make changes in their professional careers. Includes career planning advice from nearly 50 experts.

Flying Solo: A Survival Guide for the Solo Lawyer, 2nd Ed. An updated and expanded guide to the problems and issues unique to the solo practitioner.

How to Start and Build a Law Practice, 3rd Ed. Jay Foonberg's classic guide has been updated and expanded. Included are more than 10 new chapters on marketing, financing, automation, practicing from home, ethics and professional responsibility.

Last Frontier: Women Lawyers as Rainmakers. Explains why rainmaking is different for women than men and focuses on ways to improve these skills. Shares the experiences of four women who have successfully built their own practices.

Lawyer's Guide to the Internet. A no-nonsense guide to what the Internet is (and isn't), how it applies to the legal profession, and the different ways it can—and should—be used.

Leveraging with Legal Assistants. Reviews the changes that have led to increased use of legal assistants and the need to enlarge their role further. Learn specific ways in which a legal assistant can handle a substantial portion of traditional lawyer work.

Making Partner: A Guide for Law Firm Associates. Written by a managing partner, this book offers guidelines and recommendations designed to help you increase your chances of making partner.

Planning the Small Law Office Library. A step-by-step guide to planning, building, and managing a small law office library. Includes case studies, floor plans, and questionnaires.

Practical Systems: Tips for Organizing Your Law Office. It will help you get control of your in-box by outlining systems for managing daily work.

Results-Oriented Financial Management: A Guide to Successful Law Firm Financial Performance. How to manage "the numbers," from setting rates and computing billable hours to calculating net income and preparing the budget. Over 30 charts and statements to help you prepare reports.

Survival Skills for the Practicing Lawyer. Includes 29 articles from *Law Practice Management* magazine for the attorney with little or no management responsibilities.

Through the Client's Eyes: New Approaches to Get Clients to Hire You Again and Again. Includes an overview of client relations and sample letters, surveys, and self-assessment questions to gauge your client relations acumen.

The Time Trap. A classic book on time management published by the American Management Association. This guide focuses on "The Twenty Biggest Time Wasters" and how you can overcome them.

Win-Win Billing Strategies. Represents the first comprehensive analysis of what constitutes "value," and how to bill for it. You'll learn how to initiate and implement different billing methods that make sense for you and your client.

TQM in Action: One Firm's Journey Toward Quality and Excellence. A guide to implementing the principles of Total Quality Management in your law firm.

Winning with Computers, Part 1. Addresses virtually every aspect of the use of computers in litigation. You'll get an overview of products available and tips on how to put them to good use. For the beginning and advanced computer user.

Winning with Computers, Part 2. Expands on the ways you can use computers to manage the routine and not-so-routine aspects of your trial practice. Learn how to apply general purpose software and even how to have fun with your computer.

Women Rainmakers' 101+ Best Marketing Tips. A collection of over 130 marketing tips suggested by women rainmakers throughout the country. Includes tips on image, networking, public relations, and advertising.

WordPerfect® in One Hour for Lawyers. This is a crash course in the most popular word processing software package used by lawyers. In four easy lessons, you'll learn the basic steps for getting a simple job done.

WordPerfect® Shortcuts for Lawyers: Learning Merge and Macros in One Hour. A fast-track guide to two of WordPerfect's more advanced functions: merge and macros. Includes 4 lessons designed to take 15 minutes each.

Your New Lawyer, 2nd Ed. A complete legal employer's guide to recruitment, development, and management of new lawyers. Updated to address the many changes in the practice of law since the 1983 edition.

Order Form

Qty	Title	LPM Price	Regular Price	Total
_____	ABA Guide to Int'l Business Negotiations (511-0331)	$74.95	$84.95	$_____
_____	ABA Guide to Legal Marketing (511-0341)	69.95	79.95	$_____
_____	ACCESS 1994 (511-0327)	29.95	34.95	$_____
_____	Becoming Computer Literate (511-0342)	32.95	39.95	$_____
_____	Beyond the Billable Hour (511-0260)	69.95	79.95	$_____
_____	Breaking Traditions (511-0320)	64.95	74.95	$_____
_____	Changing Jobs, 2nd Ed. (511-0334)	49.95	59.95	$_____
_____	Flying Solo, 2nd Ed. (511-0328)	59.95	69.95	$_____
_____	How to Start & Build a Law Practice, 3rd Ed. (511-0293)	32.95	39.95	$_____
_____	Last Frontier (511-0314)	9.95	14.95	$_____
_____	Lawyer's Guide to the Internet (511-0343)	24.95	29.95	$_____
_____	Leveraging with Legal Assistants (511-0322)	59.95	69.95	$_____
_____	Making Partner (511-0303)	14.95	19.95	$_____
_____	Planning the Small Law Office Library (511-0325)	29.95	39.95	$_____
_____	Practical Systems (511-0296)	24.95	34.95	$_____
_____	Results-Oriented Financial Management (511-0319)	44.95	54.95	$_____
_____	Survival Skills for the Practicing Lawyer (511-0324)	39.95	49.95	$_____
_____	Through the Client's Eyes (511-0337)	69.95	79.95	$_____
_____	The Time Trap (511-0330)	14.95	14.95	$_____
_____	TQM in Action (511-0323)	59.95	69.95	$_____
_____	Win-Win Billing Strategies (511-0304)	89.95	99.95	$_____
_____	Winning with Computers, Part 1 (511-0294)	89.95	99.95	$_____
_____	Winning with Computers, Part 2 (511-0315)	59.95	69.95	$_____
_____	Winning with Computers, Parts 1 & 2 (511-0316)	124.90	144.90	$_____
_____	Women Rainmakers' 101+ Best Marketing Tips (511-0336)	14.95	19.95	$_____
_____	WordPerfect® in One Hour for Lawyers (511-0308)	9.95	14.95	$_____
_____	WordPerfect® Shortcuts for Lawyers (511-0329)	14.95	19.95	$_____
_____	Your New Lawyer, 2nd Ed. (511-0312)	74.95	84.95	$_____

* HANDLING
$2.00-$9.99........$2.00
10.00-24.99........$3.95
25.00-49.99........$4.95
50.00 +..............$5.95

**TAX
DC residents add 5.75%
IL residents add 8.75%
MD residents add 5%

SUBTOTAL: $_____
*HANDLING: $_____
**TAX: $_____
TOTAL: $_____

PAYMENT

☐ Check enclosed (Payable to the ABA)   ☐ Bill Me

☐ Visa   ☐ MasterCard   Account Number: _____-_____-_____-_____

Exp. Date: _____ Signature _____

Name _____

Firm _____

Address _____

City_____ State_____ ZIP _____

Phone number_____

Mail to: ABA, Publication Orders, P.O. Box 10892, Chicago, IL 60610-0892

PHONE: (312) 988-5522
Or FAX: (312) 988-5568

BOOK

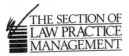

THE SECTION OF LAW PRACTICE MANAGEMENT

CUSTOMER COMMENT FORM

Title of Book:_____

We've tried to make this publication as useful, accurate, and readable as possible. Please take 5 minutes to tell us if we succeeded. Your comments and suggestions will help us improve our publications. Thank you!

1. How did you acquire this publication:

☐ by mail order   ☐ at a meeting/convention   ☐ as a gift

☐ by phone order   ☐ at a bookstore   ☐ don't know

☐ other: (describe) _____

Please rate this publication as follows:

	Excellent	Good	Fair	Poor	Not Applicable
Readability: Was the book easy to read and understand?	☐	☐	☐	☐	☐
Examples/Cases: Were they helpful, practical? Were there enough?	☐	☐	☐	☐	☐
Content: Did the book meet your expectations? Did it cover the subject adequately?	☐	☐	☐	☐	☐
Organization and clarity: Was the sequence of text logical? Was it easy to find what you wanted to know?	☐	☐	☐	☐	☐
Illustrations/forms/checklists: Were they clear and useful? Were there enough?	☐	☐	☐	☐	☐
Physical attractiveness: What did you think of the appearance of the publication (typesetting, printing, etc.)?	☐	☐	☐	☐	☐

Would you recommend this book to another attorney/administrator? ☐ Yes ☐ No

How could this publication be improved? What else would you like to see in it?

_____

_____

_____

Do you have other comments or suggestions? _____

_____

_____

Name _____

Firm/Company _____

Address _____

City/State/Zip _____

Phone _____

Firm Size: _____ Area of specialization: _____

We appreciate your time and help.

Fold

NO POSTAGE
NECESSARY
IF MAILED
IN THE
UNITED STATES

BUSINESS REPLY MAIL

FIRST CLASS   PERMIT NO. 16471   CHICAGO, ILLINOIS

POSTAGE WILL BE PAID BY ADDRESSEE

AMERICAN BAR ASSOCIATION
PPM, 8th FLOOR
750 N. LAKE SHORE DRIVE
CHICAGO, ILLINOIS 60611–9851

Fold